Fodor's 2003

W9-CFQ-836

Montréal and Québec City

The Guide
for All Budgets

Completely
Updated

Where to Stay, Eat,
and Explore

On and Off
the Beaten Path

When to Go,
What to Pack

Maps, Travel Tips,
and Web Sites

Fodor's Travel Publications • New York, Toronto, London, Sydney, Auckland
www.fodors.com

Fodor's Montréal and Québec City 2003

EDITORS: Chris Swiac, Shannon Kelly

Editorial Contributors: Carolyn Jackson, Paul Karr, Melanie Reffes, Elizabeth Thompson, Katherine Thompson, Julie Waters, Paul Waters
Editorial Production: Ira-Neil Dittersdorf
Maps: David Lindroth, *cartographer;* Rebecca Baer and Robert Blake, *map editors*
Design: Fabrizio La Rocca, *creative director;* Guido Caroti, *art director;* Jolie Novak, *senior picture editor;* Melanie Marin, *photo editor*
Cover Design: Pentagram
Production/Manufacturing: Yexenia (Jessie) Markland
Cover Photo (Ste-Anne Street, Québec City): Tibor Bognar

Copyright

Copyright © 2003 by Fodors LLC

Fodor's is a registered trademark of Random House, Inc. All rights reserved under International and Pan-American Copyright Conventions. Published in the United States by Fodor's Travel Publications, a unit of Fodors LLC, a subsidiary of Random House, Inc., and simultaneously in Canada by Random House of Canada Limited, Toronto. Distributed by Random House, Inc., New York.

No maps, illustrations, or other portions of this book may be reproduced in any form without written permission from the publisher.

ISBN 1–4000–1095–0

ISSN 1525–5867

Important Tip

Although all prices, opening times, and other details in this book are based on information supplied to us at press time, changes occur all the time in the travel world, and Fodor's cannot accept responsibility for facts that become outdated or for inadvertent errors or omissions. So **always confirm information when it matters,** especially if you're making a detour to visit a specific place.

Special Sales

Fodor's Travel Publications are available at special discounts for bulk purchases for sales promotions or premiums. Special editions, including personalized covers, excerpts of existing guides, and corporate imprints, can be created in large quantities for special needs. For more information, contact your local bookseller or write to Special Markets, Fodor's Travel Publications, 1745 Broadway, New York, NY 10019. Inquiries from Canada should be directed to your local Canadian bookseller or sent to Random House of Canada, Ltd., Marketing Department, 2775 Matheson Boulevard East, Mississauga, Ontario L4W 4P7. Inquiries from the United Kingdom should be sent to Fodor's Travel Publications, 20 Vauxhall Bridge Road, London SW1V 2SA, England.

PRINTED IN THE UNITED STATES OF AMERICA

10 9 8 7 6 5 4 3 2 1

CONTENTS

On the Road with Fodor's *iv–v*
Smart Travel Tips A to Z *viii–xxx*

1   **Destination: Montréal and Québec City**   *1*

Francophones in the New World 2
What's Where 6
Pleasures and Pastimes 7
Fodor's Choice 8

2   **Montréal**   *10*

Exploring Montréal 16
Dining 51
Lodging 62
Nightlife and the Arts 71
Outdoor Activities and Sports 78
Shopping 81
Montréal A to Z 90

3   **Québec City**   *96*

Exploring Québec City 98
Dining 120
Lodging 128
Nightlife and the Arts 133
Outdoor Activities and Sports 136
Shopping 140
Side Trips from Québec City 143
Québec City A to Z 150

4   **Province of Québec**   *155*

The Laurentians 162
The Eastern Townships 173
Charlevoix 186
The Gaspé Peninsula 193
Province of Québec A to Z 196

Index   *201*

Maps

Montréal and Québec City *vi–vii*
Montréal *12–13*
Vieux-Montréal *19*
Downtown Montréal (Centre-Ville) and Golden Square Mile *30*
Quartier Latin and Parc du Mont-Royal *40*
Olympic Park and Botanical Garden *47*
Montréal Dining *54–55*
Montréal Lodging *66–67*
Montréal Métro *94*
Metropolitan Québec City *100–101*
Upper and Lower Towns (Haute-Ville, Basse-Ville) *104–105*
Outside the Walls *114*
Québec City Dining and Lodging *122–123*
Île d'Orléans and Côte de Beaupré *144*
Lower Québec *158–159*
The Laurentians (les Laurentides) *163*
Eastern Townships (les Cantons de l'Est) and Montérégie *176*
Charlevoix *187*
Gaspé Peninsula (Gaspésie) *194*

ON THE ROAD WITH FODOR'S

A trip takes you out of yourself. Concerns of life at home completely disappear, driven away by more-immediate thoughts—about, say, what marvels will beguile the next day, or where you'll have dinner. That's where Fodor's comes in. We make sure that you know all your options, so that you don't miss something around the next bend just because you didn't know it was there. Mindful that the best memories of your trip might have nothing to do with what you came to Montréal and Québec City to see, we guide you to sights large and small all over the region. You might set out to tour Montréal's Olympic Park or stroll Québec City's Plains of Abraham, but back at home you find yourself unable to forget sharing coffee and pastries at a neighborhood *marché,* exploring narrow cobblestone streets, or sampling maple-syrup treats. With Fodor's at your side, serendipitous discoveries are never far away.

About Our Writers

Our success in showing you every corner of Montréal and Québec is a credit to our extraordinary writers. Although there's no substitute for travel advice from a good friend who knows your style, our contributors are the next best thing—the kind of people you would poll for travel advice if you knew them.

Writer and editor **Carolyn Jackson,** a native Torontonian, lived in the Caribbean for several years before being transplanted to Québec in 1990. She is still finding new and intriguing places to explore in "*la belle province.*" Carolyn updated most of the Province of Québec chapter.

Editor and guidebook writer **Paul Karr** has covered Vienna, Denmark, Northern Italy, and a host of other far-flung places. Since the mid-1990s, he has lived part-time in Montréal, which, he insists, produces the world's best bagels. Paul updated Smart Travel Tips as well as the Laurentians section of the Province of Québec chapter for this guide.

Travel writer and broadcaster **Melanie Reffes,** who hails from New Jersey, hangs her chapeau in Montréal these days. She travels the world for various radio and TV programs and has penned stories for several publications, including the *Montréal Gazette.* Melanie updated the nightlife, sports, outdoor activities, and Montréal A to Z sections of the Montréal chapter.

Elizabeth Thompson covers the Canadian government as an Ottawa-based reporter for the *Montréal Gazette.* Her Fodor's beat is Québec City, where she lived for many years.

Montréal resident **Katherine Thompson** travels extensively as part of her job at a Canadian airline. A Cordon Bleu–trained chef, she turns her attentions to her city's shopping scene for this book.

Paul Waters and Julie Waters are a travel-writing team from Montréal, most of which they cover for Fodor's. Paul is an editorial-board member at the *Montréal Gazette;* Julie works for various trade travel magazines.

You can rest assured that you're in good hands—and that no property mentioned in the book has paid to be included. Each has been selected strictly on its merits, as the best of its type in its price range.

How to Use this Book

Up front is Smart Travel Tips A to Z, arranged alphabetically by topic and loaded with tips, Web sites, and contact information. Destination: Montréal and Québec City helps get you in the mood for your trip. Subsequent chapters in *Montréal and Québec City* are arranged regionally. The two city chapters begin with exploring information, with a section for each neighborhood (each recommending a good tour and listing sights alphabetically). All regional chapters are divided geographically; within each area, towns are covered in logical geographical order, and attractive stretches of road between them are indicated by the designation En Route. To help you decide what you'll have time to visit, all chapters begin with our writers' favorite itineraries. (Mix itineraries from several chapters, and you can put together a really exceptional trip.) The A to Z section that ends every chapter lists additional resources.

Icons and Symbols

★ Our special recommendations
✕ Restaurant
🖫 Lodging establishment
✕🖫 Lodging establishment whose restaurant warrants a special trip
⚿ Campgrounds
🐤 Good for kids (rubber duck)
☞ Sends you to another section of the guide for more information
⊠ Address
☎ Telephone number
🕓 Opening and closing times
💵 Admission prices (those we give apply to adults; substantially reduced fees are almost always available for children, students, and senior citizens)

Numbers in white and black circles ③ ❸ that appear on the maps, in the margins, and within the tours correspond to one another.

For hotels, you can assume that all rooms have private baths, phones, TVs, and air-conditioning unless otherwise noted and that all hotels operate on the European Plan (with no meals) if we don't specify another meal plan. We always list a property's facilities but not whether you'll be charged extra to use them, so do ask what's included. For restaurants, it's always a good idea to book ahead; we mention reservations only when they're essential or are not accepted. All restaurants we list are open daily for lunch and dinner unless stated otherwise; dress is mentioned only when men are required to wear a jacket or a jacket and tie. Look for an overview of local dining-out habits in Smart Travel Tips A to Z and in the Pleasures and Pastimes section after each chapter introduction.

Don't Forget to Write

Your experiences—positive and negative—matter to us. If we have missed or misstated something, we want to hear about it. We follow up on all suggestions. Contact the Montréal and Québec City editor at editors@fodors.com or c/o Fodor's, 1745 Broadway, New York, NY 10019. And have a fabulous trip!

Karen Cure

Karen Cure
Editorial Director

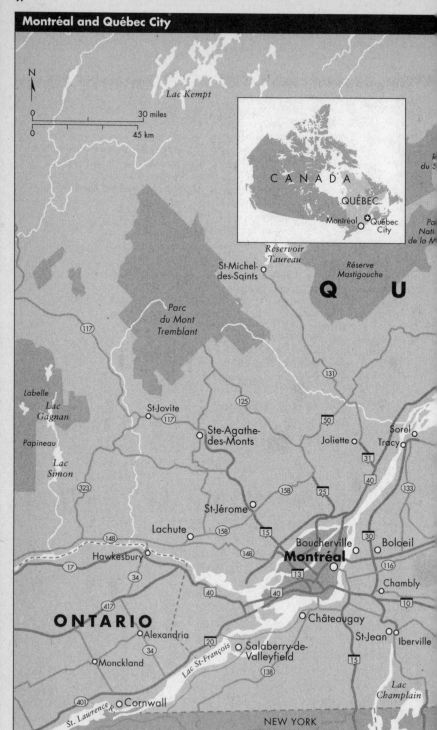

N

0 _____ 30 miles
0 _____ 45 km

Lac Kempt

CANADA

QUÉBEC

Montréal ○ ✦ Québec City

Réservoir Taureau

Réserve Mastigouche

St-Michel-des-Saints

Q **U**

Parc du Mont Tremblant

(117)

Labelle

Lac Gagnan

St-Jovite ○ (117)

(125)

(131)

(50)

Joliette ○

Sorel ○

Tracy ○

Papineau

Ste-Agathe-des-Monts

(31)

Lac Simon

(323)

(158)

(25)

(40)

(133)

St-Jérome ○

Lachute ○ (158)

(15)

Boucherville ○

Boloeil ○

(148)

Hawkesbury ○

(148)

Montréal

(30)

(116)

(17)

(34)

(13)

Chambly ○

(417)

(40)

(40)

ONTARIO

○ Alexandria

(34)

Lac St-François

(20)

Salaberry-de-Valleyfield

(15)

Châteaugay ○

St-Jean ○○ Iberville

(10)

○ Monckland

(138)

Lac Champlain

(401)

St. Lawrence R. ○ Cornwall

NEW YORK

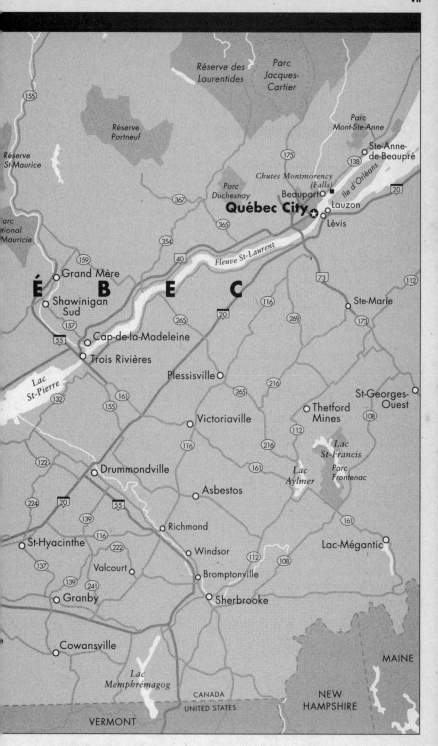

ESSENTIAL INFORMATION

AIR TRAVEL

BOOKING

When you book **look for nonstop flights** and **remember that "direct" flights stop at least once.** Try to avoid connecting flights, which require a change of plane. Two airlines may operate a connecting flight jointly, so ask if your airline operates every segment of the trip; you may find that the carrier you prefer flies you only part of the way. To find more booking tips and to check prices and make on-line flight reservations, log on to www.fodors.com.

CARRIERS

When flying internationally, you must usually choose between a domestic carrier, the national flag carrier of the country you are visiting, and a foreign carrier from a third country. National flag carriers have the greatest number of nonstops. Domestic carriers may have better connections to your hometown and serve a greater number of gateway cities. Third-party carriers may have a price advantage.

Of the major U.S. and U.K. airlines, American, British Airways, Delta, Northwest, and US Airways serve Montréal; United flies to Montréal and Québec City.

More specifically, US Airways has six nonstop flights daily from New York's LaGuardia Airport to Montréal's Dorval Airport. Air Canada has the most nonstop flights, and flies to Dorval Airport and Québec City's Jean LeSage Airport from 57 U.S. cities.

Regularly scheduled flights to Montréal and Québec City are available on Air Canada and the regional feeder airlines associated with it. Since the end of 1999, when it took over the smaller, financially troubled Canadian Airlines, Air Canada has dominated

90% of Canada's airline industry. A few upstart carriers, such as Air Tango and JetsGo, have entered the fray to compete with Air Canada.

From the United Kingdom, Canadian charter line Air Transat offers flights to Montréal, though not in winter. This carrier also flies between many major Canadian cities. Air Canada's Air Tango and JetsGo are both budget carriers who book only via their Web sites. JetsGo flies only within Canada, and Air Tango serves only three cities outside of Canada: Las Vegas, Ft. Lauderdale, and Orlando.

For regulations and for the locations of air bases that allow private flights, check with the regional tourist agencies for charter companies and with the District Controller of Air Services in Québec City. Private pilots should obtain information from the Canada Map Office, which has the "Canada Flight Supplement" (lists of airports with Canada Customs services) as well as aeronautical charts.

➤ MAJOR AIRLINES: **Air Canada** (☎ 888/247–2262, WEB www.aircanada.ca). **American Airlines** (☎ 800/433–7300, WEB www.aa.com). **British Airways** (☎ 800/247–9297, 0845/722–2111, WEB www.britishairways.com). **Continental** (☎ 800/525–0280, WEB www.continental.com). **Delta** (☎ 800/241–4141, WEB www.delta.com). **Northwest** (☎ 800/225–2525, WEB www.nwa.com). **United** (☎ 800/241–6522, WEB www.united.com). **US Airways** (☎ 800/428–4322, WEB www.usair.com).

➤ SMALLER AIRLINES: **Air Tango** (☎ 800/315–1390, WEB www.flytango.com). **Air Transat** (☎ 877/872–6728). **JetsGo** (☎ 866/448–5888, WEB www.jetsgo.com).

CHECK-IN AND BOARDING

Always **ask your carrier about its check-in policy.** Plan to arrive at the airport about two hours before your scheduled departure time for domestic flights and 2½ to 3 hours before international flights. Assuming that not everyone with a ticket will show up, airlines routinely overbook planes. When everyone does, airlines ask for volunteers to give up their seats. In return, these volunteers usually get a certificate for a free flight and are rebooked on the next flight out. If there are not enough volunteers, the airline must choose who will be denied boarding. The first to get bumped are passengers who checked in late and those flying on discounted tickets, so **get to the gate and check in as early as possible,** especially during peak periods.

Always **bring a government-issued photo I.D. to the airport;** even when it's not required, a passport is best. You will be asked to show it before you are allowed to check in. U.S. Customs and Immigration maintains an office at the Montréal airports; U.S.-bound passengers should arrive early enough to clear customs before their flight. Make sure you arrive at the airport at least two hours before your flight departs.

Security measures at Canadian airports are similar to those in the United States. Be sure you're not carrying anything that could be construed as a weapon: a letter opener, Swiss Army knife, or a toy weapon, for example. Arriving passengers from overseas flights might find a beagle in a green coat sniffing their luggage; he's looking for forbidden agricultural products.

Departing passengers in Montréal must pay a $15 airport-improvement fee before boarding.

CUTTING COSTS

The least expensive airfares to Montréal and Québec City are priced for round-trip travel and must usually be purchased in advance. Airlines generally allow you to change your return date for a fee; most low-fare tickets, however, are nonrefundable. It's smart to **call a number of airlines,** and when you are quoted a good price, **book it on the spot**—the same fare may not be available the next day. Always **check different routings** and

look into using alternate airports. Also, price off-peak flights, which may be significantly less expensive than others. Travel agents, especially low-fare specialists (☞ Discounts & Deals), are helpful.

Consolidators are another good source. They buy tickets for scheduled international flights at reduced rates from the airlines, then sell them at prices that beat the best fare available directly from the airlines. Sometimes you can even get your money back if you need to return the ticket. Carefully read the fine print detailing penalties for changes and cancellations, purchase the ticket with a credit card, and **confirm your consolidator reservation with the airline.**

➤ CONSOLIDATORS: **Cheap Tickets** (☎ 800/377–1000 or 888/922–8849, WEB www.cheaptickets.com). **Discount Airline Ticket Service** (☎ 800/576–1600). **Up & Away Travel** (☎ 212/889–2345). **World Travel Network** (☎ 800/409–6753).

ENJOYING THE FLIGHT

State your seat preference when purchasing your ticket, and then repeat it when you confirm and when you check in. For more legroom, you can request one of the few emergency-aisle seats at check-in, if you are capable of lifting at least 50 pounds—a Federal Aviation Administration requirement of passengers in these seats. Seats behind a bulkhead also offer more legroom, but they don't have under-seat storage. Don't sit in the row in front of the emergency aisle or in front of a bulkhead, where seats may not recline.

If you have dietary concerns, **ask for special meals when booking.** These can be vegetarian, low-cholesterol, or kosher, for example. It's a good idea to pack some healthy snacks and a small (plastic) bottle of water in your carry-on bag. On long flights, try to maintain a normal routine, to help fight jet lag. At night, **get some sleep.** By day, **eat light meals, drink water** (not alcohol), and **move around the cabin** to stretch your legs. For additional jet-lag tips consult *Fodor's FYI: Travel Fit & Healthy* (available at bookstores everywhere).

None of the major airlines or charter lines permit smoking.

FLYING TIMES

Flying time to Montréal is 1½ hours from New York, 2 hours from Chicago, 4½ hours from Dallas, 6 hours from Los Angeles, 6½ hours from London, and 22 hours from Sydney.

HOW TO COMPLAIN

If your baggage goes astray or your flight goes awry, complain right away. Most carriers require that you **file a claim immediately.** The Aviation Consumer Protection Division of the Department of Transportation publishes *Fly-Rights,* which discusses airlines and consumer issues and is available on-line. At PassengerRights.com, a Web site, you can compose a letter of complaint and distribute it electronically.

➤ AIRLINE COMPLAINTS: **Aviation Consumer Protection Division** (⊠ U.S. Department of Transportation, Room 4107, C-75, Washington, DC 20590, ☎ 202/366–2220, WEB www.dot.gov/airconsumer). **Federal Aviation Administration Consumer Hotline** (☎ 800/322–7873).

RECONFIRMING

Check the status of your flight before you leave for the airport. You can do this on your carrier's Web site, by linking to a flight-status checker (many Web booking services offer these), or by calling your carrier or travel agent. Always confirm international flights at least 72 hours ahead of the scheduled departure time.

AIRPORTS

Dorval International Airport (YUL) and Mirabel International Airport (YMX) serve Montréal, and the small Jean Lesage International Airport (YQB) serves Québec City. Newer Mirabel is primarily used for a limited number of charter flights, while the older Dorval handles most other flights. Chances are, you're arriving at Dorval.

➤ AIRPORT INFORMATION: **Dorval International Airport** (⊠ 975 blvd. René-Vachon, Dorval, ☎ 514/394–7377). **Jean Lesage International Airport** (⊠ 510 rue Principale, Ste-Foy, ☎ 418/640–2600). **Mirabel International Airport** (⊠ 12600 rue Aérogare, Mirabel, ☎ 514/394–7377).

BIKE TRAVEL

Despite Canada's harsh climate and demanding landscape, long-distance bicycle travel is very popular, especially in Québec. Some terrain is steep and hilly, but it's always varied and interesting. Québec is in the middle of developing the Route Verte, a 3,500-km (2,170-mi) network of trails covering the southern half of the province. In many areas, some of the prettiest roads have dirt or gravel surfaces, which make a hybrid bike more practical than a road bike. Bicycle rentals are readily available in all major cities, in recreational areas (the Québec Laurentians, for example), and in resort towns.

Nationally, the Trans-Canada Trail—linking the Atlantic to both the Pacific and Arctic oceans—will allow bicycles along much of its length when the project is finished. Though cyclists aren't allowed on most multiple-lane, limited-access highways, much of the Trans-Canada Highway is a two-lane blacktop with broad, paved shoulders that are widely used by cyclists crossing the country. There are also plenty of secondary roads that see little traffic (and almost no truck traffic).

For maps and information on bicycle routes, consult the provincial tourist information offices. Bikes can be rented around the cities and province, anything from mountain bikes to hybrids to touring cycles; cost is usually $10 to $25 per day.

BIKES IN FLIGHT

Most airlines accommodate bikes as luggage, provided they are dismantled and boxed; check with individual airlines about packing requirements. Airlines sell bike boxes, which are often free at bike shops, for about US$15 (bike bags start at US$100). International travelers often can substitute a bike for a piece of checked luggage at no charge; otherwise, the cost is about US$100. Domestic and Canadian airlines charge US$40–US$80 each way.

BOAT AND FERRY TRAVEL

A fast hydrofoil, the *Dauphin*, runs from Montréal to Québec City daily during summer. Travel time is 2 hours each way, and the boat runs from June through mid-September.

FARES & SCHEDULES

Cost for a one-way ticket on the Dauphin fast ferry from Montréal to Québec is $80 to $90; a round-trip ticket is $130 to $150. Although the boat runs daily, the ticket office at Montréal's Quai Jacques-Cartier—where the boat departs—is only open weekends from 10–6. Weekdays, call the toll-free number below and reserve a seat.

➤ BOAT & FERRY INFORMATION: **Le Dauphin** (⊠ Quai Jacques-Cartier, Montréal, ☎ 514/288–4499 or 877/648–4499, WEB www.dauphins.ca).

BUSINESS HOURS

Business hours are uniform throughout the province. Businesses do not close on the following Monday when a holiday falls on a weekend.

BANKS & OFFICES

Most banks in the province of Québec are open Monday through Thursday 10–3 and Friday 10–5 or 6. Some banks are open longer hours and also on Saturday morning. All banks are closed on national holidays. Most banks (and some gas stations) have automatic teller machines (ATMs) that are accessible around the clock.

Government offices are generally open 9–5; some close for an hour around noon. Official post offices are open 8–5 weekdays and 9–noon on Saturdays. Postal outlets in city pharmacies—of which there are a dozen or so in Montréal—may stay open as late as 9 PM even on Saturdays.

GAS STATIONS

Most highway and city gas stations in the province of Québec are open daily (although there's rarely a mechanic on duty Sunday) and some are open around the clock. In small towns, gas stations are often closed on Sunday, although they may take turns staying open.

MUSEUMS AND SIGHTS

Hours at museums vary, but most open at 10 or 11 and close in the evening. Some smaller museums close for lunch. Many museums are closed on Monday; some make up for it by staying open late on Wednesday, often waiving admission.

The days when all churches were always open are gone; vandalism, theft, and the drop in general piety have seen to that. But the major churches in Montréal and Québec City—the Basilique Notre-Dame-de-Montréal, for example—are open daily, usually about 9–6.

PHARMACIES

The province's pharmacies are uniformly open from 9–5, but in Montréal and Québec City a few are open 24 hours; most close around 10 PM or 11 PM.

SHOPS

Stores, shops, and supermarkets usually are open Monday through Saturday 9–6, although in Montréal and Québec City, supermarkets are often open 7:30 AM–9 PM and some food stores are open around the clock. Most liquor stores are closed on Sundays, with a few exceptions. Shops often stay open Thursday and Friday evenings, most malls until 9 PM. Convenience stores tend to be open 24 hours a day, seven days a week.

BUS TRAVEL

The bus is an essential form of transportation in Québec, especially if you want to visit out-of-the-way towns that do not have airports or rail lines.

There are approximately 20 private bus lines serving the province in all; Orléans Express is probably the most useful, as it offers regular service between Montréal and Québec City with a relatively new fleet of clean, comfortable buses. Limocar is another bus line serving the ski resorts of the Laurentians and Eastern Townships. Greyhound Lines and Voyageur offer interprovincial service and are reasonably timely and comfortable, if not exactly plush. Smoking isn't permitted on any buses.

CUTTING COSTS

Greyhound's Canada Coach Pass Plus gives you access to Québec and the Maritime Provinces. Passes must be purchased in Canada at a Greyhound terminal. They represent an excellent value for travelers who want to wander the highways and byways of the country, packing a lot of miles into a relatively short period of time. However, for occasional, short daytrips (from Montréal to Québec City, for example) they're hardly worth it.

FARES AND SCHEDULES

Bus terminals in Montréal and Québec City are usually efficient operations, with service all week and plenty of agents on hand to handle ticket sales. In villages and some small towns, the bus station is simply a counter in a local convenience store, gas station, or snack bar. Getting information on schedules beyond the local ones is sometimes difficult in these places. In rural Québec, it's advisable to **bring along a French-English dictionary,** although most merchants and clerks can handle a simple ticket sale in English.

PAYING

In major bus terminals, most bus lines accept at least some of the major credit cards. Some smaller lines require cash or take only Visa or MasterCard. All accept travelers' checks in U.S. or Canadian currency with suitable identification, but it's advisable to exchange foreign currency (including U.S. currency) at a bank or exchange office. To buy a ticket in really small centers, it's best to use cash.

RESERVATIONS

Most bus lines do not accept reservations. You should plan on picking up your tickets at least 45 minutes before the bus's scheduled departure time.

➤ BUS INFORMATION: **Greyhound Lines** (✉ 877 Greyhound Way SW, Calgary, AB T3C 3V8, ☎ 800/661–8747 in Canada; 800/231–2222 in the U.S., WEB www.greyhound.ca). **Limocar** (✉ 505 Est blvd. Maisonneuve, Montréal, QC H2L 1Y4, ☎ 514/845–8899 Eastern Townships; 450/681–4111 Laurentians). **Orléns Express** (✉ 505 Est blvd. Maisonneuve, Montréal, QC H2L 1Y4,

☎ 514/395–4000). **Voyageur** (✉ 505 Est blvd. Maisonneuve, Montréal, QC H2L 1Y4, ☎ 514/842–2281).

CAMERAS AND PHOTOGRAPHY

To catch Québec at its most dramatically beautiful, consider a winter trip. City and country take on new glamour when they're frosted with snow.

The *Kodak Guide to Shooting Great Travel Pictures* (available at bookstores everywhere) is loaded with tips.

➤ PHOTO HELP: **Kodak Information Center** (☎ 800/242–2424, WEB www.kodak.com).

EQUIPMENT PRECAUTIONS

Don't pack film and equipment in checked luggage, where it is much more susceptible to damage. X-ray machines used to view checked luggage are becoming much more powerful and therefore are much more likely to ruin your film. Try to **ask for hand inspection of film,** which becomes clouded after repeated exposure to airport X-ray machines, and **keep videotapes and computer disks away from metal detectors.** Always **keep film, tape, and computer disks out of the sun.** Carry an extra supply of batteries, and **be prepared to turn on your camera, camcorder, or laptop** to prove to airport security personnel that the device is real.

CAR RENTAL

Rates in Montréal run from about $30 to $45 a day for an economy car with air-conditioning and unlimited kilometers. If you prefer a manual-transmission car, check whether the rental agency of your choice offers stick shifts; some companies, such as Avis, don't in Canada.

➤ MAJOR AGENCIES: **Alamo** (☎ 800/522–9696; WEB www.alamo.com). **Avis** (☎ 800/331–1084; 800/879–2847 in Canada; 02/9353–9000 in Australia; 09/526–2847 in New Zealand; 0870/606–0100 in the U.K.; WEB www.avis.com). **Budget** (☎ 800/527–0700; 0870/156–5656 in the U.K.; WEB www.budget.com). **Dollar** (☎ 800/800–6000; 0124/622–0111 in the U.K., where it's affiliated with Sixt; 02/9223–1444 in Australia; WEB www.dollar.com). **Hertz** (☎ 800/654–

3001; 800/263–0600 in Canada; 020/ 8897–2072 in the U.K.; 02/9669– 2444 in Australia; 09/256–8690 in New Zealand; WEB www.hertz.com). **National Car Rental** (☎ 800/227– 7368; 020/8680–4800 in the U.K.; WEB www.nationalcar.com).

CUTTING COSTS

Renting at the airports in Québec City and Montréal is usually more expensive than renting elsewhere in the cities.

For a good deal, **book through a travel agent who will shop around.** Also, **price local car-rental companies**— whose prices may be lower still, although their service and maintenance may not be as good as those of major rental agencies—and **research rates on-line.** Remember to ask about required deposits, cancellation penalties, and drop-off charges if you're planning to pick up the car in one city and leave it in another. If you're traveling during a holiday period, also make sure that a confirmed reservation guarantees you a car.

➤ LOCAL AGENCIES: **Via Route** (✉ Montréal, ☎ 514/521–5221 or 888/ 842–7388, WEB www.viaroute.com).

INSURANCE

When driving a rented car you are generally responsible for any damage to or loss of the vehicle. You may also be liable for any property damage or personal injury that you may cause while driving. Before you rent, see what coverage you already have under the terms of your personal auto-insurance policy and credit cards.

REQUIREMENTS AND RESTRICTIONS

In Canada, you must get an international driver's license before arriving if you are from any country except the U.S. International driving permits (IDPs) are available from the American and Canadian automobile associations and, in the United Kingdom, from the Automobile Association and Royal Automobile Club. These international permits, valid only in conjunction with your regular driver's license, are universally recognized; having one may save you a problem with local authorities.

In Québec, drivers under 25 often have to pay a surcharge of $5 a day. Rental-car companies have not set an upper age limit. Most rental companies don't allow you to drive gravel roads. Crossing into the U.S. is allowed. Child seats are compulsory for children ages 5 and under.

SURCHARGES

Before you pick up a car in one city and leave it in another, **ask about drop-off charges or one-way service fees,** which can be substantial. Note, too, that some rental agencies charge extra if you return the car before the time specified in your contract. To avoid a hefty refueling fee, **fill the tank just before you turn in the car,** but be aware that gas stations near the rental outlet may overcharge. It's almost never a deal to buy the tank of gas in the car when you rent it; the understanding is that you'll return it empty, but some fuel usually remains.

CAR TRAVEL

Canada's highway system is excellent. It includes the Trans-Canada Highway, which uses several numbers and is the longest highway in the world— running about 8,000 km (5,000 mi) from Victoria, British Columbia, to St. John's, Newfoundland, using ferries to bridge coastal waters at each end. It passes through Montréal and Québec City.

FROM THE U.S.

Drivers must carry owner registration and proof of insurance coverage, which is compulsory in Canada. The Canadian Non-Resident Inter-Provincial Motor Vehicle Liability Insurance Card, available from any U.S. insurance company, is accepted as evidence of financial responsibility in Canada, but you're not required to have one. The minimum liability in Québec is $50,000. If you are driving a car that is not registered in your name, carry a letter from the owner that authorizes your use of the vehicle.

The U.S. Interstate Highway System leads directly into Canada: I–91 and I–89 from Vermont to Québec, and I–87 from New York to Québec. Many smaller highways cross between the two countries as well.

➤ INSURANCE INFORMATION: **Insurance Bureau of Canada** (☎ 416/362–9528; 800/387–2880 in Canada, WEB www.ibc.ca).

EMERGENCY SERVICES

Dial 911 in an emergency. Contact CAA, the Canadian Automobile Association, in the event of a flat, dead battery, empty gas tank, or other car-related mishap. Automobile Association of America membership includes CAA service.

➤ EMERGENCY INFORMATION: **CAA** (☎ 800/222–4357 or 514/861–7111, WEB www.caa.com).

GASOLINE

At this writing, gas prices in Canada are on the rise; the per-liter price is 85¢. Distances are always shown in kilometers, and gasoline is always sold in liters. (A gallon has 3.8 liters.) Lead-free is called *sans plomb*. Major credit cards are widely accepted; paying for gas is the same as it is in the U.S., and you can often pay at the pump. Receipts are provided if you want one—ask for a *facture*. Fuel comes in several grades, denoted in Montréal by bronze, silver, and gold colors and in other areas of the province by the words *reguliere* and *superieure*.

ROAD CONDITIONS

In Montréal and Québec City, the jumble of bicycle riders, delivery vehicles, taxis, and municipal buses can be chaotic. In the countryside at night, roads are lit at exit points from major highways and are otherwise dark. Roads in the province are not very good—be prepared for some spine-jolting bumps and potholes, and check tire pressure once in awhile. Also, in wintertime, be aware of changing road conditions: Montréal streets are kept mostly clear of snow and ice, but once outside the city the situation quickly denigrates. Locals are notorious for exceeding the speed limit, so keep an eye on your mirrors.

RULES OF THE ROAD

By law, you are required to wear seat belts even in the back seat (and to use infant seats). Radar-detection devices are illegal in Québec, and just having one in your car is illegal. Speed limits, given in kilometers, are usually within the 90–110 kph (50–68 mph) range outside the cities.

Right turns on red signals are illegal in the province of Québec. Driving with a blood-alcohol content of .08 percent or higher is illegal and earns a stiff fine. Headlights are compulsory in inclement weather.

➤ CONTACTS: **Ministère des Transports du Québec** (☎ 514/873–2605, WEB www.mtq.gouv.qc.ca).

CHILDREN IN QUÉBEC

Travelers crossing the border with children should **carry identification for them** similar to that required by adults (i.e., passport or birth certificate). Children traveling with one parent or other adult should **bring a letter of permission** from the other parent, parents, or legal guardian. Divorced parents with shared custody rights should **carry legal documents establishing their status.**

If you are renting a car, don't forget to **arrange for a car seat** when you reserve. For general advice about traveling with children, consult *Fodor's FYI: Travel with Your Baby* (available in bookstores everywhere).

FLYING

If your children are two or older, **ask about children's airfares.** As a general rule, infants under two not occupying a seat fly at greatly reduced fares or even for free. When booking, **confirm carry-on allowances** if you're traveling with infants. In general, for babies charged 10%–50% of the adult fare you are allowed one carry-on bag and a collapsible stroller; if the flight is full, the stroller may have to be checked or you may be limited to less.

Experts agree that it's a good idea to use safety seats aloft for children weighing less than 40 pounds. Airlines set their own policies: U.S. carriers usually require that the child be ticketed, even if he or she is young enough to ride free, since the seats must be strapped into regular seats. Do **check your airline's policy about using safety seats during takeoff and landing.** Safety seats are not allowed everywhere in the plane, so get your seat assignments as early as possible.

When reserving, **request children's meals or a freestanding bassinet** (not available at all airlines) if you need them. But note that bulkhead seats, where you must sit to use the bassinet, may lack an overhead bin or storage space on the floor.

LODGING

Most hotels in Canada allow children under a certain age to stay in their parents' room at no extra charge, but others charge for them as extra adults; be sure to **find out the cutoff age for children's discounts.**

SIGHTS & ATTRACTIONS

Places that are especially appealing to children are indicated by a rubber-duckie icon (☺) in the margin.

CONSUMER PROTECTION

Whether you're shopping for gifts or purchasing travel services, **pay with a major credit card** whenever possible, so you can cancel payment or get reimbursed if there's a problem (and you can provide documentation). If you're doing business with a particular company for the first time, **contact your local Better Business Bureau and the attorney general's offices** in your state and (for U.S. businesses) the company's home state as well. Have any complaints been filed? Finally, if you're buying a package or tour, always **consider travel insurance** that includes default coverage (☞ Insurance).

➤ BBBs: **Council of Better Business Bureaus** (✉ 4200 Wilson Blvd., Suite 800, Arlington, VA 22203, ☎ 703/276–0100, FAX 703/525–8277, WEB www.bbb.org).

CUSTOMS AND DUTIES

When shopping abroad, **keep receipts** for all purchases. Upon reentering the country, **be ready to show customs officials what you've bought.** If you feel a duty is incorrect, appeal the assessment. If you object to the way your clearance was handled, note the inspector's badge number. In either case, first ask to see a supervisor. If the problem isn't resolved, write to the appropriate authorities, beginning with the port director at your point of entry.

U.S. Customs and Immigration has preclearance services in Montréal at both major airports. This allows U.S.-bound air passengers to depart their airplane directly on arrival at their U.S. destination without further inspection and delays.

IN AUSTRALIA

Australian residents who are 18 or older may bring home A$400 worth of souvenirs and gifts (including jewelry), 250 cigarettes or 250 grams of tobacco, and 1,125 ml of alcohol (including wine, beer, and spirits). Residents under 18 may bring back A$200 worth of goods. Prohibited items include meat products. Seeds, plants, and fruits need to be declared upon arrival.

➤ INFORMATION: **Australian Customs Service** (Regional Director, ✉ 3rd Floor Tower, Sydney Central Building, 477 Pitt St., Sydney, NSW 2000, ☎ 02/6275–6666, FAX 02/9213–4043, WEB www.customs.gov.au).

IN CANADA

American and British visitors may bring in the following items duty-free: 200 cigarettes, 50 cigars, and 7 ounces of tobacco; 1 bottle (1.1 liters or 40 imperial ounces) of liquor or wine, or 24 355-ml (12-ounce) bottles or cans of beer for personal consumption. Any alcohol and tobacco products in excess of these amounts is subject to duty, provincial fees, and taxes. You can also bring in gifts up to a total value of $750.

A deposit is sometimes required for trailers (refunded upon return). Cats and dogs must have a certificate issued by a licensed veterinarian that clearly identifies the animal and certifies that it has been vaccinated against rabies during the preceding 36 months. Seeing-eye dogs are allowed into Canada without restriction. Plant material must be declared and inspected. There may be restrictions on some live plants, bulbs, and seeds. With certain restrictions or prohibitions on some fruits and vegetables, visitors may bring food with them for their own use, providing the quantity is consistent with the duration of the visit.

Canada's firearms laws are significantly stricter than those in the United States. All handguns and semiautomatic and fully automatic weapons are prohibited and cannot be brought into the country. Sporting rifles and shotguns may be imported provided they are to be used for sporting, hunting, or competition while in Canada. All firearms must be declared to Canada Customs at the first point of entry. Failure to declare firearms will result in their seizure, and criminal charges may be made. Regulations require visitors to have a confirmed "Firearms Declaration" to bring any guns into Canada; a fee of $50 applies, good for one year. For more information, contact the Canadian Firearms Centre.

➤ INFORMATION: **Revenue Canada** (⊠ 2265 St. Laurent Blvd. S, Ottawa, ON K1G 4K3, ☎ 204/983–3500; 800/461–9999 in Canada, WEB www.ccra.gc.ca). **Canadian Firearms Centre** (☎ 800/731–4000, WEB www.cfc-ccaf.gc.ca).

IN NEW ZEALAND

All homeward-bound residents may bring back NZ$700 worth of souvenirs and gifts; passengers may not pool their allowances, and children can claim only the concession on goods intended for their own use. For those 17 or older, the duty-free allowance also includes 4.5 liters of wine or beer; one 1,125-ml bottle of spirits; and either 200 cigarettes, 250 grams of tobacco, 50 cigars, *or* a combination of the three up to 250 grams. Meat products, seeds, plants, and fruits must be declared upon arrival to the Agricultural Services Department.

➤ INFORMATION: **New Zealand Customs** (⊠ Head Office, The Customhouse, 17–21 Whitmore St., Box 2218, Wellington, ☎ 09/359–6655, FAX 09/359–6735, WEB www.customs.govt.nz).

IN THE U.K.

From countries outside the European Union, including Canada, you may bring home, duty-free, 200 cigarettes or 50 cigars; 1 liter of spirits or 2 liters of fortified or sparkling wine or liqueurs; 2 liters of still table wine; 60 ml of perfume; 250 ml of toilet water; plus £145 worth of other goods, including gifts and souvenirs. Prohibited items include meat products, seeds, plants, and fruits.

➤ INFORMATION: **HM Customs and Excise** (⊠ St. Christopher House, Southwark, London SE1 OTE, ☎ 0845/010–9000 within the U.K., 020/8929–0152, WEB www.hmce.gov.uk).

IN THE U.S.

U.S. residents who have been out of the country for at least 48 hours (and who have not used the US$800 allowance or any part of it in the past 30 days) may bring home US$800 worth of foreign goods duty-free; the duty-free allowance drops to US$200 for fewer than 48 hours.

U.S. residents 21 and older may bring back 1 liter of alcohol duty-free. In addition, regardless of your age, you are allowed 200 cigarettes and 100 non-Cuban cigars. Antiques, which the U.S. Customs Service defines as objects more than 100 years old, enter duty-free, as do original works of art done entirely by hand, including paintings, drawings, and sculptures. You may also send packages home duty-free, with a limit of one parcel per addressee per day (except alcohol or tobacco products or perfume worth more than US$5). You can mail up to US$200 worth of goods for personal use; label the package PERSONAL USE and attach a list of its con-tents and their retail value. If the package contains your used personal belongings, mark it PERSONAL GOODS RETURNED to avoid paying duties. You may send up to US$100 worth of goods as a gift; mark the package UNSOLICITED GIFT. Mailed items do not affect your duty-free allowance on your return.

➤ INFORMATION: **U.S. Customs Service** (for inquiries, ⊠ 1300 Pennsylvania Ave. NW, Washington, DC 20229, WEB www.customs.gov, ☎ 202/354–1000; for complaints, ⊠ Customer Satisfaction Unit, 1300 Pennsylvania Ave. NW, Room 5.5A, Washington, DC 20229; for registration of equipment, ⊠ Office of Passenger Programs, 1300 Pennsylvania Ave. NW, Room 5.4D, Washington, DC 20229, ☎ 202/927–0530).

DINING

The restaurants we list are the cream of the crop in each price category. Properties indicated by a ✕🏠 are lodging establishments whose restaurant warrants a special trip.

French–Canadian fast food follows the same concept as American fast food, though roasted chicken is also quite popular—and *poutine* (fries topped with gravy and/or cheese curds) is wildly popular.

Local chains to watch for include St.-Hubert, which serves barbecued chicken, and La Belle Province and Valentine, which both serve up artery-clogging hamburgers, hot dogs, and fries. As an antidote, try the Montréal chain Le Commensal—it's completely vegetarian, and it's excellent.

RESERVATIONS AND DRESS

Reservations are always a good idea; we mention them only when they're essential or not accepted. Book as far ahead as you can, and reconfirm as soon as you arrive. (Large parties should always call ahead to check the reservations policy.) We mention dress only when men are required to wear a jacket or a jacket and tie.

WINE, BEER, AND SPIRITS

You can find lots of good local microbrews, such as Unibroue's Fin du Monde, bottled in local supermarkets and on tap in bars. The locally produced hard cider P.O.M. is also excellent. The official provincial liquor store, SAQ, stocks a wide choice of wines and is also the only place you can buy hard liquor; most SAQ stores are open regular business hours.

DISABILITIES AND ACCESSIBILITY

Travelers with disabilities don't have the same blanket legal protection in Canada that they have in the United States. Indeed, some facilities aren't easy to use in a wheelchair—the subway system in Montréal, for example, and city buses just about everywhere. However, thanks to increased awareness and government-incentive programs, most major attractions— museums, churches, theaters—are equipped with ramps and lifts to handle wheelchairs. National and provincial institutions—parks, public monuments, and government buildings—almost always are accessible.

The Canadian Paraplegic Association National Office has information about touring in Canada. Kéroul, which was founded by travelers with disabilities to promote tourism in Québec among people in similar circumstances, rates hotels and attractions, organizes trips, and lobbies for improved facilities.

To file a complaint about transportation obstacles at Canadian airports (including flights), railroads, or ferries, contact the Director, Accessible Transportation Directorate, at the Canadian Transportation Agency (www.cta-otc.gc.ca).

➤ LOCAL RESOURCES: **Canadian Paraplegic Association National Office** (✉ 1101 Prince of Wales Dr., Ottawa, ON K2C 3W7, ☎ 613/723–1033, WEB www.canparaplegic.org). **Kéroul** (✉ Box 1000, Branch M, Montréal, QC H1V 3R2, ☎ 514/252–3104, WEB www.keroul.qc.ca).

RESERVATIONS

When discussing accessibility with an operator or reservations agent, **ask hard questions.** Are there any stairs, inside *or* out? Are there grab bars next to the toilet *and* in the shower/tub? How wide is the doorway to the room? To the bathroom? For the most extensive facilities meeting the latest legal specifications, **opt for newer accommodations.** If you reserve through a toll-free number, consider also calling the hotel's local number to confirm the information from the central reservations office. Get confirmation in writing when you can.

➤ COMPLAINTS: **Aviation Consumer Protection Division** (☞ Air Travel) for airline-related problems. **Departmental Office of Civil Rights** (for general inquiries, ✉ U.S. Department of Transportation, S-30, 400 7th St. SW, Room 10215, Washington, DC 20590, ☎ 202/366–4648, FAX 202/366–9371, WEB www.dot.gov/ost/docr/index.htm). **Disability Rights Section** (✉ U.S. Department of Justice, Civil Rights Division, Box 66738, Washington, DC 20035-6738, ☎ 800/514–

0301, for ADA inquiries; WEB www. usdoj.gov/crt/ada/adahom1.htm).

TRAVEL AGENCIES

In the United States, the Americans with Disabilities Act requires that travel firms serve the needs of all travelers. Some agencies specialize in working with people with disabilities.

➤ TRAVELERS WITH MOBILITY PROBLEMS: **Access Adventures** (✉ 206 Chestnut Ridge Rd., Rochester, NY 14624, ☎ 585/889–9096, dltravel@ prodigy.net), run by a former physical-rehabilitation counselor. **CareVacations** (✉ No. 5, 5110–50 Ave., Leduc, Alberta T9E 6V4, Canada, ☎ 780/ 986–6404 or 877/478–7827, FAX 780/ 986–8332, WEB www.carevacations. com), for group tours and cruise vacations. **Flying Wheels Travel** (✉ 143 W. Bridge St., Box 382, Owatonna, MN 55060, ☎ 507/451–5005 or 800/535–6790, FAX 507/451–1685, WEB www.flyingwheelstravel.com).

DISCOUNTS AND DEALS

Be a smart shopper and **compare all your options** before making decisions. A plane ticket bought with a promotional coupon from travel clubs, coupon books, and direct-mail offers or purchased on the Internet may not be cheaper than the least expensive fare from a discount ticket agency. And always keep in mind that what you get is just as important as what you save.

DISCOUNT RESERVATIONS

To save money, **look into discount reservations services** with Web sites and toll-free numbers, which use their buying power to get a better price on hotels, airline tickets, even car rentals. When booking a room, always **call the hotel's local toll-free number** (if one is available) rather than the central reservations number—you'll often get a better price. Always ask about special packages or corporate rates.

When shopping for the best deal on hotels and car rentals, **look for guaranteed exchange rates,** which protect you against a falling dollar. With your rate locked in, you won't pay more, even if the price goes up in the local currency.

➤ AIRLINE TICKETS: ☎ 800/AIR– 4LESS.

➤ HOTEL ROOMS: **Hotel Reservations Network** (☎ 800/715–7666, WEB www.hoteldiscount.com). **RMC Travel** (☎ 800/245–5738, WEB www. rmcwebtravel.com). **Steigenberger Reservation Service** (☎ 800/223– 5652, WEB www.srs-worldhotels.com). **Turbotrip.com** (☎ 800/473–7829, WEB www.turbotrip.com).

PACKAGE DEALS

Don't confuse packages and guided tours. When you buy a package, you travel on your own, just as though you had planned the trip yourself. Fly/drive packages, which combine airfare and car rental, are often a good deal.

EMBASSIES AND CONSULATES

All embassies are in Ottawa. Emergency information is given in the A to Z section at the end of each chapter. The U.S. consulate in Montréal is open weekdays 8:30–noon and Wednesday also 2–4.

➤ AUSTRALIA: **Australian High Commission** (✉ 50 O'Connor St., Suite 710, Ottawa, ☎ 613/236–0841).

➤ NEW ZEALAND: **New Zealand High Commission** (✉ 99 Bank St., Suite 727, Ottawa, ☎ 613/238–5991).

➤ UNITED KINGDOM: **British High Commission** (✉ 80 Elgin St., Ottawa, ☎ 613/237–1530).

➤ UNITED STATES: **U.S. Consulate General** (✉ 1155 rue Saint-Alexandre, Montréal, QC H27 1Z2; mailing address: Box 65 Postal Station Desjardins, Montréal H5B 1G1, ☎ 514/ 398–9695). **U.S. Consulate General** (✉ B.P. 939, 2 pl. Terrasse Dufferin, behind Château Frontenac, Québec QC G1R 4T9). **U.S. Embassy** (✉ 490 Sussex Dr., Ottawa ON K1N 1G8, ☎ 613/238–5335).

GAY AND LESBIAN TRAVEL

Canada is generally a fairly tolerant country, and same-sex couples should face few problems in major metropolitan areas. The former Catholic bastion of Montréal actively and avidly competes for gay visitors, and has a large, visible, and very active gay and lesbian community.

Montréal's gay community is centered in Le Village, a cluster of bars, restaurants, boutiques, and antiques shops in the once run-down area between rues Amherst and Papineau. The annual Parade de la Fierté Gaie et Lesbienne, on the first weekend in August, is one of the city's biggest parades and ends a week of gay cultural activities. The community supports three magazines—*Fugues, RG,* and *Gazelle.*

For details about the gay and lesbian scene, consult *Fodor's Gay Guide to the USA* (available in bookstores everywhere).

➤ GAY- & LESBIAN-FRIENDLY TRAVEL AGENCIES: **Different Roads Travel** (✉ 8383 Wilshire Blvd., Suite 902, Beverly Hills, CA 90211, ☎ 323/651–5557 or 800/429–8747, FAX 323/651–3678, lgernert@tzell.com). **Kennedy Travel** (✉ 314 Jericho Turnpike, Floral Park, NY 11001, ☎ 516/352–4888 or 800/237–7433, FAX 516/354–8849, WEB www.kennedytravel.com). **Now, Voyager** (✉ 4406 18th St., San Francisco, CA 94114, ☎ 415/626–1169 or 800/255–6951, FAX 415/626–8626, WEB www.nowvoyager.com).

GUIDEBOOKS

Plan well and you won't be sorry. Guidebooks are excellent tools—and you can take them with you. You may want to check out pocket-size *City-pack Montréal,* which includes a foldout map and is available at on-line retailers and bookstores everywhere.

HOLIDAYS

Canadian national holidays are as follows: New Year's Day (Jan. 1), Good Friday (late March or early April), Easter Monday (the Monday following Good Friday), Victoria Day (May 21), Canada Day (July 1), Labour Day (September 2), Thanksgiving (October 14), Remembrance Day (November 11), Christmas, and Boxing Day (December 26). St. Jean Baptiste Day (June 24) is a provincial holiday.

INSURANCE

The most useful travel-insurance plan is a comprehensive policy that includes coverage for trip cancellation and interruption, default, trip delay, and medical expenses (with a waiver for preexisting conditions).

Without insurance you will lose all or most of your money if you cancel your trip, regardless of the reason. Default insurance covers you if your tour operator, airline, or cruise line goes out of business. Trip-delay covers expenses that arise because of bad weather or mechanical delays. Study the fine print when comparing policies.

U.K. residents can buy a travel-insurance policy valid for most vacations taken during the year in which it's purchased (but check preexisting-condition coverage). British and Australian citizens need extra medical coverage when traveling overseas.

Always **buy travel policies directly from the insurance company;** if you buy them from a cruise line, airline, or tour operator that goes out of business you probably will not be covered for the agency or operator's default, a major risk. Before making any purchase, **review your existing health and home-owner's policies** to find what they cover away from home.

➤ TRAVEL INSURERS: In the U.S.: **Access America** (✉ 6600 W. Broad St., Richmond, VA 23230, ☎ 800/284–8300, FAX 804/729–6021 or 800/346–9265, WEB www.etravelprotection.com). **Travel Guard International** (✉ 1145 Clark St., Stevens Point, WI 54481, ☎ 800/826–1300; 715/345–0505 international callers, FAX 800/955–8785, WEB www.travelguard.com).

➤ INSURANCE INFORMATION: In the U.K.: **Association of British Insurers** (✉ 51 Gresham St., London EC2V 7HQ, ☎ 020/7600–3333, FAX 020/7696–8999, WEB www.abi.org.uk). In Canada: **RBC Travel Insurance** (✉ 6888 Financial Dr., Tower 1, Mississauga, Ontario L5A 2Y9, ☎ 905/791–8700 or 800/668–2487, FAX 905/813–4704, WEB www.rbcinsurance.com). In Australia: **Insurance Council of Australia** (✉ Level 3, 56 Pitt St., Sydney, NSW 2000, ☎ 02/9253–5100, FAX 02/9253–5111, WEB www.ica.com.au). In New Zealand: **Insurance Council of New Zealand** (✉ Level 7, 111–115 Customhouse Quay, Box 474, Wellington, ☎ 04/

472–5230, FAX 04/473–3011, WEB
www.icnz.org.nz).

LANGUAGE

Although Canada has two official
languages—English and French—the
province of Québec has only one.
French is the language you hear most
often on the streets in Québec; it is
also the language of government,
businesses, and schools. Only in Montréal, the Ottawa Valley, and the Eastern Townships is English more widely
spoken. Most French Canadians speak
English as well, but it is useful to **learn
a few French phrases** before you go.
Canadian French has many distinctive
words and expressions, but it's no
more different from the language of
France than North American English is
from the language of Great Britain.

LANGUAGES FOR TRAVELERS

A phrase book and language-tape set
can help get you started. *Fodor's
French for Travelers* (available at
bookstores everywhere) is excellent.

LODGING

In Montréal and Québec City, you
have a choice of luxury hotels, mod-
erately priced modern properties, and
smaller older hotels with perhaps
fewer conveniences but more charm.
Options in smaller towns and in the
country include large, full-service
resorts; small, privately owned hotels;
roadside motels; and bed-and-breakfasts. Even here you need to make
reservations at least on the day on
which you plan to pull into town.

Expect accommodations to cost more
in summer than in the off-season
(except for places such as ski resorts,
where winter is high season). When
making reservations, **ask about
special deals and packages.** Big-city
hotels that cater to business travelers
often offer weekend packages, and
many city hotels offer rooms at up to
50% off in winter. If you're planning
to visit Montréal or Québec City or a
resort area in high season, **book well
in advance.** Also be aware of any
special events or festivals that may
coincide with your visit and fill every
room for miles around. For resorts
and lodges, consider the winter ski-
season high as well and plan accordingly.

The lodgings we list are the cream of
the crop in each price category. We
always list the facilities that are
available, but we don't specify
whether they cost extra; when pricing
accommodations, always ask what's
included and what costs extra. Properties are assigned price categories
based on the range from their least-
expensive standard double room at
high season (excluding holidays) to
the most expensive. Properties
marked ✕☐ are lodging establishments whose restaurants warrant a
special trip.

Assume that hotels operate on the
European Plan (EP, with no meals)
unless we specify that they use the
Continental Plan (CP, with a Continental breakfast), **Modified American
Plan** (MAP, with breakfast and dinner), or the **Full American Plan** (FAP,
with all meals).

APARTMENT & VILLA RENTALS

If you want a home base that's roomy
enough for a family and comes with
cooking facilities, **consider a furnished
rental.** These can save you money,
especially if you're traveling with a
group. Home-exchange directories
sometimes list rentals as well as
exchanges.

➤ INTERNATIONAL AGENTS: **Hide-
aways International** (✉ 767 Islington
St., Portsmouth, NH 03801, ☎ 603/
430–4433 or 800/843–4433, FAX 603/
430–4444, WEB www.hideaways.com;
membership US$129).

➤ RENTAL LISTINGS: The *Gazette* is
Montréal's daily newspaper, and has
the best rental listings in town; log on
at www.montrealgazette.com. A good
weekly free paper with more rental
listings is *Hour,* at www.hour.ca.

BED-AND-BREAKFASTS

Bed-and-breakfasts can be found in
both the country and the cities. For
assistance in booking these, **contact
the provincial tourist board,** which
either has a listing of B&Bs or can
refer you to an association that can
help you secure reservations. Be sure
to **check out the B&B's Web site,**
which may have useful information,
although you should also find out
how up-to-date it is. Room quality
varies from house to house as well,

so you can **ask to see a room before making a choice.**

CAMPING

Campgrounds in Québec range from rustic woodland settings far from the nearest paved road to facility-packed open fields full of sleek motor homes next to major highways. Some of the best sites are in national and provincial parks—well cared for, well equipped, and close to plenty of nature and activity programs for both children and adults. The campgrounds in the coastal regions of Québec are particularly beautiful. Campers tend to be working- or middle-class families with a fair sprinkling of seniors, but their tastes and practices are as varied as the campsites they favor. Some see camping simply as a way to get practical, low-cost lodgings on a road trip, while other, more sedentary campers move into one campground with as much elaborate equipment as they can and set up for a long stay. Wilderness camping for hikers and canoeists is available in national and provincial parks.

HOME EXCHANGES

If you would like to exchange your home for someone else's, **join a home-exchange organization,** which will send you its updated listings of available exchanges for a year and will include your own listing in at least one of them. It's up to you to make specific arrangements.

➤ EXCHANGE CLUBS: **HomeLink International** (✉ Box 47747, Tampa, FL 33647, ☎ 813/975–9825 or 800/638–3841, FAX 813/910–8144, WEB www.homelink.org; $106 per year).

HOSTELS

No matter what your age, you can **save on lodging costs by staying at hostels.** In some 4,500 locations in more than 70 countries around the world, Hostelling International (HI), the umbrella group for a number of national youth-hostel associations, offers single-sex, dorm-style beds and, at many hostels, rooms for couples and family accommodations. Membership in any HI national hostel association, open to travelers of all ages, allows you to stay in HI-affiliated hostels at member rates; one-

year membership is about US$25 for adults (C$35 for a two-year minimum membership in Canada, £12.50 in the U.K., A$52 in Australia, and NZ$40 in New Zealand); hostels run about US$10–$25 per night. Members have priority if the hostel is full; they're also eligible for discounts around the world, even on rail and bus travel in some countries.

➤ ORGANIZATIONS: **Hostelling International—American Youth Hostels** (✉ 733 15th St. NW, Suite 840, Washington, DC 20005, ☎ 202/783–6161, FAX 202/783–6171, WEB www.hiayh.org). **Hostelling International—Canada** (✉ 400–205 Catherine St., Ottawa, Ontario K2P 1C3, ☎ 613/237–7884; 800/663–5777 in Canada, FAX 613/237–7868, WEB www.hihostels.ca). **Youth Hostel Association of England and Wales** (✉ Trevelyan House, Dimple Rd., Matlock, Derbyshire DE4 3YH, U.K., ☎ 0870/8708808, FAX 01629/592702, WEB www.yha.org.uk). **Youth Hostel Association Australia** (✉ 10 Mallett St., Camperdown, NSW 2050, ☎ 02/9565–1699, FAX 02/9565–1325, WEB www.yha.com.au). **Youth Hostels Association of New Zealand** (✉ Level 3, 193 Cashel St., Box 436, Christchurch, ☎ 03/379–9970, FAX 03/365–4476, WEB www.stayyha.com).

HOTELS

Canada doesn't have a national government rating system for hotels, but Québec's tourism ministry rates the province's hotels; the stars are more a reflection of the number of facilities than of the hotel's performance. Hotels are rated zero to three stars, with zero stars representing minimal comfort and few services, and three stars being the very best.

All hotels listed have private bath unless otherwise noted.

➤ TOLL-FREE NUMBERS: **Best Western** (☎ 800/528–1234, WEB www.bestwestern.com). **Choice** (☎ 800/221–2222, WEB www.choicehotels.com). **Clarion** (☎ 800/252–7466, WEB www.clarionhotel.com). **Comfort Inn** (☎ 800/228–5150, WEB www.comfortinn.com). **Hilton** (☎ 800/445–8667, WEB www.hilton.com). **Holiday Inn** (☎ 800/465–4329, WEB www.basshotels.com). **Inter-**

Continental (☎ 800/327–0200, WEB www.intercontil.com). **Marriott** (☎ 800/228–9290, WEB www.marriott.com). **Omni** (☎ 800/843–6664, WEB www.omnihotels.com). **Quality Inn** (☎ 800/228–5151, WEB www.qualityinn.com). **Radisson** (☎ 800/333–3333, WEB www.radisson.com). **Ramada** (☎ 800/228–2828; 800/854–7854 international reservations, WEB www.ramada.com or www.ramadahotels.com). **Renaissance Hotels & Resorts** (☎ 800/468–3571, WEB www.renaissancehotels.com/). **Ritz-Carlton** (☎ 800/241–3333, WEB www.ritzcarlton.com). **Sheraton** (☎ 800/325–3535, WEB www.starwood.com/sheraton). **Wyndham Hotels & Resorts** (☎ 800/822–4200, WEB www.wyndham.com).

MAIL AND SHIPPING

In Canada you can buy stamps at the post office or from vending machines in most hotel lobbies, railway stations, airports, bus terminals, many retail outlets, and some newsstands. If you're sending mail to or within Canada, **be sure to include the postal code** (six digits and letters). Note that the suite number often appears before the street number in an address, followed by a hyphen.

The postal abbreviation for Québec is QC.

POSTAL RATES

Within Canada, postcards and letters up to 30 grams cost 48¢; between 31 grams and 50 grams, the cost is 77¢; and between 51 grams and 100 grams, the cost is 96¢. Letters and postcards to the United States cost 65¢ for up to 30 grams, 90¢ for between 31 and 50 grams, and $1.40 for up to 100 grams. Prices include GST (Goods and Services Tax).

International mail and postcards run $1.25 for up to 30 grams, $1.75 for 30 to 50 grams, and $3 for 51 to 100 grams.

RECEIVING MAIL

Visitors may have mail sent to them c/o General Delivery in the town they are visiting, for pickup in person within 15 days, after which it will be returned to the sender.

SHIPPING PARCELS

Shops will often ship purchases home; if so, you may not have to pay the steep provincial taxes. By courier, a package will take only a few days, but via regular Canada Poste mail it can often take a week—or more—for packages to reach the U.S. Be sure to address everything properly and wrap it securely.

MEDIA

NEWSPAPERS AND MAGAZINES

Maclean's and *Saturday Night* are Canada's two main general-interest magazines. Both cover arts and culture as well as politics. Canada has two national newspapers, the *National Post* and the *Globe and Mail*—both are published in Toronto and both are available at newsstands in major foreign cities, especially the big weekend editions, which are published on Saturday. The arts-and-entertainment sections of both papers have advance news of major events and exhibitions across the country. Both also have Web sites with limited information on cultural events. For more-detailed information, it is advisable to rely on metropolitan papers. Montréal's daily newspaper is the *Montréal Gazette*; Québec's is *Le Soleil*. For entertainment listings, try the *Montréal Mirror* or *Voir* (www.voir.ca), a French-language newspaper that publishes both Montréal and Québec City editions.

RADIO AND TELEVISION

U.S. television dominates Canada's airwaves. In border areas—where most Canadians live—Fox, PBS, NBC, CBS, and ABC are readily available. Canada's two major networks, the state-owned Canadian Broadcasting Corporation (CBC) and the private CTV, and the smaller Global Network broadcast a steady diet of U.S. sitcoms and dramas in prime time with only a scattering of Canadian-produced dramas and comedies. The selection of Canadian-produced current-affairs programs, however, is much wider. The CBC also has a parallel French-language network, Radio-Canada. Canadian cable subscribers have the usual vast menu of specialty channels to choose from, including the all-news outlets operated by CTV and CBC.

The CBC operates the country's only truly national radio network, in both French and English. The daily schedule is rich in news, current-affairs, discussion programs, and classical music.

MONEY MATTERS

Throughout this book, unless otherwise stated, all prices, including dining and lodging, are given in Canadian dollars. The price of a cup of coffee ranges from less than $1 to $2.50 or more, depending on how upscale or downscale the place is; beer costs $3 to $7 in a bar; a smoked-meat sandwich costs about $5 to $6; and museum admission can cost anywhere from nothing to $15.

Prices throughout this guide are given for adults. Substantially reduced fees are almost always available for children, students, and senior citizens. For information on taxes, *see* Taxes.

ATMS

ATMs are available in most bank, trust-company, and credit-union branches across the province, as well as in many convenience stores, malls, and gas stations.

CREDIT CARDS

Throughout this guide, the following abbreviations are used: **AE**, American Express; **D**, Discover; **DC**, Diners Club; **MC**, MasterCard; and **V**, Visa.

➤ REPORTING LOST CARDS: **American Express** (☎ 800/528–4800). **Diners Club** (☎ 800/234–6377). **Discover** (☎ 800/347–2683). **MasterCard** (☎ 800/307–7309). **Visa** (☎ 800/336–8472).

CURRENCY

U.S. dollars are accepted in much of Canada (especially in communities near the border). However, to get the most favorable exchange rate, **exchange at least some of your money into Canadian funds at a bank or other financial institution.** Traveler's checks (some are available in Canadian dollars) and major U.S. credit cards are accepted in most areas.

The units of currency in Canada are the Canadian dollar (C$) and the cent, in almost the same denominations as U.S. currency ($5, $10, $20, 1¢, 5¢, 10¢, 25¢, etc.). The $1 and $2 bill are no longer used; they have been replaced by $1 and $2 coins (known as a "loonie," because of the loon that appears on the coin, and a "toonie," respectively). At this writing, the exchange rate is US$1 to C$1.53, £1 to C$2.25, €1 to C$1.45, A$1 to 87 Canadian cents, and NZ$1 to 75 Canadian cents.

CURRENCY EXCHANGE

For the most favorable rates, **change money through banks.** Although ATM transaction fees may be higher abroad than at home, ATM rates are excellent because they are based on wholesale rates offered only by major banks. You won't do as well at exchange booths in airports or rail and bus stations, in hotels, in restaurants, or in stores. To avoid lines at airport exchange booths, **get a bit of local currency before you leave home.**

➤ EXCHANGE SERVICES: **International Currency Express** (☎ 888/278–6628 orders, WEB www.foreignmoney.com). **Thomas Cook Currency Services** (☎ 800/287–7362 orders and retail locations, WEB www.us.thomascook.com).

OUTDOORS AND SPORTS

BICYCLING

Cycling is wildly popular in Montréal and, indeed, throughout Québec province. You can rent a cycle almost anywhere, and bike lanes and touring itineraries are common not only in Montréal but even in small country towns.

➤ ASSOCIATION: **Canadian Cycling Association** (✉ 702–2197 Riverside Dr., Ottawa, ON K1H 7X3, ☎ 613/248–1353, FAX 613/248–9311, WEB www.canadian-cycling.com).

CANOEING AND KAYAKING

The provincial tourist office can be of assistance, especially in locating an outfitter to suit your needs. You may also contact the Canadian Recreational Canoeing Association.

➤ ASSOCIATION: **Canadian Recreational Canoeing Association** (✉ Box 398, Merrickville, ON K0G 1N0, ☎ 613/269–2910 or 888/252–6292, FAX 613/269–2908, WEB www.paddlingcanada.com).

CLIMBING/MOUNTAINEERING

➤ ASSOCIATION: **Alpine Club of Canada** (✉ Box 8040, Canmore, AB T1W 2T8, ☎ 403/678–3200, FAX 403/678–3224, WEB www.alpineclubofcanada.ca).

GOLF

Locals golf fanatically in almost any weather, but the summer is short here, and most courses don't stay officially open very long; you may have trouble getting a tee time on a summer weekend as a result. Call ahead. Courses and practice ranges can be found everywhere, from mountains and lakes to the city.

➤ ASSOCIATION: **Royal Canadian Golf Association** (✉ 2070 Hadwen Rd., Mississauga, ON L5K 2T3, ☎ 905/849–9700, FAX 905/845–7040, WEB www.rcga.org).

HIKING

➤ ASSOCIATION: **Fédération Québécoise de la Marche** (Québec Walking Federation; ✉ 4545 av. Pierre-de-Coubertin, Montréal H1V 3R2, ☎ 514/252–3157, 866/252–2065 within Québec).

TENNIS

➤ ASSOCIATION: **Tennis Canada** (✉ 3111 Steeles Ave. W, Downsview, ON M3J 3H2, ☎ 416/665–9777, FAX 416/665–9017, WEB www.tenniscanada.com).

PACKING

If you plan on camping or hiking in the deep woods in summer, **always carry insect repellent,** especially in June, which is black-fly season. Winters are snowy and cold; bring sweaters, boots, gloves, and thermal underwear.

In your carry-on luggage, **pack an extra pair of eyeglasses or contact lenses and enough of any medication** you take to last the entire trip. You may also ask your doctor to write a spare prescription using the drug's generic name, since brand names may vary from country to country. In luggage to be checked, **never pack prescription drugs or valuables.** And don't forget to carry with you the addresses of offices that handle refunds of lost traveler's checks. Check

Fodor's How to Pack (available in bookstores everywhere) for more tips.

To avoid customs and security delays, carry medications in their original packaging. Don't pack any sharp objects in your carry-on luggage, including knives of any size or material, scissors, manicure tools, and corkscrews, or anything else that might arouse suspicion.

CHECKING LUGGAGE

You are allowed one carry-on bag and one personal article, such as a purse or a laptop computer. Make sure that everything you carry aboard will fit under your seat or in the overhead bin. Get to the gate early, so you can board as soon as possible, before the overhead bins fill up.

If you are flying internationally, note that baggage allowances may be determined not by piece but by weight—generally 88 pounds (40 kilograms) in first class, 66 pounds (30 kilograms) in business class, and 44 pounds (20 kilograms) in economy.

Airline liability for baggage is limited to US$2,500 per person on flights within the United States. On international flights it amounts to US$9.07 per pound or US$20 per kilogram for checked baggage (roughly US$640 per 70-pound bag) and US$400 per passenger for unchecked baggage. You can buy additional coverage at check-in for about US$10 per US$1,000 of coverage, but it excludes a rather extensive list of items, shown on your airline ticket.

Before departure, **itemize your bags' contents** and their worth, and label the bags with your name, address, and phone number. (If you use your home address, cover it so potential thieves can't see it readily.) Inside each bag, **pack a copy of your itinerary.** At check-in, **make sure that each bag is correctly tagged** with the destination airport's three-letter code. If your bags arrive damaged or fail to arrive at all, file a written report with the airline before leaving the airport.

PASSPORTS AND VISAS

When traveling internationally, **carry your passport** even if you don't need one (it's always the best form of I.D.)

and **make two photocopies of the data page** (one for someone at home and another for you, carried separately from your passport). If you lose your passport, promptly call the nearest embassy or consulate and the local police.

U.S. passport applications for children under age 14 require consent from both parents or legal guardians; both parents must appear together to sign the application. If only one parent appears, he or she must submit a written statement from the other parent authorizing passport issuance for the child. A parent with sole authority must present evidence of it when applying; acceptable documentation includes the child's certified birth certificate listing only the applying parent, a court order specifically permitting this parent's travel with the child, or a death certificate for the non-applying parent. Application forms and instructions are available on the Web site of the U.S. State Department's Bureau of Consular Affairs (www.travel.state.gov).

ENTERING CANADA

Citizens and legal residents of the United States do not need a passport or a visa to enter Canada, but proof of citizenship (a birth certificate or valid passport) and some form of photo identification will be requested. Naturalized U.S. residents should carry their naturalization certificate. Permanent residents who are not citizens should carry their "green card." U.S. residents entering Canada from a third country must have a valid passport, naturalization certificate, or "green card."

Citizens of the United Kingdom need only a valid passport to enter Canada for stays of up to six months.

PASSPORT OFFICES

The best time to apply for a passport or to renew is in fall and winter. Before any trip, check your passport's expiration date, and, if necessary, renew it as soon as possible.

➤ AUSTRALIAN CITIZENS: **Australian State Passport Office** (☎ 131–232, WEB www.dfat.gov.au/passports).

➤ NEW ZEALAND CITIZENS: **New Zealand Passport Office** (☎ 04/494–0700 or 04/474–8100 application procedures, WEB www.passports.govt.nz).

➤ U.K. CITIZENS: **London Passport Office** (☎ 0870/521–0410, WEB www.ukpa.gov.uk) for application procedures and emergency passports.

SENIOR-CITIZEN TRAVEL

To qualify for age-related discounts, **mention your senior-citizen status up front** when booking hotel reservations (not when checking out) and before you're seated in restaurants (not when paying the bill). Be sure to have identification on hand. When renting a car, ask about promotional car-rental discounts, which can be cheaper than senior-citizen rates.

➤ EDUCATIONAL PROGRAMS: **Elderhostel** (✉ 11 Ave. de Lafayette, Boston, MA 02111-1746, ☎ 877/426–8056, FAX 877/426–2166, WEB www.elderhostel.org). **Interhostel** (✉ University of New Hampshire, 6 Garrison Ave., Durham, NH 03824, ☎ 603/862–1147 or 800/733–9753, FAX 603/862–1113, WEB www.learn.unh.edu).

SHOPPING

Montréal has some of the most varied shopping in Canada. The city owes its founding to the fur trade and is still the fur capital of Canada; it's also a good place to hunt for antiques and to buy clothes direct from manufacturers.

Some smaller regions and towns have become known for particular products. Farmers in rural Québec produce more than 75% of the world's supply of maple syrup and often have roadside stands where you can buy sugar, taffy, and syrup.

SMART SOUVENIRS

Québec pop and folk music is linguistically distinctive, and French-Canadian stars range from rock hunks such as Roch Voisine to passionate chansoniers Félix Leclerc and Gilles Vigneault. Cistercian monks in the Lac St-Jean area of northern Québec make chocolate-covered blueberries in summer. They're available all over the province but vanish almost as quickly as they're made. However, you can purchase other, less-perishable blueberry products from this area year-round.

WATCH OUT

Americans should note that it is illegal for them to buy Cuban cigars and to take them home.

STUDENTS IN CANADA

Persons under 18 years of age who are not accompanied by their parents should **bring a letter from a parent or guardian** giving them permission to travel to Canada.

➤ I.D.s & SERVICES: STA Travel (WEB www.sta.com). Travel Cuts (✉ 187 College St., Toronto, Ontario M5T 1P7, Canada, ☎ 416/979–2406; 800/ 667–2887 in Canada, FAX 416/979– 0956, WEB www.travelcuts.com).

TAXES

A goods and services tax (GST) of 7% applies on virtually every transaction in Canada except for the purchase of basic groceries.

In addition to imposing the GST, Québec levies a sales tax from 6% to 12% on most items purchased in shops, on restaurant meals, and sometimes on hotel rooms.

GST REFUNDS

You can **get a GST refund** on purchases taken out of the country and on short-term accommodations of less than one month, but not on food, drink, tobacco, car or motor-home rentals, or transportation; rebate forms, which must be submitted within 60 days of leaving Canada, may be obtained from certain retailers, duty-free shops, customs officials, or from the Canada Customs and Revenue Agency. Instant cash rebates up to a maximum of C$500 are provided by some duty-free shops when you leave Canada, and, in most cases, goods that are shipped directly by the vendor to the purchaser's home are not taxed. Refunds are paid out in U.S. dollars for U.S. citizens, Canadian dollars for everyone else. Always **save your original receipts** from stores and hotels (not just credit-card receipts), and **be sure the name and address of the establishment is shown on the receipt.** Original receipts are not returned. To be eligible for a refund, receipts must

total at least $200, and each individual receipt must show a minimum purchase of $50.

➤ INFORMATION: Canada Customs and Revenue Agency (✉ Visitor Rebate Program, Summerside Tax Centre, 275 Pope Rd., Suite 104, Summerside, PE C1N 6C6, ☎ 902/ 432–5608; 800/668–4748 in Canada, WEB www.ccra-adrc.gc.ca).

PROVINCIAL TAX REFUNDS

Québec offers a sales-tax rebate system similar to the federal one. For provincial tax refunds, **call the provincial toll-free visitor information lines for details** (☞ Visitor Information). Most provinces do not tax goods shipped directly by the vendor to the visitor's home address.

TIME

Montréal and Québec City are both in the Eastern Standard Time zone. Los Angeles is three hours behind local time and Chicago is one hour behind. Sydney is 14 hours ahead; London is five hours ahead.

TIPPING

Tips and service charges are not usually added to a bill in Canada. In general, tip 15% of the total bill. This goes for waiters, waitresses, barbers and hairdressers, and taxi drivers. Porters and doormen should get about $2 a bag. For maid service, leave at least $2 per person a day ($3 in luxury hotels).

TOURS AND PACKAGES

Because everything is prearranged on a prepackaged tour or independent vacation, you spend less time planning—and often get it all at a good price.

BOOKING WITH AN AGENT

Travel agents are excellent resources. But it's a good idea to collect brochures from several agencies, as some agents' suggestions may be influenced by relationships with tour and package firms that reward them for volume sales. If you have a special interest, **find an agent with expertise in that area**; the American Society of Travel Agents (ASTA; ☞ Travel Agencies) has a database of specialists worldwide.

Make sure your travel agent knows the accommodations and other services of the place being recommended. Ask about the hotel's location, room size, beds, and whether it has a pool, room service, or programs for children, if you care about these. Has your agent been there in person or sent others whom you can contact?

Do some homework on your own, too: local tourism boards can provide information about lesser-known and small-niche operators, some of which may sell only direct.

BUYER BEWARE

Each year consumers are stranded or lose their money when tour operators—even large ones with excellent reputations—go out of business. So **check out the operator.** Ask several travel agents about its reputation, and try to **book with a company that has a consumer-protection program.** (Look for information in the company's brochure.) In the United States, members of the National Tour Association and the United States Tour Operators Association are required to set aside funds to cover your payments and travel arrangements in the event that the company defaults. It's also a good idea to choose a company that participates in the American Society of Travel Agents' Tour Operator Program (TOP); ASTA will act as mediator in any disputes between you and your tour operator.

Remember that the more your package or tour includes the better you can predict the ultimate cost of your vacation. Make sure you know exactly what is covered, and **beware of hidden costs.** Are taxes, tips, and transfers included? Entertainment and excursions? These can add up.

➤ TOUR-OPERATOR RECOMMENDATIONS: **American Society of Travel Agents** (☞ Travel Agencies). **National Tour Association** (NTA; ✉ 546 E. Main St., Lexington, KY 40508, ☎ 859/226–4444 or 800/682–8886, WEB www.ntaonline.com). **United States Tour Operators Association** (USTOA; ✉ 275 Madison Ave., Suite 2014, New York, NY 10016, ☎ 212/599–6599 or 800/468–7862, FAX 212/599–6744, WEB www.ustoa.com).

THEME TRIPS

The companies listed below offer multiday tours in Canada. Additional local or regionally based companies that have different-length trips with these themes are listed in each chapter, either with information about the town or in the A to Z section that concludes the chapter.

➤ ADVENTURE: **Gorp Travel** (✉ Box 1486, Boulder, CO 80306, ☎ 303/444–2622 or 877/440–4677, FAX 303/635–0658, WEB www.gorptravel.com).

➤ BICYCLING: **Backroads** (✉ 801 Cedar St., Berkeley, CA 94710-1800, ☎ 510/527–1555 or 800/462–2848, FAX 510/527–1444, WEB www.backroads.com). **Vermont Bicycle Touring** (✉ Box 711, Bristol, VT 05443-0711, ☎ 800/245–3868 or 802/453–4811, FAX 802/453–4806, WEB www.vbt.com). **Les Voyages du Tour de l'Île** (✉ 1251 rue Rachel Est, Montréal, QC H2J 2J9, ☎ 514/521–8356 or 888/899–1111, FAX 514/512–5711, WEB www.velo.qc.ca).

➤ SPAS: **Spa-Finders** (✉ 91 5th Ave., Suite 600, New York, NY 10003-3039, ☎ 212/924–6800 or 800/255–7727, WEB www.spafinders.com).

➤ WALKING/HIKING: **New England Hiking Holidays** (✉ Box 1648, North Conway, NH 03860, ☎ 603/356–9696 or 800/869–0949, WEB www.nehikingholidays.com).

TRAIN TRAVEL

Amtrak has daily service from New York's Penn Station to Montréal, with connections to Canadian rail line VIA Rail's Canadian routes. The slow ride takes up to 10 hours, and tickets cost $55 to $68 one-way. VIA Rail trains run from Montréal to Québec City often, and take three hours. Smoking is not allowed on these trains.

CUTTING COSTS

Check out the 30-day North American RailPass offered by Amtrak and VIA Rail. It allows unlimited coach–economy travel in the U.S. and Canada. You must indicate the itinerary when purchasing the pass. The cost is $1,004 from June to October 15, $702 at other times.

➤ TRAIN INFORMATION: **Amtrak** (☎ 800/872–7245). **VIA Rail Canada**

(☎ 888/842–7245, 514/989–2626, or 418/692–3940).

TRANSPORTATION
AROUND QUÉBEC

A car allows you to explore the province fully. Bicycling is quite popular throughout Québec, so bring your bike, or, if you have one, a bike rack for your rental car should you want to rent a bike. Buses can transport you between cities and towns, though they make many stops. Train service is efficient but expensive, as is short-hop air service.

TRAVEL AGENCIES

A good travel agent puts your needs first. Look for an agency that has been in business at least five years, emphasizes customer service, and has someone on staff who specializes in your destination. In addition, **make sure the agency belongs to a professional trade organization.** The American Society of Travel Agents (ASTA)—the largest and most influential in the field with more than 24,000 members in some 140 countries—maintains and enforces a strict code of ethics and will step in to help mediate any agent-client disputes involving ASTA members if necessary. ASTA (whose motto is "Without a travel agent, you're on your own") also maintains a Web site that includes a directory of agents. (If a travel agency is also acting as your tour operator, *see* Buyer Beware *in* Tours & Packages.)

➤ LOCAL AGENT REFERRALS: **American Society of Travel Agents** (ASTA; ✉ 1101 King St., Suite 200, Alexandria, VA 22314, ☎ 800/965–2782 24-hr hot line, FAX 703/739–3268, WEB www.astanet.com). **Association of British Travel Agents** (✉ 68–71 Newman St., London W1T 3AH, ☎ 020/7637–2444, FAX 020/7637–0713, WEB www.abtanet.com). **Association of Canadian Travel Agents** (✉ 130 Albert St., Suite 1705, Ottawa, Ontario K1P 5G4, ☎ 613/237–3657, FAX 613/237–7052, WEB www.acta.net). **Australian Federation of Travel Agents** (✉ Level 3, 309 Pitt St., Sydney, NSW 2000, ☎ 02/9264–3299, FAX 02/9264–1085, WEB www.afta.com.au). **Travel Agents' Association of New Zealand** (✉ Level 5, Tourism and Travel House, 79 Boulcott St., Box 1888, Wellington 10033, ☎ 04/499–0104, FAX 04/499–0786, WEB www.taanz.org.nz).

VISITOR INFORMATION

➤ TOURIST INFORMATION: **Canadian Tourism Commission** (☎ 613/946–1000, WEB www.canadatourism.com). **Tourisme Québec** (✉ C.P. 979, Montréal, H3C 2W3, ☎ 877/266–5687, WEB www.bonjourquebec.com).

➤ IN THE U.K.: **Québec Tourism** (✉ PO Box 1839, Maidenhead, Berkshire SL6 1AJ, ☎ 08705/561–205). **Visit Canada Center** (✉ 62–65 Trafalgar Sq., London, WC2 5DY, ☎ 0891/715–000, 50p per minute peak rate and 45p per minute cheap rate).

WEB SITES

Do check out the World Wide Web when planning your trip. You'll find everything from weather forecasts to virtual tours of famous cities. Be sure to **visit Fodors.com** (www.fodors.com), a complete travel-planning site. You can research prices and book plane tickets, hotel rooms, rental cars, vacation packages, and more. In addition, you can post your pressing questions in the Travel Talk section. Other planning tools include a currency converter and weather reports, and there are loads of links to travel resources.

For festival information, check out Festival Seeker (www.festivalseeker.com).

WHEN TO GO

Montréal and Québec City are liveliest in summer, when the weather is warm and festivals kick in by the dozen. Nights can be chilly. The long winter is cold, snowy, and slushy. In Montréal, it's a good opportunity to explore the underground malls that run beneath the city. In Québec City, you do as the locals do: bundle up and get on with your business. Winter festivals, some of the best in the world, help take the edge off the season. (Be careful of ice on sidewalks, tall buildings, bridges, and roadways, which can be quite hazardous.) Spring is short and normally chilly, while fall can be either beautifully crisp or gray, dull, and rainy.

Hilly and mountainous regions, such as the Eastern Townships and the Laurentians, tend to be colder and windier than Montréal, as befits their higher elevations.

CLIMATE

The following are average daily maximum and minimum tempera- tures for Montréal. Québec City tends to be as much as 10 degrees colder, especially in winter, due to its more northerly position.

➤ FORECASTS: **Weather Channel Connection** (☎ 900/932–8437), 95¢ per minute from a Touch-Tone phone.

MONTRÉAL

Jan.	23F	– 5C	May	65F	18C	Sept.	68F	20C
	9	–13		48	9		53	12
Feb.	25F	– 4C	June	74F	23C	Oct.	57F	14C
	12	–11		58	14		43	6
Mar.	36F	2C	July	79F	26C	Nov.	42F	6C
	23	– 5		63	17		32	0
Apr.	52F	11C	Aug.	76F	24C	Dec.	27F	– 3C
	36	2		61	16		16	– 9

FESTIVALS AND SEASONAL EVENTS

Québec has always been able to find a reason to party. Québec City celebrates one of the world's most brutal winters with a carnival that includes a boat race across an ice-choked river. Throughout the province, the rest of the year is full of festivals celebrating jazz, international folklore, film, classical music, fireworks, comedy, and hot-air balloons. The provincial tourist board has more information about these and other festivals.

➤ JAN.–FEB.: **La Fête des Neiges** (☎ 800/797–4537, WEB www. fetedesneiges.com) is Winter Carnival in Montréal. It lasts about two weeks and takes place at Parc Jean Drapeau on the river, in the east end of the city. Québec City's **Carnaval de Québec** (WEB www.carnaval.qc.ca) is an 11-day festival of winter-sports competitions, ice-sculpture contests, and parades. **Festival Montréal en Lumière** (WEB www.montrealhighlights. com), a festival of mostly classical music, takes place on Montréal's Place des Artes during the last two weeks of February.

➤ APR.: **Sugaring-off parties** celebrate the maple-syrup season throughout the province, but especially north and east of Montréal.

➤ JUNE: Some of the world's best drivers compete in the **Grand Prix** (WEB www.grandprix.ca) in Montréal. The renowned **Fringe Festival** (WEB www.montrealfringe.ca) brings world-renowned playwrights, acting troupes, dancers, and musicians to Montréal.

➤ JULY: **Festival International de Jazz de Montréal** (☎ 514/790–1245 or 800/361–4595) draws more than 2,000 musicians from all over the world for an 11-day series. **Québec International Summer Festival** offers entertainment in the streets and parks of old Québec City. Montréal's world-famous **Juste pour Rire** (Just for Laughs; ☎ 514/845–3155 or 888/ 244–3155, WEB www.hahaha.com) comedy festival features international comics, in French and English, from the second through third weeks of July. At **Festival Orford** (☎ 888/310– 3665, WEB www3.sympatico.ca/arts. orford), international artists perform in Orford Park's music center (about an hour east of Montréal) throughout August. The **Coup Rogers** tennis tournament brings top professional players to Montréal.

➤ AUG.: Montréal's **World Film Festival** (☎ 514/848–3883, WEB www. ffm-montreal.org) continues to grow in popularity. **St-Jean-sur-Richelieu's Hot Air Balloon Festival** (☎ 450/ 347–9555, WEB www.montgolfieres. com) is the largest gathering of hot-air balloons in Canada. In mid-

August (Aug. 9–17 in 2003), the **Fêtes de la Nouvelle France** (☎ 418/694–3319, WEB www.nouvellefrance.qc.ca) re-creates the days of the French regime with markets and artisans in the Old Town district of Québec City.

➤ SEPT.: The **Québec International Film Festival** (☎ 418/523–3456, WEB www.telegraphe.com/fifq) is screened in Québec City. The **Gatineau Hot Air Balloon Festival** (WEB www.vielle.gatineau.qc.ca), held Labor Day weekend, brings together hot-air balloons from across Canada, the United States, and Europe.

➤ OCT.: Farmers' markets, arts-and-crafts fairs, and activities such as weekend hikes are part of the **Festival of Colors,** which celebrates autumn throughout the province of Québec.

1 DESTINATION: MONTRÉAL AND QUÉBEC CITY

Francophones in the New World

What's Where

Pleasures and Pastimes

Fodor's Choice

FRANCOPHONES IN THE NEW WORLD

QUÉBEC IS THE LARGEST and oldest of Canada's provinces, covering 600,000 square miles of land and waterways, one-sixth of Canada's land. Of Québec's 6,627,000 inhabitants, 5,300,000 are French-speaking—over 80% of the French-speaking population of Canada. Although Montréal and Québec City are linked by their history and culture, no two cities could be more different.

History buffs and romantics will want to roam the winding cobblestone streets of Québec City, the capital of the province. Its French colonial history is evident in its architecture, silver-spired churches, and grand cathedrals. In Montréal the Old World meets the New with French bistros and postmodern skyscrapers vying for the limelight. Québec may be the center of the province's government, but Montréal is the business center. Much like New York City, Montréal has attracted a large immigrant population, and its ethnic diversity can be seen in its wide range of restaurants and enclaves. It is not only considered the Canadian center for book publishing, the film industry, and architecture and design; it's also considered the unrivaled bagel capital of Canada.

Montréal's and Québec City's histories are inextricably linked. Montréal sits on the site that was called Hochelaga by the Indians who lived there. Québec City was known as Stadacona. In 1534 Jacques Cartier, a young sea captain setting out to find a passage to China, came upon Canada and changed the course of events in the region forever. He returned in the following year seeking gold. But this time he found a wide river, sailed down it, and arrived at Stadacona, an Indian village. He admired the location of the village perched on the cliffs overlooking a *kebec,* the Algonquin word for a narrowing of the waters. He continued along to Hochelaga, which eventually became Montréal.

More than 1,000 surprised Iroquois greeted the Frenchman. It would take two centuries of fierce battles before the French made peace with the Iroquois people. Perhaps the violent meeting of the French explorers and the Canadian natives discouraged the French, because no more exploring was done until 1608, when Samuel de Champlain established a French settlement at Stadacona.

Throughout the 17th century, the French opened up Canada and some of what became the United States, using both Montréal and Québec City as convenient trading posts and strategic military locations. They discovered and mapped a vast area stretching from Hudson Bay to the Gulf of Mexico. *Coureurs de bois* (fur traders), missionaries, and explorers staked out this immense new territory.

During this time, France tamed and populated its new colonies across the ocean with the firm hand of *seigneurs,* aristocrats to whom the king distributed land. In turn, the seigneurs swore loyalty to the king, served in the military, maintained manor houses, ceded land to tenant farmers, and established courts to settle local grievances. Seigneuries were close-knit, with sons and fathers able to establish farms within the same territory. In addition, the Roman Catholic Church's influence was strong in these communities. Priests and nuns provided medical care and education, and oversaw business arrangements among the farmers and between French-speaking traders and English-speaking merchants. *Survivance,* the survival of the French people and their culture, was the doctrine of the church. Couples were told to have large families, and they did. Until the 1950s, 10 to 12 children in a family was the norm, not the exception.

THE SEVEN YEARS' WAR between England and France marked the second half of the 18th century. In 1756, France sent the commander Louis-Joseph, Marquis de Montcalm, to secure the frontier of New France and consolidate the new territory of Louisiana. Although Montcalm, leading a French and Indian expedition, was able to secure the Ohio Valley, turn Lake Ontario into a French waterway, and secure Fort Carillon (now Ticonderoga) on Lake Champlain, the tides began to turn in 1759 with the arrival of a large British fleet to the shores of Québec City, commanded by James Wolfe.

After bombarding the city for several weeks, Wolfe and his 4,000 men decided the fate of Canada in a vicious battle that lasted 20 minutes. The British won, but both leaders were mortally wounded. Today, in Québec City's Governors Park, there is a unique memorial to these two army men—the only statue in the world commemorating both victor and vanquished of the same battle. A year later the French regained the city of Québec, but they were soon forced to withdraw when English ships arrived with supplies and reinforcements. The French were driven back to Montréal, where a large British army defeated them in 1760. In 1763, the Treaty of Paris ceded Canada to Britain. France preferred to give up the new country to preserve its sugar islands, which it believed were of greater value. At that time, all the French civil administrators, as well as the principal landowners and businessmen, returned to France. Of the leaders of New France, only the Roman Catholic clergy remained, and they became more important to the peasant farmers than ever before.

Québec's trouble was in no way over with the Treaty of Paris. In 1774, the British Parliament passed the Québec Act. It extended Québec's borders, hemming in the northernmost of the independence-minded British colonies to the south. The Roman Catholic Church's authority and the seigneurial landlord system were maintained under the act, leaving traditional Québecois life fairly intact. But the American colonists were furious with the passing of the Québec Act and hoped to incite a revolt in Québec against British rule. After the American War of Independence broke out in 1775, Generals Richard Montgomery and Benedict Arnold led American troops that took over Montréal and set up headquarters in the Château de Ramezay, home of the British governor (and now a museum). The Americans then attempted to capture Québec City, but they had misunderstood the Catholic Royalist heritage of the Canadians. Québecois did not share the Americans' love of independence and republicanism. Rather than incite a revolt, the Americans managed to draw the Canadians and British together. The Canadians stood with the British in

Québec City to fight off the invasions. Montgomery died in the attack and Arnold fled. The following year, British forces arrived and recaptured Montréal.

A number of British and American settlers left Albany in New York and settled in Montréal. They began to press the authorities, as did other British colonists west of the Ottawa River, to introduce representative government.

The British responded with the Constitutional Act of 1791, which divided Québec into two provinces, Upper and Lower Canada, west and east of the Ottawa. The act provided for nominated legislative councils and elected assemblies, like those that had existed in the English colonies. The first election was held the following year.

E LECTED GOVERNMENT WAS a novelty to the French Canadians, who had never known democracy and had been shielded from the French Revolution of 1789. But democracy suited them well, and before long there was a rising demand for more rights. Heading the movement for greater rights was Louis Joseph Papineau, who was also leader of the French-speaking majority in the legislative assembly. He demanded that the English *château clique*, which made up the governor's council, should be subject to elections as the assembly was. In 1834, he and his associates issued a long list of grievances, "The 92 Resolutions." Papineau lost the support of many of his own associates, and that of the leaders of the church. The British responded with their own "10 resolutions" and refused elections to the council. That same year crops failed and unemployment spread. General unrest led to clashes between the English and young French *Patriotes* in Montréal. Soon a general insurrection broke out. Patriote irregulars fought British troops at St. Charles and St. Eustache near Montréal.

In spite of bad feelings, the upheavals led to major legislative changes in 1841. England passed the Act of Union, which produced a united Canada. Québec was now known as Canada East, while Upper Canada became Canada West. Each sent an equal number of representatives to the elected assembly; the governor was not responsible to the assembly, but rather to the Colonial Office in London. This continued to bridle both English and French members of the assembly.

Toward the end of the 1700s, the fur trade declined so much that Montréal almost faced economic disaster. But in Europe the demand for lumber increased, and Québec had lots of it. As a result, Montréal became the major trading center in British North America, helped by the fact that New York and New England had seceded from Britain.

Then the flood of immigration from Britain started, so much so that by the mid-1800s, Montréal was transformed into a predominantly English city. About 100,000 Irish immigrants came to work in Montréal's flour mills, breweries, and shipyards, which had sprung up on the shores of the river and the Lachine Canal, begun in 1821. By 1861, working-class Irish made up a third of Montréal's population. Within the next 80 years, Polish, Hungarian, Italian, Chinese, Ukrainian, Greek, Armenian, Spanish, Czech, Japanese, German, and Portuguese immigrants, escaping from poverty and political hardships, arrived by the thousands, seeking freedom in the New World. By 1867, more than a half million immigrants had arrived from Europe, pushing Canada's population to more than 2 million. The demand for union came from all the provinces of British North America to increase trade and economic prosperity, to increase their military strength in case of attack from the United States, to create a government capable of securing and developing the Northwest (the vast lands west of Canada West), and to make possible the building of a railway that would contribute to the realization of all these ambitions.

The Dominion of Canada was created on July 1, 1867, by an act of British Parliament, known as the British North America (BNA) Act. It divided the province of Canada into Québec and Ontario and brought in Nova Scotia and New Brunswick. Manitoba joined in 1870, British Columbia in 1871, Prince Edward Island in 1873, Alberta and Saskatchewan in 1905, and Newfoundland in 1949. The BNA Act also enshrined French as an official language. The province of Québec, like the other provinces, was given far-reaching responsibilities in social and civil affairs.

THE ENTENTE between the French and the English in Canada was viable until World War I strained it. At the outbreak of the war, the two groups felt equally supportive of the two European motherlands. Many volunteered, and a totally French regiment, the Royal 22nd, was created. But two things ended the camaraderie.

On the battlefields of Europe, Canadians, along with Australians, formed the shock troops of the British Empire and died horribly, by the thousands. More than 60,000 Canadians died in the war, a huge loss for a country of 7.5 million. In 1915, Ontario passed Regulation 17, severely restricting the use of French in its schools. It translated into an anti-French stand and created open hostility. The flow of French Canadians into the army became a trickle. Then Prime Minister Robert Borden ordered the conscription of childless males to reinforce the ailing Canadian corps. A wider conscription law loomed in Ottawa, resulting in an outcry in Québec led by nationalist, journalist, and politician Henry Bourassa (grandson of patriot Louis Joseph Papineau). The nationalists claimed that conscription was a device to diminish the French-speaking population. When, in 1917, conscription did become law, Québec was ideologically isolated from the rest of Canada.

The crisis led to the formation of the Union Nationale provincial party in 1936, initially a reformist party. Under its leader Maurice Duplessis, it held control until 1960 and was characterized by lavish patronage, strong-arm methods, fights with Ottawa, and nationalistic sloganeering. Duplessis believed that to survive, Québecois should remain true to their traditions. Duplessis deterred industrial expansion in Québec, which went to Ontario, and slowed the growth of reformist ideas until his death and the flowering of the Quiet Revolution.

The population of Québec had grown to 6 million, but the province had fallen economically and politically behind Canada's English majority. Under Duplessis and the Union Nationale party, French-language schools and universities were supervised by the church and offered courses in the humanities rather than in science and economics. Francophones (French-speaking Québeckers) were denied any chance of real business education unless they attended English institutions. As a result, few of them held top positions in industry or finance. On a general cultural basis, the country overwhelmingly reflected Anglo-Saxon attitudes rather than an Anglo-French mixture.

In 1960 the Liberal Party under Jean Lesage swept to power. Though initially occupied with social reform, it soon turned to economic matters. In 1962, Lesage's minister of natural resources, René Lévesque, called for the nationalization of most of the electricity industry, which up to then had been in private hands. This was the first step toward economic independence for Québec. The financiers of Montréal's St. James Street, the heart of the business district, opposed it, but ordinary Québecois were enthusiastic. In 1965, Lévesque's ministry established a provincial mining company to explore and develop the province's mineral resources.

Meanwhile U.S. capital poured into Québec, as it did everywhere else in Canada. With it came American cultural influence, which increased Québecois' expectations of a high standard of living. English-speaking citizens remained in firm control of the large national corporations headquartered in Montréal. Indeed it became clear that they had no intention of handing power over to the French. Few Francophones were promoted to executive status. Successive provincial governments became increasingly irritated by the lack of progress.

The discontent led to a dramatic radicalization of Québec politics. A new separatist movement arose that hoped to make Québec a distinct state by breaking away from the rest of the country. The most extreme faction of the movement was the Front de Libération du Québec (FLQ). It backed its demands with bombs and arson, culminating in the kidnapping and murder of Québec Cabinet Minister Pierre Laporte in October 1970.

The federal government in Ottawa, under Prime Minister Pierre Elliot Trudeau, himself a French-speaking Québecois, imposed the War Measures Act. This permitted the police to break up civil disorders and arrest hundreds of suspects and led to the arrest of the murderers of Laporte.

The political crisis calmed down, but it left behind vibrations that affected all of the country. The federal government redoubled its efforts to correct the worst grievances of the French Canadians. Federal funds flowed into French schools outside Québec to support French-Canadian culture in the other provinces. French Canadians were appointed to senior positions in the government and crown corporations. The federal government dramatically increased its bilingual services to the population.

In Québec from the mid-1970s, the Liberal government and then the Parti Québecois, elected in 1976 and headed by René Lévesque (who had left the Liberal Party in 1967 and helped found the Parti Québecois), replaced the English language with the French language in Québec's economic life. In 1974, French was adopted as the official language of Québec. This promoted French-language instruction in the schools and made French the language of business and government. The Parti Québecois followed up in 1977 with the Charter of the French Language, which established deadlines and fines to help enforce the program to make French the chief language in all areas of Québec life. The charter brought French into the workplace; it also accelerated a trend for English companies to relocate their headquarters outside Québec, particularly in and near Toronto. The provincial government is working to attract new investment to Québec to replace those lost jobs and revenues.

The Parti Québecois proposed to go further by taking Québec out of the confederation, provided that economic ties with the rest of Canada could be maintained. Leaders in the other provinces announced that such a scheme would not be acceptable. A referendum was held in 1980 for the authority to negotiate a sovereignty association with the rest of Canada. Québec voters rejected the proposal by a wide margin. In 1985, the Parti Québecois government was defeated at the polls by the Liberal Party, headed by Robert Bourassa.

Bourassa was committed to keeping Québec within Canada until the collapse of the Meech-Lake Accord, a three-year attempt to integrate Québec into the Canadian constitution, in 1990. Bourassa then vowed to put the interests of the province before those of the country, even if this meant separation. The Québec Bélanger-Campeau commission, set up to study the future of Québec in Canada, concluded that the province should be recognized as a "sovereign state," although it would remain part of the Canadian Federation given certain conditions. However, the federal and provincial governments did not reach an agreement. In a 1995 referendum, Québecois decided by a narrow margin to remain part of the Federation. Support for independence hovers between 30% and 40%—not enough to accomplish it, but certainly enough to remain a force.

ALTHOUGH FRENCH IS the official language of Québec, Québec also has a large English-speaking population (676,000), particularly in Montréal, the Ottawa Valley, and the Eastern Townships. They are descendants of those English, Irish, and Scots who landed here after the conquest of New France, and of immigrants from other nations whose main language is English. English-speaking Montréalers founded and financed a variety of great institutions including universities, museums, hospitals, orchestras, and social agencies, as well as a number of national and multinational corporations in the worlds of banking and finance, transportation, natural resources, and distilled spirits.

Half a million immigrants from Europe, Asia, Latin America, and the Caribbean also live in Québec. People from 80 countries have made their new homes in the province. In proportion to its population, this land, along with the rest of Canada, has welcomed the greatest number of fugitives from political and economic unrest in recent decades. Between 1968 and 1982, for example, 60,000 immigrants arrived from Czechoslovakia, Haiti, Uganda, Lebanon, Chile, and Southeast Asia. A much larger wave of immigrants—from Italy, Greece, and Eastern Europe—had arrived following World War II.

The native people of Québec number more than 40,000. Nearly 30,000 of Québec's Amerindians live in the villages within reserved territories in various parts of Québec, where they have exclusive fishing and hunting rights. The Inuit people (Eskimo) number over 5,000 and live in villages scattered along the shores of James Bay, Hudson Bay, Hudson Strait, and Ungava Bay. They have abandoned their igloos for prefabricated houses, but they still make their living by trapping and hunting.

The French Canadians of Québec, often called Latins of the North, have an ever-sparkling joie de vivre, especially at the more than 400 festivals and carnivals they celebrate each year. Even the long winter does not dampen their good spirits. The largest festival splash is on June 24, which was originally the Feast of Saint John the Baptist. Now it is called La Fête Nationale (National Day). Everyone celebrates the long weekend by building roaring bonfires and dancing in the streets.

February brings Québec City's Winter Carnival, an 11-day-long noisy and exciting party. Chicoutimi also has a winter carnival in which residents of the city celebrate and dress up in period costumes. In September international canoe races are held in Mauricie, and in August an international swim gets under way across Lac-Saint-Jean. Trois-Rivières celebrates the summer with automobile races through its streets, and Valleyfield is the scene of international regattas.

WHAT'S WHERE

Québec City and Montréal share a language and a river, but, like jealous sisters, the two cities seldom see eye to eye. Montréal, the younger and edgier of the two, is a brassy island metropolis where commercial towers overshadow the domes of older faiths and whose bars and cafés buzz with dozens of languages. Québec City, on the other hand, is more solidly French and moves at a slower, more bureaucratic pace (it is the provincial capital, after all). It's also the more graceful of the two, a walled city straight out of a fairy tale, with mansard roofs, dormer windows, and winding cobbled streets. Although Québec City and Montréal seldom have anything good to say about each other, they do complement each other. Visit only one and you miss half the story of French Canada.

The province of Québec is huge—at 600,000 square mi, it's nearly three times the size of France—and its staggeringly varied landscape stretches from pastoral valleys at its southern edge to arctic tundra in the far north. The Charlevoix region alone, which has long inspired artists, includes mountains that touch down on the shores of the St. Lawrence River, valleys and plateaus, and cliffs cut by waterfalls and streams. The province's vast maple forests bring glorious color to fall and sweetness to spring, when sap is collected and boiled into syrup, that mainstay of Québecois dishes. The wildlife is as varied as the terrain: caribou, black bear, and moose live on the Gaspé Peninsula and in other parts of the province; a massive colony of gannets summers on Île Bonaventure, off the peninsula's tip; and blue, beluga, and other whales come to eat and breed in the Saguenay River and at the mouth of its fjord. The Laurentians, north of Montréal, encompass thousands of miles of wilderness, but for many people the draw is Mont-Tremblant and its world-class ski slopes. In a southern corner of the province, the Eastern Townships, with their covered bridges, village greens, country inns, and church steeples, are reminiscent of New England. You can ski, golf, and eat well in these vacation communities.

PLEASURES AND PASTIMES

Dining

Canadian fine dining really began in Québec, where eating out in a good restaurant with a good bottle of wine has long been a traditional part of life. Montréal can claim many superb restaurants that serve both classic and innovative French cuisine. The city's varied population has also made it rich in ethnic restaurants from delis to Asian eateries. Québec City has a narrower range of choices, but good French and Québecois fare are available, and some fine new restaurants have opened recently. In the countryside a number of inns, including some in the Eastern Townships, provide food that can compete with any served in the cities for freshness and creativity. Hearty meat pies, pâtés, and creative uses of maple syrup are traditional specialties throughout the province. When you're in Québec, do as the locals do and order the table d'hôte, a several-course package deal that is often cheaper and may give you a chance to sample some special dishes.

French Heritage

To visit Québec is to encounter more than 450 years of French civilization in North America. The well-preserved streets of Vieux-Montréal and the Upper and Lower Towns of Québec City hold centuries-old buildings filled with history. Churches such as the Basilique Notre-Dame-de-Québec in Québec City, the Basilique Notre-Dame-de-Montréal in Montréal, and the Basilique Ste-Anne-de-Beaupré in Ste-Anne-de-Beaupré tell part of the story. Excellent museums, including the Musée d'Archéologie Pointe-àCallière in Montréal and the Musée de la Civilisation and the Musée de Québec in Québec City, add further insight. But history is alive in Québec: in the language, the people, and the arts. Whether you're sitting in a café, walking through a beautiful botanical garden, or just strolling the city streets at night, you'll enter a different culture.

The Great Outdoors

Most Canadians live in towns and cities within 325 km (200 mi) of the American border, but the country has a splendid backyard to play in. Even major cities like Montréal and Québec City are just a few hours drive from a wilderness full of rivers, lakes, and mountains, and lovely rural areas are even closer. It's easy to combine a visit to Québec's cities with a side trip to the countryside. The Laurentian Mountains, with the revitalized Mont-Tremblant ski resort, are just an hour north of Montréal, and the hills and lakes of the bucolic Eastern Townships lie to the city's southeast. The Ile d'Orléans, just 15 minutes from Québec City, embodies the traditional lifestyle of rural Québec and is well worth exploring. The lovely villages, mountains, and waterfalls of the Charlevoix stretch along the north shore of the St. Lawrence River from Ste-Anne-de-Beaupré to the Saguenay River.

Shopping

Distinctively Canadian items include furs and fashions from Montréal, wood carvings from rural Québec, and antiques (the best are in Montréal). The weak Canadian dollar has made shopping even more appealing.

ANTIQUES➤ On the whole, prices for antiques are lower in Canada than in the United States. Shops along Montréal's rue Sherbrooke Ouest stock everything from ancient maps to fine crystal; stores along rue Notre-Dame Ouest and rue Amherst sell antiques from Napoléonic-period furniture to 1950s bric-a-brac.

MAPLE SYRUP➤ Eastern Canada is famous for its sugar maples. The trees are tapped in early spring, and the sap is collected in buckets to be boiled into maple syrup. This natural confection is sold all year. You can also buy maple taffy, candy, and even liqueur. Avoid the tourist shops and department stores; for the best prices, stop at farm stands and markets.

NATIVE CANADIAN ART➤ Interest has been growing in the highly collectible art and sculpture of the Inuit, usually rendered in soapstone. For the best price and a guarantee of authenticity, purchase Inuit and other native crafts in the province where they originate. Many styles are now attributed to certain tribes and are mass-produced for sale in galleries and shops miles away from their regions of origin. At the very top galleries you can be assured of getting pieces done by individual artists, though the prices will be higher than in the provinces of origin. The Canadian government has registered the symbol of an igloo as a mark of a work's authenticity. Be sure this Canadian government sticker or tag is attached before you make your purchase.

FODOR'S CHOICE

Even with so many special places in Montréal and Québec City, Fodor's writers and editors have their favorites. Here are a few that stand out.

Dining
L'Eau à la Bouche, Ste-Adèle. Nouvelle cuisine meets traditional Québecois cooking at the restaurant of this Bavarian-style inn in the lower Laurentians. $$$$

Caprices de Nicholas, Montréal. The two art nouveau–inspired rooms of this French restaurant are magnificent, but the most romantic tables are in the soaring plant-filled atrium. $$$–$$$$

Toqué!, Montréal. At the city's most fashionable restaurant, the sometimes whimsical kitchen takes its inspiration from market-fresh ingredients. $$$–$$$$

L'Initiale, Québec City. The eight-course *menu gastronomique* is a meal to remember, but all of the sophisticated French fare fits this bill. The gracious service enhances the experience. $$$

L'Echaudé, Québec City. Sunday shoppers favor the three-course brunch at this chic bistro between the financial and antiques districts. Desserts are fabulous. $$–$$$

Brioche Lyonnaise, Montréal. Start your day at the quintessential Quartier-Latin café with a buttery brioche and a bowl of steaming café au lait. $–$$

Schwartz's Delicatessen, Montréal. The smoked meat at this deli, officially the Montréal Hebrew Delicatessen, is the city's best. Don't ask for a menu (there isn't one) and, unless you don't mind long lines, don't go during the lunch hour. $–$$

Historic Sights
Basilique Notre-Dame-de-Montréal, Montréal. The 3,800-seat neo-Gothic church has a star-studded blue vaulted ceiling, stained-glass windows from Limoges, and a 7,000-pipe organ.

Basilique Ste-Anne-de-Beaupré, Ste-Anne-de-Beaupré. The monumental basilica with two granite steeples, 18 altars, 22 chapels, and more than 200 stained-glass windows draws hordes of pilgrims who come to worship Québec's patron saint.

Maison St-Gabriel, Montréal. St. Marguerite Bourgeoys' religious order used this stone farm structure, a rare example of 17th-century rural architecture, to train young orphaned French girls to become the wives and mothers of New France.

Plains of Abraham, Québec City. The site of the 1759 battle between the French and the British that decided the fate of New France is now part of a large park overlooking the St. Lawrence River.

Vieux-Québec, Québec City. The immaculately preserved old town, veined with narrow winding streets, is small and dense, steeped in more than four centuries of history and French tradition.

Lodging

Auberge Hatley, North Hatley. With floral prints on the beds and windows, the guest rooms in this 1903 country manor near Lake Massawippi are a bit of Provence. The first-rate restaurant uses produce from the inn's greenhouse and has a serious wine cellar. $$$$

Fairmont Le Château Frontenac, Québec City. Its history and architecture make this castle of a hotel overlooking the St. Lawrence one of the city's most recognizable landmarks. $$$$

Hotel Dominion 1912, Québec City. Modern and uncluttered, guest rooms in this former warehouse building include special design touches such as swing-out night tables. The lobby is more chic living room than hotel. $$$$

Loews Hôtel Vogue, Montréal. Behind the hotel's facade of polished rose granite and tall windows are elegant rooms with silk upholstery and lacy duvets. $$$$

Auberge du Vieux-Port, Montréal. Tall windows and exposed beams lend charm to this inn in an 1880s building in Vieux-Montréal, overlooking the Vieux-Port. Rooms have brass beds and stone or brick walls. $$$–$$$$

Auberge de la Fontaine, Montréal. Two adjoining turn-of-the-20th-century residences in the trendy Plateau Mont-Royal district reveal a riot of color inside—purple, red, yellow, green—but the hotel is delightful. A few rooms have private balconies. $$–$$$

Auberge les Passants du Sans Soucy, Montréal. Brass beds, stone walls, exposed beams, soft lighting, whirlpool baths, and flowers galore create a romantic mood at this rue St-Paul gem in a former warehouse. $$

Parks and Gardens

Jardin Botanique, Montréal. This botanical garden, with 181 acres of gardens in summer and 10 greenhouses open all year, has one of the best bonsai collections in the West and the largest Ming-style garden outside Asia.

Parc Jean-Drapeau, Montréal. Stretching across two islands in the middle of the St. Lawrence River, this urban playground includes a major amusement park, a casino, acres of flower gardens, and a beach.

Parc du Mont-Royal, Montréal. The Frederick Law Olmsted–designed park encompasses 494 acres of forest and paths in the heart of the city.

2 MONTRÉAL

Traces of this island city's long history are found everywhere, from the 17th-century buildings in Vieux-Montréal to grand churches and verdant parks such as Mont-Royal. But Montréal, with its romantic and elegant atmosphere, is also full of very modern pleasures: fine dining, whether you want French cuisine or any kind of ethnic fare; good shopping for everything from antiques to high fashion; and nightlife, arts events, and festivals that provide diversions year-round.

By Paul and
Julie Waters

MONTRÉAL IS CANADA'S most romantic metropolis, an island city that seems to favor grace and elegance over order and even prosperity, a city full of music, art, and joie de vivre. It is rather like the European capital Vienna—past its peak of power and glory, perhaps, but still a vibrant and beautiful place full of memories, dreams, and festivals.

That's not to say Montréal is ready to fade away. It may not be so young anymore—2002 marked its 360th birthday—but it remains Québec's largest city and an important port and financial center. Its office towers are full of young Québecois entrepreneurs ready and eager to take on the world. The city's four universities—two English and two French—and a host of junior colleges add to this youthful zest. (A 1999 study by local McGill University showed that Montréal's population had the highest proportion of students of any city in North America— 3.48 per hundred, just a whisker ahead of Boston with 3.47.)

Montréal is the only French-speaking metropolis in North America and the second-largest French-speaking city in the world, but it's a tolerant place that over the years has made room for millions of immigrants who speak dozens of languages. Today about 15% of the 3.1 million people who live in the metropolitan area claim English as their mother tongue, and another 15% claim a language that's neither English nor French. The city's gentle acceptance has made it one of the world's most livable cities.

The city's grace, however, has been sorely tested. Since 1976, Montréal has endured the election (twice) of a separatist provincial government, a law banning all languages but French on virtually all public signs and billboards, and four referenda on the future of Québec and Canada. The latest chapter in this long constitutional drama was the cliff-hanger referendum on Québec independence on October 30, 1995. In that showdown Québecois voters chose to remain part of Canada, but by the thinnest of possible margins. More than 98% of eligible voters participated, and the final province-wide result was 49.42% in favor of independence and 50.58% against. In fact, 60% of the province's Francophones voted in favor of establishing an independent Québec. But Montréal, where most of the province's Anglophones and immigrants live, bucked the separatist trend and voted nearly 70% against independence.

The drama has cooled; since 1998 the separatist government has turned its attention to the economy, and Montréal has prospered accordingly. Indeed, Montréal has emerged stronger and more optimistic. And why not? It's a city that's used to turmoil. It was founded by the French, conquered by the British, and occupied by the Americans. It has a long history of reconciling contradictions and even today is a city of contrasts. The glass office tower of La Maison des Coopérants, for example, soars above a Gothic-style Anglican cathedral that squats gracefully in its shadow. The neo-Gothic facade of the Basilique Notre-Dame-de-Montréal glares across Place d'Armes at the pagan temple that's the head office of the Bank of Montréal. And while pilgrims still crawl up the steps of the Oratoire St-Joseph on one side of Mont-Royal, thousands of their fellow Catholics line up to get in to the very chic Casino de Montréal on the other side—certainly not what the earnest French settlers who founded Montréal envisioned when they landed on the island in May 1642.

Those 54 pious men and women under the leadership of Paul de Chomedey, sieur de Maisonneuve, hoped to do nothing less than

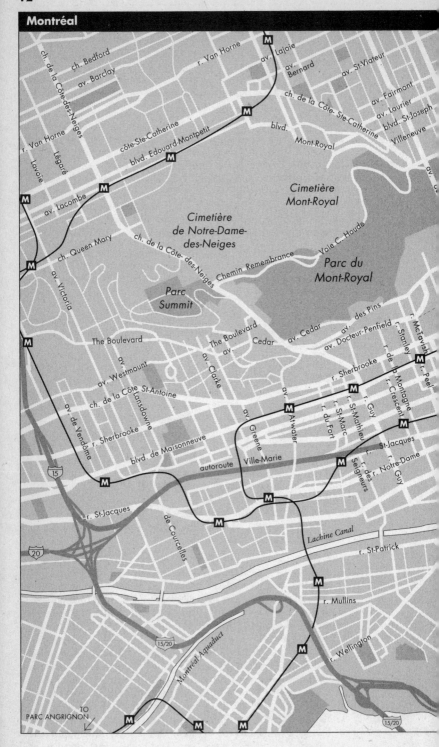

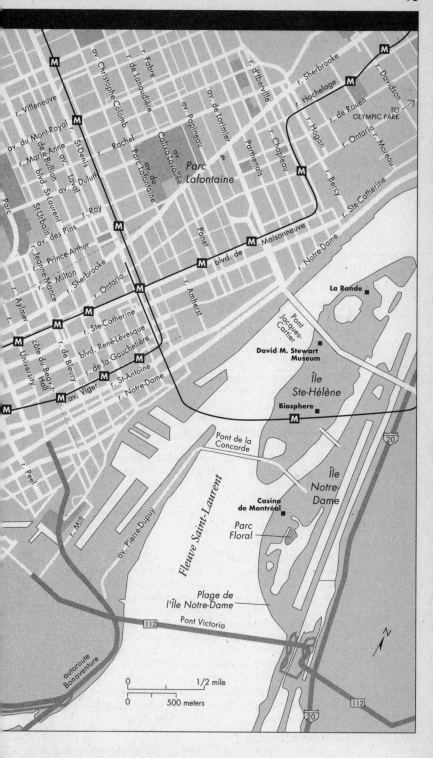

av. Christophe-Colomb
av. de Lanaudière
r. Fabre
r. d'Iberville
r. Sherbrooke
r. Hochelaga
Davidson
TO OLYMPIC PARK
r. de Rouen
av. du Mont-Royal
Villeneuve
r. de Lorimier
av. Papineau
av. Calixa-Lavallée
Hogan
Ontario
r. Moreau
Marie-Anne
de-Bullion
av. Loval
av. Laval
St-Denis
Rachel
av. du Parc-Lafontaine
Parc Lafontaine
Parthenais
r. Chapleau
r. Bercy
Ste-Catherine
blvd. St-Laurent
Duluth
r. Roy
r. des Pins
St-Urbain
av. des Pins
Panel
blvd. de Maisonneuve
r. Notre-Dame
Prince-Arthur
Jeanne-Mance
Milton
r. Sherbrooke
r. Ontario
r. Amherst
La Ronde
av. Aylmer
Parc
r. Ste-Catherine
blvd. René-Lévesque
de la Gauchetière
Pont Jacques-Cartier
David M. Stewart Museum
côte du Beaver-Hall
University
r. de Bleury
av. Viger
r. St-Antoine
r. Notre-Dame
Île Ste-Hélène
Biosphere
Pont de la Concorde
20
Île Notre-Dame
r. Peel
Mill
Fleuve Saint-Laurent
Casino de Montréal
Parc Floral
av. Pierre-Dupuy
Plage de l'Île Notre-Dame
Pont Victoria
112
autoroute Bonaventure
0   1/2 mile
0   500 meters
20
112

create a new Christian society. They named their settlement Ville-Marie in honor of the mother of Christ and set out to convert the natives. The heroism of two women—Jeanne Mance, a French noblewoman who arrived with de Maisonneuve, and Marguerite Bourgeoys, who came 11 years later—marked those early years. Jeanne Mance, working alone, established the Hôpital Hôtel-Dieu de St-Joseph, still one of the city's major hospitals. In 1659 she invited members of a French order of nuns to help her in her efforts. That order, the Religieuses Hospitalières de St-Joseph, now has its motherhouse in Montréal and is the oldest nursing group in the Americas. Marguerite Bourgeoys, with Jeanne Mance's help, established the colony's first school and taught both French and native children how to read and write. Bourgeoys founded the Congrégation de Notre Dame, a teaching order that still has schools in Montréal, across Canada, and around the world. She was canonized by the Roman Catholic Church in 1982.

Piety wasn't the settlement's only raison d'être, however. Ville-Marie was ideally located to be a commercial success as well. It was at the confluence of two major transportation routes—the St. Lawrence and Ottawa rivers—and fur trappers used the town as a staging point for their expeditions. But the city's religious roots were never forgotten. Until 1854, long after the French lost possession of the city, the island of Montréal remained the property of the Sulpicians, an aristocratic order of French priests. The Sulpicians were responsible for administering the colony and for recruiting colonists. They still run the Basilique Notre-Dame-de-Montréal and are still responsible for training priests for the Roman Catholic archdiocese.

The French regime in Canada ended with the Seven Years' War—what Americans call the French and Indian War. British troops took Québec City in 1759, and Montréal fell less than a year later. The Treaty of Paris ceded all New France to Britain in 1763, and soon English and Scottish settlers poured into Montréal to take advantage of the city's geography and economic potential. By 1832, Montréal was a leading colonial capital of business, finance, and transportation and had grown far beyond the walls of the old settlement. Much of that business and financial leadership has since moved to Toronto, the upstream rival Montrealers love to hate.

Pleasures and Pastimes

Dining
Montrealers are passionate about food. They love to dine on classic dishes in restaurants such as Les Halles and Chez La Mère Michel, or swoon over culinary innovations in places like Toqué! and Area, but they can be equally passionate about humbler fare. They'll argue with some heat about where to get the juiciest smoked meat (the city's beloved version of corned beef), the crispiest barbecued chicken, and the soggiest *stimés* (steamed hot dogs). There's great French food here, but also some of North America's most innovative chefs, who seamlessly blend French discipline, Asian and Latin flavors, and the freshest of local ingredients. Over the years, immigrants from all over the world—notably Jews from Eastern Europe, Greeks, Thais, Chinese, Portuguese, and especially Italians—have added to the mix; the city's restaurants represent more than 75 ethnic groups.

Faith and History
Reminders of the city's long history are found everywhere, including in its churches. Some buildings in Vieux-Montréal (Old Montréal, or the old city) date from the 17th century. Other parts of the city are full of examples of Victorian architecture. Museums such as the Musée Mc-

Cord de l'Histoire Canadienne, the Musée d'Archéologie de la Pointe-à-Callière, and the Stewart Museum in the Old Fort on Île Ste-Hélène attest to the city's fascination with its past.

Montréal's two most popular attractions are the oratory dedicated to St. Joseph on the north side of Mont-Royal and the Basilique Notre-Dame-de-Montréal, dedicated to his wife, in the old city. These are just two of dozens of churches built in the days when the Québecois were among the most devout Roman Catholics. Other gems include St. Patrick's Basilica and the Chapelle Notre-Dame-de-Lourdes. In working-class neighborhoods, parish churches can be as grand as some cathedrals.

Festivals

Summer and fall are one succession of festivals, beginning in late June with the Festival International de Jazz, when as many as a million fans descend on the city to hear more than 1,000 musicians, including such giants as the guitarist John Scofield and the tenor saxophonist Joe Lovano. In mid-summer there are the World Film Festival and the lively Just for Laughs Comedy Festival in the Vieux-Port (old port) area. Other festivals celebrate beer, alternative films, French-language music and song from around the world, and international cuisine. In late June and July the skies over the city waterfront light up with color and flame as fireworks teams from around the world vie for prizes in the International Fireworks Competition.

Lodging

Montréal's downtown has its share of big, comfortable hotels, but the little inns and auberges along the cobbled streets of Vieux-Montréal offer charm as well as a dose of history. As recently as 1990, you couldn't stay in the old city; now more than a dozen establishments have sprung up, ranging from modern hotels to an 18th-century stone inn that once housed Benjamin Franklin.

Nightlife

Montréal's reputation as a place to visit for a night on the town dates back at least to Prohibition days, when hordes of thirsty Americans from south of the border would flood the city every weekend to eat, drink, and be merry. African-American jazz musicians and singers in particular loved the place because they could stay, dine, and imbibe where they wanted, free of most of the race restrictions they faced back home. Dozens of dance and jazz clubs and bistros line downtown streets, and the city has hundreds of bars where you can go to argue about sports, politics, and religion until the wee hours of the morning. Much of the action takes place along rue St-Denis and adjacent streets in the eastern part of the city or on rues Bishop, Crescent, and de la Montagne in the downtown area. The scene is constantly shifting; last year's hot spot can quickly become this year's has-been. The best and easiest way to figure out what's in is to stroll along rue St-Denis or rue Bishop at about 10:30 PM and look for the place with the longest line and the rudest doorman.

Shopping

Thanks to the development of the Underground City, shopping is a year-round sport in Montréal. Subterranean passageways and the Métro link this vast complex, which is heated in winter, air-conditioned in summer, and includes two major department stores, at least a dozen huge shopping malls, and more than 1,000 boutiques. Antiques, hand-crafted jewelry, avant-garde fashions, vintage clothing, leather goods, sleek home furnishings—the variety of goods keeps things interesting above and below ground. Add to this Montréal's status as one of the fur capitals of the world and it's easy to see why the city is a shopping destination. For Americans there's the added bonus of the U.S. dollar's continued strength against the Canadian currency.

EXPLORING MONTRÉAL

The Île de Montréal (Island of Montréal) sits in the St. Lawrence River and is 51 km (32 mi) long and 14 km (9 mi) wide. It gets its name from the 764-ft-high Mont-Royal, which provides the only rise in the landscape and which is known by residents simply as "the mountain." The 24 suburbs on the island were absorbed into the city of Montréal in 2002, forming one mega-city—much to the dismay of many proud suburbanites. A belt of off-island suburbs sits on the south shore of the St. Lawrence, and just to the north across the narrow Rivière des Prairies, on an island of its own, is Laval, a suburb that has become the second-largest city in the province. But the countryside is never far away. The pastoral Eastern Townships, first settled by Loyalists fleeing the American Revolution, are less than an hour's drive away, and the Laurentians, an all-season playground full of lakes and ski hills, are even closer.

For a good overview of the city, head for the lookout at the Chalet du Mont-Royal. You can drive most of the way, park, and walk ½ km (¼ mi), or hike all the way up from chemin de la Côte-des-Neiges or avenue des Pins. Look directly out—southeast—from the belvedere to see, at the foot of the hill, the McGill University campus and, surrounding it, the skyscrapers of downtown Montréal. Just beyond, along the bank of the river, are the stone houses of Vieux-Montréal. Hugging the south shore on the other side of the river are îles Ste-Hélène and Notre-Dame, sites of La Ronde amusement park, the Biosphère, and the Casino de Montréal; acres of parkland; and the Lac de l'Île Notre-Dame public beach—all popular excursions. To the east are rue St-Denis and the Quartier Latin, with its rows of French and ethnic restaurants, bistros, chess hangouts, designer boutiques, antiques shops, and art galleries. Even farther east you can see the flying-saucer–shape Olympic Stadium with its leaning tower.

Montréal is easy to explore. Streets, subways, and bus lines are clearly marked. The city is divided by a grid of streets roughly aligned east–west and north–south. (Montréal takes its directions from the flow of the river rather than the compass, so this grid is tilted about 40 degrees off—to the left of—true north, meaning that west is actually southwest and so on.) North–south street numbers begin at the St. Lawrence River and increase as you head north; east–west street numbers begin at boulevard St-Laurent, which divides Montréal into east and west halves. The city is not so large that seasoned walkers can't see all the districts around the base of Mont-Royal on foot. Nearly everything else is easily accessible by the city's clean and quiet bus and Métro (subway) system. If you're planning to visit a number of museums, look into the city's museum pass (available at museums and Centre Info-Touriste).

Numbers in the text correspond to numbers in the margin and on the Vieux-Montréal, Downtown Montréal (Centre-Ville) and Golden Square Mile, Quartier Latin and Parc du Mont-Royal, and Olympic Park and Botanical Garden maps.

Great Itineraries

Getting a real feel for this bilingual, multicultural city takes some time. An ideal stay is seven days, but even three days of walking and soaking up the atmosphere is enough time to visit Mont-Royal, explore Vieux-Montréal, do some shopping, and perhaps visit the Parc Olympique.

It also includes enough nights for an evening of bar-hopping on rue St-Denis or rue Crescent and another for a long, luxurious dinner at one of the city's excellent restaurants.

IF YOU HAVE 3 DAYS
Any visit to Montréal should start with Mont-Royal, Montréal's most enduring symbol. Afterward wander down to avenue des Pins and then through McGill University to downtown. Make an effort to stop at the Musée des Beaux-Arts and St. Patrick's Basilica. On Day 2, explore Vieux-Montréal, with special emphasis on the Basilique Notre-Dame-de-Montréal and the Musée d'Archéologie Pointe-à-Callière. On Day 3 you can either visit the Parc Olympique (recommended for children) or stroll through the Quartier Latin.

IF YOU HAVE 5 DAYS
Start with a visit to Parc du Mont-Royal. After viewing the city from the Chalet du Mont-Royal, visit the Oratoire St-Joseph. You should still have enough time to visit the Musée des Beaux-Arts before dinner. That leaves time on Day 2 to get in some shopping as you explore downtown, with perhaps a visit to the Centre Canadien d'Architecture. Spend all of Day 3 in Vieux-Montréal, and on Day 4 stroll through the Quartier Latin. On Day 5, visit the Parc Olympique and then do one of three things: visit the islands, take a ride on the Lachine Rapids, or revisit some of the sights you missed in Vieux-Montréal or downtown.

IF YOU HAVE 7 DAYS
A week gives you enough time for the five-day itinerary while expanding your Vieux-Montréal explorations to two days and adding a shopping spree on rue Chabanel and a visit to the Casino de Montréal.

Vieux-Montréal

When Montréal's first European settlers arrived by river in 1642, they stopped to build their houses just below the treacherous Lachine Rapids that blocked the way upstream. They picked a site near an old Iroquois settlement on the bank of the river nearest Mont-Royal. In the mid-17th century, Montréal consisted of a handful of wood houses clustered around a pair of stone buildings, all flimsily fortified by a wooden stockade. For almost three centuries this district—bounded by rues Berri and McGill on the east and west, rue St-Jacques on the north, and the river to the south—was the financial and political heart of the city. Government buildings, the largest church, the stock exchange, the main market, and the port were here. The narrow but relatively straight cobblestone streets were lined with solid, occasionally elegant houses, office buildings, and warehouses—also made of stone. In the early days a thick stone wall with four gates protected the city against native people and marauding European powers. Montréal quickly grew beyond the bounds of its fortifications, however, and by World War I the center of the city had moved toward Mont-Royal. Dominion Square (now Square Dorchester) became the new heart of Montréal. For the next two decades Vieux-Montréal (Old Montréal), as it became known, was gradually abandoned, the warehouses and offices emptied. In 1962 the city began studying ways to revitalize Vieux-Montréal, and a period of renovations and restorations began.

Today Vieux-Montréal is a center of cultural life and municipal government. Most of the summer activities revolve around Place Jacques-Cartier, which becomes a pedestrian mall with street performers and outdoor cafés, and the Vieux-Port, one of the city's most popular recreation spots. The Orchestre Symphonique de Montréal performs summer concerts at Basilique Notre-Dame-de-Montréal, and English-language plays are staged in the Centaur Theatre in the old stock-exchange building. This district has museums devoted to history, religion, and the arts. It also has a growing number of boutiques and hotel beds, especially in the quieter, western part of the neighborhood.

A Good Walk

Take the Métro to the Square-Victoria station and follow the signs to the **Centre de Commerce Mondial de Montréal** ①, one of the city's more appealing enclosed spaces, with a fountain and frequent art exhibits. Exit on the north side of the complex onto rue St-Antoine and turn right. The building across the street just to the east is the Palais de Congrèes, a vast convention center that sprawls across the Ville Marie Expressway and will fill six city blocks when an expansion project is completed in 2003. Turn right on rue St-Pierre, walk south to **rue St-Jacques** and turn left. The pale-yellow stone building with the third-story columns catercorner across the junction is the former headquarters of the **Royal Bank of Canada** ②. Walking east, you see the Victorian office buildings of the country's former financial center. The area can seem deserted on weekends, when the business and legal offices close down, but things get livelier closer to the waterfront.

Walk the few blocks to **Place d'Armes** ③, a square that was the site of battles with the Iroquois in the 1600s and later became the center of Montréal's Haute-Ville, or Upper Town. Horse-drawn calèches are available at the south end of the square; on the north side is the **Bank of Montréal** ④, an impressive building with Corinthian columns. The **Basilique Notre-Dame-de-Montréal** ⑤, one of the most beautiful churches in North America, dominates the south end of Place d'Armes. The low, more retiring stone building behind a wall to the west of the basilica is the **Vieux Séminaire** ⑥, Montréal's oldest building. Unlike the basilica, it is closed to the public. To the east of the basilica is **rue St-Sulpice,** one of the first streets in Montréal, and catercorner from it is the art deco Aldred Building, the first building in Montréal to exceed 10 stories. Next to that is a nine-story red-stone tower built in 1888 by a New York life-insurance company. One block farther east on rue Notre-Dame, just past boulevard St-Laurent and on the left, rises the black glass–sheathed **Palais de Justice** ⑦ (1971), the courthouse. The large domed building at 155 rue Notre-Dame Est is the **Vieux Palais de Justice** ⑧ (1857). Criminal cases used to be heard in the **Edifice Ernest-Cormier** ⑨, the imposing building across the street with the stately columns and grand bronze doors. Today it's a musical conservatory. Just east of it, at 160 rue Notre-Dame Est, is the Maison de la Sauvegarde, one of the city's oldest houses. The Vieux Palais de Justice abuts the small **Place Vauquelin** ⑩, named after an 18th-century naval hero. North of this square is Champ-de-Mars, a former military parade ground and now a public park crisscrossed by archaeologists' trenches. The ornate building on the east side of Place Vauquelin is the Second Empire–style **Hôtel de Ville** ⑪, or City Hall, built in 1878.

You're in a perfect spot to explore **Place Jacques-Cartier** ⑫, the square that is the heart of Vieux-Montréal. On its north end, at the western corner of rue Notre-Dame, is a tourist-information office operated by the Office des Congrès et du Tourisme du Grand Montréal. Two- and three-story stone buildings that were originally homes or hotels line both sides of the square. In summer, the one-block rue St-Amable, near the bottom of the square, becomes a marketplace for local jewelers, artists, and other craftspeople.

Retrace your steps to the north end of Place Jacques-Cartier and continue east on rue Notre-Dame. On the right at the corner of rue

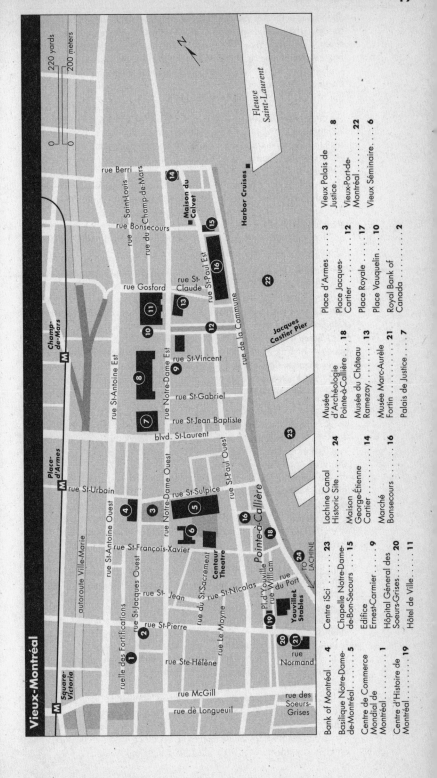

Vieux-Montréal

220 yards

200 meters

Fleuve Saint-Laurent

Harbor Cruises

rue Berri

rue Saint-Louis

rue Bonsecours

rue du Champ-de-Mars

Maison du Calvet

rue Gosford

rue St-Claude

rue St-Paul Est

Champ-de-Mars **M**

Place-d'Armes **M**

rue St-Antoine Est

rue St-Vincent

rue Notre-Dame Est

rue St-Gabriel

rue St-Jean Baptiste

blvd. St-Laurent

rue St-Antoine Ouest

rue Notre-Dame Ouest

rue St-Sulpice

rue St-Paul Ouest

rue St-Urbain

autoroute Ville-Marie

rue St-François-Xavier

Centaur Theatre

Pointe-à-Callière

Square Victoria **M**

ruelle des Fortifications

rue St-Jacques Ouest

rue St- Jean

rue du St-Sacrement

rue St-Nicolas

Pl. d'Youville

rue William

rue du Port

TO LACHINE

Youville Stables

rue St-Pierre

rue Le Moyne

rue Ste-Hélène

rue Normand

rue McGill

rue de Longueuil

rue des Soeurs-Grises

Jacques Castier Pier

rue de la Commune

St-Claude is the **Musée du Château Ramezay** ⑬, built as the residence of the 11th governor of Montréal, Claude de Ramezay, and now a museum. Continue on rue Notre-Dame toward rue Berri; on the right just before you reach the intersection are two houses from the mid-19th century that have been transformed into the **Maison George-Étienne Cartier** ⑭, a museum honoring one of the leading figures in the founding of the Canadian federation in 1867.

When you come out of the museum, walk south on rue Berri to rue St-Paul and then start walking west again, back toward the center of the city. The first street on your right is rue Bonsecours, one of the oldest in the city. On the corner is the charming Maison du Calvet, now a restaurant and small but opulent bed-and-breakfast (called Pierre du Calvet AD 1725). Opposite it is the charming **Chapelle Notre-Dame-de-Bon-Secours** ⑮, founded by St. Marguerite Bourgeoys, Montréal's first schoolteacher. The long, domed building beyond the chapel is the **Marché Bonsecours** ⑯, a public market with exhibits on Montréal in the hall upstairs and boutiques specializing in regional crafts and Québecois fashions downstairs.

Restaurants, shops with Québecois handicrafts, and nightclubs line rue St-Paul for almost 20 blocks. Eight blocks past Place Jacques-Cartier, rue St-Paul leads to **Place Royale** ⑰, the oldest public square in Montréal. Behind the Old Customs House on the square are the **Pointe-à-Callière,** a small park that commemorates the settlers' first landing, and the **Musée d'Archéologie Pointe-à-Callière** ⑱, Montréal's premier museum of history and archaeology. A 1½-block walk down rue William takes you to the 19th-century Youville Stables, a set of low stone buildings enclosing a garden that served as warehouses and never as a shelter for animals.

Across rue William from the stables is the old fire station that houses the **Centre d'Histoire de Montréal** ⑲, a museum that chronicles the day-to-day life of Montrealers throughout the years. Now walk south on rue St-Pierre toward the harbor. You pass the ruins of the **Hôpital Général des Soeurs-Grises** ⑳, which served as a shelter for homeless children in the 18th and 19th centuries. Next to the ruins is the charming **Musée Marc-Aurèle Fortin** ㉑, a gallery dedicated to the works of one of Québec's most distinctive landscape artists. Just south of the museum, rue St-Pierre ends at rue de la Commune, across the street from the **Vieux-Port-de-Montréal** ㉒, a pleasant and popular waterfront park that makes a fitting close to any walk in Vieux-Montréal. If you have time, you can arrange for a harbor excursion or a daring ride on the Lachine Rapids. The Vieux-Port is also home to the **Centre iSci** ㉓, Montréal's state-of-the-art science center. At the western end of the port area is the entrance to the **Lachine Canal Historic Site** ㉔, a canal-turned-park that has the city's most popular bicycle path.

TIMING

If you walk briskly and don't stop, you could get through this route in under an hour. A more realistic and leisurely pace takes about 90 minutes (still without stopping), or longer in winter when the streets are icy. Comfortable shoes are a must for the cobblestone streets. The Basilique Notre-Dame is one of Montréal's most famous landmarks and deserves at least a 45-minute visit; Château Ramezay deserves the same. The Pointe-à-Callière museum could keep an enthusiastic history buff occupied for a whole day, so give it at least two hours. If you do visit any museums, check ahead for seasonal hours.

Sights to See

❹ Bank of Montréal. The head office of Canada's oldest chartered bank is a temple to business and finance. It's housed in a neoclassical structure built on Place d'Armes in 1847 and remodeled by the renowned New York architectural firm McKim, Mead & White in 1905. The central dome and Corinthian columns give it the air of an ancient Greek or Roman sanctuary, a stark contrast to the Gothic glory of the Catholic Basilique Notre-Dame-de-Montréal across the square. If anything, the bank's interior is even more templelike. In the main entrance, a 20-ft statue stands like an ancient goddess amid a forest of dark marble columns supporting an intricate coffered ceiling. She actually represents Patria—or "homeland"—and stands as a memorial to the war dead of 1914–18. The bank's tellers work in an immense room surrounded by more marble columns. A one-room museum recounts the early history of banking in Canada. ⊠ *119 rue St-Jacques, Vieux-Montréal,* ☎ *514/877–7373.* ☒ *Free.* ☉ *Weekdays 10–4. Métro: Place-d'Armes.*

★ ❺ Basilique Notre-Dame-de-Montréal (Notre-Dame Basilica). James O'Donnell, the American Protestant architect who designed this 3,800-seat temple, was so pleased with his handiwork that he converted to Roman Catholicism. Everything about the basilica, which opened in 1829, is on a grand scale. The twin towers of its new-Gothic facade are 228 ft high, and the western tower holds one of the largest bells in North America. The interior isn't so much Gothic as neo-Romanesque, with stained-glass windows, pine and walnut carvings, and a blue vaulted ceiling studded with thousands of 24-karat gold stars. The stained-glass windows are from Limoges and commemorate episodes of Montréal's history. Life-size wooden carvings of Ezekiel and Jeremiah sit under the opulently decorated pulpit with its intricately twisting staircase. Side altars honor—among others—St. Marguerite d'Youville, Canada's first native-born saint; St. Marguerite Bourgeoys, Canada's first schoolteacher; and a group of Sulpician priests who were martyred in Paris during the French Revolution.

As the northwest corner of the church has been glassed off to make a small prayer room away from the noise of the visiting hordes, the magnificent baptistery, decorated with frescoes by Ozias Leduc, is difficult to see. With more than 7,000 pipes, the Casavant pipe organ is one of the largest on the continent. If you want only to hear the organ roar, drop in for the 11 AM solemn Mass on Sunday and pay special attention to the recessional. Behind the main altar is the **Sacré-Coeur Chapel** (Sacred Heart Chapel), destroyed by fire in 1978 and rebuilt in five styles. Its dominant feature is the huge modern bronze sculpture that forms the backdrop for the altar. The chapel is often called the Wedding Chapel, because hundreds of Montrealers get married in it every year. The wedding of pop diva Céline Dion to her manager in 1994, however, filled the main church, as did the state funeral of former Prime Minister Pierre Elliot Trudeau in 2000. In the evening, the darkened nave is transformed into a backdrop for a state-of-the-art light-and-sound show, which depicts the history of Montréal and showcases the church's extraordinary art.

Notre-Dame is an active house of worship and visitors are asked to dress accordingly (i.e., no shorts or bare midriffs). Tours aren't permitted during the Sunday masses (at 9, 11 AM, 12:30, and 4:30 PM) in the main church and the chapel can't be viewed during the 12:15 and 5 PM weekday masses. ⊠ *116 rue Notre-Dame Ouest, Vieux-Montréal,* ☎ *514/849–1070,* 🕸 *www.basiliquenddm.org.* ☒ *$2, including guided tour.* ☉ *8–5 daily; 20-min tours in French and English every* *hr July–Sept., every 2 hrs (or by prior arrangement) Oct.–June. Métro: Place-d'Armes.*

❶ Centre de Commerce Mondial de Montréal (Montréal World Trade Center). The narrow, soaring atrium houses boutiques, a food court, frequent art exhibits, and Montréal's own chunk of the Berlin Wall, complete with graffiti. Photographers often use the fountain and reflecting pond at the west end as a backdrop for fashion shoots and wedding groups. The semi-reclining statue of Amphitrite (Poseidon's wife) overlooking the fountain is an 18th-century piece and comes from the municipal fountain of St-Mihiel-de-la-Meuse in France. The complex covers a block of the run-down ruelle des Fortifications, a narrow lane that marks the place where the city walls stood. Developers glassed it in and sandblasted and restored 11 of the 19th-century buildings that lined it. One of them—the **Nordheimer,** at the southeastern end of the complex—is worth a look. It now forms part of the Hôtel Inter-Continental Montréal. To see it, climb the stairs to the hotel lobby and cross the footbridge. The building's dark woodwork and suggestive Celtic-style mosaics reflect the romantic tastes of the Scottish businessmen who ran Victorian Montréal. The building also once housed a small concert hall where such luminaries as Sarah Bernhardt and Maurice Ravel performed. ✉ *747 Sq. Victoria, Vieux-Montréal,* ☎ *514/982–9888. Métro: Square-Victoria.*

☺ ⓳ Centre d'Histoire de Montréal (Montréal History Center). Video games, sound tracks, and more than 300 artifacts re-create the day-to-day life of the men and women who have lived in Montréal from pre-colonial to modern times. Some of the most touching exhibits depict family life in Montréal's working-class tenements in the 20th century. You can sit in a period-furnished living room and listen to a 1940s radio broadcast that includes the play-by-play of a hockey game and the recitation of the rosary, or you can step into a phone booth and eavesdrop on a young working-class couple arranging a date. ✉ *335 pl. d'Youville, Vieux-Montréal,* ☎ *514/872–3207,* 🕸 *www2.ville.montreal.qc. ca/chm/engl/chma.htm.* 🎫 *$6.50.* ☼ *Tues.–Sun. 10–5. Métro: Place-d'Armes or Square-Victoria.*

☺ ㉓ Centre iSci. The "i" stands for interactive, the "Sci" for science, and together they spell the name of Montréal's science center, which fills more than 600,000 square ft on the old King Edward Pier. The center's two main exhibition halls—Eureka and Technocity—were overhauled in 2002. Each uses puzzles, quizzes, games of strategy and skill, and hands-on experiments, as well as lectures and demonstrations, to explore various aspects of such scientific and technological themes as medicine, aerospace, computers, communications and media, natural resources, and engineering. The center also encompasses three IMAX film theaters and the giant-screen, interactive Immersion Studios theater—complete with digital projection system and "surround sound"—where audience members use touch screens to vote on the twists and turns of the story. The center also includes Porto Fiorentino, a 1,000-seat family restaurant that overlooks the harbor and presents interactive culinary activities and piano concerts. The neighboring food court teaches lessons about nutrition and agriculture. In summer, ship containers serve as outdoor boutiques with a science message—for example, the watch boutique demonstrates the use of liquid quartz, and the jewelry boutique might explain the formation of amber. ✉ *Quai King Edward, Vieux-Montréal,* ☎ *514/496–4724 or 877/496–4724,* 🕸 *www. isci.ca.* 🎫 *Exhibit halls and Immersion Studios $10; IMAX $12; exhibit halls, Immersion Studios, and IMAX $17.* ☼ *June 17–Sept. 8,*

Mon.–Thurs. 10–5, weekends 10–9; Sept. 9–June 16, Tues.–Sun. 10–5. Métro: Place-d'Armes or Champ-de-Mars.

⑮ Chapelle Notre-Dame-de-Bon-Secours (Our Lady of Lourdes Chapel). St. Marguerite Bourgeoys dedicated the original waterfront chapel on this site to the Virgin Mary in 1657. (Montréal's founder, Paul de Chomedey, sieur de Maisonneuve, apparently helped cut the timber.) Fire destroyed that structure and the present stone chapel dates to 1771. A renovation project in 1998 revealed beautiful 18th-century murals that had been covered up with more-recent pictures. The chapel has always had a special place in the hearts of mariners. It was built to house a statue of Notre-Dame-de-Bon-Secours (Our Lady of Good Hope), credited with the rescue of those in peril at sea. A larger-than-life statue of the Virgin graces the steeple of the present building, facing the river with arms outstretched in welcome. Mariners who survived the perils of ocean crossings in the 18th and 19th centuries often came to the church to thank the Virgin for her help and to leave votive lamps in the shape of small model ships as tokens of appreciation. Many of them still hang from the ceiling, and the chapel is usually referred to simply as the Église des Matelots, or the Sailors' Church. You may climb the steeple to the "aerial," a tiny chapel where mariners came to pray for safe passage. The adjacent **Musée Marguerite Bourgeoys** explores the life of the saint and the history of Montréal, with an emphasis on education. ⊠ *400 rue St-Paul Est, Vieux-Montréal,* ☎ *514/282–8670,* WEB *www.marguerite-bourgeoys.com.* ⊡ *Chapel free; museum $6.* ☉ *May–Oct., daily 10–5; Nov.–mid-Jan. and mid-Mar.–Apr., daily 11–3:30; mid-Jan.–mid-Mar., open only for Sun. mass. Métro: Champ-de-Mars.*

⑨ Edifice Ernest-Cormier. The columned neoclassical building erected in 1926 as the city's main criminal court is today the home of the Québec Court of Appeal. The building had served as a music conservatory for 32 years, starting in 1970. Its massive bronze doors are richly carved and the vast main hall has dome-shape skylights and travertine facing. *100 rue Notre-Dame Est, Vieux-Montréal,* ☎ *no phone. Métro: Champ-de-Mars.*

⑳ Hôpital Général des Soeurs-Grises. These ruins of the hospital the Frères Charon established in 1694 have been preserved as a memorial to Canada's first native-born saint, Marguerite d'Youville, who took over the hospital in 1747 and ran it until it burned down in 1765. The bare stone walls once formed the west wing and the transept of the chapel. The gold script on the one facing the street is a re-creation of the letters patent signed by Louis XIV establishing the hospital. St. Marguerite founded the Soeurs de la Charité, better known as the Soeurs Grises, or gray nuns. In the shadow of the Hôpital Général des Soeurs-Grises is the **Maison de Mère d'Youville** (☎ 514/842–9411; ask for Sr. Marguerite D'Aoust), which houses a small retreat operated by the Soeurs Grises as well as some remarkable reminders of St. Marguerite's days, such as the old kitchen where she worked, with its enormous fireplace and big stone sink, the stone floor of the room that served as North America's first external clinic or outpatients' department, and the room where St. Marguerite died. The house isn't open to the general public, but guided tours can be arranged. Tours are free, but donations are accepted. ⊠ *138 rue St-Pierre, Vieux-Montréal,* ☎ *no phone. Métro: Square-Victoria.*

⑪ Hôtel de Ville. President Charles de Gaulle of France marked Canada's centennial celebrations in 1967 by standing on the central balcony of Montréal's ornate City Hall on July 24 and shouting *Vive le Québec libre"* ("Long live free Québec"), much to the delight of the fledgling separatist movement. Perhaps he got carried away because he felt so at home—the Second Empire–style city hall, built in 1878, is modeled on the one in Tours, France. Free guided tours are available daily 9–5 in June, July, and August, and the main hall is used for occasional exhibitions. ✉ *275 rue Notre-Dame Est, Vieux-Montréal,* ☎ *514/872–3355.* ☉ *Main hall, daily 9–5. Métro: Champ-de-Mars.*

OFF THE   **LACHINE** – This district's name began as a joke. Robert Cavalier de La
BEATEN PATH   Salle, the first seigneur to hold land west of the Lachine Rapids, was obsessed with finding a westward passage to the Orient. His persistent and unsuccessful attempts led his fellow colonists to refer to his lands derisively as La Chine, or China.

Lachine has the oldest standing house on the Île de Montréal: the Mayson LeBer–LeMoyne, built by Montréal merchants Jacques LeBer and Charles LeMoyne between 1669 and 1685. Now the **Musée de Lachine** (Lachine Museum), it houses Lachine's historical collections, including artifacts and documents dating from colonial times. It and its outbuildings also serve as a showcase for local and regional artists. ✉ *110 chemin LaSalle, Lachine,* ☎ *514/634–3471 Ext. 346,* FAX *514/637–6784.* ✉ *Free.* ☉ *Wed.–Sun. 11:30–4:30.*

An old stone warehouse on the Lachine waterfront that dates from 1802 is now the **Fur Trade in Lachine National Historic Site.** This museum recalls the salad days when Lachine's position upstream from the rapids made it an important center in the fur trade: the site is stocked with bales of pelts ready for shipment to England and trade goods—blankets, flour, tea, axes, firearms—for the area trappers. ✉ *1255 blvd. St-Joseph, Lachine,* ☎ *514/637–7433 or 514/283–6054,* WEB *www.parkscanada.pch.gc.ca/fourrure.* ✉ *$2.50.* ☉ *Apr.–mid-Oct., daily 10–12:30 and 1–6 (closed Mon. AM); mid-Oct.–late Nov., Wed.–Sun. 9:30–12:30 and 1–5.*

🖑 ❷❹ **Lachine Canal Historic Site.** It was a group of prescient French priests who first tried to dig a canal to move cargo around the treacherous Lachine Rapids, but they had neither the royal approval nor the money to finish the job. That didn't happen until 1825, when the Lachine Canal opened, linking Montréal's harbor to Lac St-Louis and the Ottawa River. For more than 150 years, the canal was one of Canada's most vital waterways, but it was rendered obsolete in 1959 when the St. Lawrence Seaway opened, making it possible for large cargo ships to move freely from the sea to the Great Lakes. The Lachine Canal was subsequently closed to navigation and became an illicit dumping ground for old cars and the victims of underworld killings, while the area around it degenerated into an industrial slum.

In 1988, however, the federal government planted lawns and trees along the old canal and transformed it into a long, thin park linking the Vieux-Port to Lachine, one of the island's oldest municipalities and the spot where the St. Lawrence widens to become Lac St-Louis. In spring, summer, and fall, hundreds of Montrealers ride or skate the 9-mi bicycle path to picnic in Lachine's lakefront park or dine in one of the century-old buildings along the waterfront. The path, which in winter hosts cross-country skiiers, is the first link in the more than 60 mi of bike trails that constitute the **Pôle des Rapides** (☎ 514/732–7303).

Since 2002, the canal has been opened to pleasure craft, and you can take a shuttle boat between Vieux-Montréal and Lachine. The canalside factories and warehouses—most now abandoned or converted into offices or housing—provide an insight into the city's early industrial development. A permanent exhibition at the **Lachine Canal Interpretation Centre** explains the history and construction of the canal. The center, on the western end of the canal, is free and open daily (except Monday morning) mid-May to September 1, 10–noon and 1–6. ☎ *514/637–7433,* WEB *www.parkscanada.pch.gc.ca/canallachine.* ▣ *Free.* ☉ *Sunrise–sunset.*

🟤 **Maison George-Étienne Cartier.** The two houses of this museum explore the private and public life of George-Étienne Cartier, the statesman who persuaded French-speaking Québecers to join the Canadian federation when it was formed in 1867. In the east house, which focuses on Cartier's political career, you can listen to recordings of him and his contemporaries argue the pros and cons of confederation or learn about the importance of Cartier's role in the building of the colony's first railways. Next door, where the Cartier family lived in the 1860s, you can listen to portions of taped conversation from "servants" gossiping about the lives of their master and mistress. The residence is furnished in the opulently fussy style favored by the 19th-century bourgeois. From mid-November to mid-December, Victorian decorations festoon the home. ✉ *458 rue Notre-Dame Est, Vieux-Montréal,* ☎ *514/283-2282 or 800/463-6769,* WEB *www.parkscanada.pch.gc.ca/cartier.* ▣ *$3.25.* ☉ *Late May–early Sept., daily 10–6; early Sept.–mid-Dec. and Apr.–late-May, Wed.–Sun. 10–noon and 1–5. Métro: Champ-de-Mars.*

OFF THE
BEATEN PATH

MAISON ST-GABRIEL – A rare example of 17th-century rural architecture deep in working-class Pointe-St-Charles houses one of the city's most overlooked museums. It was here that St. Marguerite Bourgeoys and her religious order trained the *filles du roy* (literally "daughters of the king") to be the wives and mothers of New France; these were young orphan girls sent from France to find husbands and help populate the colony. The two-story stone structure with its complex roof beams—one of the few authentic 17th-century roofs in North America—and huge attics has been restored to show the kind of life these young girls had and the kind of training they received in cooking and child-rearing from their devout instructors. The kitchen is equipped with a rare black-stone sink and an ingenious waste-water disposal system. Several items that belonged to St. Marguerite are also on display, including a writing desk she used. ✉ *2146 pl. Dublin, Pointe-St-Charles,* ☎ *514/935–8136,* WEB *www.maisonsaint-gabriel.qc.ca.* ▣ *$5.* ☉ *June 24–Labor Day, Tues.–Sun. 10–5 (guided tours every hour); early Sept.–Dec. 20 and Feb. 15–June 23, Tues.–Sat. 1:30–3:30 and Sun. 1–5.*

🟤 **Marché Bonsecours.** The graceful, neoclassical building dominates the waterfront of Vieux-Montréal. It was built of gray stone in the 1840s to serve as the city's main market. Its main entrance, on rue St-Paul, has a portico supported by six cast-iron Doric columns imported from England. Two rows of meticulously even, sashed windows and a silvery dome complete the building's distinctive features; because of the slope of the land, the building's waterfront side appears more massive than the long, low frontage along rue St-Paul. A market until the early 1960s, the building was then converted into municipal offices. A 1998 refurbishing transformed it into a public space with an exhibition hall (usually open Tues.–Sun. 10–7) on the second floor for history and culture displays. The bright, airy ground floor facing rue St-Paul and the lower floor facing the waterfront house restaurants as well as shops and boutiques with a focus on local crafts and fashions. ✉ *350 rue St-Paul Est, Vieux-Montréal,* ☎ *514/872–7730,* WEB *www.marchebonsecours.qc.ca. Métro: Champ-de-Mars.*

★ ☚ 🟤 **Musée d'Archéologie Pointe-à-Callière.** The exhibits in this imposing, ship-like building near the Pointe-à-Callière park take you right to the foundations of New France—the museum is built over the excavated remains of structures dating to Montréal's beginnings. Visits usually start with an audio-visual show that gives an overview of the area's history from the Ice Age to the present. When that's over, you descend deep below street level to the bank of the Rivière St-Pierre that once flowed past the site and was where the first settlers built their homes and traded with the local natives. One of the most impressive finds the archaeologists unearthed was the city's first Catholic cemetery, with some tombstones still intact. From there, you wander through the stone foundations of an 18th-century tavern and a 19th-century insurance building. Filmed figures from the past appear on ghostly screens. The museum's excellent gift shop, full of interesting books on Montréal's history as well as pictures and reproductions of old maps, engravings, and other artifacts, is in the Old Customs House, a lovely, neoclassical gray-stone building erected in 1836. An industrial exhibit is housed in the 1915 Youville Pumping House, across the street from the main building. ⊠ *350 pl. Royale, Vieux-Montréal,* ☏ *514/872–9150,* 𝖂𝖤𝖡 *www.musee-pointe-a-calliere.qc.ca.* 🎫 *$9.50.* ☉ *July–Aug., weekdays 10–6, weekends 11–5; Sept.–June, Tues.–Fri. 10–5, weekends 11–5. Métro: Place-d'Armes.*

🖑 **⑬ Musée du Château Ramezay.** French governors, British conquerors, and American occupiers have all lived in this little stone castle. The 11th governor of Montréal, Claude de Ramezay, built it in 1702, and the Compagnie des Indes Occidentales (the French West Indies Company) took it over in 1745 and stored precious furs in the basement vaults. The British used it as headquarters after their conquest in 1760, and so did the American commanders Richard Montgomery and Benedict Arnold, whose troops occupied the city during their 1775–76 campaign to conquer Canada. Benjamin Franklin, who came north in a failed attempt to persuade the Québecois to join the American Revolution, stayed here during that winter adventure. With its thick stone walls, steeply pitched roof, and dormer windows, the château has the air of a Norman castle. Two squat stone towers added in the late 18th century contribute to the effect. The building became a museum of city and provincial history in 1895 and has been restored to the style of Governor de Ramezay's day. The public rooms on the ground floor are gracefully elegant. Of particular interest is the Salon Nantes, with 18th-century Louis XV–style mahogany paneling carved by the French architect Germain Boffrand and imported from the Compagnie des Indes's head office in Nantes about 1750. The main-floor displays are somewhat staid—uniforms, documents, and furniture—but a series of tableaux in the basement vividly depicts the everyday lives of the city's early European settlers, and the château's garden has been planted in a typical colonial fashion. The museum's collection is fairly eclectic, however. One of its most prized possessions, for example, is a bright-red automobile that was produced at the turn of the 20th century by the De Dion-Bouton company for the city's first motorist. ⊠ *280 rue Notre-Dame Est, Vieux-Montréal,* ☏ *514/861–3708,* 𝖂𝖤𝖡 *www.chateauramezay.qc.ca.* 🎫 *$6.* ☉ *June–Sept., daily 10–6; Oct.–May, Tues.–Sun. 10–4:30. Métro: Champ-de-Mars.*

NEED A BREAK?
In summer, few places are livelier than **Place Jacques-Cartier,** just around the corner from the Musée du Château Ramezay. You can stop at a *terasse* (sidewalk café) for a beer or a coffee, or just sit on a bench amid the flower vendors and listen to the street musicians. If you're really daring, you might try *poutine,* Québec's contribution to junk-food culture. It consists of french fries covered with cheese curds and smothered in gravy—an acquired taste.

★ **㉑ Musée Marc-Aurèle Fortin.** Heavy clouds, higgledy-piggledy villages, and lush, fantastic trees crowd the painted landscapes in this little museum dedicated to the work of Marc-Aurèle Fortin (1888–1970), one of the pioneers of modern art in Québec. Fortin experimented wildly with different techniques. For example, he painted some of his works on canvases that he'd prepainted with gray to emphasize the warm light of the countryside; others he painted on black backgrounds to create dramatic contrasts. Fortin painted some cityscapes, but he is best known for his rich and bountiful landscapes of the Laurentians, the Gaspé, and the Charlevoix region. ⊠ *118 rue St-Pierre, Vieux-Montréal,* ☎ *514/ 845–6108.* ☑ *$4.* ☉ *Tues.–Sun. 11–5. Métro: Square-Victoria.*

❼ Palais de Justice. Lawyers in elaborate gowns and cravats and judges in scarlet-trimmed robes decide points of law in this black-glass tower built in 1971 as the main courthouse for the judicial district of Montréal. Criminal law in Canada falls under federal jurisdiction and is based on British common law, but civil law is a provincial matter. Québec's is based on France's Napoleonic Code, which governs all the minutiae of private life—from setting up a company and negotiating a mortgage to drawing up a marriage contract and registering the names of children. Although the building doesn't offer tours, you can drop in to any courtroom and see how justice is dispensed in Montréal. Proceedings are usually in French—defendants in criminal cases can choose which official language they wish to be tried in. ⊠ *1 rue Notre-Dame Est, Vieux-Montréal. Métro: Place-d'Armes or Champ-de-Mars.*

❸ Place d'Armes. Montréal's founder, Paul de Chomedey, slew an Iroquois chief in a battle here in 1644 and was wounded in return. His statue stands in a fountain in the middle of the square. Tunnels beneath the square protected the colonists from the winter weather and provided an escape route; unfortunately they are too small and dangerous to visit. ⊠ *Bordered by rues Notre-Dame Ouest, St-Jacques, and St-Sulpice, Vieux-Montréal. Métro: Place-d'Armes.*

★ ⑫ Place Jacques-Cartier. Musicians, magicians, and acrobats entertain the summer crowds that congregate in this historic square in the heart of Vieux-Montréal. The restaurants lining the square serve everything from hot dogs to escargot to their patrons, who sit in open-air terasses watching the passing scene. The 1809 monument at the top of the square was the first monument in the British Empire erected to honor Lord Nelson's victory over Napoléon Bonaparte's French navy at Trafalgar. The campaign to raise money for it was led not by patriotic British residents of Montréal but by the Sulpician priests, who didn't have much love for the Corsican emperor either; the priests were engaged in delicate land negotiations with the British government at the time and eager to show what good subjects they were. ⊠ *Bordered by rues Notre-Dame Est and de la Commune, Vieux-Montréal. Métro: Champ-de-Mars.*

⑰ Place Royale. The oldest public square in Montréal served as a public market during the French regime and later became a Victorian garden. The neoclassical Vielle Douane (Old Customs House) on its south side serves as the gift shop for the Musée d'Archéologie Pointe-à-Callière. ⊠ *Bordered by rues St-Paul Ouest and de la Commune, Vieux-Montréal. Métro: Place-d'Armes.*

⑩ Place Vauquelin. The statue in this little square is of Admiral Jacques Vauquelin, a naval hero of the French regime. In summer, foot-weary visitors often soak their feet in the fountain. ⊠ *Between rues St-Antoine Est and Notre-Dame Est, near rue Gosford, Vieux-Montréal. Métro: Champ-de-Mars.*

Pointe-à-Callière. A little stream used to flow into the St. Lawrence here, and it was on this point of land between the two waters that the colonists landed their four boats on May 17, 1642. A flood almost washed away the settlement the next Christmas. When it was spared, Paul de Chomedey, Sieur de Maisonneuve, placed a cross on top of Mont-Royal as thanks to God. ⊠ *Bordered by rues de la Commune and William, Vieux-Montréal. Métro: Place-d'Armes.*

② **Royal Bank of Canada.** The last landmark of Montréal's gilded age is this 22-story tower in pale-yellow stone designed by New York architects York & Sawyer. The building's main banking hall has a coffered ceiling and is decorated with the arms of the eight provinces that made up Canada when the bank was built in 1928. ⊠ *369 rue St-Jacques, Vieux-Montréal,* ☎ *514/874–2459.* 🎫 *Free.* ☉ *Weekdays 10–4. Métro: Place-d'Armes.*

Rue St-Jacques. Popular with filmmakers, the stretch of rue St-Jacques between rue McGill and boulevard St-Laurent is often decked out as Main Street U.S.A., complete with American flags, English signs, and period cars. Stone nymphs, angels, and goddesses decorate the Victorian office buildings lining this stretch, which once served as the financial heart of Canada.

Rue St-Sulpice. A plaque on the eastern side of rue St-Sulpice—one of the oldest streets in Montréal—marks the spot, at No. 445 (near rue St-Paul), where in 1644 Jeanne Mance built the Hôpital Hôtel-Dieu de St-Joseph, the city's first hospital.

❽ **Vieux Palais de Justice.** The old courthouse, a domed building in the Classical Revival style, was built in 1857. It once housed the civil courts but is now a warren of city offices. The sculpture group on the lawn at the west end of the building depicts Ste. Marguerite Bourgeoys, Montréal's first schoolteacher, playing with a group of children. ⊠ *155 rue Notre-Dame Est, Vieux-Montréal,* ☎ *no phone. Métro: Champ-de-Mars.*

㉒ **Vieux-Port-de-Montréal.** In warm weather, skateboarders, strollers, cyclists, and street performers crowd the revitalized old port, where private operators offer harbor cruises and raft rides on the Lachine Rapids. (Bicycles and in-line skates are available for rent at shops along rue de la Commune.) A ferry takes pedestrians to the park on Île Ste-Hélène, and in winter, visitors can skate on a huge outdoor rink in the Vieux-Port. The **King Edward Pier** is the home of iSci, Montréal's innovative science center. If you feel up to it, you may climb the 192 steps to the top of the **Clock Tower,** erected at the eastern end of the waterfront in memory of merchant mariners killed during World War I, for a good view of the waterfront and the islands. Every couple of years or so, Montréal's Cirque du Soleil comes home to pitch its blue-and-yellow tent in the Vieux-Port. ☎ *514/496–7678 or 800/ 971–7678,* 🌐 *www.oldportofmontreal.com. Métro: Place-d'Armes or Champ-de-Mars.*

❻ **Vieux Séminaire.** Montréal's oldest building was constructed in 1685 as a headquarters for the Sulpician priests who owned the island of Montréal until 1854. It's still a residence for the Sulpicians who administer the basilica. The clock on the roof over the main doorway is the oldest (pre-1701) public timepiece in North America. Behind the seminary building is a garden that is closed to the public, as is the seminary itself. ⊠ *116 rue Notre-Dame Ouest, behind wall west of Basilique Notre-Dame-de-Montréal, Vieux-Montréal. Métro: Place-d'Armes.*

Downtown

On the surface, Montréal's downtown, or *centre-ville,* is much like the downtown core of many other major cities—full of life and noisy traffic, its streets lined with department stores, boutiques, bars, restaurants, strip clubs, amusement arcades, and bookstores. In fact, however, much of the area's activity goes on beneath the surface, in Montréal's Cité Souterrain (Underground City). Development of this unique endeavor began in 1966 when the Métro opened. Now it includes (at last count) seven hotels, more than 1,500 offices and 1,600 boutiques, 30 movie theaters, 200 restaurants, three universities, two colleges, two train stations, a skating rink, 40 banks, a bus terminal, an art museum, a complex of concert halls, the home ice arena of the Montréal Canadiens, and a cathedral. All this is linked by Métro lines and more than 30 km (19 mi) of well-lighted, boutique-lined passages that protect shoppers and workers from the hardships of winter and the heat of summer. A traveler arriving by train could book into a fine hotel and spend a week shopping, dining, and going to a long list of movies, plays, concerts, sports events, and discos without once stepping outside.

A Good Walk

The start of this walk is designed for moles—it's underground—but it gives you an idea of the extent of the Underground City. Start at the McGill Métro station, one of the central points in the Underground City. It's linked to office towers and two of the "Big Three" department stores, Simons and La Baie (the third is Ogilvy). Passages also link the station to major shopping malls such as Le Centre Eaton, Les Promenades de la Cathédrale, and Place Montréal Trust.

Follow the signs from the station to Le Centre Eaton and then descend yet another floor to the tunnel that leads to **Place Ville-Marie** ㉕. The mall complex underneath this cruciform skyscraper was the first link in the Underground City. From here head south via the passageways toward Fairmont Le Reine Elizabeth hotel, which straddles the entrance to the Gare Centrale (Central Station). Walk through the station and follow the signs marked MÉTRO/PLACE BONAVENTURE until you see a sign for Le 1000 rue de la Gauchetière, a skyscraper that's home to the **Atrium le Mille de la Gauchetière** ㉖, which houses an indoor ice rink. Return to the tunnels and again follow signs to the Bonaventure Métro station and then to the Canadian Pacific Railway Company's **Windsor Station** ㉗, with its massive stone exterior. The rail station and the Place Bonaventure Métro station below it are all linked to **Centre Bell** ㉘, the home of the Montréal Canadiens.

By now—having covered 10 city blocks and visited two train stations, a couple of malls, a major hotel, an office tower, and the city's most important sports shrine without once emerging from cover—you're probably ready for some fresh air. Exit the Underground City at the north end of Windsor Station and cross rue de la Gauchetière to **St. George's** ㉙, the prettiest Anglican church in the city. Just to the east, across rue Peel, is **Place du Canada** ㉚, a park. Cross the park and rue de la Cathédrale to **Cathédrale Marie-Reine-du-Monde** ㉛, which is modeled after St. Peter's Basilica in Rome. People sometimes call the gray granite building across boulevard René-Lévesque from the cathedral the Wedding Cake, because it rises in tiers of decreasing size and has lots of columns, but its real name is the **Sun Life Building** ㉜. The park just north of boulevard René-Lévesque and facing the Sun Life Building is **Square Dorchester** ㉝, for years the heart of Montréal. The Dominion Square Building at the north end of the park houses the Centre-Infotouriste, the main center for visitor information about the city and the province. Backtrack across the park to rue Peel and walk north to rue Ste-Catherine. Many regard this intersection as the heart of downtown.

Turn right and walk east along rue Ste-Catherine, pausing to admire the view at the corner of avenue McGill College. Look north up this

30

Downtown Montréal (Centre-Ville) and Golden Square Mile

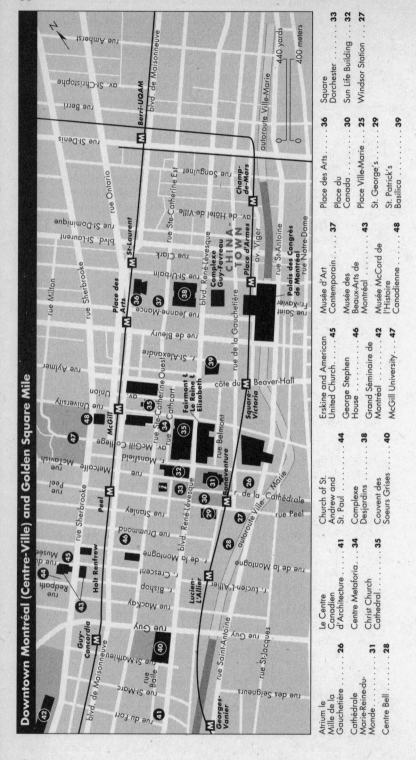

broad boulevard and you can see the Victorian-era buildings of the McGill University campus, with Mont-Royal looming in the background. The grim-looking gray castle high on the slope to the right is the Royal Victoria Hospital. On the south side of rue Ste-Catherine is **Centre Metaforia** ㉞, which offers visitors a "virtual voyage" to the bottom of the sea. One block more brings you to the Eatons department store, where this whole adventure started, and next to that is **Christ Church Cathedral** ㉟, the main church of the Anglican diocese of Montréal.

You can end your stroll here or continue six blocks farther east on rue Ste-Catherine to **Place des Arts** ㊱, Montréal's main theater complex. The **Musée d'Art Contemporain** ㊲, the modern-art museum, is also part of the complex. While still in Place des Arts, follow the signs to the tunnel below rue Ste-Catherine to **Complexe Desjardins** ㊳, headquarters of Québec's credit-union movement. Walk through the complex's bright airy mall to boulevard René-Lévesque. Here you have a choice: go east and then south on boulevard St-Laurent to explore **Chinatown**, or turn right and walk west for four blocks to visit **St. Patrick's Basilica** ㊴, mother church of the city's English-speaking Roman Catholics.

TIMING

Walking this route at a brisk pace takes 90 minutes, at minimum. The Musée d'Art Contemporain is worth at least two hours, so set aside at least half a day and preferably a full day.

Sights to See

㉖ **Atrium le Mille de la Gauchetière.** Skating is a passion in Montréal, and you can do it year-round in this skyscraper atrium. During daylight hours, natural light illuminates the indoor ice rink, which is surrounded by cafés, a food court, and a winter garden. Skate rentals and lockers are available. There are skating lessons Friday and Saturday, disco skating Saturday night, and scheduled ice shows. To find the rink once you're inside the building, it might help to remember the French word for skating rink, *patinoire.* ⊠ *1000 rue de la Gauchetière, Downtown,* ☎ *514/395–0555,* WEB *www.le1000.com.* ⊠ *$5; skate rental $4.50.* ☉ *Canadian Thanksgiving–Easter, Sun.–Thurs. 11:30–9, Fri. 11:30 AM–7, Sat. 10 AM–midnight; Easter–Canadian Thanksgiving, Sun. and Tues.–Fri. 11:30–6, Sat. 10–10. Métro: Bonaventure.*

㉛ **Cathédrale Marie-Reine-du-Monde** (Mary Queen of the World Cathedral). When Roman Catholic Bishop Ignace Bourget (1799–1885) picked this site in the heart of the city's Protestant neighborhood as the spot for his new cathedral, many of his co-religionists thought he was mad. But the bishop was determined to assert the Church's authority—and its loyalty to Rome—in the British-ruled city. So he built a quarter-scale replica of St. Peter's Basilica, complete with a quite magnificent reproduction of Bernini's ornate baldachin over the main altar and an ornately coffered ceiling. The figures on the roof don't, as many think, represent the apostles, but rather the patron saints of the Montréal parishes that contributed to the construction. Victor Bourgeau, the architect who created the interior of Basilique Notre-Dame in Vieux-Montréal, thought the idea of the cathedral's design terrible but completed it after the original architect proved incompetent. All Montréal's bishops are entombed in the mortuary chapel on the east side of the nave, where a reclining figure of Bishop Bourget holds the place of honor. One last symbol of the bishop's loyalty to the Roman pontiff is a plaque on a pillar in the northeast corner honoring local residents who went to Italy to defend the Papal States from Garibaldi. A huge accompanying painting shows the Papal Zouaves fighting off a nationalist attack. ⊠ *1071 rue de la Cathédrale (enter through main doors on blvd. René-Lévesque), Downtown,* ☎ *514/866–1661.* ⊠ *Free.*

⊘ *Mass weekdays at 7, 7:30, 8 AM, 12:10 PM, and 5; Mon. also at 7 PM; Sat. at 8 AM, 12:10 PM, 5, and 7:30; Sun. at 9:30, 11 AM with choir, 12:15 PM, and 5. Métro: Bonaventure or Peel.*

㉘ Centre Bell. The Montréal Canadiens, the hockey team fans call simply *les Glorieux*, have been playing in this brown-brick building since 1996, when it was built to replace the Forum that had been the Canadiens' home since 1917. Guided tours include a visit to the Canadiens' dressing room when possible. ⊠ *1260 rue de la Gauchetière Ouest, Downtown,* ☎ *514/932–2582, 514/925–5656 tours.* ⊡ *Tour $8.* ⊘ *Tours daily at 11:15 and 2:45 in English, and 9:45 and 1:15 in French. Métro: Bonaventure or Lucien-L'Allier.*

㉞ Centre Metaforia. Metaforia Inc. has used the prizewinning technology it developed for Lisbon's 1998 World's Fair to re-create a 45-minute voyage to an underwater base to explore the ruins of an ancient civilization. Participants make the journey via computer-generated effects, including group and individual interaction segments, 3-D images, vibrating seats, and stereo-display helmets. The center, in a converted theater, also includes a wide array of computer games, restaurants, interactive displays, and boutiques, as well as a climbing wall. ⊠ *698 rue Ste-Catherine Ouest, Downtown,* ☎ *514/878–6382,* ⓦⓔⓑ *www.metaforia.com/an.* ⊡ *$15 weekdays, $20 weekends.* ⊘ *Thurs. noon–10, Fri.–Sat. noon–11, Sun. noon–7.*

Chinatown. The Chinese first came to Montréal in large numbers after 1880, following the construction of the transcontinental railroad. They settled in an 18-block area between boulevard René-Lévesque and avenue Viger to the north and south, and near rue de Bleury and avenue Hôtel de Ville on the west and east, an area now full of mainly Chinese and Southeast Asian restaurants, food stores, and gift shops. *Métro: Place-d'Armes.*

NEED A
BREAK?
Pho Bang New York (⊠ 970 blvd. St-Laurent, Chinatown, ☎ 514/954–2032) is the best of the small Vietnamese restaurants on the edge of Chinatown that specialize in traditional noodle soups. For less than $5 (cash only), you get soup, a plate of crispy vegetables, and a small pot of tea. The iced coffee with condensed milk is worth trying.

㉟ Christ Church Cathedral. The gargoyles and grand Gothic entrance of the seat of Montréal's Anglican bishop are a welcome break in the unrelenting strip of commercial rue Ste-Catherine. The church, built in 1859 and patterned on Snettisham Parish Church in Norfolk, England, is the architectural sister of the cathedral in Fredericton, New Brunswick. The church has had its problems: it was built on unstable ground, and in 1927 the community had to pull down the stone steeple because it was too heavy and sinking fast. Thirteen years later, the church leaders replaced it with a much lighter structure with aluminium plates molded to simulate stone. In 1988 the diocese assured the stability of both soil and finances by leasing its land and air rights to developers, who then built **La Maison des Coopérants,** a 34-story office tower behind the cathedral, and a huge retail complex, **Les Promenades de la Cathédrale,** below it. Inside, the pillars that support the cathedral's Gothic arches are crowned with carvings of the types of foliage to be found on Mont-Royal at the time the church was built. At the four corners of the nave are sculpted heads representing the four Evangelists. The stained-glass windows behind the main altar were installed in the early 1920s as a memorial to the dead of World War I and show scenes from the life of Christ. On the wall just above and to the left of the pulpit is the Coventry Cross; it's made of nails taken from the ruins of

Britain's Coventry Cathedral, destroyed by bombing in 1940. The church has a quiet, graceful interior and hosts frequent organ recitals and concerts. ⊠ *635 rue Ste-Catherine Ouest, Downtown,* ☏ *514/843–6577,* WEB *www.montreal.anglican.org/cathedral.* ⊠ *Free.* ☉ *Daily 8–6. Métro: McGill.*

❸❽ Complexe Desjardins. The devoutly Catholic Alphonse Desjardins founded Québec's credit-union movement early in the 20th century to rescue his impoverished compatriots from debt and misery. The humble "peoples' bank" has grown into a major financial institution with headquarters in the towers above this boutique-rich mall. The large galleria on the ground floor hosts everything from displays of law-enforcement technology to sessions of gospel song. ⊠ *Bordered by rues Ste-Catherine, Jeanne-Mance, and St-Urbain and blvd. René-Lévesque, Downtown,* ☏ *514/845–4636 or 514/281–1870. Métro: Place-d'Armes or Place des Arts.*

♨ ❸❼ Musée d'Art Contemporain. In 1948, a group of Québec artists led by Paul-Émile Borduas (1905–60) and Jean-Paul Riopelle (1923–2002) signed *Le Refus Global,* a political–artistic manifesto that renounced the political and religious establishment of the day and revolutionized art in the province. The spirit of these Automatistes, as they called themselves, is at the heart of this museum, which includes 72 Borduas paintings and 80 Riopelle paintings in its permanent collection of more than 5,000 works. But the exhibits explore all facets of contemporary work by living artists—paintings, sculptures, installations, multimedia. The museum often has weekend programs, with many child-oriented activities, and almost all are free. Hours for guided tours vary. ⊠ *185 rue Ste-Catherine Ouest, Downtown,* ☏ *514/847–6226,* WEB *www.macm.org.* ⊠ *$6; free after 6 PM Wed.* ☉ *Tues. and Thurs.–Sun. 11–6, Wed. 11–9. Métro: Place des Arts.*

❸❻ Place des Arts. The government-subsidized complex of five very modern theaters offers guided tours of the halls and backstage to groups of at least 15. ⊠ *175 rue Ste-Catherine Ouest, Downtown,* ☏ *514/842–2112 tickets, 514/285–4270 information, 514/285–4200 tours,* WEB *www.pda.qc.ca. Métro: Place des Arts.*

❸⓪ Place du Canada. Separatists and federalists have both used this pleasant green park to make political statements. In 1992, nationalists with a macabre sense of humor decapitated the statue of Sir John A. Macdonald, Canada's first prime minister. In October 1995, a rally for Canadian unity drew more than 300,000 participants from across the country, a demonstration that was at least partly responsible for preserving a slim victory for the pro-unity forces in the subsequent referendum on independence for Québec. At the south end of Place du Canada is Le Marriott Château Champlain, often called "the Cheese Grater" because of its rows and rows of half-moon-shape windows. ⊠ *Bordered by blvd. René-Lévesque and rues de la Gauchetière, Peel, and de la Cathédrale, Downtown. Métro: Bonaventure.*

❷❺ Place Ville-Marie. The cross-shape 1962 office tower was Montréal's first modern skyscraper; the mall complex underneath it was the first link in the Underground City. ⊠ *Bordered by blvd. René-Lévesque and rues Mansfield, Cathcart, and University, Downtown,* ☏ *514/866–6666. Métro: McGill or Bonaventure.*

NEED A BREAK? The once grim passageways at the back of Gare Centrale just below the escalators leading to Place Ville-Marie today house a trendy food court, **Les Halles de la Gare** (⊠ 895 rue de la Gauchetière Ouest, ☏ no phone). The food available includes some of the city's best bread and pastries, salads, and sandwiches made with fresh terrines and pâtés. If it's nice out, you can take your snack up the escalator to the mall under Place Ville-Marie and then up the stairs in the middle of its food court to the terrace, a wide area with a fine view.

....

㉙ St. George's Anglican Church. The dim interior of this pretty little Anglican church built in 1872 seems a world away from the Centre Bell—the modern temple to professional ice hockey just across the street—but several prominent National Hockey League players regularly drop in for a few minutes of quiet meditation before joining the action on the ice. The double hammer-beam roof is one of the largest of its type in the world, and the unique column-free interior, which combines elements of both English and French Gothic styles, is embellished with English wood-carving and illuminated with fine stained-glass windows. ⊠ *1101 rue Stanley, Downtown,* ☎ *514/866–7113.* ☞ *Free.* ⊙ *Tues.–Sun. 8:30–4:30; Sun. services at 9 and 10:30* AM. *Métro: Bonaventure.*

㉚ St. Patrick's Basilica. Rarely visited by sightseers, this 1847 church is one of the purest examples of the Gothic Revival style in Canada. It is to Montréal's English-speaking Catholics what the Basilique Notre-Dame is to the city's French-speaking Catholics. The church's colors are soft, and the vaulted ceiling glows with green and gold mosaics. The old pulpit has panels depicting the apostles, and a huge lamp decorated with six 6-ft-tall angels hangs over the main altar. The tall, slender columns that support the roof are actually pine logs lashed together and decorated to look like marble. The Canadian poet Émile Nelligan (1879–1941) was baptized in the font installed in front of the side altar on the east side of the sanctuary. The pew used by Thomas Darcy McGee—a father of confederation who was assassinated in 1868—is marked with a small Canadian flag. Visitors named after some obscure saint might well be able to find their namesake's portrait in the 170 painted panels on the walls of the nave. The church is three blocks east of Place Ville-Marie. ⊠ *460 blvd. René-Lévesque Ouest, Downtown,* ☎ *514/866–7379,* WEB *www.sympatico.ca/stpatricksmtl.* ☞ *Free.* ⊙ *Daily 8:30–6. Métro: Square-Victoria.*

㉝ Square Dorchester. Until 1870, a Catholic burial ground occupied this downtown park, and bodies still are buried beneath the grass. The statuary includes a monument to the Boer War and statues of the Scottish poet Robert Burns and Sir Wilfrid Laurier, Canada's first French-speaking prime minister. ⊠ *Bordered by rues Peel, Metcalfe, and Mc-Tavish and blvd. René-Lévesque, Downtown. Métro: Bonaventure or Peel.*

㉜ Sun Life Building. During World War II, Britain stored its financial reserves and the Crown jewels in the basement under the Montréal headquarters of the Sun Life Assurance Co.—what was then the largest building in the British Commonwealth. Stroll past the Corinthian columns for a look at the grand main hall with its rosy marble walls and brass-doored elevators. ⊠ *1155 rue Metcalfe, Downtown,* ☎ *514/866–6411. Métro: Bonaventure.*

㉗ Windsor Station. This proud stone building was once the eastern passenger terminus for the Canadian Pacific Railway, Canada's first transcontinental link. Alas, today it's a trainless shell; its vast, glass-roofed concourse—with its splendid bronze monument to the dead of World War I and its huge patio—serves no ostensible purpose save to shelter a barbershop, a coffee shop, and a barbecue-chicken restaurant. ⊠ *1100 rue de la Gauchetière, Downtown,* ☎ *no phone. Métro: Bonaventure.*

Golden Square Mile

As Montréal grew in confidence and economic might in the 19th century, the city's prosperous merchant class moved north, building lavish stone homes on Mont-Royal. In fact, at the turn of the 20th century, the people who lived here (mostly of Scottish descent) controlled 70% of the country's wealth. Their baronial homes and handsome churches—Protestant, of course—covered the mountain north of rue Sherbrooke roughly between avenue Côte-des-Neiges and rue University.

Humbler residents south of rue Sherbrooke referred to the area simply as the Square Mile, a name immortalized in novelist Hugh MacLennan's *Two Solitudes* (1945). The Square Mile was eventually "gilded" by the newspaper columnist Al Palmer in the 1950s, long after its golden age had passed. (Proud Square Milers like the actor Christopher Plummer still bridle at the extra adjective.) Many of the palatial homes have been leveled to make way for high-rises and office towers, but architectural gems still stud the area, and rue Sherbrooke remains the city's most elegant street.

This walk takes in much of the Square Mile along with an area named Shaughnessy Village, to the southwest (bounded roughly by rues Atwater and Guy to the west and east and rue Sherbrooke and boulevard René-Lévesque to the north and south). The village takes its name from the very lush Shaughnessy Mansion on boulevard René-Lévesque, a house that would fit in quite comfortably up the hill in the Square Mile. But whereas most of the Shaughnessy family's 19th-century neighbors were well-off businesspeople and professionals who lived in elegantly comfortable homes, they certainly weren't wealthy enough to make it into the Square Mile.

A Good Walk

Start at the Guy-Concordia Métro station at the rue Guy exit. The statue just north of the station on the little triangular slice of land in the middle of boulevard de Maisonneuve portrays Norman Bethune, a McGill University–trained doctor from Gravenhurst, Ontario, who served with the Loyalists in the Spanish civil war and died in China in 1939 while serving with Mao's Red Army. Walk south on rue Guy to rue Ste-Catherine and turn right. The long building on the south side of the street used to be a car dealership and bowling alley until it was transformed into the Faubourg Ste-Catherine, an enclosed market selling specialty and ethnic foods, pastries, and bagels.

At rue St-Mathieu, turn left and head south. The huge gray building on the left side of the street is **Couvent des Soeurs Grises** ㊵, the motherhouse of an order of nuns founded by St. Marguerite d'Youville, Canada's first native-born saint. Across from the convent, turn right onto rue Baile and into the heart of Shaughnessy Village. The family mansion the area is named for now forms part of **Le Centre Canadien d'Architecture** ㊶. Many of the area's town houses and mansions were torn down during the 1960s to make way for boxy high-rises, but a few remain. Note, for example, the fine row of stone town houses just across rue Baile from the architecture center.

Turn right on rue du Fort and walk north four blocks to rue Sherbrooke. On the north side of the street is a complex of fine neoclassical buildings in a shady garden. This is the **Grand Séminaire de Montréal** ㊷, which trains priests for Montréal's Roman Catholic parishes. The two stone towers on the property are among the oldest buildings on the island. In 1928, the anticlerical Freemasons built the grandly Greek Masonic Temple, across the street at No. 1859.

Walk east along stately rue Sherbrooke, past rows of old town houses holding exclusive shops and galleries, to the **Musée des Beaux-Arts de Montréal** ㊸. The city's main art collection, which includes works from around the world, is housed here, in two buildings facing each other across rue Sherbrooke. Two fine Protestant churches frame the museum's neo-Classical Michal and Renata Hornstein Pavilion, which is on the north side of the street. To the west is the neo-Gothic **Church of St. Andrew and St. Paul** ㊹, and to the east is the red-stone **Erskine and American United Church** ㊺, which has the largest collection of Louis Comfort Tiffany–signed stained-glass windows outside the United States. A few blocks east on rue Sherbrooke, at the corner of rue de la Montagne, is the small and exclusive Holt Renfrew department store. Dozens of popular bars and bistros are ensconced in the old row houses lining rue de la Montagne and the two streets just west of it, rues Crescent and Bishop, between boulevard René-Lévesque and rue Sherbrooke. The area once encompassed the playing fields of the Montréal Lacrosse and Cricket Grounds and later became an exclusive suburb lined with millionaires' row houses.

One block east on the south side of rue Sherbrooke at rue Drummond is the Ritz-Carlton, the grande dame of Montréal hotels. Catercorner from the Ritz is Le Château (1926), a huge, copper-roofed apartment building that looks somewhat like a cross between a French Renaissance château and a Scots castle. It's one of the few samples of gracious living on rue Sherbrooke. Others worth looking at are the Corby House and the Maison Louis-Joseph Forget, at 1201 and 1195 rue Sherbrooke Ouest, respectively. One of the area's most magnificent homes, however, is on rue Drummond a couple of blocks south of Sherbrooke. The **George Stephen House** ㊻ was built for the founder of the Canadian Pacific Railway and is now the private Mount Stephen Club.

The campus of **McGill University** ㊼ is on the north side of rue Sherbrooke three blocks east of the Ritz-Carlton. Opposite its main gate is the Banque Commerciale Italienne (888 rue Sherbrooke Ouest), housed in a beautiful neo-Elizabethan house built in 1906 for Dr. William Alexander Molson, a scion of Montréal's most famous brewing family. Another block east is the **Musée McCord de l'Histoire Canadienne** ㊽, one of the best history museums in Canada.

TIMING

You need at least 90 minutes for a brisk walk, but you could easily spend a day or more in the area, which is rich in cultural sights such as the Musée des Beaux-Arts, the Musée des Art Décoratifs, and the Musée McCord de l'Histoire Canadienne, all of which deserve visits.

Sights to See

㊶ **Le Centre Canadien d'Architecture** (Canadian Center for Architecture). Phyllis Lambert, an heiress to the Seagram liquor fortune and an architect of some note, was the genius behind this temple to the art of building. She had a hand in designing the ultramodern U-shaped structure of gray limestone and filled it with her vast collection of drawings, photographs, plans, books, documents, and models; the library alone has more than 165,000 volumes. The center's six large and well-lit exhibition rooms present a series of rotating exhibits that focus on the work of a particular architect or on a particular style. Some can be forbiddingly academic, but more-playful exhibits have looked at such subjects as dollhouses and American lawn culture. The two arms of the center wrap around a grandly ornate mansion built in 1874 for the family of the president of the Canadian Pacific Railway, Sir Thomas Shaughnessy. It has a remarkable art nouveau conservatory with an intricately decorated ceiling. On a tiny piece of land across the street is an amusing sculpture garden. ⊠ *1920 rue Baile, Shaughnessy Village,* ☎ *514/939–7000,* WEB *www.cca.qc.ca.* ⌑ *$6.* ☉ *Oct.–May, Wed.–Sun. 11–6, Thurs. until 8; June–Sept., Tues.–Sun. 11–5, Thurs. until 9. Métro: Guy-Concordia or Georges-Vanier.*

㊹ Church of St. Andrew and St. Paul. Soaring above the white-stone communion table at the head of the 220-ft nave of this neo-Gothic church is a glorious stained-glass window of the risen Christ, installed as a memorial to the soldiers of the Royal Highland Regiment of Canada (Black Watch) killed in World War I. The William Morris Co. made two of the side windows to a design by pre-Raphaelite artist Sir Edward Burne-Jones. The church, which has Montréal's largest organ—a four-manual Casavant with 6,911 pipes—and a fine choir, is open for Sunday services. To see it at other times, ask the secretary at the side entrance at 3415 rue Redpath. ⊠ *Rue Sherbrooke Ouest at rue Redpath, Square Mile,* ☎ *514/843–3431,* WEB *www.standrewstpaul.com.* ⌑ *Free.* ☉ *Sun. service at 11 AM; other times by arrangement. Métro: Guy-Concordia.*

㊵ Couvent des Soeurs Grises. The *soeurs grises,* or "gray nuns," have a beautiful Romanesque chapel and a small museum dedicated to their saintly founder, Marguerite d'Youville (1701–71), in this rambling, gray-stone convent. The nuns moved here in 1874, after their residence and hospital in Vieux-Montréal burned down. The name of the order, which still administers hospitals, shelters for battered women, and halfway houses, had nothing to do with the color of the good sisters' habits. Their founder started looking after the city's down-and-outs after her unhappy marriage to a whiskey trader ended in widowhood. Her late husband's profession and the condition of many of her clients earned her and her colleagues the sobriquet "soeurs grises," which is slang for tipsy nuns. The order ran a public hospital and shelters for abandoned children, opened the city's first nursing schools, and, indeed, adopted gray habits. ⊠ *1185 rue St-Mathieu, Shaughnessy Village,* ☎ *514/937–9501.* ⌑ *By donation.* ☉ *Tues.–Sun. 1:30–4:30. Métro: Guy-Concordia or Georges-Vanier.*

㊺ Erskine and American United Church. Various marbles adorn the sanctuary of this massive, neo-Romanesque church (built in 1894). Its greatest treasures, however, are the 24 Tiffany windows. The church is open for Sunday services. To see the interior and the Tiffany windows at other times, go to the avenue du Musée entrance, ring the bell, and ask politely. ⊠ *Rue Sherbrooke Ouest at av. du Musée, Square Mile,* ☎ *514/849–3286.* ⌑ *Free.* ☉ *Sun. service at 11 AM; other times by arrangement. Métro: Guy-Concordia.*

㊻ George Stephen House. Scottish-born George Stephen, founder of the Canadian Pacific Railway, spent $600,000 to build this impressive home in 1883—an almost unimaginable sum at the time. He imported artisans from all over the world to panel its ceilings with Cuban mahogany, Indian lemon tree, and English oak and to dress its walls in marble, onyx, and gold. The house is a private club now (the Mount Stephen Club), but most Sundays visitors can drop in for a guided tour or, with reservations, a sumptuous brunch ($25) of braised duck or roast beef served to the accompaniment of live music. ⊠ *1440 rue Drummond, Square Mile,* ☎ *514/849–7338.* ☉ *Sun. by reservation. Closed to non-members mid-July–Aug. Métro: Peel or Guy-Concordia.*

㊷ Grand Séminaire de Montréal. St. Marguerite Bourgeoys used one of the two stone towers visible from the street to set up a school for Native Canadian girls in the 17th century. The gardens of the 1860 seminary, which trains priests for the Roman Catholic archdiocese, are private, but a little area by the gates has three plaques that explain the towers' history in French. The neoclassical chapel is open for mass at 10:30 every Sunday morning from September through June. ⊠ *2065 rue Sherbrooke Ouest, Square Mile,* ☎ *no phone.* ☉ *Sun. service at 10:30 AM. Métro: Guy-Concordia.*

🖐 ㊼ **McGill University.** James McGill, a wealthy Scottish fur trader and merchant, bequeathed the money and the land for this institution, which opened in 1828 and is perhaps the finest English-language university in the nation. The student body numbers 15,000, and the university is best known for its medical and engineering schools. A tree-lined road leads from the Greek Revival Roddick Gates to the austerely beautiful neoclassical Arts Building—the university's original building—at the northern end of the campus. The templelike building to the west of the Arts Building houses the delightful **Redpath Museum of Natural History,** which has an eclectic collection of dinosaur bones, old coins, African art, and shrunken heads. Under the trees to the east of the main drive, a bronze James McGill hurries across campus holding his tricorn hat against the wind. ⊠ *845 rue Sherbrooke Ouest, Square Mile,* ☎ *514/398–4455, 514/398–4086 museum,* ⓦⓔⓑ *www.mcgill.ca.* ☜ *Free.* ☉ *Museum: Sept.–May, Mon.–Thurs. 9–5; June–Aug., weekdays 9–5. Métro: McGill or Peel.*

NEED A BREAK?   The campus of **McGill University** (⊠ 845 rue Sherbrooke Ouest, Square Mile, ☎ 514/398–4455, ⓦⓔⓑ www.mcgill.ca) is an island of green in a sea of traffic and skyscrapers. On a fine day you can sit on the grass in the shade of a 100-year-old tree and let the world drift by.

★ ㊸ **Musée des Beaux-Arts de Montréal** (Museum of Fine Arts). The oldest museum in the country was founded by a group of English-speaking Montrealers in 1860. The art collection is housed in two buildings—the older neoclassical **Michal and Renata Hornstein Pavilion,** on the north side of rue Sherbrooke, and the glittering glass-fronted **Jean-Noël-Desmarais Pavilion,** across the street. The two buildings, connected by underground tunnels, hold a large collection of European and North American fine and decorative art; ancient treasures from Europe, the Near East, Asia, Africa, and America; art from Québec and Canada; and Native American and Inuit artifacts. The museum is particularly strong in 19th-century works and has one of the finest collections of Canadian paintings, prints, and drawings. It also has a gift shop, an art-book store, a restaurant, a cafeteria, and a gallery from which you can buy or rent paintings by local artists. Since 2001, the museum has absorbed the collection of the Musée des Arts Décoratifs, including prototypes of Frank Gehry's bentwood furniture for Knoll and designs by Charles and Ray Eames. ⊠ *1380 rue Sherbrooke Ouest, Square Mile,* ☎ *514/285–2000,* ⓦⓔⓑ *www.mbam.qc.ca.* ☜ *Permanent collection free, special exhibitions $12.* ☉ *Tues.–Sun. 11–6 (special exhibitions stay open until 9 PM Wed.). Métro: Guy-Concordia.*

★ 🖐 ㊽ **Musée McCord de l'Histoire Canadienne.** A grand, eclectic attic of a museum, the McCord documents the life of ordinary Canadians, using costumes and textiles, decorative arts, paintings, prints and drawings, and the 450,000-print-and-negative Notman Photographic Archives, which highlight 19th-century life in Montréal. One series of photographs, for example, portrays the prosperous members of the posh Montréal Athletic Association posing in snowshoes on the slopes of Mont-Royal all decked out in Hudson Bay coats and woolen hats. Each of the hundreds of portraits was shot individually in a studio and then painstakingly mounted on a picture of the snowy mountain to give the impression of a winter outing. There are guided tours (call for times), a reading room and documentation center, a gift shop and bookstore, and a café. ⊠ *690 rue Sherbrooke Ouest, Square Mile,* ☎ *514/398–7100,* WEB *www.musee-mccord.qc.ca.* ⊠ *$8.50.* ⊙ *Tues.–Fri. 10–6, weekends 10–5. Métro: McGill.*

Quartier Latin and Plateau Mont-Royal

Early in the 20th century, rue St-Denis cut through a bourgeois neighborhood of large, comfortable residences. The Université de Montréal was established here in 1893, and the students and academics who moved into the area dubbed it the Quartier Latin, or Latin Quarter. The university eventually moved to a larger campus on the north side of Mont-Royal, and the area went into decline. It revived in the early 1970s, largely as a result of the 1969 opening of the Université du Québec à Montréal and the launch of the International Jazz Festival in the summer of 1980. Plateau Mont-Royal, the trendy neighborhood just north of the Quartier Latin, shared in this revival. Residents are now a mix of immigrants and young professionals eager to find a home they can renovate close to the city center. The Quartier Latin and Plateau Mont-Royal are home to rows of French and ethnic restaurants, charming bistros, coffee shops, designer boutiques, antiques shops, and art galleries. When night falls, these streets are always full of omnilingual hordes—young and not so young, rich and poor, established and still studying.

Many of the older residences in this area have graceful wrought-iron balconies and twisting staircases that are typical of Montréal. They were built that way for practical reasons. The buildings are what Montrealers call duplexes or triplexes, that is, two or three residences stacked one atop the other. To save interior space, the stairs to reach the upper floors were put outside. The stairs and balconies are treacherous in winter, but in summer they are often full of families and couples gossiping, picnicking, and partying. If Montrealers tell you they spend the summer in Balconville, they mean they don't have the money or the time to leave town and won't get any farther than their balcony.

A Good Walk

Begin at the Berri-UQAM Métro stop. The "UQAM" in the subway name is pronounced "oo-kam" by local Francophones and "you-kwam" by local Anglophones. It refers to the **Université du Québec à Montréal** ㊾, whose modern but nondescript brick campus fills up much of three city blocks between rues Sanguinet and Berri. A few splendid, stone fragments of the old Église St-Jacques—demolished to make way for the school—have been incorporated into the buildings, notably the main steeple, which still chimes out the hours. A more substantial religious monument that has survived intact right in UQAM's resolutely secularist heart is the ornate **Chapelle Notre-Dame-de-Lourdes** ㊿, on rue Ste-Catherine.

Just west of rue St-Denis is the Cinémathèque Québecoise, which includes one of the largest cinematic reference libraries in the world. Around the corner is the headquarters of the National Film Board of Canada, home of a robot-serviced screening room. A half block north on rue St-Denis stands the 2,500-seat **Théâtre St-Denis** ⑤, the city's second-largest auditorium. Continue north on rue St-Denis to the **Bibliothèque Nationale du Québec** ㊷, on the left.

Continue north to rue Sherbrooke and turn left. At boulevard St-Laurent turn left again for the **Musée Juste pour Rire** ㊼, one of the few museums in the world dedicated to humor. Backtrack east on rue

Quartier Latin and Parc du Mont-Royal

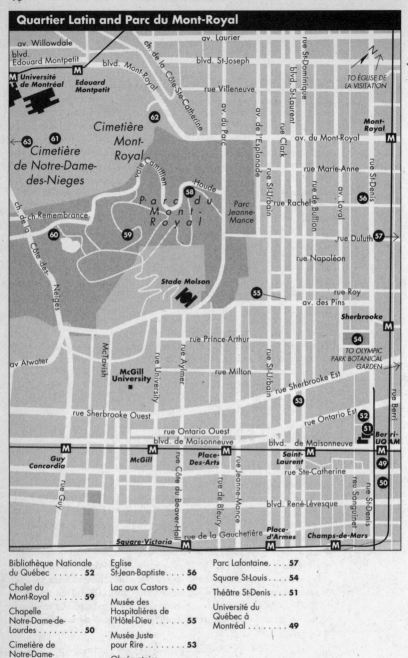

Sherbrooke, turn left on rue St-Denis, and walk north to **Square St-Louis** ㉔, a lovely green space.

The stretch of **rue Prince-Arthur** beginning at the western end of Square St-Louis and continuing several blocks west is a center of youth culture. When you reach **boulevard St-Laurent,** take a right and stroll north through Montréal's ethnic diversity. This area was still partly rural in the mid-19th century, with lots of fresh air, which made it healthier than overcrowded Vieux-Montréal. So in 1861 the Hôpital Hôtel-Dieu, the hospital Jeanne Mance founded in the 17th century, moved into a building at what is now the corner of avenue des Pins and rue St-Urbain, two blocks west of boulevard St-Laurent. Hôtel-Dieu, one of the city's major hospitals, is still here, and next to it is the **Musée des Hospitalières de l'Hôtel-Dieu** ㉕, which gives a remarkable picture of the city's early days.

A few blocks north on boulevard St-Laurent, turn right on rue Duluth, an intriguing strip of ethnic restaurants with outdoor terraces, crafts shops, and clothing boutiques. Turn left on avenue Henri-Julien and walk north for a block to see the **Église St-Jean-Baptiste** ㉖ on rue Rachel, a neoclassical monument to the piety of working-class French-Canadians at the beginning of the 20th century. Walk east another nine blocks on rue Rachel and you come to **Parc Lafontaine** ㉗, the smallest of Montréal's three major parks. After exploring the park's 100 acres, walk south to rue Sherbrooke Est, turn right, and then walk west on rues Sherbrooke and Cherrier to the Sherbrooke Métro station to complete the walk. Or head farther west to explore Parc du Mont-Royal.

TIMING

This is a comfortable afternoon walk, lasting perhaps three hours, or longer if you linger for an hour or so in the Musée des Hospitalières and spend some time shopping. There's a bit of a climb from boulevard de Maisonneuve to rue Sherbrooke.

Sights to See

㉒ **Bibliothèque Nationale du Québec** (Québec National Library). Québec's official archives have long outgrown this fine Beaux-Arts structure built to house them in 1915, and will move to a new, purpose-built building on rue Berri across from the bus terminal in 2004. However, the rooms of this graceful building will continue to play host to numerous artistic, cultural, and literary exhibits. ✉ *1700 rue St-Denis, Quartier Latin,* ☎ *514/873–1100.* ☉ *Tues.–Sat. 9–5. Métro: Berri-UQAM.*

Boulevard St-Laurent. Depending on how you look at it, this street divides the city into east and west or it's where east and west meet. After the first electric tramway was installed on boulevard St-Laurent, working-class families began to move in. In the 1880s the first of many waves of Jewish immigrants escaping pogroms in Eastern Europe arrived. They called the street The Main, as in "Main Street." The Jews were followed by Greeks, other Eastern Europeans, Portuguese, and, most recently, Latin Americans. The 10 blocks north of rue Sherbrooke are filled with delis, junk stores, restaurants and luncheonettes, and clothing stores, as well as fashionable boutiques, bistros, cafés, bars, nightclubs, bookstores, and galleries. The block between rues Roy and Napoléon is particularly rich in delights. *Métro: St-Laurent, Sherbrooke, or Mount-Royal.*

㉚ **Chapelle Notre-Dame-de-Lourdes** (Our Lady of Lourdes Chapel). The tiny Roman Catholic chapel is one of the most ornate pieces of religious architecture in the city. It was built in 1876 and decorated with brightly colored murals by the artist Napoléon Bourassa. The chapel is a dazzling mixture of Roman and Byzantine styles. ⊠ *430 rue Ste-Catherine Est, Quartier Latin.* ⊙ *Daily 8–5. Métro: Berri-UQAM.*

56 **Église St-Jean-Baptiste** (St. John the Baptist Church). The neoclassical facade of this immense parish church hides a sumptuously baroque-revival interior with a baldachin of pink marble and gilded wood shelters a white marble altar. The church, dedicated in 1904 to the patron saint of French Canada, seats 3,000 and has a powerful Casavant organ, which makes it popular for concerts and choir recitals. The parishioners who paid for this magnificent church and worshipped in it were largely working-class men and women with large families. ⊠ *309 rue Rachel Est, Plateau Mont-Royal.* ⊙ *Mass Sat. 5 PM, Sun. 10 AM and 11:30 AM. Métro: Mont-Royal.*

OFF THE BEATEN PATH

ÉGLISE DE LA VISITATION DE LA BIENHEUREUSE VIERGE MARIE – Far to the north on the banks of Rivière des Prairies is the oldest extant church on the island of Montréal, the Church of the Visitation of the Blessed Virgin Mary. Its stone walls were raised in the 1750s, and the beautifully proportioned Palladian front was added in 1850. The task of decorating lasted from 1764 until 1837, with simply stunning results. The altar and the pulpit are as ornate as wedding cakes and as delicate as starlight. The church's most notable treasure is a rendering of the Visitation attributed to Pierre Mignard, a painter in the 17th-century court of Louis XIV. The church is a 15-minute walk from the Henri Bourassa Métro station, but the trek is worth it. Parkland surrounds the church, and the nearby Îles de la Visitation (reachable by footbridge) make a delightful walk. ⊠ *1847 blvd. Gouin Est, Sault-au-Récollet,* ☎ *514/388–4050.* ▨ *Free.* ⊙ *Daily 10–11:30 and 2–4. Métro: Henri Bourassa.*

55 **Musée des Hospitalières de l'Hôtel-Dieu.** More than just a fascinating exhibit on the history of medicine and nursing, this museum captures the spirit of an age. France in the 17th century was consumed with religious fervor, and aristocratic men and women often built hospitals, schools, and churches in distant lands. The nuns of the Religieuses Hospitalières de St-Joseph who came to Montréal in the mid-17th century to help Jeanne Mance run the Hôpital Hôtel-Dieu were good examples of this fervor, and much of their spirit is evident in the letters, books, and religious artifacts displayed here. Pay special attention to the beautiful wooden stairway in the museum's entrance hall. ⊠ *201 av. des Pins Ouest, Plateau Mont-Royal,* ☎ *514/849–2919.* ▨ *$5.* ⊙ *Mid-June–mid-Oct., Tues.–Fri. 10–5, weekends 1–5; mid-Oct.–mid-June, Wed.–Sun. 1–5. Métro: Sherbrooke.*

NEED A BREAK?

The homey, cash-only **Café Santropol** (⊠ 3990 rue St-Urbain, Plateau Mont-Royal, ☎ 514/842–3110) serves hearty soups, cake, salads, and unusual high-rise sandwiches garnished with fruit (the Jeanne Mance mixes pineapples and chives in cream cheese). One percent of the profits goes to charity, and the staff runs a meals-on-wheels program.

53 **Musée Juste pour Rire** (Just for Laughs Museum). Here's one of the few museums in the world to be dedicated to laughter. Its multimedia exhibits explore and celebrate humor by drawing you into their plots. Some visiting exhibits have a serious side, too. There's a large collection of humor videos, a cabaret where budding comics can test their material, and a restaurant where you can watch old tapes while you eat. ⊠ *2111 blvd. St-Laurent, Quartier Latin,* ☎ *514/845–5105,* WEB *www.hahaha.com.* ▨ *$5.* ⊙ *Weekends (year-round) 10–5; June–Sept., Tues.–Fri. 9–5; Sept.–June, Thurs.–Fri. 9–3. Métro: Sherbrooke or Berri-UQAM.*

57 **Parc Lafontaine.** Montréal's two main cultures are reflected in the lay-out of this popular park: the eastern half is pure French, with paths, gardens, and lawns laid out in geometric shapes; the western half is very English, with meandering paths and irregularly shaped ponds that follow the natural contours of the land. In summer there are bowling greens, tennis courts, an open-air theater (Théâtre Verdure) with free arts events, and two artificial lakes with paddleboats. In winter the two lakes form a large skating rink. The park is named for Sir Louis-Hip-polyte Lafontaine (1807–64), a pioneer of responsible government in Canada. His statue graces a plot on the park's southwestern edge. ⊠ *3933 av. Parc Lafontaine, Plateau Mont-Royal,* ☎ *514/872–9800.* ☉ *Daily 9* AM–10 PM. *Métro: Sherbrooke or Mont-Royal.*

Rue Prince-Arthur. In the 1960s, the young people who moved to the neighborhood transformed this street into a small hippie bazaar of cloth-ing, leather, and smoke shops. It remains a center of youth culture, al-though it's much tamer and more commercial these days. The city turned the blocks between avenue Laval and boulevard St-Laurent into a pedestrian mall. Hippie shops have metamorphosed into inexpensive Greek, Vietnamese, Italian, Polish, and Chinese restaurants and little neighborhood bars. *Métro: Sherbrooke.*

54 **Square St-Louis.** The elegant square has a fountain, benches, and trees and is surrounded by 19th-century homes built in the large, comfort-able style of the Second Empire. Originally a reservoir, these blocks be-came a park in 1879 and attracted upper-middle-class families and artists. French-Canadian poets were among the most famous creative people to occupy the houses back then, and the neighborhood today is home to painters, filmmakers, musicians, and writers. On the wall of 336 Square St-Louis you can see—and read, if your French is good—a long poem by Michel Bujold. ⊠ *Bordered by av. Laval and rue St-Denis between rue Sherbrooke Est and av. des Pins Est, Quartier Latin. Métro: Sherbrooke.*

51 **Théâtre St-Denis.** With 2,500 seats, this is the second-largest audito-rium in Montréal (after Salle Wilfrid Pelletier in Place des Arts). Sarah Bernhardt is one of the many famous performers who have graced its stage. ⊠ *1594 rue St-Denis, Quartier Latin,* ☎ *514/849–4211. Métro: Berri-UQAM.*

49 **Université du Québec à Montréal.** Part of a network of campuses set up by the provincial government in 1969, UQAM encompasses a se-ries of massive, modern brick buildings clogging much of the three city blocks bordered by rues Sanguinet and Berri and boulevards de Maison-neuve and René-Lévesque. The splendid fragments of Gothic grandeur sprouting up among the modern brick hulks are all that's left of Église St-Jacques. ⊠ *Bordered by rues Sanguinet and Berri and blvds. de Maisonneuve and René-Lévesque, Plateau Mont-Royal,* ☎ *514/987– 3000. Métro: Berri-UQAM.*

Parc du Mont-Royal

Frederick Law Olmsted, the codesigner of New York City's Central Park, designed Parc du Mont-Royal, 494 acres of forest and paths in the heart of Montréal. Olmsted believed that communion with nature could cure body and soul, and the park follows the natural topogra-phy and accentuates its features, in the English style. You can jog, cycle, or stroll the miles of paths, or just scan the horizon from one of two lookouts. Horse-drawn transport is popular year-round: sleigh rides in winter and calèche rides in summer. On the eastern side of the hill stands the 100-ft steel cross that is the symbol of the city. Not far away from the park and perched on a neighboring crest of the same mountain is the Oratoire St-Joseph, a shrine that draws millions every year.

A Good Tour

Begin by taking the Métro's Orange Line to the Mont-Royal station and transfer to Bus 11 (be sure to get a transfer—*correspondence* in French—from a machine before you get on the Métro). The No. 11 drives right through the Parc du Mont-Royal on the voie Camillien Houde. Get off at the **Obsérvatoire de l'Est** ⑤⑧, a lookout. Climb the stone staircase at the end of the parking lot and follow the trails to the **Chalet du Mont-Royal** ⑤⑨, a baronial building with a terrace that overlooks downtown Montréal. The next stop is **Lac aux Castors** ⑥⓪, and there are at least three ways to get to this lake. You can take the long way and walk down the steep flight of stairs at the east end of the terrace and then turn right to follow the gravel road that circles the mountain. The shortest way is to leave the terrace at the west end and follow the crowds along the road. The middle way is to leave at the east end, but then to turn off the main road and follow one of the shaded paths that lead through the woods and along the southern ridge of the mountain.

Across chemin Remembrance from Lac aux Castors is what looks like one vast cemetery. It is in fact two cemeteries—one Protestant and one Catholic. The **Cimetière Mont-Royal** ⑥① is toward the east in a little valley that cuts off the noise of the city; it's the final resting place of Anna Leonowens, the real-life heroine of *The King and I*. The yellow-brick buildings and tower on the north side of the mountain beyond the cemetery belong to the Université de Montréal, the second-largest French-language university in the world, with nearly 60,000 students. If you're now humming "Getting to Know You," you'll probably change your tune to Canada's national anthem when you enter the **Cimetière de Notre-Dame-des-Neiges** ⑥②; the composer of "O Canada," Calixa Lavallée, is buried here.

Wander northwest through the two cemeteries, and you eventually emerge on chemin Queen Mary on the edge of a decidedly lively area of street vendors, ethnic restaurants, and boutiques. Walk west on Queen Mary across chemin Côte-des-Neiges, and you come to Montréal's most grandiose religious monument, the **Oratoire St-Joseph** ⑥③. Across the street is the ivy-covered Collège Notre Dame, where the oratory's founder, Brother André, worked as a porter. Today it's an important private school (now coed) and one of the few in the city that still accept boarders. After visiting the church, retrace your steps to chemin Côte-des-Neiges and walk to the Côte-des-Neiges station to catch the Métro.

TIMING

Allot the better part of a day for this tour, longer if you plan on catching some rays or ice-skating in the park.

Sights to See

★ ⑤⑨ **Chalet du Mont-Royal.** The view here overlooks downtown Montréal. In the distance you can see Mont-Royal's sister mountains—monts St-Bruno, St-Hilaire, and St-Grégoire. These isolated peaks—called the Montérégies, or Mountains of the King—rise dramatically from the flat countryside. Be sure to take a look inside the chalet, especially at the murals depicting scenes from Canadian history. There's a snack bar in the back. ⊠ *Off voie Camillien-Houde, Mont-Royal.* ☉ *Daily 9–5.*

⑥② **Cimetière de Notre-Dame-des-Neiges** (Our Lady of the Snows Cemetery). The largest Catholic graveyard in the city is the final resting place of hundreds of prominent artists, poets, intellectuals, politicians, and clerics. Among them is Calixa Lavallée (1842–91), who wrote "O Canada." Many of the monuments and mausoleums—scattered along 55 km (34 mi) of paths and roadways—are the work of leading artists. There are no tours of the cemetery, but a book at the reception gates lists locations of certain graves. ⊠ *4601 chemin Côte-des-Neiges, Mont-Royal,* ☎ *514/735–1361. Métro: Université de Montréal.*

61 Cimetière Mont-Royal. The Mont-Royal Cemetery was established in 1852 by the Anglican, Presbyterian, Unitarian, and Baptist churches and was laid out like a landscaped garden with monuments that are genuine works of art. The most famous permanent guest here is Anna Leonowens, who was governess to the children of the King of Siam and the real-life model for the heroine of the musical *The King and I.* There are no tours of the cemetery. ⊠ *1297 chemin de la Forêt, Mont-Royal,* ☎ *514/279–7358.* ☉ *Daily 10–6. Métro: Edouard Montpetit.*

OFF THE
BEATEN PATH
☙

COSMODOME – The adventure of space exploration is the focus of this interactive center in suburban Laval, about a 30-minute drive from downtown. It's loaded with such kid-pleasing exhibits as replicas of rockets and space ships and a full-size mock-up of the space shuttle Endeavor. There are films—some of them shown on a 360-degree screen—demonstrations, and games. Next door to the Cosmodome is the **Space Camp** (☎ 800/565–2267), a training center for amateur astronauts 9 or older that is affiliated with the U.S. Space Camp in Georgia. ⊠ *2150 autoroute des Laurentides, Laval,* ☎ *450/978–3600,* WEB *www.cosmodome.org.* ☞ $11.50. ☉ *June 24–Aug., daily 10–6; Sept.–June 23, Tues.–Sun. 10–6.*

☙ 60 Lac aux Castors (Beaver Lake). In summer, children can float boats in this lake reclaimed from boggy ground. It makes a fine skating rink in winter. ⊠ *Off chemin Remembrance, Mont-Royal. Métro: Edouard Montpetit.*

58 Obsérvatoire de l'Est. This lookout gives a spectacular view of the east end of the city and the St. Lawrence River. ⊠ *Voie Camillien-Houde, Mont-Royal.*

63 Oratoire St-Joseph. St. Joseph's Oratory, a huge domed church perched high on a ridge of Mont-Royal, is the largest shrine in the world dedicated to the earthly father of Jesus. It's the result of the persistence of a remarkable little man named Brother André Besette, who was a porter in the school run by his religious order. The son of very poor farmers, he dreamed of building a shrine dedicated to St. Joseph—Canada's patron saint—and began in 1904 by building a little chapel. Miraculous cures were reported and attributed to St. Joseph's intercession, and Brother André's project caught the imagination of Montréal. The result is one of the most important shrines in North America.

The octagonal copper dome on top of the church is one of the biggest in the world—146 ft tall and 125 ft in diameter—and the church has a magnificent mountainside setting with sweeping views over the north of the city and the Laurentian foothills in the distance. It's also home to Les Petits Chanteurs de Mont-Royal, the city's finest boys' choir. The modern concrete interior is a soaring dim cave full of rows of folding metal chairs and not much in the way of art or color except for some striking stained-glass windows made by Marius Plamondon. The Montréal sculptor Henri Charlier is responsible for the huge crucifix, the elongated wooden statues of the apostles in the transepts, and the main altar.

In the more modest crypt church at the base of the stairs leading to the main church, a larger-than-life white marble statue of St. Joseph dominates the main altar. Behind the crypt is a room that glitters with hundreds of votive candles lighted in honor of St. Joseph; the walls are hung with crutches discarded by the cured. Just beyond is the simple tomb of Brother André, who was beatified in 1982. His heart is displayed in a glass case upstairs in one of the galleries sandwiched between the crypt and the main church.

High on the mountain beside the main church is a beautiful garden, commemorating the Passion of Christ with life-size representations of the 14 traditional Stations of the Cross. Carillon, choral, and organ concerts are held weekly in summer. The church's front door is 300 steps above street level (many pilgrims climb them on their knees), but a major construction project under way at this writing is to link the church to the street-level parking lot with escalators and elevators. ⊠ *3800 chemin Queen Mary, Côte-des-Neiges,* ☎ *514/733–8211,* WEB *www.saint-joseph.org.* ✉ *Free.* ☉ *Mid-Sept.–mid-May, daily 7–5:30; mid-May–mid-Sept., daily 7 AM–9 PM. Métro: Côte-des-Neiges.*

Olympic Park and Botanical Garden

The giant Stade Olympique and the leaning tower that supports the stadium's roof dominate the skyline of the eastern part of town. But the area has more to recommend it than the stadium complex: there are the Jardin Botanique (Botanical Garden); the Insectarium, the world's largest museum dedicated to bugs; and Parc Maisonneuve, which is an ideal place for a stroll or a picnic. You can reach the Parc Olympique (Olympic Park) and the botanical garden via the Pie-IX or Viau Métro stations; a free shuttle links the latter, which is nearer the stadium entrance, with the Jardin Botanique, Biodôme, and Parc Olympique.

A Good Tour

Start with a ride on the Métro's Green Line and get off at the Viau station, which is only a few steps from the main entrance to the 70,000-seat **Stade Olympique** ⑥④, a stadium built for the 1976 summer games. A trip to the top of the **Tour Olympique** ⑥⑤, the world's tallest tilting structure, gives you a view up to 80 km (50 mi) on a clear day. The six pools of the **Centre Aquatique** ⑥⑥ are under the tower.

Next to the tower is the **Biodôme** ⑥⑦, where you can explore both a rain forest and an arctic landscape. Continuing your back-to-nature experience, cross rue Sherbrooke to the north of the park (or take the free shuttle bus) to reach the enormous **Jardin Botanique** ⑥⑧. The botanical complex includes the **Insectarium** ⑥⑨ and the 5-acre Montréal-Shanghai Lac de Rêve, an elegant Ming-style garden.

After you've looked at the flowers, return to boulevard Pie-IX, which runs along the western border of the gardens. The name of this traffic artery (and the adjoining Métro station) puzzles thousands of visitors every year. The street is named for the 19th-century pope Pius IX, or Pie IX in French. It's pronounced Pee-neuf, however, which isn't at all how it looks to English speakers. At rue Sherbrooke cross boulevard Pie-IX and walk east to rue Jeanne-d'Arc past the lavish **Château Dufresne** ⑦⑩, a pair of attached mansions built as family homes by two brothers in 1916.

TIMING

To see all the sights at a leisurely pace, you need a full day.

Sights to See

☞ ⑥⑦ **Biodôme.** Not everyone thought it was a great idea to transform an Olympic bicycle-racing stadium into a natural-history exhibit, but the

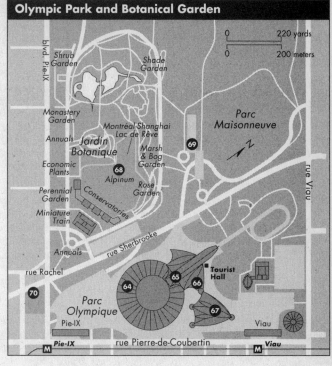

result is one of the city's most popular attractions. It combines four ecosystems—the boreal forest, tropical forest, polar world, and St. Lawrence River—under one climate-controlled dome. You follow protected pathways through each environment, observing flora and fauna of each ecosystem. A word of warning: the tropical forest really is tropical. If you want to stay comfortable, dress in layers. ⊠ *4777 av. Pierre-de-Coubertin, Hochelaga-Maisonneuve,* ☎ *514/868–3000,* WEB *www.biodome.qc.ca.* ⌨ *$10.* ☺ *July–Aug., daily 9–7; Sept.–June, daily 9–5. Métro: Viau.*

 **66** **Centre Aquatique.** Olympic swimmers competed here in 1976, but now anyone can use four of the six pools. One is for games such as water polo, the others are for laps. Volleyball courts also are available. ⊠ *4141 av. Pierre-de-Coubertin, Hochelaga-Maisonneuve,* ☎ *514/252–4622.* ⌨ *$3.30.* ☺ *Weekdays 2–9, weekends 1–4. Métro: Pie-IX or Viau.*

70 **Château Dufresne.** The adjoining homes of a pair of shoe manufacturers, Oscar and Marius Dufresne, provide a revealing glimpse into the lives of Montréal's Francophone bourgeoisie in the early 20th century. The brothers built this Beaux Arts palace in 1916 along the lines of the Petit-Trianon in Paris and lived in it with their families—Oscar in the eastern half and Marius in the western half. The residences include oak staircases with gilded rails, marble-tile floors, stained-glass windows, and coffered ceilings. Murals by Guido Nincheri, an artist who also decorated many of the city's most beautiful churches, adorn the walls. Of particular charm are the delicate domestic scenes on the walls of the Petit Salon, where Madame Oscar Dufresne would entertain her friends. Her brother-in-law, on the other side of the house, relaxed with his male friends in a smoking room decked out like a Turkish lounge. During the house's incarnation as a boys' school, the Eudist priests, who ran the place, covered the room's frieze of frolicking nymphs and satyrs with a modest curtain that their charges lifted at every opportunity. ✉ *2929 rue Jeanne-d'Arc, Hochelaga-Maisonneuve,* ☎ *514/256–4636.* 🎟 *$6.* ☉ *Tues.–Fri. 9:30–noon and 1:30–4:30, weekends 10–5. Métro: Pie-IX.*

🐾 **69** **Insectarium.** A bug-shape building in the ☞ **Jardin Botanique** houses more than 250,000 insect specimens. Most are mounted, but colorful butterflies fly free in the butterfly room, and there are ant and bee exhibits, too. In February you can taste such delicacies as deep-fried bumblebees. ✉ *4581 rue Sherbrooke Est, Hochelaga-Maisonneuve,* ☎ *514/872–1400,* 🌐 *www.ville.montreal.qc.ca/insectarium.* 🎟 *May–Oct. $10, Nov.–Apr. $7.50; includes Jardin Botanique admission.* ☉ *May–mid-June and Sept. 10–Apr., daily 9–5; mid-June–Sept. 9, daily 9–7. Métro: Pie-IX or Viau.*

★ 🐾 **68** **Jardin Botanique.** This botanical garden, with 181 acres of plantings in summer and 10 exhibition greenhouses open all year, is the second-largest attraction of its kind in the world (after England's Kew Gardens). Founded in 1931, the garden has more than 26,000 species of plants. Among the 30 thematic gardens are a rose garden and an alpine garden; the poisonous-plant garden is a favorite. Traditional tea ceremonies are held in the Japanese Garden, which also has one of the best bonsai collections in the West. The Tree House exhibit center in the arboretum explores the world of the forest. The Jardin des Premier Nations, or the First Nations Garden, includes such indigenous plants and trees as silver birch, maples, Labrador, and tea and jack-in-the-pulpit. Other highlights are the 5-acre Montréal–Shanghai Lac de Rêve, the largest Ming-style Chinese garden outside Asia, with seven elegant pavilions and a 30-ft rock garden built around a pool, and the ☞ **Insectarium.** ✉ *4101 rue Sherbrooke Est, Hochelaga-Maisonneuve,* ☎ *514/872–1400,* 🌐 *www.ville.montreal.qc.ca/jardin.* 🎟 *May–Oct. $10, Nov.–Apr. $7.50; includes Insectarium admission.* ☉ *May–Oct., daily 9–7, Nov.–Apr., daily 9–5. Métro: Pie-IX or Viau.*

OFF THE
BEATEN PATH

MAISONNEUVE – Olympic organizers weren't the first dream-makers to have big plans for this socially cohesive but economically depressed neighborhood. At the beginning of the 20th century, when the district was a hard-working, booming industrial center with its own municipal government, civic leaders wanted to transform it into a model city with broad boulevards, grandiose public buildings, and fine homes. World War I and the Depression killed those plans, but a few fine fragments of the grand dream survive, just three blocks south of the Olympic site. The magnificent Beaux Arts public market with its 20-ft-tall bronze statue of a farm woman stands at the northern end of tree-lined avenue Morgan. Farmers and butchers have moved into a modern building next door; the old market is now a community center and the site of shows and concerts in the summer. Monumental staircases and a heroic rooftop sculpture embellish the public baths across the street; the **Théâtre Denise Pelletier,** at the corner of rue Ste-Catherine Est, has a lavish Italianate interior; **Fire Station No. 1,** at 4300 rue Notre-Dame Est, was inspired by Frank Lloyd Wright's Unity Temple in suburban Chicago; and the sumptuously decorated **Église Très-Saint-Nom-de-Jésus** has one of the most powerful organs in North America. **Tourisme Maisonneuve** (✉ *4375 rue Ontario Est, Hochelaga-Maisonneuve,* ☎ *514/256–4636*) has information about the area. *Métro: Pie-IX or Viau.*

64 **Stade Olympique.** The stadium, built for the 1976 Summer Olympics, is beautiful to look at but not very practical. It's hard to heat, and the retractable fabric roof, supported by the tower, has never worked properly. Nevertheless, it's home to the Expos of baseball's National League and is used for events like Montréal's annual car show. ✉ *4141 av. Pierre-de-Coubertin, Hochelaga-Maisonneuve,* ☏ *514/252–8687,* WEB *www.rio.gouv.qc.ca. Métro: Pie-IX or Viau.*

㉖ Tour Olympique. A trip to the top of this tower, the world's tallest tilting structure, is very popular; a two-level cable car can whisk 90 people up the exterior of the 890-ft tower. On a clear day you can see up to 80 km (50 mi) from the tower-top observatory. Daily guided tours of the Olympic complex leave from the **Tourist Hall** (☏ 514/252–8687) in the base of the Tour Olympique. Tours at 12:40 and 3:40 are in English and tours at 11 and 2 are in French; cost is $5.25. ✉ *Av. Pierre-de-Coubertin, Hochelaga-Maisonneuve,* ☏ *514/252–4141 Ext. 5246 for tour and tower-ride arrangements.* 🎫 *$9; $12 including tour of Olympic complex. Métro: Pie-IX or Viau.*

The Islands

Expo '67—the world's fair staged to celebrate the centennial of the Canadian federation—was the biggest party in Montréal's history, and it marked a defining moment in the city's evolution as a modern metropolis. That party was held on two islands in the middle of the St. Lawrence River—Île Ste-Hélène, which was formed by nature, and Île Notre-Dame, which was created with the stone rubble excavated from Montréal's Métro. The two islands are still a playground. Together they form **Parc Jean-Drapeau** (☏ 514/872–4537, WEB www.parcjeandrapeau.com/en), named for the visionary mayor who brought the world's fair to Montréal, and encompass a major amusement park, acres of flower gardens, a beach with clean filtered water, and the Casino de Montréal. There's history, too, at the Old Fort, where soldiers in colonial uniforms display the military skills of ancient wars. In winter you can skate on the old Olympic rowing basin or slide down iced trails on an inner tube.

A Good Walk

Start at the Parc Jean-Drapeau station on the Métro's Yellow Line. The first thing you see when you emerge is the huge geodesic dome that houses **Biosphère,** an environmental exhibition center. From the Biosphère walk to the northern shore and then east to the Old Fort, now the **Stewart Museum.** Just east of the Old Fort past the Pont Jacques-Cartier (Jacques Cartier Bridge) is **La Ronde,** an amusement park.

Now cross over to the island's southern shore and walk back along the waterfront to the Cosmos Footbridge, which leads to Île Notre-Dame. On the way you pass the Hélène de Champlain restaurant, which probably has the prettiest setting of any restaurant in Montréal, and the military cemetery of the British garrison stationed on Île Ste-Hélène from 1828 to 1870.

Île Notre-Dame is laced with a network of canals and ponds, and the grounds are brilliant with flower gardens left from the 1980 Floralies Internationales flower show. Most of the Expo '67 buildings are gone, the victims of time and weather. One that has remained, however, is the fanciful French Pavilion. It and the neighboring Québec Pavilion have been turned into the **Casino de Montréal.** A five-minute walk west of the casino is the Lac de l'Île Notre-Dame, site of **Plage de l'Île Notre-Dame,** Montréal's only beach. In mid-June Île Notre-Dame is the site of the Air Canada Grand Prix du Canada, a top Formula 1 international auto race at the **Circuit Gilles Villeneuve.**

After your walk you can return to the Métro or walk back to the city via the Pont de la Concorde and the Parc de la Cité du Havre to Vieux-Montréal. If you walk, you can see Habitat '67, an irregular pile of concrete blocks on avenue Pierre-Dupuy that was designed by Moshe Safdie and built as an experiment in housing for Expo '67. The private apartment complex resembles an updated version of a Hopi cliff dwelling.

TIMING

This is a comfortable two-hour stroll, but the Biosphère and the Old Fort (try to time your visit to coincide with a drill display) deserve at least an hour each, and you should leave another half hour to admire the flowers. Children are likely to want to spend a whole day at La Ronde, but in summer the best time to go is in the evening, when it's cooler. Try to visit the casino on a weekday, when the crowds are thinnest.

Sights to See

Biosphère. An environmental center in the huge geodesic dome designed by Buckminster Fuller as the American Pavilion at Expo '67 successfully brings fun to an earnest project—heightening awareness of the St. Lawrence River system and its problems. ⊠ *Île Ste-Hélène,* ☎ *514/ 496–8300,* WEB *www.biosphere.ec.gc.ca/bio.* ☞ *$8.50.* ☉ *June–Sept., daily 10–6; Oct.–May, Tues.–Sat. 10–4. Métro: Parc Jean-Drapeau.*

★ **Casino de Montréal.** The government has tried to capture the elegance of Monte Carlo here, one of the biggest gambling palaces in the world. This stunning complex—originally the French Pavilion for Expo '67, Montréal's world's fair—glitters with glass and murals and offers stunning city views. The casino, which is open around the clock, has a strict dress code and houses four restaurants, including Nuances, and a bilingual cabaret theater. ⊠ *1 av. du Casino, Île Notre-Dame,* ☎ *514/392– 2746 or 800/665–2274. Métro: Parc Jean-Drapeau (then Bus 167).*

Circuit Gilles Villeneuve. All the big names in motor sports gather at this track every summer for the Air Canada Grand Prix, one of the racing season's most important Formula 1 events. One of the veterans of the Formula 1 circuit is local hero Jacques Villeneuve, who won the world championship in 1997. The track is named for his father, Gilles, who was killed in a racing crash in Belgium in 1982. In late August 2002, the track also staged the first annual Molson Indy of Montréal, part of the CART FedEx Championship Series in automobile racing. ⊠ *Île Notre-Dame,* ☎ *800/797–4537. Métro: Parc Jean-Drapeau.*

☉ **Plage de l'Île Notre-Dame.** The swimming beach is an oasis, with clear, filtered river water and an inviting stretch of lawn and trees; it's often filled to capacity in summer, however. Lifeguards are on duty, a shop rents swimming and boating paraphernalia, and there are picnic areas and a restaurant. ⊠ *West side of Île Notre-Dame, Île Notre-Dame,* ☎ *514/872–4537.* ☞ *$7.50. Métro: Parc Jean-Drapeau.*

☉ **La Ronde.** This world-class amusement park has Ferris wheels, boat rides, simulator-style rides, and the second-highest roller coaster in the world. Six Flags, the U.S. company that owns the park, has been refurbishing the aging infrastructure and adding rides. Its first major addition, opened in summer 2002, is the Vampire, a looping roller coaster that sends its riders hurtling upside down at speeds of up to 50 mph. The popular **International Fireworks Competition** (☎ 514/935–5161, 800/361–4595 in Canada, 800/678–5440), which takes place weekends and a couple of weeknights in late June and July, is held here. ⊠ *Eastern end of Île Ste-Hélène,,* ☎ *514/872–6222.* ☞ *$27.81; grounds only $18.69.* ☉ *May, weekends 10–8; June 1–14, daily 10–8; June 15– Sept. 2, daily 10:30–11. Métro: Parc Jean-Drapeau.*

☉ **Stewart Museum at the Fort.** In summer the grassy parade square of the fine stone Old Fort comes alive with the crackle of colonial musket fire. The French are represented by the Compagnie Franche de la Marine and the British by the kilted 78th Fraser Highlanders, one of the regiments that participated in the conquest of Québec in 1759. The fort itself, built to protect Montréal from American invasion, is now a museum that tells the story of colonial life in Montréal through displays of old firearms, maps, and uniforms. The two companies of colonial soldiers raise the flag every day at 11, practice their maneuvers at 1, put on a combined display of precision drilling and musket fire at 2:30, and lower the flag at 5. Children can participate. ⊠ *Just west of Pont Jacques-Cartier, Île Ste-Hélène,* ☎ *514/861–6701,* WEB *www.stewart-museum.org.* 🎟 *Early May–mid-Oct. $7, mid-Oct.– early May $6.* ◷ *Early May–mid-Oct., daily 10–6; mid-Oct.–early May, Wed.–Mon. 10–5. Métro: Parc Jean-Drapeau.*

DINING

When you dine out, you can order à la carte, but look for the table d'hôte, a two- to four-course package deal. It's usually more economical, often offers interesting special dishes, and may also take less time to prepare. If you want to splurge with your time and money, indulge yourself with the *menu dégustation,* a five- to seven-course tasting menu executed by the chef. It generally includes soup, salad, fish, sherbet (to refresh the taste buds), a meat dish, dessert, and coffee or tea. At the city's finest restaurants, such a meal for two, along with a good bottle of wine, can cost more than $200 and last four hours; it's worth every cent and every second.

A word about language: menus in many restaurants are bilingual, but some are in French only. If you don't understand what a dish is, don't be shy about asking; a good server will be delighted to explain. If you feel brave enough to order in French, remember that in French an entrée is an appetizer and what English speakers call an entrée is a *plat principal,* or main dish.

CATEGORY	COST*
$$$$	over $32
$$$	$22–$32
$$	$13–$22
$	under $13

*per person, in Canadian dollars, for a main course at dinner

Cafés

$-$$ ✕ **Brioche Lyonnaise.** The quintessential Quartier Latin café—it opened
★ in 1980—is in a semibasement with stone walls across the street from the Théatre St-Denis. A display case holds some of the city's finest pastries, all loaded with butter, cream, pure fruit, and a dusting of sugar. The butter brioche and a bowl of steaming café au lait make for one of the city's finest breakfasts, but heartier fare is available, too. Table d'hôte meals are served at lunch and dinner, and the place stays open until midnight. The atrium in the back and a terasse are open in fine weather. ⊠ *1593 rue St-Denis, Quartier Latin,* ☎ *514/842–7017. MC, V. Métro: Berri-UQAM.*

$-$$ ✕ **Claude Postel.** Claude Postel closed his well-regarded French restau-
★ rant in the late 1980s and moved to Toronto, but in the early 1990s he lended his name to staff members who opened this *patisserie– chocolatier.* Its sandwiches (on first-rate bread), pastries, pâtés, coffees, and limited selection of prix-fixe meals (braised veal, poached salmon, vegetable-and-orange soup) are popular with discriminating clerks and lawyers in nearby offices. In summer, there's richly flavored ice

cream. The place closes at 6 PM. ⊠ *75 rue Notre-Dame Ouest,, Vieux-Montréal,* ☎ *514/844–8750. MC, V. Métro: Place-d'Armes.*

$ ✕ **Les Gâteries.** The revered Montréal playwright Michel Tremblay is reputed to be among the writers and artists who take their morning espresso in this comfortable little café facing Square St-Louis. The menu is decidedly more Montréalais than European with such local favorites as bagels, muffins, maple-syrup pie, and toast with *cretons* (a coarse, fatty kind of pâté made with pork) sharing space with baguettes and croissants. ⊠ *3443 rue St-Denis, Plateau Mont-Royal,* ☎ *514/843–6235. MC, V. Métro: Sherbrooke.*

$ ✕ **St-Viateur Bagel & Café.** Even expatriate New Yorkers come to prefer Montréal's light, crispy, and slightly sweet bagel over its leaden Manhattan cousin. St-Viateur's wood-fired brick ovens have been turning out some of the best since 1959. The dough is boiled in honey-sweetened water before baking. With coffee and smoked salmon, these bagels make a great breakfast. ⊠ *1127 av. Mont-Royal Est, Plateau Mont-Royal,* ☎ *514/528–6361. No credit cards. Métro: Mont-Royal.*

Canadian

$ ✕ **Binerie Mont-Royal.** That rarest of the city's culinary finds—authentic Québecois food—is the specialty at this tiny restaurant. The fare includes stews made with meatballs and pigs' feet, various kinds of *tourtière* (meat pie), and, of course, pork and beans. It's cheap, filling, and charming. ⊠ *367 av. Mont-Royal Est, Plateau Mont-Royal,* ☎ *514/ 285–9078. No credit cards. No dinner weekends. Métro: Mont-Royal.*

$ ✕ **Chalet Barbecue.** In the early 1950s, Swiss-born Marcel Mauron and French-born Jean Detanne built a large brick oven in this west-end location and pioneered a Montréal tradition: crispy, spit-barbecued chicken served with a slightly spicy, gravylike sauce and mountains of french fries. There are dozens of imitators all over the city, but no one does it better. Many of the restaurant's customers order their meals to go. ⊠ *5456 rue Sherbrooke Ouest, Notre-Dame-de-Grace,* ☎ *514/489– 7235. MC, V. Métro: Vendôme.*

$ ✕ **Chez Clo.** Here, deep in east-end Montréal, where seldom is heard an English word, is authentic Québecois food. A meal in this unpretentious neighborhood diner could start with a bowl of the best pea soup in the city, followed by a slab of tourtière. The dessert specialty is *pudding au chomeur* (literally, pudding for the unemployed), a kind of shortcake smothered in a thick brown-sugar sauce. The service is noisy and friendly and the clientele mostly local. ⊠ *3199 rue Ontario Est, Hochelaga-Maisonneuve,* ☎ *514/522–5348. No credit cards. Métro: Pie IX.*

Chinese

$$–$$$$ ✕ **Orchidée de Chine.** Diners feast on such delectables as baby bok choy with mushrooms, perfumed spareribs, feather-light fried soft-shell crabs with black-bean sauce, and steamed, gingery grouper. The elegant, glassed-in dining room has a great view on a busy, fashionable sidewalk; a more intimate room is in the back. ⊠ *2017 rue Peel, Downtown,* ☎ *514/287–1878. Reservations essential. AE, DC, MC, V. Closed Sun. No lunch Sat. Métro: Peel.*

$–$$ ✕ **Maison Kam Fung.** You get Chinatown's most reliable dim-sum lunch at this bright, airy restaurant. Every day from 10 to 3, waiters push a parade of trolleys through the restaurant, carting treats such as firm dumplings stuffed with pork and chicken, stir-fried squid, and delicate shrimp-filled pastry envelopes. ⊠ *1008 rue Clark, Chinatown,* ☎ *514/878–2888. AE, DC, MC, V. Métro: Place-d'Armes.*

$ ✕ **Bon Blé Riz.** The food in this little restaurant is flamboyantly Chinese, but the prices are as modest as the unpretentious decor. Sizzling shrimp with onion, green pepper, and carrot, and finely chopped lamb served with celery and bamboo shoots in a peppery anise-flavored sauce are two of the intriguing dishes. The Beijing-style dumplings are good starters. ⊠ *1437 blvd. St-Laurent, Downtown,* ☎ *514/844–1447. AE, DC, MC, V. Métro: St-Laurent.*

Contemporary

$$$–$$$$ ✕ **Cube.** Fish dishes like roasted striped bass in a lemon-herb broth
★ and starters such as wild-mushroom tart with arugula and cheddar are served in a chic-casual room with gray concrete walls, picture windows, and flickering purple candles. Skip the disappointing cheese offerings—only one from Québec—and try the house-made ice cream. ⊠ *Hotel St. Paul, 355 rue McGill, Vieux-Montréal,* ☎ *514/876–2823. Reservations essential. AE, DC, MC, V. Métro: Square-Victoria.*

$$$–$$$$ ✕ **Mediterraneo.** Sandstone floors, a space-age metallic ceiling, and huge windows that wrap around two walls set off some of the trendiest food in Montréal. Dinner could start with a plate of grilled king herring and mushrooms and continue with a veal chop served with sweetbreads and wild-mushroom sauce. ⊠ *3500 blvd. St-Laurent, Plateau Mont-Royal,* ☎ *514/844–0027. Reservations essential. AE, MC, V. No lunch. Métro: Sherbrooke.*

$$$–$$$$ ✕ **Toqué!** Toqué's innovative co-owner and chef, Normand Laprise,
★ has achieved a level of celebrity in Montréal equaled only by the captain of the Canadiens hockey team. His menu changes constantly, depending on whim and what ingredients are available. A cold summer soup from fresh green tomatoes might be replaced in winter with a fluffy cake of bronzed potatoes, goat cheese, and spinach. Main courses could range from quail with raspberry sauce to butter-bean stew with cumin and jalapeño peppers. The portions don't look big but are surprisingly filling. And the desserts—crème brûlée, almond-crusted blueberry pie, chocolate mille-feuille—are worth saving space for. ⊠ *3842 rue St-Denis, Plateau Mont-Royal,* ☎ *514/499–2084. Reservations essential. AE, DC, MC, V. No lunch. Métro: Sherbrooke.*

$$–$$$$ ✕ **Globe.** Frosted lighting fixtures, potted palms, and red-velvet banquettes adorn this fashionable haunt of successful thirtysomethings. The vegetables are organic, the meat and poultry free-range, and the portions generous. Slow-cooked meats—rabbit, baby back ribs in red-wine sauce—are best bets. The menu also includes alphabet soup and home-fried potatoes. ⊠ *3455 blvd. St-Laurent, Plateau Mont-Royal,* ☎ *514/284–3823. AE, DC, MC, V. No lunch. Métro: St-Laurent.*

$$$ ✕ **Chorus.** Gold-framed mirrors, dark-blue walls, and halogen lamps give this two-level restaurant a very modern air. So does the menu, which offers starters such as a beet-and-cheese mille-feuille with mustard sprouts and main dishes like rabbit stuffed with shiitake mushrooms, sesame seeds, and cabbage. ⊠ *2424 rue St-Denis, Quartier Latin,* ☎ *514/841–8080. Reservations essential. AE, DC, MC, V. No lunch weekends and July 1–Sept. 1. Métro: Sherbrooke.*

$$$ ✕ **La Chronique.** Yellow walls and minimalist decor make an understated
★ backdrop for some of Montréal's most adventurous cooking. Owner-chef Marc de Canck seamlessly blends lightened French fare with Japanese, Chinese, and creole flashes. Starters like sashimi salmon rubbed with coarsely ground pepper, coriander, and mustard seed could precede pan-fried mahimahi served with thin slices of goat cheese–filled eggplant, for example, or veal sweetbreads with chorizo. ⊠ *99 av. Laurier Est, Laurier,* ☎ *514/271–3095. Reservations essential. AE, DC, MC, V. Closed Sun.–Mon. No lunch Sat. Métro: Mont-Royal.*

54

Montréal Dining

Ⓜ Edouard-Montpetit

ch. de la Côte-Ste-Catherine

blvd.

av. Laurier 61 6

blvd. St-Josep

Mont-Royal

Villeneuve

Cimetière Mont-Royal

voie C. Houde

Parc du Mont-Royal

❶ chemin Remembrance

av. des Pins

av. Cedar

av. Cedar

av. Docteur-Penfield

rue du Musée

rue Redpath

rue Simpson

rue de la

rue Stanley

rue Pee

rue Sherbrooke

❹

Ⓜ Guy-Concordia

❿ ⓫ ⓭

av. Atwater

❷

Atwater

Ⓜ Maisonneuve

blvd. de Maisonneuve

rue du Fort

rue St-Marc

rue St-Mathieu

rue Guy

❺

❾

❼ ❽

Montagne

rue Bishop

rue MacKay

rue Crescent

rue Dr

Ⓜ Lucien-L'Allier

❸

av. Greene

av. Greene

rue Ste-Catherine

blvd. Dorchester

blvd. René-Lévesque

autoroute Ville-Marie

rue St-Antoine

rue des Seigneurs

rue St-Jacques

Ⓜ Georges-Vanier

rue Notre-Dam

Lionel-Groulx

Ⓜ

❻

Parc
Lafontaine

1/2 mile
500 meters

rue Villeneuve

Mont-
Royal **M**

rue St-Denis

av. Mont-Royal

rue Marie-Anne

av. du Parc

blvd. St-Laurent

de Bullion

av. Laval

St-Urbain

rue Rachel

rue Roy

Duluth

av. Berri

av. du Parc Lafontaine

av. Colborne-Lavallée

av. Papineau

rue Sherbrooke

av. de Lorimier

Cherrier

Sherbrooke **M**

av. des Pins

rue Prince-Arthur

rue Jeanne-Mance

rue Milton

rue Sherbrooke

rue Aylmer

St-Christophe

Robin

Panel

Amherst

Beaudry **M**

de Maisonneuve

rue Ste-Catherine

St-Hubert

Berri-
UQAM **M**

blvd.

rue Ontario

av. du Président Kennedy

St-Laurent **M**

Place
des Arts **M**

av. Victoria

av. Union

McGill **M**

McGill

Col. Mansfield

Metcalfe

City Councillors

côte du Beaver-Hall

r. Cathcart

rue de Bleury

rue University

blvd. René-Lévesque

rue de la Gauchetière

Champ-
de-Mars **M**

Peel

Belmont

Square-
Victoria **M**

Bonaventure **M**

av. Viger

Place-
d'Armes **M**

rue St-Antoine

rue Notre-Dame

rue St-Paul

rue S-Fr-Xavier

rue de la Commune

rue McGill

autoroute Bonaventure

rue de la Montagne

rue Peel

rue Ottawa

rue Murray

Fleuve Saint-Laurent

$$-$$$ ✕ **Area.** Items on the short menu in this tiny 38-seat restaurant in Le
  ★   Village are categorized as cold, hot, or sweet. Sweetbreads in a gin-
        gerbread crust and cabbage salad are among the suggested starters. Main
        dishes include chicken leg stuffed with pistachio paste. Desserts are
        equally inventive. ⊠ *1429 rue Amherst, Village,* ☎ *514/890–6691.*
        Reservations essential. AE, DC, MC, V. Closed Mon. No lunch week-
        ends. Métro: Beaudry.

$$-$$$ ✕ **Bazou.** The name means "jalopy," and a car theme appears in both
        the decor and the table d'hôte menu. To start, for example, you can
        have *crevettes* Thais Suzuki, shrimp cooked with peanut butter, coriander,
        chili, and fried spinach; the duo Maserati main dish is cannelloni with
        four meats and sauce *napolitaine,* a tomato sauce. ⊠ *2004 Hôtel de*
        Ville, Village, ☎ *514/982–0853. AE, MC, V. No lunch. Métro: Beaudry.*

Continental

$$$-$$$$ ✕ **Beaver Club.** This grand old institution traces its roots to a 19th-
          century social club for the trading and banking elite, and its wood pan-
          eling, formal settings, and starched, veteran servers give it the air of
          an exclusive men's club. No one does a better job with such classics
          as roast beef, grilled chops, poached salmon, and Cornish hens. The
          bar serves the best martini in the city. ⊠ *Fairmont Le Reine Elizabeth,*
          900 blvd. René-Lévesque Ouest, Downtown, ☎ *514/861–3511. Jacket*
          and tie. AE, D, DC, MC, V. Closed Sun. and July. No dinner Mon.;
          no lunch Sat. and in Aug. Métro: Bonaventure.

Delicatessens

$-$$ ✕ **Schwartz's Delicatessen.** Its proper name is the Montréal Hebrew
        Delicatessen, but everyone calls it Schwartz's. The smoked meat (cured
        in-house) is the city's best, and the tender steaks come with grilled-liver
        appetizers. Waiters are briskly efficient; the furniture is a bit shabby.
        Don't ask for a menu (there isn't one) and avoid the lunch hour—lines
        are long even on the most brutal winter days. ⊠ *3895 blvd. St-Lau-*
        rent, Plateau Mont-Royal, ☎ *514/842–4813. Reservations not ac-*
        cepted. No credit cards. Métro: Sherbrooke.

$ ✕ **Bens.** This big, brassy deli is a Montréal institution, with 1950s decor
        and green and yellow walls hung with photos of celebrity customers.
        Sadly, the food isn't what it once was, though this is still a good place
        for a late-night snack. ⊠ *990 blvd. de Maisonneuve Ouest, Downtown,*
        ☎ *514/844–1000. Reservations not accepted. MC, V. Métro: Peel.*

French

$$$$ ✕ **Nuances.** The magnificent view of Montréal over the river is the best
        reason to eat in this formal, paneled restaurant at the Casino de Mont-
        réal. The items on the menu—scallops with shallots and caviar, orange
        and spice–marinated duck, and crisp-skinned pigeon—are often good
        but much pricier than similar fare in town. ⊠ *1 av. de Casino, Île Notre-*
        Damel, ☎ *514/392–2708. Reservations essential. AE, DC, MC, V. No*
        lunch. Métro: Parc Jean-Drapeau.

$$$-$$$$ ✕ **Caprices de Nicolas.** Antique furniture, plush seats, stained-glass
  ★   lamps, and dainty china make this restaurant one of Montréal's most
          luxurious. Its two art nouveau–inspired rooms are magnificent, but the
          most romantic tables are in the soaring, three-story atrium filled with
          tropical plants (reserved for nonsmokers). The poached sea bass is
          exquisite, as is the salmon pavé with onion preserves and currants.
          Meatier dishes include Alberta beef with an herb crust and pistachio
          gravy. ⊠ *2072 rue Drummond, Downtown,* ☎ *514/282–9790. Reser-*
          vations essential. AE, DC, MC, V. No lunch. Métro: Peel.

$$$–$$$$ ✕ **Chez la Mère Michel.** A fine gray-stone town house provides a staid front for one of the city's most elegant dining rooms: big, well-spaced tables; large, comfy chairs; and bright paintings and murals. Chef-owner Micheline Delbuguet—the Mère Michel of the name—presides over a kitchen that turns out such flawlessly executed examples of classic French cuisine as Dover sole meunière and coq au vin (made with a rooster—not a chicken). Save room for such desserts as soufflé Grand Marnier and poached pears in an almond basket. ✉ *1209 rue Guy, Downtown,* ☎ *514/934–0473. Reservations essential. AE, DC, MC, V. Closed Sun. No lunch Mon. and Sat. Métro: Guy-Concordia.*

$$$–$$$$ ✕ **Les Halles.** Main dishes such as grapefruit Marie-Louise with scallops and lobster or roasted duck with pears sit comfortably beside the chef's ventures into nouvelle cuisine, such as his lobster with herbs and butter. The desserts are classic—the Paris-Brest, a puff pastry with praline cream inside, is one of the best in town. Mirrors, murals, and light colors are part of the Paris-market decor. ✉ *1450 rue Crescent, Downtown,* ☎ *514/844–2328. Reservations essential. AE, DC, MC, V. Closed Sun. No lunch. Métro: Guy-Concordia or Peel.*

$$$–$$$$ ✕ **Les Remparts.** A stone-walled cellar under the Auberge du Vieux-Port showcases innovative French cooking in an atmosphere redolent of Nouvelle France. The restaurant gets its name from an ancient lump of gray stone unearthed during renovations to the building in 1994—it once formed part of the city wall. Dishes include braised deer shanks, semi-smoked salmon with sweet-potato gratin, and wild-mushroom risotto. ✉ *93 rue de la Commune Est, Vieux-Montréal,* ☎ *514/392–1649. AE, DC, MC, V. Métro: Place d'Armes.*

$$–$$$$ ✕ **Le Caveau.** Among the towers of downtown is an eccentric Victorian house where buttery sauces, creamy desserts, and fairly reasonable prices have survived the onslaught of nouvelle cuisine. The restaurant gets its name from its warm and comfortable low-ceiling cellar, but claustrophobes can dine on the upper two floors amid sculptures and paintings. A main course might be rabbit cooked with sweet wine, spices, and raisins, or rack of lamb crusted with bread crumbs, mustard, garlic, and herbs. A children's menu—rare in restaurants of Le Caveau's caliber—is available. ✉ *2063 av. Victoria, Downtown,* ☎ *514/844–1624. AE, DC, MC, V. No lunch weekends. Métro: McGill.*

$$–$$$$ ✕ **Guy and Dodo Morali.** Lots of art decorates this comfortable restaurant in the Cours Mont-Royal shopping plaza. In summer, dining spills out onto a little terrace on rue Metcalfe. The daily table d'hôte menu is the best bet, with openers such as lobster bisque followed by *agneau en croûte* (lamb in a pastry) with thyme sauce, or fillet of halibut with leeks. For dessert try the *tatan* (apples and caramel with crème anglaise). ✉ *Les Cours Mont-Royal, 1444 rue Metcalfe, Downtown,* ☎ *514/842–3636. Reservations essential. AE, D, DC, MC, V. Closed Sun. No lunch weekends. Métro: Peel.*

$$$
★ ✕ **Le Passe-Partout.** The opening hours are eccentric, the location is relatively remote, and the room is a simple peach-color rectangle with about 40 seats, but the food is worth the trek to the residential West End. Chef James McGuire is one of the city's best, and his short, handwritten menu might include such starters as smoked salmon, potage of curried sweet potatoes, and perhaps a venison terrine. Main dishes include swordfish steak served with a purée of red cabbage, or the signature dish—rosy slices of crisp-skinned duck with pineapple pieces and tangy orange sauce. ✉ *3857 blvd. Décarie, Notre-Dame-de-Grace,* ☎ *514/487–7750. Reservations essential. AE, DC, MC, V. Closed Mon., Sun., and Wed. No dinner Tues. No lunch Fri.–Sat. Métro: Villa Maria.*

$$–$$$ ✕ **Bistro Boris.** A huge, tree-shaded terasse hidden behind the restored facade of a burned-out building is one of the best alfresco dining areas in the city. The bistro fare includes blood pudding, grilled fish, and chops, served with salad or fries. There is an indoor part, as well, which is just fine in winter. ✉ *465 rue McGill, Vieux-Montréal,* ☎ *514/848–9575. AE, D, DC, MC, V. Métro: Square-Victoria.*

$$–$$$ ✕ **Bistro Gourmet.** At chef Gabriel Ohana's tiny but richly atmospheric bistro, you can try such classics as rack of lamb with garlic, roasted shallot, and a stuffed broiled tomato; fillet of beef in a sauce spiked with blue cheese; and breast of duck over a wine-stewed pear. ✉ *2100 rue St-Mathieu, Downtown,* ☎ *514/846–1553. AE, D, DC, MC, V. No lunch weekends. Métro: Guy-Concordia.*

$$–$$$ ✕ **Bonaparte.** A cheerful fireplace and walls richly trimmed in impe-
★ rial purple and hung with sketches of Napoleonic soldiers set the tone, and the menu features traditional French dishes served with a light touch. You could start with a wild-mushroom ravioli seasoned with fresh sage and move on to a lobster stew flavored with vanilla and served with a spinach fondue, or a roast rack of lamb in port sauce. Lunch is a good value. Upstairs is a little auberge. ✉ *443 rue St-François-Xavier, Vieux-Montréal,* ☎ *514/844–4368. AE, D, DC, MC, V. No lunch weekends. Métro: Place-d'Armes.*

$–$$$ ✕ **Le Paris.** Every city should have a Le Paris. Its crowded dining
★ room, with big tables and age-dimmed paint, is as comfortable as the reasonably priced bourgeois fare that streams out of the kitchen. The *brandade de morue*—salt cod, potatoes, garlic, and cream—is famous, and dishes such as grilled boudin (blood sausage), calves' liver *meunière* (dusted with flour and sautéed), and tripe satisfy the soul. Desserts range from creamy pastries to comfort dishes like stewed rhubarb and *île flottant* (basically meringue floating in a sea of custard). ✉ *1812 rue Ste-Catherine Ouest, Downtown,* ☎ *514/937–4898. AE, DC, MC, V. No lunch Sun. Métro: Guy-Concordia.*

$–$$ ✕ **L'Express.** This Paris-style bistro has mirrored walls, a smoky atmosphere, and noise levels that are close to painful on weekends. But the food is good (even if the tiny crowded tables barely have room to accommodate it), the service fast, and the prices reasonable. The steak tartare with french fries, the salmon with sorrel, and the calves' liver with tarragon are marvelous. Jars of gherkins, fresh baguettes, and cheeses aged to perfection make the pleasure last longer. L'Express has one of the best and most original wine cellars in town. ✉ *3927 rue St-Denis, Plateau Mont-Royal,* ☎ *514/845–5333. Reservations essential. AE, DC, MC, V. Métro: Sherbrooke.*

Greek

$$$–$$$$ ✕ **Milos.** Don't let the nets and floats hanging from the ceiling fool you: this isn't a simple taverna but rather a first-class Greek restaurant. Paul Newman and Bette Midler are among the admirers who enjoyed Milos so much that they persuaded its eponymous owner to open a branch in New York City. The real display is the octopus, squid, shrimp, crabs, oysters, and sea urchins. The main dish is usually fish grilled over charcoal and seasoned with parsley, capers, and lemon juice. The fish are priced by the pound ($23–$32), and you can order one large fish to serve two or more. You can also find lamb and veal chops, cheeses, and olives. Milos is a healthy walk from the Laurier Métro. ✉ *5357 av. du Parc, Mile-End,* ☎ *514/272–3522. Reservations essential. AE, D, DC, MC, V. No lunch weekends. Métro: Laurier.*

$$–$$$ ✕ **Mythos Ouzerie.** Scores of incipient Zorbas come to this brick-lined semibasement every weekend to eat, drink, dance, and make merry in a Pan-inspired atmosphere of chaos and frenzy. The food is good every night—unctuous moussaka, plump stuffed vine leaves, grilled mushrooms, braised lamb, grilled squid—but go Thursday, Friday, or Saturday night when the live and very infectious bouzouki music makes it impossible to remain seated. If you want to burn those calories before you have a chance to digest them, this is the place. ⊠ *5318 av. Park, Mile-End,* ☎ *514/270–0235. AE, MC, V. No lunch. Métro: Laurier.*

$–$$$ ✗ **Rotisserie Panama.** No one seems to know why this big, noisy Greek taverna is named for a Latin American country, but who cares? It offers some of the best grilled meat in Montréal, at prices so reasonable you'll do a double take. The chicken and crispy lamb chops are excellent and on weekends you can order roasted baby lamb. The more adventurous might try the *kokoretsi* (various organ meats wrapped in intestines and grilled on a spit) or the *patsas,* a full-flavored tripe soup. And although the chefs specialize in meats, they have a deft hand with grilled fish and octopus as well. ⊠ *789 rue Jean-Talon Ouest, Mile-End,* ☎ *514/276–5223. AE, MC, V. Métro: Parc.*

Indian

$–$$ ✗ **Gandhi.** Standards like butter chicken, shrimp curry, and lamb vindaloo are served in a pleasant sunny room with yellow walls and immaculate white linen. ⊠ *230 rue St-Paul Ouest, Vieux-Montréal,* ☎ *514/845–5866. AE, MC, V. Métro: Place-d'Armes or Square-Victoria.*

$ ✗ **Le Taj.** The cuisine of the north of India, less spicy and more refined than that of the south, is showcased here. The tandoori ovens seal in the flavors of the grilled meat and fish. Among the vegetarian dishes are the *taj-thali,* which includes lentils, basmati rice, and *saag panir,* spicy white cheese with spinach. A nine-course lunch buffet is less than $10, and at night there's an "Indian feast" for $20. The desserts—pistachio ice cream or mangoes—are often decorated with pure silver leaves. ⊠ *2077 rue Stanley, Downtown,* ☎ *514/845–9015. AE, MC, V. Métro: Guy-Concordia.*

Italian

$$$–$$$$ ✗ **Il Mulino.** Nothing about the decor or the location of this family-run restaurant in Little Italy hints at the delights within. The antipasti alone—grilled mushrooms, stuffed eggplant, pizza, broiled scallops—are worth the trip. The pasta, too, is excellent, especially the agnolotti and the gnocchi. Main dishes include simply prepared lamb chops, veal, and excellent fish. ⊠ *236 rue St-Zotique Est, Little Italy,* ☎ *514/273–5776. Reservations essential. AE, DC, MC, V. Closed Sun.–Mon. Métro: de Castelnau.*

$$–$$$$ ✗ **Da Emma.** Massive stone pillars and wooden beams give this family-run restaurant on the Vieux-Port a genuinely Roman feel. So does the food. Seafood antipasto (squid, mussels, shrimp, and octopus drizzled with olive oil), fettuccine with porcini mushrooms, and suckling pig roasted with garlic and rosemary are among the highlights. ⊠ *777 rue de la Commune Ouest, Vieux-Montréal,* ☎ *514/392–1568. AE, D, DC, MC, V. No lunch Sat. Métro: Square-Victoria.*

$$–$$$ ✗ **Da Vinci.** The pioneering Mazzaferros were among the first to give Montrealers a taste for anchovies and take-out pizzas. You can no longer get an "all-dressed to go" (a pizza with everything) but you can sit down in the family's romantic Victorian town house and enjoy gnocchi with lamb ragù or seafood risotto and then follow that with cannoli. ⊠ *1180 rue Bishop, Downtown,* ☎ *514/874–2001. Reservations essential. AE, DC, MC, V. Closed Sun. Métro: Guy-Concordia.*

$$ ✗ **Tre Marie.** Hearty Italian family fare—think veal stew and baccala (salt cod) with polenta—is the trademark of this modest but very popular establishment opened in 1966 by sisters Rosina and Maria Fabrizio. ⊠ *6934 rue Clark, Little Italy,* ☎ *514/277–9859. Reservations essential. AE, DC, MC, V. Métro: de Catelnau.*

Japanese

$$–$$$ ✕ **Azuma.** The closest thing Montréal has to a Japanese bistro, Azuma keeps the price of its ultrafresh sushi and sashimis reasonable. ✉ *5264 blvd. St-Laurent, Laurier,* ☎ *514/271–5263. AE, DC, MC, V. Closed Mon. Métro: Laurier.*

$$–$$$ ✕ **Katsura.** Stick to impeccably fresh sushi at this stylish restaurant and you won't go wrong. Items include the spicy Kamikaze Roll—salmon, avocado, fried onion, and Masago roe. ✉ *2170 rue de la Montagne, Downtown,* ☎ *514/849–1172. Reservations essential. AE, DC, MC, V. No lunch weekends. Métro: Peel or Guy-Concordia.*

Middle Eastern

$$–$$$ ✕ **Restaurant Daou.** René Angelil and wife Céline Dion favor this casual spot, which serves some of the city's best Lebanese food—hummus with ground meat, stuffed grape leaves, and delicately seasoned kabobs. ✉ *519 rue Faillon, Villeray,* ☎ *514/276–8310. MC, V. Closed Mon. Métro: Parc.*

$–$$ ✕ **Alep.** Graze on *mouhamara* (pomegranate and walnuts), *sabanegh* (spinach and onions), *fattouche* (salad with pita and mint), and *yalanti* (vine leaves stuffed with rice, chickpeas, walnuts, and tomatoes) in a pleasant stone-walled room draped with ivy and full of young couples. Kabobs dominate the main courses. ✉ *199 rue Jean-Talon Est, Villeray,* ☎ *514/270–6396. MC, V. Closed Mon. Métro: Jean-Talon or de Castelnau.*

Peruvian

$–$$ ✕ **Pucapuca.** Dark green walls and Latin music give this bargain restaurant a vaguely junglelike atmosphere, and its mostly young aficionados give it a cheery air. But it's the Peruvian cooking and the great value that keep the crowds coming. The owner, Ciro Wong, serves up a particularly fine version of the classic Peruvian *papa huancaina,* a boiled potato covered with a spicy cheese sauce. Other items on the menu include grilled beef heart, rabbit with roasted peanuts, and grilled shark. ✉ *5400 blvd. St-Laurent, Plateau Mont-Royal,* ☎ *514/272–8029. No credit cards. Closed Sun.–Mon. Métro: Laurier.*

Polish

$–$$ ✕ **Café Stash.** On chilly nights many Montrealers turn to Café Stash in Vieux-Montréal for sustenance—for pork chops or duck, hot borscht, pierogi, or cabbage and sausage—in short, for all the hearty specialties of a Polish kitchen. Diners sit on pews from an old chapel at refectory tables from an old convent. ✉ *200 rue St-Paul Ouest, Vieux-Montréal,* ☎ *514/845–6611. AE, MC, V. Métro: Place-d'Armes.*

Portuguese

$$–$$$$ ✕ **Café Ferreira.** This high-ceilinged room with pale-yellow walls is decorated with antique pottery and bottles of aged port. It makes an elegant setting for the "haute" version of Portuguese cuisine. The traditional *caldo verde,* or green soup, shares space on the menu with grilled fresh sardines; baked salt cod topped with a tomato, onion and pepper salsa; and *arroz di marisco,* a paellalike dish rich with seafood, garlic, and onions. *1446 rue Peel, Downtown,* ☎ *514/848–0988. AE, MC, V. No lunch Sat. Métro: Peel.*

$ ✕ **Chez Doval.** Chicken and sometimes sardines, grouper, and squid sizzle on the open grill behind the bar. They can be eaten in the noisy, bright tavern or in the quieter, softly lit dining room. A guitarist works both rooms on weekends. *150 rue Marie Anne Est, Plateau Mont-Royal,* ☎ *514/843–3390. AE, MC, V. Métro: Mont-Royal.*

Seafood

$$–$$$$ ✕ **Maestro S.V.P.** Wine-red walls, etched glass, and a chalked menu board give this seafood spot a real bistro ambience. The musical instruments on the walls match the playfulness of the cooking. Oysters are the specialty—dozens of kinds from all over the world are always in stock. The rest of the menu is impressive, too—variations on mussels-and-fries, an excellent poached salmon with mango butter, and a bountiful fish and seafood pot-au-feu in a tomato-basil sauce. Appetizers include tender calamari as well as shrimp dipped in beer batter and rolled in shredded coconut, with a marmalade and horseradish sauce. ✉ *3615 blvd. St-Laurent, Plateau Mont-Royal,* ☎ *514/842–6447. AE, DC, MC, V. No lunch weekends. Métro: Sherbrooke.*

$$–$$$ ✕ **Chez Delmo.** The long, shiny wooden bar is crammed at lunchtime with lawyers and businesspeople gobbling oysters and fish. In the back is a more relaxed and cheerful dining room. The poached salmon with hollandaise is a nice slab of perfectly cooked fish served with potatoes and broccoli. Also excellent are the arctic char and the Dover sole. ✉ *211–215 rue Notre-Dame Ouest, Vieux-Montréal,* ☎ *514/849–4061. Reservations essential. AE, DC, MC, V. No dinner Mon. Closed Sun., 3 wks in Aug. and Christmas–mid-Jan. Métro: Place-d'Armes.*

Steak

$$$–$$$$ ✕ **Moishe's.** The Lighter brothers still age their big, marbled steaks in their own cold rooms for 21 days before charcoal-grilling them, just the way their father did when he opened Moishe's in 1938. There are other things on the menu, such as lamb and grilled arctic char—but people come for the beef. The selection of single-malt Scotches is exquisite. ✉ *3961 blvd. St-Laurent, Plateau Mont-Royal,* ☎ *514/ 845–3509. AE, DC, MC, V. No lunch. Métro: St.-Laurent.*

$–$$ ✕ **Magnan.** Defiantly masculine, this tavern in working-class Pointe St-Charles didn't give women full run of the place until 1988. Before that they were tolerated only in a small, coed dining room. The decor is upscale warehouse, with TV sets noisily stuck on sports. You can't beat the roast beef and steaks, though; everyone from dock workers to corporate executives comes here. The salmon pie is a delightfully stodgy filler that makes great picnic fare. Also on the menu are pigs' feet (*pattes de cochon*) and soul-satisfying desserts like sugar pie. In summer the tavern adds Québec lobster to its menu and turns its parking lot into an outdoor dining area. Excellent beer from several local microbreweries is on tap. ✉ *2602 rue St-Patrick, Pointe St-Charles,* ☎ *514/935–9647. AE, DC, MC, V. Métro: Charlevoix.*

$–$$ ✕ **Mr. Steer.** This unpretentious restaurant with vinyl booths and plain beige walls has several things going for it: a great location in the heart of the downtown shopping district, friendly if brisk service, and the best hamburgers in Montréal. The thick, juicy, almost globular patties, discreetly seasoned and served slightly *saignant* (rare) with a wide choice of almost unnecessary dressings and garnishes, are a worthy replacement for steak—although that's available, too, at reasonable prices. ✉ *1198 rue Ste-Catherine Ouest, Downtown,* ☎ *514/866–3233. MC, V. Métro: Peel.*

Thai

$–$$ ✕ **Chao Phraya.** The huge front window of this bright, airy restaurant with its subtle flashes of Asian decor overlooks fashionable rue

Laurier, from which it draws many of its upscale customers. They come to feast on such classics as crunchy, multiflavored *poe pia* (imperial rolls), *pha koung* (grilled-shrimp salad), and fried halibut in red curry with lime juice. ⊠ *50 rue Laurier Ouest, Laurier,* ☎ *514/272–5339. Reservations essential. AE, DC, MC, V. No lunch. Métro: Laurier.*

$–$$ ✕ **Salsa Thai.** The portions are generous and the prices reasonable at this popular Thai eatery on Square Dorchester. Among the appealing choices are hot-and-sour seafood soup with coconut milk; squid salad with onion, hot chilies, and mint leaves; and deep-fried whole pomfret (butterfish). Frogs' legs are fried with pepper, garlic, and sesame seeds; beef with *satay* sauce (a peanut-based sauce) comes on a sizzling-hot plate. ⊠ *1237 rue Metcalfe, Downtown,* ☎ *514/874–9047. MC, V. Métro: Peel.*

Vegetarian

$–$$ ✕ **Chu Chai.** Vegetarians can usually dine well in any Thai restaurant, even one that serves plenty of meat and fish dishes. But the chefs at Chu Chai—rigorously vegan in their cooking—see no reason vegetarians shouldn't be able to enjoy the same classic Thai dishes as their meat-eating compatriots. So they cook up such delicacies as "duck" salad with pepper and mint leaves, "fish" with three hot sauces, and "beef" with yellow curry and coconut milk, substituting soy and seitan (a firm, chewy meat substitute made from wheat gluten) for the offending flesh. ⊠ *4088 rue St-Denis, Plateau Mont-Royal,* ☎ *514/ 843–4194. Reservations essential. AE, DC, MC, V. Métro: Sherbrooke or Mont-Royal.*

$–$$ ✕ **Le Commensal.** The food at this Montréal-grown chain of vegetarian restaurants—heavy on salads, sandwiches, couscous, and delightfully "meaty" bean dishes—is served buffet style and sold by weight. There are at least seven outlets on the island, all of them big and bright with modern furniture; the nicest is on the second floor of a downtown building with big windows overlooking busy, fashionable rue McGill College. There's also one on rue St-Denis in the heart of the busy nightclub and shopping district and another on chemin Queen-Mary near the Oratoire St-Joseph. ⊠ *1205 rue McGill College, Downtown,* ☎ *514/871–1480. AE, DC, MC, V. Métro: McGill. Branch:* ⊠ *1720 rue St-Denis, Plateau Mont-Royal,* ☎ *514/845–2627. AE, DC, MC, V. Métro: St.-Laurent. Branch:* ⊠ *3715 chemin Queen-Mary, Côte-des-Neiges,* ☎ *514/733–9755. AE, DC, MC, V. Métro: Côte-des-Neiges.*

LODGING

Keep in mind that during peak season (May through August), finding a bed without reserving can be difficult. From mid-November to early April, rates often drop, and throughout the year many hotels have two-night, three-day double-occupancy packages that offer substantial discounts.

CATEGORY	COST*
$$$$	over $200
$$$	$150–$200
$$	$100–$150
$	under $100

All prices are for a standard double room at high season—excluding 7.5% provincial sales tax, 7% goods-and-services tax (GST), and a $2.30 city tax—in Canadian dollars.

$$$$ ★ 🏨 **Bonaventure Hilton International.** The large Hilton occupies the top three floors of the Place Bonaventure exhibition center. From the outside, the massive building is uninviting, but you step off the elevator into an attractive reception area flanked by an outdoor swimming pool (heated year-round) and 2½ acres of rooftop gardens. The rooms have sleek modern furniture and pastel walls. The location gives you excellent access to the Métro and the Underground City. ✉ *1 pl. Bonaventure, Downtown, H5A 1E4,* ☎ *514/878–2332 or 800/267–2575,* FAX *514/028–1442,* WEB *www.hilton.com. 360 rooms, 7 suites. Restaurant, room service, in-room data ports, minibars, room TVs with movies and video games, pool, gym, bar, shops, concierge, business services, meeting rooms, parking (fee), some pets allowed (fee). AE, D, DC, MC, V. EP. Métro: Bonaventure.*

$$$$ 🏨 **Château Versailles.** The two mansions that make up this luxury property were built at the turn-of-the-20th-century for some of the city's leading families. The hotel's rich decor and sumptuous furnishings reflect the Beaux Arts style of the architecture, which features high ceilings and plaster moldings. The marble fireplaces in many of the guest rooms and public rooms aren't just decorative—they actually work. ✉ *1659 rue Sherbrooke Ouest, Square Mile, H3H 1E3,* ☎ *514/933–3611 or 800/933–8111,* FAX *514/933–8401,* WEB *www.versailleshotels. com. 63 rooms, 2 suites. Restaurant, room service, in-room data ports, minibars, gym, sauna, bar, baby-sitting, dry cleaning, laundry service, concierge, business services, parking (fee). AE, DC, MC, V. CP. Métro: Guy-Concordia.*

$$$$ 🏨 **Fairmont Le Reine Elizabeth.** The Gare Centrale (the train station) is under this hotel, so it's no wonder the lobby is like a railroad station, with hordes marching this way and that. Upstairs, however, the rooms are modern, spacious, and spotless, with lush pale carpets, striped Regency wallpapers, and chintz bedspreads. The Penthouse floors—20 and 21—have business services, and the Gold Floor has its own elevator, check-in, and concierge. The hotel, host to many convention groups, is also home to the classic Beaver Club restaurant. ✉ *900 blvd. René-Lévesque Ouest, Downtown, H3B 4A5,* ☎ *514/861–3511 or 800/441–1414,* FAX *514/954–2256,* WEB *www.fairmont.com. 964 rooms, 100 suites. 2 restaurants, in-room data ports, some microwaves, cable TV with movies and video games, indoor pool, health club, hair salon, 3 bars, baby-sitting, concierge, concierge floors, meeting rooms, parking (fee), some pets allowed (fee). AE, D, DC, MC, V. EP. Métro: Bonaventure.*

$$$$ 🏨 **Hôtel Gault.** The street is gaslit and the facade is 19th-century, but the loft-style rooms in this boutique property are modern, with Tibetan rugs, concrete floors, minimalist decor, and bathrooms with heated floors. ✉ *449 rue Ste-Hélène, Vieux-Montréal, H2V 2K9,* ☎ *514/904–1616 or 866/904–1616,* WEB *www.hotelgault.com. 25 rooms, 5 suites. In-room data ports, minibars, cable TV with movies, gym, parking (fee). AE, D, DC, MC, V. CP. Métro: Square-Victoria.*

$$$$ 🏨 **Hôtel le Germain.** The hotelier Christiane Germain turned a dowdy, outdated, downtown office building into a sleekly luxurious boutique hotel that includes two huge two-story apartments. The earth-tone rooms showcase Québec-designed bed and bathroom furnishings in dark, dense tropical woods. All rooms have individual sound systems, three phones, and an iron and ironing board; some have grand views of the skyscrapers along avenue du Président-Kennedy or of Mont-Royal. ✉ *2050 rue Mansfield, Downtown, H3A 1Y9,* ☎ *514/849–2050 or 877/333–2050,* FAX *514/849–1437,* WEB *www.hotelgermain.com. 99 rooms, 2 apartments. Room service, in-room data ports, minibars, cable TV, gym, bar, parking (fee). AE, DC, MC, V. CP. Métro: Peel or McGill.*

$$$$ ⊞ **Hotel Nelligan.** Verses by Émile Nelligan, Québec's most revered poet, decorate the stone and brick walls in this boutique hotel on fashionable rue St-Paul. The hotel takes up two adjoining stone buildings—both built in the 1850s—one block north of the Vieux-Port and a block south of the Basilique Notre-Dame-de-Montréal. Some suites have terraces with river views. In summer, breakfast is served on the rooftop terrace. Complimentary wine and cheese are served every afternoon. ⊠ *106 rue St-Paul Ouest, Vieux-Montréal, H2Y 1Z3,* ☎ *514/788–2040 or 877/788–2040,* FAX *514/788–2041,* WEB *www.hotelnelligan.com. 37 rooms, 27 suites. Restaurant, room service, in-room data ports, in-room cable TV, gym, massage, bar, Internet, meeting rooms, parking (fee). AE, D, DC, MC, V. CP. Métro: Place d'Armes.*

$$$$ ⊞ **Hôtel Le St. James.** What used to be the Mercantile Bank of Canada is now a hotel lavishly furnished with antiques and antique reproductions. One of the rooms, with 20-ft ceilings and lovingly restored murals of hydroelectric dams and waterfalls, was a boardroom. There's no dining room but the hotel's kitchen provides 24-hour room service and light meals and afternoon tea are available on the ground floor or the balcony of the two-story lobby bar, which used to be the main banking room. Guest rooms include large marble bathrooms with separate tubs and showers and have Bang & Olufsen sound systems; some rooms and suites have gas fireplaces. ⊠ *355 rue St-Jacques, Vieux-Montréal, H2Y 1N9,* ☎ *866/841–3111 or 514/841–3111,* FAX *514/841–1232,* WEB *www.lhw.com. 64 rooms, 21 suites. Room service, in-room data ports, room TVs with movies, gym, spa, bar, library, concierge, meeting rooms, parking (fee). AE, D, DC, MC, V. EP. Métro: Place d'Armes.*

$$$$ ⊞ **Hotel St. Paul.** Stark white walls and huge shuttered windows give the standard rooms in this converted 19th-century office building a light, ethereal feel. All guest rooms have separate sitting areas with sleek leather furniture. The hotel's Cube restaurant offers some of the city's most innovative dining. ⊠ *355 rue McGill, H2Y 2E8, Vieux-Montréal,* ☎ *514/380–2222 or 866/380–2222,* FAX *514/380–2200,* WEB *www.hotelstpaul. com. 96 rooms, 24 suites. Restaurant, room service, in-room data ports, in-room fax, minibars, in-room cable TV with movies, gym, massage, bar, business services. AE, D, DC, MC, V. EP. Métro: Square-Victoria.*

$$$$ ⊞ **Loews Hôtel Vogue.** Tall windows and a facade of polished rose gran-
 ★ ite grace this chic hotel in the heart of downtown. The lobby's focal point, L'Opéra Bar, has an expansive bay window overlooking the trendy rue de la Montagne. Guest-room furnishings are upholstered with striped silk, and the beds are draped with lacy duvets. The bathrooms have whirlpool baths, TVs, and phones. ⊠ *1425 rue de la Montagne, Downtown, H3G 1Z3,* ☎ *514/285–5555 or 800/465–6654,* FAX *514/ 849–8903,* WEB *www.loewshotels.com. 126 rooms, 16 suites. Restaurant, room service, in-room data ports, in-room fax, minibars, cable TV, gym, sauna, bar, meeting rooms, parking (fee). AE, D, DC, MC, V. EP. Métro: Peel.*

$$$$ ⊞ **Pierre du Calvet** AD **1725.** Merchant Pierre du Calvet—a notorious
 ★ republican and Freemason—entertained Benjamin Franklin behind the stone walls of this 18th-century home in Vieux-Montréal. Today it's an almost all-suites B&B luxuriously decorated with antique furniture and Oriental rugs. The French restaurant is first-rate, and the glassed-in garden, filled with flowers and potted plants, is lovely. ⊠ *405 rue Bonsecours, Vieux-Montréal, H2Y 3C3,* ☎ *514/282–1725,* FAX *514/282–0546,* WEB *www.pierreducalvet.ca. 1 room, 8 suites. Dining room, in-room data ports, no room TVs, library, meeting room, parking (fee). AE, D, DC, MC, V. BP. Métro: Champ-de-Mars.*

$$$$ ⊞ **Ritz-Carlton.** The guest rooms at Montréal's grandest hotel are a suc-
 ★ cessful blend of Edwardian style—all rooms have marble baths and some

suites have working fireplaces—and modern amenities. Careful and personal attention are hallmarks of the Ritz-Carlton's service: your shoes are shined, there's fresh fruit in your room, and everyone calls you by name. Power meals are the rule at Le Café de Paris, which also serves a formal afternoon tea. ✉ *1228 rue Sherbrooke Ouest, Square Mile, H3G 1H6,* ☎ *514/842–4212, 800/363–0366, 800/241–3333,* FAX *514/842–3383,* WEB *www.ritzcarlton.com. 185 rooms, 45 suites. Restaurant, room service, in-room data ports, minibars, cable TV with video games, gym, bar, concierge, business services, parking (fee), some pets allowed (fee). AE, DC, MC, V. EP. Métro: Peel or Guy-Concordia.*

$$$$ 🏨 **Le St. Sulpice.** The Basilique Notre-Dame-de-Montréal is next door
★ and the comfortable lobby lounge and bar open onto a courtyard garden that's one of the rare green spots in Vieux-Montréal's stony landscape. The lodgings—all huge suites with queen-size beds, feather duvets, leather armchairs, and casement windows that actually open—are housed in a structure built in 2002 to fit into the old neighborhood; the gym and business center are in an adjoining 19th-century building. Some suites have fireplaces and balconies. ✉ *414 rue St-Sulpice, Vieux-Montréal, H2Y 2V5,* ☎ *514/288–1000 or 877/785–7423,* FAX *514/288–0077,* WEB *www.lesaintsulpice.com. 108 suites. Room service, minibars, microwaves, in-suite cable TV with movies and video games, gym, massage, business services, meeting rooms, parking (fee), some pets allowed (fee). AE, D, DC, MC, V. BP. Métro: Place-d'Armes.*

$$$–$$$$ 🏨 **Auberge du Vieux-Port.** The rooms' stone and brick walls date to
★ the 1880s and their tall casement windows overlook either fashionable rue St-Paul or the Vieux-Port. Brass beds and massive exposed beams add to the period feel. In summer, you can watch the fireworks competitions from a rooftop terrace. A full breakfast is served in Les Remparts, the hotel's French restaurant. ✉ *97 rue de la Commune Est, Vieux-Montréal, H2Y 1J1,* ☎ *514/876–0081 or 888/660–7678,* FAX *514/876–8923,* WEB *www.aubergeduvieuxport.com. 27 rooms. Restaurant, in-room data ports, parking (fee), some pets allowed (fee); no smoking. AE, DC, MC, V. BP. Métro: Place d'Armes or Champ-de-Mars.*

$$$–$$$$ 🏨 **Delta Montréal.** The Delta has the city's most complete exercise and pool facility and an extensive business center. The hotel's public areas spread over two stories and look a bit like a French château, with a huge baronial chandelier and gold patterned carpets. Rooms are big, with plush broadloom, mahogany-veneer furniture, and windows that overlook the mountain or downtown. The Cordial Music bar serves lunch on weekdays. ✉ *475 av. du Président-Kennedy, Downtown, H3A 1J7,* ☎ *514/286–1986 or 800/268–1133,* FAX *514/284–4306,* WEB *www.deltamontreal.com. 453 rooms, 8 suites. Restaurant, in-room data ports, minibars, cable TV with video games, 1 indoor and 1 outdoor pool, gym, sauna, squash, bar, recreation room, baby-sitting, concierge, business services, meeting rooms, parking (fee), some pets allowed (fee). AE, D, DC, MC, V. EP. Métro: McGill or Place des Arts.*

$$$–$$$$ 🏨 **Hotel Inter-Continental Montréal.** On the edge of Vieux-Montréal, this luxury hotel is part of the Montréal World Trade Center, a block-long retail and office development. Rooms are in a modern 26-story brick tower with fanciful turrets and pointed roofs. They're large, with lush carpets, pastel walls, heavy drapes, and big windows overlooking downtown or Vieux-Montréal and the waterfront. The bathrooms have separate marble tubs and showers. The main lobby is home to Le Continent, which serves fine international cuisine. A footbridge across the Trade Center's mall links the hotel with the 18th-century Nordheimer Building, which houses many of the hotel's public rooms. ✉ *360 rue St-Antoine Ouest, Vieux-Montréal, H2Y 3X4,* ☎ *514/987–9900 or 800/827–0200,* FAX *514/847–8730,* WEB *www.montreal.interconti.com. 332 rooms, 25 suites. 3 restaurants, room service, in-room data ports,*

Montréal Lodging

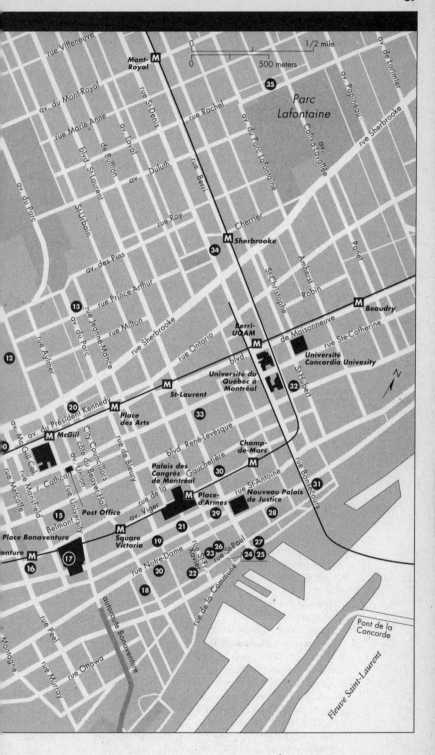

0   1/2 mile
0   500 meters

Mont-Royal

rue Villeneuve

av. du Mont-Royal

rue Marie-Anne

blvd. St-Laurent

de Bullion

av. Laval

rue St-Denis

av. Duluth

rue Berri

rue Rachel

Parc Lafontaine

35

av. du Parc Lafontaine

av. Calixa-Lavallée

av. Papineau

av. de Lorimier

rue Sherbrooke

St-Urbain

av. du Parc

rue Roy

Cherrier

Sherbrooke

34

av. des Pins

rue Prince-Arthur

13

av. du Parc

rue Jeanne-Mance

rue Milton

rue Sherbrooke

rue Ontario

St-Christophe

Amherst

Robin

Panet

Beaudry

12

rue Aylmer

Berri-UQAM

de Maisonneuve

rue Ste-Catherine

Université Concordia Univesity

blvd.

Université du Québec à Montréal

St-Hubert

32

20

av. du Président Kennedy

Place des Arts

St-Laurent

33

av. McGill Col.

McGill

City Councillors

côte du Beaver-Hall

rue de Bleury

blvd. René-Lévesque

Champ-de-Mars

0

r. Cathcart

rue University

Gauchetière

Palais des Congrès de Montréal

30

rue St-Antoine

Nouveau Palais de Justice

31

rue Bonsecours

rue Mansfield

rue Metcalfe

Post Office

rue de la

Place-d'Armes

29

28

15

Belmont

av. Viger

21

Place Bonaventure

Square Victoria

19

rue Notre-Dame

26

rue St-Paul

27

enture

16

17

20

rue St-François-Xavier

23

22

24 **25**

18

rue de la Commune

autoroute Bonaventure

rue Peel

rue Ottawa

Montagne

rue Murray

Pont de la Concorde

Fleuve Saint-Laurent

minibars, room TVs with movies and video games, indoor pool, health club, sauna, bar, meeting rooms, parking (fee). AE, D, DC, MC, V. EP. Métro: Square-Victoria.

$$$–$$$$ 🏨 **Hôtel de la Montagne.** A naked nymph rises out of the fountain in the lobby, and an enormous crystal chandelier hangs from the ceiling. The rooms, large and comfortable, are tamer. There's a piano bar and a rooftop terrace, and a tunnel connects the hotel to Thursdays/Les Beaux Jeudis, a popular singles bar, restaurant, and dance club. ⊠ *1430 rue de la Montagne, Downtown, H3G 1Z5,* ☎ *514/288–5656 or 800/361–6262,* ℻ *514/288–9658,* 🕸 *www.hoteldelamontagne.com. 135 rooms. 2 restaurants, room service, minibars, in-room data ports, room TVs with movies and video games, pool, bar, piano bar, concierge, meeting rooms, parking (fee), some pets allowed (fee). AE, D, DC, MC, V. EP. Métro: Peel.*

$$$–$$$$ 🏨 **Hôtel Omni Mont-Royal.** Color, flair, and marble bathrooms dress
★   up this hotel's large, sunny rooms. Opus II, a contemporary French restaurant, occupies a street-level atrium, which gives it the air of an upscale sidewalk café. A Chinese restaurant, the Zen, is in the basement. ⊠ *1050 rue Sherbrooke Est, Downtown, H3A 2R6,* ☎ *514/284–1110 or 800/843–6664,* ℻ *514/845–3025,* 🕸 *www.omnihotels.com. 275 rooms, 25 suites. 2 restaurants, room service, in-room data ports, minibars, room TVs with movies and video games, pool, health club, hot tub, sauna, parking (fee). AE, D, DC, MC, V. EP. Métro: Peel.*

$$$–$$$$ 🏨 **Hôtel Place d'Armes.** The Basilique Notre-Dame-de-Montréal is
★   just across the square and the Palais de Congrès, the convention center, is 300 ft to the north. The ornately Victorian building, once the Canadian headquarters of the Great Scottish Life Insurance Co., has been converted into a comfortable boutique hotel with a fireplace and a bar in the lobby. Furnishings are contemporary, but some of the rooms have brick or stone walls. The bathrooms are tiled in black granite and white marble, and there are four duplex suites. A rooftop terrace with a view of Chinatown and the old city adds a crowning touch. ⊠ *701 Côte de la Place d'Armes, Vieux-Montréal, H2Y 2X6,* ☎ *514/842–1887 or 888/450–1887,* ℻ *514/842–6469,* 🕸 *www.hotelplacedarmes. com. 44 rooms, 4 suites. Restaurant, room service, in-room data ports, minibars, cable TV, gym, bar, meeting rooms, parking (fee). AE, DC, MC, V. BP. Métro: Place d'Armes.*

$$$–$$$$ 🏨 **Le Marriott Château Champlain.** At the southern end of Place du Canada is this 36-floor skyscraper with distinctive half-moon-shape windows that give the rooms a Moorish feeling. The furniture is elegant and French. Underground passageways connect the Champlain with the Bonaventure Métro station and Place Ville-Marie. ⊠ *1050 rue de la Gauchetière Ouest, Downtown, H3B 4C9,* ☎ *514/878–9000 or 800/200–5909,* ℻ *514/878–6761,* 🕸 *www.marriott.com. 611 rooms, 33 suites. Restaurant, in-room data ports, minibars, cable TV with movies, indoor pool, gym, sauna, bar, meeting rooms, parking (fee); no-smoking rooms. AE, DC, MC, V. EP. Métro: Bonaventure.*

$$$–$$$$ 🏨 **Renaissance Montréal.** The L-shape brick tower has large, bright rooms, a comfortable lobby bar, and a good restaurant, but it's the location that sets it apart. It overlooks Parc du Mont-Royal, which is close enough for athletic guests to consider jogging on its trails. The McGill University campus is a five-minute walk to the west and downtown is not much farther. ⊠ *3625 av. du Parc, Downtown, H2X 3P8,* ☎ *514/288–6666 or 800/363–0735,* ℻ *514/288–2469,* 🕸 *www. renaissancehotels.com. 455 rooms. Restaurant, café, in-room data ports, minibars, cable TV with movies, pool, gym, hair salon, bar, meeting rooms; no-smoking floors. AE, D, DC, MC, V. EP. Métro: Place des Arts.*

$$$-$$$$ ⬚ **Springhill Marriott.** The modern all-suites hotel with eight stories and plenty of amenities fits seamlessly into one of the narrowest and oldest streets of Vieux-Montréal. The Vieux-Port is a five-minute walk to the south and Place Jacques-Cartier is three blocks east. ⊠ *445 rue St-Jean-Baptiste, Vieux-Montréal, H2Y 2Z7,* ☎ *514/875–4333,* FAX *514/ 875–4331,* WEB *www.springhillsuites.com. 189 suites. Restaurant, room service, in-room data ports, minibars, cable TV with movies, indoor pool, bar, meeting rooms, parking (fee). AE, D, DC, MC, V. EP. Métro: Champ-de-Mars.*

$$-$$$$ ⬚ **Le Centre Sheraton.** The busy lobby bar of the city's biggest convention hotel is a pleasant forest of potted trees. Rues Crescent and Bishop, lined with clubs and restaurants, are just a few blocks away. The 10 Club floors are geared toward business travelers. ⊠ *1201 blvd. René-Lévesque Ouest, Downtown, H3B 2L7,* ☎ *514/878–2000 or 888/627–7102,* FAX *514/878–3958,* WEB *www.starwood.com/shera-ton. 785 rooms, 40 suites. 3 restaurants, in-room data ports, minibars, cable TV with movies and video games, indoor pool, gym, hair salon, 2 bars, baby-sitting, business services, meeting rooms, parking (fee). AE, D, DC, MC, V. EP. Métro: Bonaventure or Peel.*

$$-$$$$ ⬚ **Holiday Inn Select.** This Chinatown hotel is full of surprises, from the two pagodas on the roof to the Chinese garden in the lobby. Its restaurant, Chez Chine, is excellent. An executive floor has all the usual business facilities. The hotel has a small gym, but guests also have access to a plush private health and leisure club downstairs with a whirlpool, saunas, a billiard room, and a bar. The hotel—built according to Feng Shui principles—sits catercorner to the Palais des Congrès convention center and is a five-minute walk from the World Trade Center. ⊠ *99 av. Viger Ouest, Chinatown, H2Z 1E9,* ☎ *514/878–9888 or 888/878–9888,* FAX *514/878–6341,* WEB *www.sixcontinentshotels.com. 235 rooms, 6 suites. Restaurant, in-room data ports, minibars, in-room cable TV with movies and video games, indoor pool, gym, spa, bar, business center, meeting rooms, parking (fee). AE, D, DC, MC, V. EP. Métro: Place d'Armes.*

$$-$$$$ ⬚ **Hôtel du Fort.** All rooms here have good views of the city, the river, or the mountain. The hotel is in a residential neighborhood known as Shaughnessy Village, close to shopping at the Faubourg Ste-Catherine and Square Westmount, and just around the corner from the Canadian Center for Architecture. Rates include Continental breakfast served in a charming Louis XV lounge. ⊠ *1390 rue du Fort, Shaughnessy Village, H3H 2R7,* ☎ *514/938–8333 or 800/565–6333,* FAX *514/ 938–2078,* WEB *www.hoteldufort.com. 103 rooms, 24 suites. In-room data ports, kitchenettes, cable TV, gym, bar, meeting rooms, parking (fee). AE, DC, MC, V. CP. Métro: Atwater.*

$$-$$$$ ⬚ **Hôtel de l'Institut.** Students at the Institut de Tourisme et d'Hôtellerie du Québec—the province's leading hotel school—learn the art of pampering guests at this hotel on the institute's top floors. The building is gracelessly modern, but it overlooks charming Square St-Louis. Student waiters and chefs staff the Restaurant Salle Gérard-Delage. ⊠ *3535 rue St-Denis, Quartier Latin, H2X 3P1,* ☎ *514/282–5120 or 800/ 361–5111,* FAX *514/873–9893,* WEB *www.hotel.ithq.qc.ca. 40 rooms, 2 suites. Restaurant, cable TV, parking (fee). AE, MC, V. CP. Métro: Sherbrooke.*

$$$ ⬚ **Auberge de la Place Royale.** A 19th-century stone rooming house has been converted into a waterfront B&B overlooking the Vieux-Port. A magnificent old wooden staircase links the floors. Guest rooms, furnished with antiques and antique reproductions, are spacious; some have whirlpool baths. In summer you get a full breakfast on a sidewalk terrace; in winter it's served in your room. The service is very attentive. ⊠ *115 rue de la Commune Ouest, Vieux-Montréal, H2Y 2C7,*

☎ 514/287–0522, FAX 514/287–1209, WEB *www.aubergeplaceroyale.com.*
*9 rooms, 3 suites. Café, in-room data ports, in-room VCRs, parking
(fee); no smoking. AE, DC, MC, V. BP. Métro: Place d'Armes.*

$$–$$$ ☒ **Auberge Bonaparte.** One of the finest restaurants in Vieux-Mont-
★ réal—Bonaparte—has converted the upper floors of its 19th-century
building into an inn. The guest rooms have wrought-iron or Louis
Philippe–style furniture; some have double whirlpool baths, and the
back rooms (some with balconies) have views over the private gardens
of the Basilique Notre-Dame-de-Montréal. Breakfast is served in your
room. ⊠ *447 rue St-François-Xavier, Vieux-Montréal, H2Y 2T1,* ☎
*514/844–1448, FAX 514/844–0272, WEB www.bonaparte.ca. 30 rooms,
1 suite. Restaurant, in-room data ports, cable TV, bar, meeting room,
parking (fee). AE, D, DC, MC, V. BP. Métro: Place d'Armes.*

$$–$$$ ☒ **Auberge de la Fontaine.** The decor of this small hotel overlooking
★ Parc Lafontaine sounds wild—contrasting purple and bare-brick walls,
red molding, yellow walls, green ceilings—but the hotel is delightful.
Its rooms are in two adjoining turn-of-the-20th-century residences; some
have whirlpool baths and a few have private balconies. Guests can use
the little ground-floor kitchen and take whatever they like from its re-
frigerator full of snacks. ⊠ *1301 rue Rachel Est, Plateau Mont-Royal,
H2J 2K1,* ☎ *514/597–0166 or 800/597–0597, FAX 514/597–0496, WEB
www.aubergedelafontaine.com. 18 rooms, 3 suites. Cable TV, meeting rooms, parking (fee). AE, DC, MC, V. BP. Métro: Mont-Royal.*

$$ ☒ **Auberge les Passants du Sans Soucy.** The lobby is an art gallery,
★ the building is a 19th-century fur warehouse, and the fireplace that sep-
arates the living and breakfast rooms crackles with burning wood in
winter. The rooms have brass beds, stone walls, exposed beams, soft
lighting, whirlpool baths, and lots of fresh-cut flowers. ⊠ *171 rue St-
Paul Ouest, Vieux-Montréal, H2Y 1Z5,* ☎ *514/842–2634, FAX 514/842–
2912. 9 rooms, 1 suite. Cable TV, lounge, meeting room. AE, MC, V.
BP. Métro: Square-Victoria or Place d'Armes.*

$$ ☒ **Hôtel Lord Berri.** Rooms in this hotel near the restaurants and
nightlife of rue St-Denis have modern furniture and in-room movies.
The restaurant, Il Cavaliere, serves Italian food and is popular with
locals. ⊠ *1199 rue Berri, Downtown, H2L 4C6,* ☎ *514/845–9236 or
888/363–0363, FAX 514/849–9855, WEB www.lordberri.com. 148 rooms,
6 suites. Restaurant, room TVs with movies, meeting rooms, parking
(fee); no-smoking floors. AE, DC, MC, V. EP. Métro: Berri-UQAM.*

$ ☒ **Hostelling International.** This hostel in the heart of downtown has
same-sex dorm rooms that sleep 4, 6, or 10 people. If you're not Canadian, you must have a Hostelling International membership to stay here;
however, you have the option of paying $4.60 a day for temporary mem-
bership for up to six days. Members pay $19 for a dormitory bed, non-
members (Canadians only) $25. Some rooms are available for couples
($52 members, $64 nonmembers) and families. There are kitchen facilities and lockers for valuables. Reserve early for summer. ⊠ *1030
rue MacKay, Downtown, H3G 2H1,* ☎ *514/843–3317, FAX 514/934–
3251, WEB www.hostellingmontreal.com. 243 beds. Café, laundry facilities. AE, DC, MC, V. EP. Métro: Lucien-L'Allier.*

$ ☒ **Hôtel l'Abri du Voyageur.** Price and location are this hotel's main
selling points, but Hôtel l'Abri du Voyageur also manages to squeeze
in some unassuming charm: high ceilings, bare-brick walls, original pine
and maple floors, and paintings by local artists. The hotel's three floors
are over a restaurant in a pre–World War I commercial building. Each
room has a TV and a sink. Studios with a kitchenette and private bath
also are available. ⊠ *9 rue Ste-Catherine Ouest, Downtown, H2X
1Z5,* ☎ *514/849–2922, FAX 514/499–0151, WEB www.abri-voyageur.ca.*

30 rooms with shared bath, 12 suites with private bath. Fans, cable TV, parking (fee); no air-conditioning in some rooms. AE, MC, V. EP. Métro: St-Laurent.

$ 🖫 **McGill Student Apartments.** From mid-May to mid-August, when McGill is on summer recess, you can stay in the school's dorms on the grassy, quiet campus in the heart of the city. Nightly rates are $32 for students, $38 for nonstudents (single rooms only); some more-expensive rooms include a kitchenette. As a visitor, you may use the campus swimming pool and gym facilities for a fee. The university cafeteria is also open during the week, serving breakfast and lunch. Be sure to book early. ✉ *3935 rue University, Downtown, H3A 2B4,* ☎ *514/398–6367,* FAX *514/398–6770. 1,000 rooms with shared bath. Kitchenettes (some). MC, V. Closed mid-Aug.–mid-May. EP. Métro: McGill.*

$ 🖫 **Université de Montréal Residence.** The university's student housing accepts visitors from early May to late August. It's on the opposite side of Mont-Royal from downtown and Vieux-Montréal but next to the Edouard-Monpetit Métro station. The rooms have phones for local calls; common lounges have microwaves and TVs. For a fee you may use the campus sports facilities. Rates are $23 per night or $141 per week—$87.50 a week if you book for at least three weeks. ✉ *2350 blvd. Edouard-Montpetit, Outremont, H3T 1J4,* ☎ *514/343–6531,* FAX *514/343–2353. 1,119 rooms with shared bath. MC, V. Closed late Aug.–early May. EP. Métro: Edouard-Monpetit.*

$ 🖫 **YWCA.** Very close to dozens of restaurants, the Y is downtown, one block from rue Ste-Catherine. Men can use the overnight facilities and gym, too. There are single, double, and triple rooms. If you want a room with any amenities, you must book in advance; not all the rooms come with a sink and bath. ✉ *1355 blvd. René-Lévesque Ouest, Downtown, H3G 1T3,* ☎ *514/866–9941,* FAX *514/861–1603,* WEB *www.ywca-mtl. qc.ca/. 63 rooms. Café, indoor pool, aerobics, gym, sauna. MC, V. EP. Métro: Lucien L'Allier.*

NIGHTLIFE AND THE ARTS

Updated by Paul and Julie Waters and Melanie Reffes

The Friday Preview section of the *Gazette,* the English-language daily paper, has an especially thorough list of all events at the city's concert halls, theaters, clubs, dance spaces, and movie houses. Other publications listing what's on include the *Mirror, Hour, Scope,* and *Voir* (in French), distributed free at restaurants and other public places.

For tickets to major pop and rock concerts, shows, festivals, and hockey and baseball games, you can go to the individual box offices or call **Admission** (☎ 514/790–1245 or 800/361–4595). Tickets to Théâtre St-Denis and other venues are available via **Ticketmaster** (☎ 514/790–1111).

The Arts

Circus

The **Cirque du Soleil** (☎ 514/722–2234 or 800/361–4595, WEB www. cirquedusoleil.com) is one of Montréal's great success stories. The company began revolutionizing the ancient art of circus when it opened in a blue-and-yellow striped tent on the Montréal waterfront in 1984; its shows, which since have become an international phenomenon, combine dance, acrobatics, glorious costumes, and dramatic presentation. Touring companies attract adoring crowds all over North America, Europe, and Asia. Every couple of summers, the circus sets up its tent in the Vieux-Port.

Dance

Traditional and contemporary dance companies thrive in Montréal, though many take to the road or are on hiatus in the summer. **Ballets Classiques de Montréal** (☎ 514/866–1771) performs mostly classical programs. **Les Ballets Jazz de Montréal** (☎ 514/982–6771) experiments with new musical forms. The leading Québec company is **Les Grands Ballets Canadiens** (☎ 514/849–0269). **LaLaLa Human Steps** (☎ 514/277–9090) is an avant-garde, exciting powerhouse of a group. **Margie Gillis Fondation de Danse** (☎ 514/845–3115) gives young dancers and choreographers opportunities to develop their art. **Montréal Danse** (☎ 514/871–4005) is a contemporary dance repertory company. **Ouest Vertigo Danse** (☎ 514/251–9177) stages innovative, contemporary performances. **Tangente** (☎ 514/525–5584) is a nucleus for many of the more avant-garde dance troupes.

Montréal's dancers have a downtown performance and rehearsal space, the **Agora Dance Theatre** (✉ 840 rue Cherrier Est, Downtown, ☎ 514/525–1500), affiliated with the Université du Québec à Montréal dance faculty.

Film

Several multiscreen complexes show newly released movies in both English and French. At the west end of the city is the **AMC Forum** (✉ 2313 rue Ste-Catherine Ouest, Downtown, ☎ 514/904–1274), once the home ice of the Montréal Canadiens. Its 22 screens feature plenty of Hollywood biggies, but it also shows some foreign-language and indie productions. The complex includes several restaurants, a bar, a pool room, coffee shops, and gift shops. At the **Ciné Express Café** (✉ 1926 rue Ste-Catherine Ouest, Downtown, ☎ 514/939–2463), you can drop in for a drink, a bistro-style meal, and an old flick. Montréal's main repertory cinema theater is **Cinéma du Parc** (✉ 3575 av. du Parc, Downtown, ☎ 514/281–1900). The **Cinémathèque Québecoise** (✉ 335 blvd. de Maisonneuve Est, Quartier Latin, ☎ 514/842–9763, WEB www.cinematheque.qc.ca) has a collection of 25,000 Québec, Canadian, and foreign films, as well as a display of equipment dating from the early days of film. Cinephiles looking for the best in independent productions—both Canadian and foreign—head for **Ex Centris** (✉ 3536 blvd. St-Laurent, Plateau Mont-Royal, ☎ 514/847–3536 or 877/847–3536, WEB www.ex-centris.com). Its three comfortable theaters are equipped to screen digital new-media works. Ex Centris is worth a visit just to see the huge rotating clock in the lobby and the flashy bathrooms with reflective metal walls. The most elaborate of Montréal's cinemas is the **Famous Players Paramount** (✉ 707 rue Ste-Catherine Ouest, Downtown, ☎ 514/842–5828), in the old Simpson building. It has two IMAX theaters in addition to 15 rooms with regular screens—all showing Hollywood blockbusters. The stately **Impérial** (✉ 1430 rue Bleury, Downtown, ☎ 514/848–0300), where the sumptuous decor of the golden age of movies has been retained, shows a selection of foreign and independent productions. At the **NFB Montréal** (National Film Board; ✉ 1564 rue St-Denis, Quartier Latin, ☎ 514/496–6887, WEB www.nfb.ca), cinephiles can browse through the national Film Board of Canada's collection of 6,000 documentaries, dramas, short features, and animated flicks.

Music

The city is home to one of the best chamber orchestras in Canada, **I Musici de Montréal** (☎ 514/982–6037). The **Orchestre Métropolitain de Montréal** (☎ 514/598–0870) stars at Place des Arts most weeks during the October–April season. When it's not on tour, the **Orchestre Symphonique de Montréal** (☎ 514/842–9951) plays at the Salle

Wilfrid-Pelletier at the Place des Arts. The orchestra also gives Christmas and summer concerts in Basilique Notre-Dame-de-Montréal and pop concerts at the Arena Maurice Richard in Olympic Park. For its free summertime concerts in Montréal's city parks, check the *Gazette* listings.

McGill University's **Pollack Concert Hall** (☎ 514/398–4535) presents concerts, notably by the **McGill Chamber Orchestra**. The **Spectrum** (✉ 318 rue Ste-Catherine Ouest, Downtown, ☎ 514/861–5851) is an intimate concert hall. **Stade Olympique** (✉ Olympic Park, 4141 av. Pierre-de-Coubertin, Hochelaga–Maisonneuve, ☎ 514/252–8687) hosts rock and pop concerts. The 2,500-seat **Théâtre St-Denis** (✉ 1594 rue St-Denis, Quartier Latin, ☎ 514/849–4211), the second-largest auditorium in Montréal, stages a wide range of pop-music concerts performed in both languages, from Maritime folk singer Rita MacNeil to Québecois heartthrob Roch Voisine.

Opera
L'Opéra de Montréal (☎ 514/985–2258) stages four productions a year at Place des Arts.

Theater
French speakers can find a wealth of dramatic productions. There are at least 10 major companies in town, some of which have an international reputation. The choices for Anglophones are more limited. **Théâtre Denise Pelletier** (✉ 4353 rue Ste-Catherine Est, Hochelaga-Maisonneuve, ☎ 514/253–8974) puts on a wide range of productions in a beautifully restored Italianate hall. Named for one of Québec's best-loved actors, the **Théâtre Jean Duceppe** (☎ 514/842–2112) stages major productions in the Place des Arts. **Théâtre du Nouveau Monde** (✉ 84 rue Ste-Catherine Ouest, Downtown, ☎ 514/866–8667) is the North American temple of French classics. The **Théâtre de Quat'Sous** (✉ 100 av. des Pins Est, Downtown, ☎ 514/845–7277) performs modern, experimental, and cerebral plays. Modern French repertoire is the specialty at **Théâtre du Rideau Vert** (✉ 4664 rue St-Denis, Quartier Latin, ☎ 514/844–1793).

The **Centaur Theatre** (✉ 453 rue St-François-Xavier, Vieux-Montréal, ☎ 514/288–3161), the best-known English theatrical company, stages everything from musical revues to Eugène Ionesco works in the former stock exchange building in Vieux-Montréal. **Place des Arts** (✉ 175 rue Ste-Catherine Ouest, Downtown, ☎ 514/842–2112, WEB www.pda.qc.ca) is a favorite venue for visiting productions. English-language plays can be seen at the **Saidye Bronfman Centre** (✉ 5170 chemin de la Côte Ste-Catherine, Côte-des-Neiges, ☎ 514/739–2301 or 514/739–7944), an arts center for Montréal as a whole and for the Jewish community in particular. Plays in English are presented most of the year, but in May the Yiddish Theatre Group takes over the stage. Touring Broadway productions often can be seen at the **Théâtre St-Denis** (✉ 1594 rue St-Denis, Quartier Latin, ☎ 514/849–4211), especially in summer.

Festivals

Montréal loves a party, and every year festivals are held to celebrate everything from beer to French songwriting; here are some of the largest.

At the **Concours d'Art International Pyrotechnique** (International Fireworks Competition; ☎ 514/935–5161, 800/361–4595 in Canada, 800/678–5440, WEB www.montrealfeux.com), held mostly on weekends in late June and July (call for exact dates), teams from around the world compete to see who can best light up the sky in a show that combines fire-works and music. Their launch site is La Ronde, on Île Ste-Hélène, and you can buy a ticket, which includes an amusement-park pass and a re-served seat with a view, but thousands of Montrealers fill the Jacques-Cartier Bridge to watch the show for nothing, and hundreds more take their lawn chairs and blankets down to the Vieux-Port or across the river to the park along the south shore and watch the show. They bring ra-dios to pick up the musical accompaniment for the fireworks.

Such international stars as Denzel Washington, Bette Midler, Ben Kingsley, and Charlie Sheen show up for the **Festival International des Films du Monde** (World Film Festival; ☎ 514/848–3883, WEB www.ffm-montreal.org), at the end of August and the beginning of September. They compete for the Grand Prix of the Americas. This is the only competitive North American film festival recognized by the International Federation of Film Producers' Associations and usually screens about 400 films in a dozen venues, some of them outdoors.

The **Festival International de Jazz de Montréal** (tickets: ☎ 514/790–1245, 800/361–4595 in Canada, 800/678–5440, WEB www.montrealjazzfest.com), the world's biggest jazz festival, brings together more than 1,000 musicians for more than 400 concerts over a period of nearly two weeks, from the end of June to the beginning of July. Big names who have appeared in the past include Count Basie, Ella Fitzgerald, Bill Frisell, Brad Mehldau, Lauryn Hill, Wynton Marsalis, Chick Corea, Dave Brubeck, Angie Stone, Myriam Makeba with Omara Portuondo (of the Buena Vista Social Club), and Canada's hottest singer–pianist, Diana Krall. About three-fourths of the concerts are presented free on outdoor stages for lively audiences who sing, clap, and dance to the music. You can also hear blues, Latin rhythms, gospel, Cajun, and world music. Bell Info-Jazz (☎ 514/871–1881 or 888/515–0515) answers all queries about the Festival International de Jazz de Montréal and about travel packages.

Every other September (in odd-numbered years), the **Festival International de Nouvelle Danse** (☎ 514/287–1423 tickets) brings "new" dance to various venues around town. Tickets for this event always sell quickly.

When **Festival International Nuits d'Afrique** (African Nights International Festival; ☎ 514/499–3462 information, 514/790–1245 tickets, WEB www.festnuitafric.com) was launched in 1987, 10,000 music lovers showed up. Since then, performances by big names such as Youssou N'Dour, Baaba Maal, Myriam Makeba, and King Sunny Ade have made the 10-day event one of the most important showcases of African and Caribbean culture in North America. These days as many as 120,000 people turn out on warm mid-July nights to hear and see the festival's more than 500 singers, dancers, and musicians.

Festival Juste pour Rire (Just for Laughs Comedy Festival; ☎ 514/845–2322, WEB www.hahaha.com) is held in July; the comics show up for a 12-day festival that attracts about 650 performers and 350,000 spectators. Big names in the past have included Jerry Seinfeld, Drew Carey, Marcel Marceau, and Sandra Bernhard. Canadian comics including Mike McDonald and Bowser and Blue also got their start at this festival.

The **FrancoFolies** (☎ 514/876–8989, WEB www.francofolies.com) celebrates the art of French songwriting and is one of the most important festivals of its type in the world. Such major French stars as Isabelle Boulay, Paul Piché, and Michel Rivard play to packed concert halls while lesser-known artists from all over the world play free outdoor concerts on the plaza at the Place des Arts. Performers come from just about every country and region where French is spoken—and sung—as well as from the other Canadian provinces. In all, more than 1,000 musicians perform in dozens of different styles, including rock, hip-hop, jazz, funk, and Latin.

Montréal en Lumière (Montréal Highlights; ☎ 514/288–9955, WEB www.montrealenlumiere.com) is designed to brighten the bleak days of February, both literally and figuratively. One of the main aspects of this multifaceted mid-winter festival, which began in 2000, is the art of illumination. For every festival, experts artfully illuminate a few historic buildings. Food, too, is a major ingredient in the fun. Such leading world chefs as Paul Bocuse of France come to town to give lessons and demonstrations and to take over the kitchens of some of the leading restaurants. Outdoor and indoor concerts, ice-sculpture displays, plays, dance recitals, and other cultural events are also scheduled during the festival.

Nightlife

Club Med World (⊠ 954 rue Ste-Catherine Ouest, Downtown, ☎ 514/393–3003), in a refurbished Loews movie theater, encompasses music, theater, and magic shows, and even circus acts, along with top-notch bars and restaurants. **Laser Quest** (⊠ 1226 rue Ste-Catherine Ouest, Downtown, ☎ 514/393–3000) has fog machines, music, and live-action laser-tag games on five levels. It's open late every night of the week.

Bars

Bifteck (⊠ 3702 blvd. St-Laurent, Plateau Mont-Royal, ☎ 514/844–6211) is a crowded local favorite of the hip McGill crowd and the young-at-heart boomer crowd. **Bistro au Cépage** (⊠ 212 rue Notre-Dame Ouest, Vieux-Montréal, ☎ 514/845–5436), frequented by professionals and journalists who work nearby, is lively with talk and debate all week. There's good food, too. **Brutopia** (⊠ 1219 rue Crescent, Downtown, ☎ 514/393–9277) has good pasta, salads, and steaks. The large selection of draught beer and huge platters of food make it a popular downtown meeting place. **Île Noir** (⊠ 342 rue Ontario Est, Quartier Latin, ☎ 514/982–0866) has rich wood decor and an impressive selection of single-malt whiskies. **Sofa** (⊠ 451 rue Rachel Est, Plateau Mont-Royal, ☎ 514/285–1011), as the name suggests, is a comfortable place to sip a port or a Scotch and watch the trendy Plateau people go by. **Stogie's Café and Cigars** (⊠ 2015 rue Crescent, Downtown, ☎ 514/848–0069) imports cigars directly from Cuba. The relaxed atmosphere is ripe for friendly arguments about anything you like—except the merits of smoking. **Le Swimming** (⊠ 3643 blvd. St-Laurent, Plateau Mont-Royal, ☎ 514/282–7665) is a vast upscale pool lounge ("pool hall" just isn't genteel enough) with 10 tables, including snooker. It's very popular with the young and fashionable. **Wax Lounge** (⊠ 2481 blvd. St-Laurent, Plateau Mont-Royal, ☎ 514/282–0919) is an intimate upstairs bar specializing in champagne. The couches are excellent for people-watching or just hanging out. **Winnie's** (⊠ 1455 rue Crescent, Downtown, ☎ 514/288–0623) gets its name from Winston Churchill and draws its clientele from the young and ambitious professionals and entrepreneurs who work downtown. **Whiskey Café** (⊠ 3 rue Bernard West, Plateau Mont-Royal, ☎ 514/278–2646) has an impressive menu of 20 types of port and 30 kinds of Scotch. Don't miss the high-tech bathrooms.

Casino

The **Casino de Montréal** (⊠ 1 av. du Casino, Île Notre-Dame, ☎ 514/392–2746 or 800/665–2274), Québec's first casino, is one of the world's 10 biggest, with 3,000 slot machines and 120 tables for baccarat, blackjack, and roulette. The dress code is strict, and croupiers are trained in politeness as well as math. There are some oddities for those used to Vegas: no drinking on the floor, and no tipping the croupiers. Winners can spend their money at Nuances or three other restaurants. To get to the casino, which is open around the clock, you can take a $10 cab ride from downtown, drive (parking is free), or take the Métro to the Parc Jean-Drapeau stop and then board Bus 167.

Comedy

The **Comedy Nest** (✉ AMC Forum, 2313 rue Ste-Catherine Ouest, 4th fl., Downtown, ☎ 514/932–6378) hosts established Canadian comics such as Jim Carrey and Howie Mandel along with funny up-and-comers. Dinner-and-show packages are available. **Comedyworks** (✉ 1238 rue Bishop, Downtown, ☎ 514/398–9661) is a popular spot upstairs from Jimbo's Pub that books both amateurs and professionals. Acts tend to be more risqué than those at the Comedy Nest.

Dance Clubs

Montréal's love affair with Latin dance is one of long standing; even before the current craze, the Québecois took dancing seriously.

Bar Minuit (✉ 115 rue Laurier Ouest, Plateau Mont-Royal, ☎ 514/271–2110) plays house, pop, retro, and salsa. The space is often crowded, but Wednesday night Happy Hour is especially lively. **Cactus** (✉ 4461 rue St-Denis, Plateau Mont-Royal, ☎ 514/849–0349) fuels Montréal's Latin love affair with rigorously authentic music from salsa to merengue. The floor is always packed. **Club 737** (✉ 1 Place Ville-Marie, Downtown, ☎ 514/397–0737), a two-level club high atop the city with a sweeping panoramic view and a rooftop terrace, does the disco number every Thursday, Friday, and Saturday night. It has become very popular with the mid-twenties to mid-thirties office crowd. **Jello Bar** (✉ 151 rue Ontario Est, Quartier Latin, ☎ 514/285–2621) is filled with lava lamps, loveseats, and other retro-sleek furnishings. The 52 martini flavors include chocolate-mint, the local favorite. The music ranges from swing and jazz to salsa and R&B, with live performances on weekends. **Newtown** (✉ 1476 rue Crescent, Downtown, ☎ 514/284–6555), one of the hottest clubs, is named for its owner, Formula One race-car driver Jacques Villeneuve ("Newtown" is the English translation of his name). The tri-level dance club–bar–restaurant caters to a trendy and hip crowd. Reserve early for the private outdoor terrace table. **Quai des Brumes Dancing** (✉ 4481 rue St-Denis, Plateau Mont-Royal, ☎ 514/499–0467) is the place for house and techno-rave music. There's an upstairs disco and a DJ until 3 AM. **Salsathèque** (✉ 1220 rue Peel, Downtown, ☎ 514/875–0016) is one of the most popular Latin clubs in Montréal. **Thursdays/Les Beaux Jeudis** (✉ 1449 rue Crescent, Downtown, ☎ 514/288–5656) is the primo downtown bar and disco for the professional set. The dance club opens at 10 PM.

Folk Music

Hurley's Irish Pub (✉ 1225 rue Crescent, Downtown, ☎ 514/861–4111) attracts some of the city's best Celtic musicians, dancers, and storytellers. There's never a cover charge. At **McKibbin's Irish Pub** (✉ 1426 rue Bishop, Downtown, ☎ 514/288–1580), Celtic fiddlers from all over Canada—and, indeed, the world—put in appearances. And the Irish stew is even better than the music. **Old Dublin** (✉ 1219A rue University, Downtown, ☎ 514/861–4448), the oldest Irish club in the city, presents live Celtic bands. The menu of eats includes a few Indian choices. **Yellow Door** (✉ 3625 rue Aylmer, Downtown, ☎ 514/398–6243), a Montréal folk-music institution since the 1960s and Canada's longest-running coffeehouse, is a basement club showcasing homegrown and international folk and blues acts. There's no alcohol and no smoking.

Gay Bars and Nightclubs

The main drag along rue Ste-Catherine from about rue St-Denis east to avenue Papineau pulses with eateries and clubs, especially at night. In general, the farther east you walk, the greater the emphasis on saunas and strip clubs. *Fugues* (☎ 514/845–7645, WEB www.fugues.com), a gay newspaper published in French with a smattering of articles in English, lists events. The gay and lesbian bilingual Web site **Direction Gay Québec** (WEB www.directiongayquebec.com) is extensive and thorough in its nightlife and other listings.

Agora (✉ 1160 rue Mackay, Downtown, ☎ 514/934–1428) is a gay meet-and-greet club downtown. It's usually quiet and intimate, apart from Saturday karaoke nights. **Club Bolo** (✉ 960 rue Amherst, Village, ☎ 514/849–4777) has a country-and-western theme. **Le Drugstore** (✉ 1360 rue Ste-Catherine Est, Village, ☎ 514/524–1960), a mammoth complex of eight bars on eight floors, is modeled after a real drugstore in New York City's Times Square. There's a café, bars, a newsstand, a handsome terrace, and even a couple of shops. Although the crowd includes all ages and types, this is the neighborhood's best hangout for women, who gravitate toward the basement billiards hall and the second-floor lounge. **Exotica** (✉ 417 rue St-Pierre, Vieux Montréal, ☎ 514/281–1773), the only gay club in Vieux-Montréal and the only gay Latin disco in the city, is fashionable yet friendly and has a stylish mixed-gender crowd. **Hôtel Bourbon** (✉ 1584 rue Ste-Catherine Est, Village, ☎ 514/523–4679) is a wild and rollicking full-scale entertainment center, with a cruise bar, a disco, a drag-show lounge, restaurants, and, yes, an inexpensive and clean hotel (which draws women and men). **Sisters** (✉ 1333 rue Ste-Catherine Est, Village, ☎ 514/522–4717) is populated by lipstick lesbians and their friends. This smart space, above the gay-popular Saloon Café, is primarily a hangout for bi and lesbian women, but men are admitted Sunday afternoons and sometimes on Tuesdays. **Sky Pub/Sky Club** (✉ 1474 rue Ste-Catherine Est, Village, ☎ 514/529–6969) is two hangouts in one, and arguably the busiest gay club in the city, especially among younger and stand-and-model types. Downstairs, the Sky Pub is a sprawling, mostly male cruise bar; upstairs, Sky Club is a hip disco with two small dance floors and more of a male–female mix. **Le Stud** (✉ 1812 rue Ste-Catherine Est, Village, ☎ 514/598–8243), loud and full of leather, is a men-only hangout that's open until the wee hours.

Jazz

At **Biddle's** (✉ 2060 rue Aylmer, Downtown, ☎ 514/842–8656), bassist Charles Biddle holds court Friday and Saturday nights at 10:30. The $2.50 cover charge is the best deal in town, and the ribs and chicken are pretty good. The **Upstairs Jazz Club** (✉ 1254 rue Mackay, Downtown, ☎ 514/931–6808) has intimate live jazz sets: local and imported musicians take the stage seven nights a week. Shark and salmon are two specialties on the good dinner menu.

Reggae, Rock, Hip Hop, and World

Angels (✉ 3604 blvd. St-Laurent, Plateau Mont-Royal, ☎ 514/282–9944) has live bands and Thursday-night drink specials. **Le Balattou** (✉ 4372 blvd. St-Laurent, Plateau Mont-Royal, ☎ 514/845–5447), a busy and smoky club, specializes in African and Caribbean music. Performances start late and last even later. **Blue Dog** (✉ 3958 blvd. St-Laurent, Plateau Mont-Royal, ☎ 514/848–7006) has an eclectic musical mix from reggae to rock, with the real action happening after 11 PM. **Club Soda** (✉ 1225 blvd. St-Laurent, Downtown, ☎ 514/286–1010), the granddaddy of all city rock clubs, is a high, narrow concert hall with high-tech design and 500 seats—all of them good. The club is open only for shows; phone the box office to find out what's on. **Foufounes Electriques** (⊠ 87 rue Ste-Catherine Est, Downtown, ☎ 514/844–5539) pushes the envelope with its music and its performances, which is just about what you'd expect from a club whose name means "electric buttocks" in English. **Spectrum** (⊠ 318 rue Ste-Catherine Ouest, Downtown, ☎ 514/861–5851) is the most popular performance venue for rock bands in Montréal.

OUTDOOR ACTIVITIES AND SPORTS

Updated by
Melanie Reffes

Most Montrealers would probably claim they hate winter, but the city is rich in cold-weather activities—skating rinks, cross-country-ski trails, and toboggan runs. During the warm-weather months, residents head for the tennis courts, miles of bicycle trails, golf courses, and two lakes for boating and swimming. You can even scuba dive in Montréal—in a pool, that is.

Participant Sports

Biking

Despite the bitter winters (or perhaps because of them), Montréal has fallen in love with the bicycle. More than 350 km (217 mi) of cycling paths crisscross the metropolitan area, and bikes are welcome on the first and last cars of Métro trains during non-rush hours. The most popular trail on the island begins at the Vieux-Port and follows the **Lachine Canal** to the shores of Lac St-Louis in Lachine. **Parks Canada** (☎ 514/283–6054 or 514/637–7433) conducts guided cycling tours along the Lachine Canal every summer weekend. **Le Pôle des Rapides** (☎ 514/732–7303), a network of more than 96 km (60 mi) of bicycle trails that includes the Lachine Canal trail, follows lakefronts, canals, and aqueducts. Ferries at the Vieux-Port take cyclists to Île Ste-Hélène and the south shore of the St. Lawrence River, where riders can connect to hundreds of miles of trails in the Montérégie region.

Féria du Véle de Montréal (Montréal Bike Fest; ☎ 514/288–8356, WEB www.velo.qc.ca), at the end of May, is the biggest celebration of two-wheel transport in North America. Cyclists of all ages and conditions take part in a night ride through the streets of the city, a 22-km (14-mi) ride for children, a couple of challenge races of 100 and 150 km (62 and 93 mi), and other events. It all culminates on the last day when as many as 50,000 cyclists take over the streets for the **Tour de l'Île**, a 50-km (31-mi) ride for all on a route that circles the city.

At **Le Maison des Cyclistes** (⊠ 1251 rue Rachel Est, Plateau Mont-Royal, ☎ 514/521–8356), you can drop in to sip a coffee at the Bicicletta café or to browse the maps in the adjoining boutique. Rental bikes are available here, too. **Vélo Aventure** (☎ 514/847–0666) rents bicycles at the Vieux-Port; **Velo Montréal** (⊠ 3870 Rachel Est, Rosemont, ☎ 514/236–8356) is the place to rent bicycles at the Olympic Village.

Birdwatching

The 350 bird species in Montréal can be seen from many vantage points. The **Rare Bird Alert** (☎ 514/989–5076, WEB www.pqspb.org) offers information on recent sightings and suggested birding spots.

Boating

In Montréal you can get in a boat at a downtown wharf and be crashing through Class V white water minutes later. **Lachine Rapids Tours Ltd.** (⊠ 47 rue de la Commune, or quai de l'Horloge, Vieux-Montréal,

☎ 514/284–9607) has one-hour voyages for thrill seekers through the rapids in big aluminum jet boats. Heavy-water gear is supplied. You can also choose a half-hour trip around the islands in 10-passenger boats that can go about 100 kph (62 mph). Reservations are required; trips are narrated in French and English. There are five trips daily through the rapids from May through September; the cost is $53. Rafting trips are also available.

Golf

Nearly all courses are outside the city center. **Tourisme Québec** (☎ 514/ 873–2015 or 800/363–7777, WEB www.bonjourquebec.com) can provide a complete listing of the many golf courses in the greater metropolitan area.

The **Club de Golf Métropolitain Anjou** (Anjou Metropolitan Golf Club; ✉ 9555 blvd. du Golf, Anjou, ☎ 514/353–5353, WEB www. golfmetropolitainanjou.com), about a 20-minute drive from downtown, has a par-72 18-hole championship golf course as well as an 18-hole executive course. **Golf Dorval** (✉ 2000 av. Reverchon, Dorval, ☎ 514/ 631–4653, WEB www.golfdorval.com), about a 20-minute drive from downtown, encompasses two 18-hole courses (par 70 and 72), a driving range, and two putting greens. **Le Village** (✉ Village Olympique, 4235 rue Viau, Hochelaga–Maisonneuve, ☎ 514/872–4653) is a 9-hole municipal course.

Ice-Skating

The **Parks and Recreation Department** (☎ 514/872–6211) has information about the numerous ice-skating rinks (at least 195 outdoor and 21 indoor) in the city. The rinks on Île Ste-Hélène and at the Vieux-Port are especially large. You can skate year-round in the **Atrium le Mille de la Gauchetière** (✉ 1000 rue de la Gauchetière, Downtown, ☎ 514/ 395–1000 or 514/395–0555), a skyscraper atrium. There are skating lessons Friday and Saturday, disco skating Saturday night, and scheduled ice shows.

Jogging

Most parks in the city have paths, but for running with a panoramic view, head to the dirt track in **Parc du Mont-Royal** (☎ 514/844–4928). Take rue Peel, then follow the steps up to the track. You can also run the trail along the **Lachine Canal.**

Skiing

CROSS-COUNTRY

Trails crisscross most city parks, including parks des Îles, Maisonneuve, and Mont-Royal, but the best are probably the 46 km (29 mi) in the 900-acre **Cap St-Jacques Regional Park** (✉ off blvd. Gouin, Pierrefonds, ☎ 514/280–6871), on the west end of Montréal Island about a half-hour drive from downtown. To get to the park via public transportation, take the Métro to the Henri-Bourassa stop and then the 69 Bus west. The **Lachine Canal** trail is used by cross-country skiers in winter.

DOWNHILL

You don't have to travel far from Montréal to find good downhill skiing, but you do have to travel. **Mont St-Sauveur** (☎ 514/871–0101), with a vertical drop of 700 ft, is the closest decent-size ski hill in the Laurentian Mountains, the winter and summer playground for Montrealers. It's about an hour's drive northwest of Montréal. **Bromont** (☎ 450/534–2200), about a 1¼-hour drive from the Champlain Bridge, is the closest Appalachian hill. This hill with a 1,329-ft vertical drop is in the Eastern Townships, southeast of the city.

Within Montréal, **Parc du Mont-Royal** has a small ski slope. **Mont St-Bruno** (☎ 450/653–3441), on the south shore, has a modest vertical drop of 443 ft, but it includes Québec's biggest ski school and a high-speed lift and also offers night skiing.

A "Ski-Québec" brochure is available from **Tourisme Québec** (☎ 514/873–2015 or 800/363–7777, WEB www.bonjourquebec.com).

Snorkeling and Scuba Diving

Waddell Aquatics (✉ 6356 rue Sherbrooke Ouest, Westmount, ☎ 514/482–1890 or 888/834–8464) offers rentals, lessons in a big pool, and local excursions.

Swimming

Bain Schubert (✉ 3950 blvd. St-Laurent, Plateau Mont-Royal, ☎ 514/872–2587), a renovated art deco pool has free swims throughout the day. **Centre Aquatique** (✉ 4141 av. Pierre-de-Coubertin, Hochelaga-Maisonneuve, ☎ 514/252–4622) has four indoor public pools at Olympic Park. **Centre Sportif et des Loisirs Claude-Robillard** (✉ 1000 av. Emile-Journault, Ahuntsic, ☎ 514/872–6900) has a big indoor pool. **Île Ste-Hélène** has a popular (and crowded) outdoor pool, open June to early September. **Plage de l'Île Notre-Dame** is the only natural swimming hole in Montréal. **Vieux Montréal CEGEP** (Junior College; ✉ 255 rue Ontario Est, Berri-UQAM, ☎ 514/982–3457) has a free indoor pool, open evenings Tuesday through Friday and Saturday 9 AM–3 PM.

Tennis

The Jeanne-Mance, Kent, Lafontaine, and Somerled parks have public courts. For details call the **Accèss Montréal** (☎ 514/872–6211).

Windsurfing and Sailing

You can rent sailboards and small sailboats at **L'École de Voile de Lachine** (Lachine Sailing School; ✉ 2105 blvd. St-Joseph, Lachine, ☎ 514/634–4326).

Spectator Sports

Baseball

The **Montréal Expos** (☎ 514/253–3434 or 800/463–9767), the city's National League professional baseball team, play at Olympic Stadium April through September.

Football

The **Montréal Alouettes** (☎ 514/871–2266 information, 514/871–2255 tickets) of the Canadian Football League play the Canadian version of the game—bigger field, just three downs, and a more wide-open style—under open skies at McGill University's Molson Stadium June through October. It's one of the best sporting deals in town.

Grand Prix

Air Canada Grand Prix du Canada (☎ 514/350–4731, 514/350–0000 tickets), which draws top Formula 1 racers from around the world, takes place every June at Circuit Gilles Villeneuve on Île Notre-Dame. In late August, the course is also to host the Molson Indy of Montréal, a race sanctioned by the CART FedEx Championship Series.

Hockey

The **Montréal Canadiens** (✉ 1250 rue de la Gauchetière Ouest, Downtown, ☎ 514/932–2582), winners of 23 Stanley Cups, meet National Hockey League rivals at the Centre Bell from October through April. Buy tickets in advance to guarantee a seat.

SHOPPING

Updated by
Katherine
Thompson

Montrealers *magasinent* (shop) with a vengeance, so it's no surprise that the city has 160 multifaceted retail areas encompassing some 7,000 stores. The law allows shops to stay open weekdays 9–9 and weekends 9–5. However, many merchants close evenings Monday through Wednesday and on Sunday. Many specialty service shops are closed on Monday, too. Just about all stores, with the exception of some bargain outlets and a few selective art and antiques galleries, accept major credit cards. Most purchases are subject to a federal goods and services tax (GST) of 7% as well as a provincial tax of 8%. Non-Canadians can claim a refund of some of these taxes, however.

If you think you might be buying fur, it's wise to check with your country's customs officials before your trip to find out which animals are considered endangered and cannot be imported. Do the same for Inuit carvings, many of which are made of whalebone and ivory and cannot be brought into the United States. The Canadian government has registered the symbol of an igloo as a mark of a work's authenticity. When buying Inuit art, be sure this Canadian government sticker or tag is attached before you make your purchase.

Shopping Districts

Avenue Laurier Ouest, from boulevard St-Laurent to chemin de la Côte-Ste-Catherine, is roughly an eight-block stretch dotted with fashionable and trendy shops that carry everything from crafts and clothing to books and paintings.

Boulevard St-Laurent, affectionately known as The Main, is enjoying a renewed popularity. Its restaurants, boutiques, and nightclubs cater mostly to the upscale visitor. Still, the area has managed to retain its working-class immigrant roots and vitality, resulting in a unique melding of businesses: high-fashion shops are interspersed with ethnic food stores, secondhand bookshops, and hardware stores. Indeed, a trip up this street takes you from Chinatown to Little Italy. Shoppers flock to the two blocks of avenue Mont-Royal just east of boulevard St-Laurent for secondhand and recycled clothes.

Downtown is Montréal's largest retail district. It takes in rues Sherbrooke and Ste-Catherine, boulevard de Maisonneuve, and the side streets between them. Because of the proximity and diversity of the shops, it's the best shopping bet if you're in town overnight or for a weekend. The area bounded by rues Sherbrooke, Ste-Catherine, de la Montagne, and Crescent has antiques and art galleries in addition to designer salons. Fashion boutiques and art and antiques galleries line rue Sherbrooke. Rue Crescent holds a tempting blend of antiques, fashions, and jewelry displayed beneath colorful awnings.

Rue Chabanel, in the city's north end, is the soul of Montréal's extensive garment industry. Every Saturday, from about 8:30 to 1, many of the manufacturers and importers in the area open their doors to the general public. At least they do if they feel like it. What results is part bazaar, part circus, and often all chaos—but friendly chaos. When Montrealers say "Chabanel," they mean the eight-block stretch just west of boulevard St-Laurent. The factories and shops here are tiny—dozens of them are crammed into each building. The goods seem to get more stylish and more expensive the farther west you go. For really inexpensive leather goods, sportswear, children's togs, and linens, try the shops at 99 rue Chabanel; 555 rue Chabanel offers more-deluxe options. The manufacturers and importers at 555 have their work areas on the upper floors and have transformed the mezzanine into a glitzy mall with bargains in men's suits, winter coats, knitted goods, and stylish leather jackets. A few places on Chabanel accept credit cards, but bring cash anyway. It's easier to bargain if you can flash bills, and if you pay cash, the price will often "include the tax."

Rue St-Denis, perhaps Montréal's trendiest area, has shops of all descriptions and some of the best restaurants in town. People-watching is a popular pastime as this is where the beautiful people go to see and be seen. Cutting-edge fashions can be found both in the shops and on the shoppers.

Though **Vieux-Montréal** seems choked with garish souvenir shops, shopping here can be worthwhile. Fashion boutiques and shoe stores with low to moderate prices line both rues Notre-Dame and St-Jacques, from rue McGill to Place Jacques-Cartier. Rue St-Paul also has some interesting shops. During the warm-weather months, sidewalk cafés are everywhere. Street performers are a favorite with the kids.

The fashionable place for antiquing is a formerly run-down five-block strip of **rue Notre-Dame Ouest** between rue Guy and avenue Atwater, a five-minute walk south from the Lionel-Groulx Métro station. Antiques stores have been popping up along **rue Amherst** between rues Ste-Catherine and Ontario (a five-minute walk west of the Beaudry Métro station). The area is shabbier than rue Notre-Dame but a lot less expensive. The more affluent antiques hunter might want to try **Westmount,** where the shops cater to the tastes of the executives who live in the upscale suburb.

Department Stores

La Baie (the Bay; ⊠ 585 rue Ste-Catherine Ouest, Downtown, ☎ 514/281–4422) has been a department store since 1891. It's known for its duffel coats and Hudson Bay red-green-and-white striped blankets. La Baie also sells the typical department-store goods.

Holt Renfrew (⊠ 1300 rue Sherbrooke Ouest, Downtown, ☎ 514/842–5111), an exclusive shop whose specialty is furs and fashions, has supplied coats to four generations of British royalty. When Queen Elizabeth II got married in 1947, Holt gave her a priceless Labrador mink. The store carries the pricey line of furs by Denmark's Birger Christensen, as well as the haute couture and prêt-à-porter collections of Giorgio Armani, Calvin Klein, and Chanel.

Ogilvy (⊠ 1307 rue Ste-Catherine Ouest, Downtown, ☎ 514/842–7711), founded in 1865, still stocks traditional apparel by retailers such as Aquascutum and Jaeger. The store is divided into individual designer boutiques. A kilted piper regales shoppers every day at noon.

Simons (⊠ 977 rue Ste-Catherine Ouest, Downtown, ☎ 514/282–1840), in elegant 19th-century digs, specializes in high-quality clothes for men and women, including its own highly respected house label. Simons shares its address with a 12-screen Paramount theater, an IMAX theater, a bar, and a coffee shop.

Shopping Centers and Malls

Le Complexe Les Ailes (⊠ 677 rue Ste-Catherine Ouest, Downtown, ☎ 514/288–3708) is attached to Le Centre Eaton, in the building that housed the now-extinct Eatons. Les Ailes's flagship store sells women's clothing and accessories; the other 57 retailers here include Tommy Hilfiger and Archambault, a music store.

Le Centre Eaton (⊠ 705 rue Ste-Catherine Ouest, Downtown, ☎ 514/288–3708) has a definite youthful edge, with a huge Levi's store and some trendy sporting-goods stores. The five-story mall—the largest in the downtown core, with 175 boutiques and shops—is linked to the McGill Métro station. The Instant Tax Refund service, for non-residents, is on the fourth floor.

Complexe Desjardins (✉ blvd. René-Lévesque at rue Jeanne Mance, Downtown, ☎ 514/845-4636) gets its relaxed feel from splashing fountains and exotic plants. The roughly 80 stores range from budget-clothing outlets to the exclusive Jonathan Roche Monsieur for men's fashions. To get here, take the Métro to the Place des Arts and then follow the tunnels to the multitiered atrium mall.

Les Cours Mont-Royal (✉ 1455 rue Peel, Downtown, ☎ 514/842-7777) is *très élégant*. This mall linked to the Peel and McGill Métro stations caters to expensive tastes, but even bargain hunters find it an intriguing spot for window shopping. The more than 80 shops include DKNY and Harry Rosen. Beware: the interior layout can be disorienting.

Le Faubourg Ste-Catherine (✉ 1616 rue Ste-Catherine Ouest, at rue Guy, Downtown, ☎ 514/939-3663) is a vast indoor bazaar abutting the Couvent des Soeurs Grises. It includes clothing and crafts boutiques, but it's best known as a wonderful source of quality foods—fresh bagels, pastries, fruits and vegetables, fish, meats, and some of the city's spiciest and best Chinese takeout. A dozen or so very reasonably priced lunch counters sell ethnic foods.

Le Marché Bonsecours (✉ 350 rue St-Paul Est, Vieux-Montréal, ☎ 514/872-7730), inaugurated in the 1840s in the Vieux-Montréal area, has seen many incarnations over the years. Although it has been known as the city's principal public market for more than 100 years, it also enjoyed a stint as Montréal's city hall. Completely restored, it now houses boutiques that exclusively showcase Québecois, Canadian, and First Nation's artwork, clothing, and furniture.

Le Place Montréal Trust (✉ 1500 rue McGill College, at rue Ste-Catherine Ouest, Downtown, ☎ 514/843-8000) is a gateway to Montréal's vast Underground City. Its shops tend to specialize in high-end fashion. Indigo, one of the city's better bookstores, and the local branch of the Planet Hollywood chain are also here.

Place Ville-Marie (✉ blvd. René-Lévesque and rue University, Downtown, ☎ 514/866-6666), with its 42-story cruciform towers, is where weatherproof indoor shopping began in 1962. It was also the start of the underground shopping network that Montréal now enjoys. Stylish shoppers head to the 100-plus retail outlets for lunchtime sprees. When you're ready for a food break, consider the Mövenpick Marché restaurant, where offerings range from salads and sandwiches to stir-fries and sushi; fresh juices, pastries, and wonderful coffees make it a good breakfast choice.

Les Promenades de la Cathédrale (✉ 625 rue Ste-Catherine Ouest, Downtown, ☎ 514/849-9925), directly beneath Christ Church Cathedral, has 50-plus shops. Connected to the McGill Métro station, Les Promenades includes Canada's largest Linen Chest outlet, with hundreds of bedspreads and duvets, plus aisles of china, crystal, linen, and silver. The Anglican Church's Diocesan Book Room sells an unusually good and ecumenical selection of books as well as religious objects.

Square Westmount (✉ rue Ste-Catherine Ouest and av. Greene, Westmount, ☎ 514/932-0211) serves the mountainside suburb of Westmount, home of wealthy Montrealers, including executives and former prime ministers. So it's hardly surprising that the city's finest shops are here. With more than 50 boutiques as well as the exclusive Spa de Westmount, the prospects for self-indulgence are endless. To get here, take the Métro to the Atwater station and follow the tunnel.

Specialty Shops

Antiques

L'Antiquaire Joyal (✉ 1751 rue Amherst, Downtown, ☎ 514/524–0057) gives art deco furnishings and decorations top billing.

Antiquité Landry (✉ 1726 rue Notre-Dame Ouest, Village, ☎ 514/937–7040) has French and English furniture in pine, mahogany, walnut, and maple.

Antiquités Curiosités (✉ 1769 rue Amherst, Village, ☎ 514/525–8772) has well-priced Victorian-era tables and tallboys, as well as lamps and fixtures.

Antiquités Phyllis Friedman (✉ 1476 rue Sherbrooke Ouest, Square Mile, ☎ 514/935–1991) specializes in high-quality antique English furniture and decorative accessories—Anglo-Irish glass, ceramics, crystal, and the like.

Antiquités Pour La Table (✉ 2679 rue Notre-Dame Ouest, Mile End, ☎ 514/989–8945) has an extensive selection of antique porcelain, crystal, and linens of only the finest quality—all impeccably preserved and beautifully displayed. This is not the place to replace your missing pieces, however, as the pieces are mostly in complete sets.

Cité Déco (✉ 1761 rue Amherst, Village, ☎ 514/528–0659) sells furnishings of the 1930s, '40s, and '50s, with lots of chrome and blonde wood.

Coach House (✉ 1325 av. Greene, Westmount, ☎ 514/937–6191) is a source for antique silverware.

Galerie Jacques Germain (✉ 200 av. Laurier Ouest, Downtown, ☎ 514/278–6575) is the place to go for antique tribal art.

Galerie Tansu (✉ 1622 rue Sherbrooke Ouest, Downtown, ☎ 514/846–1039) offers 18th- and 19th-century porcelain and ceramic objects, furnishings from Japan and China, and Tibetan chests and carpets.

Héritage Antique Métropolitain (✉ 1646 rue Notre-Dame Ouest, Mile End, ☎ 514/931–5517) has many clocks and lamps as well as elegant English and French furniture. You can't turn your head without spotting another beautiful object.

Lapidarius (✉ 1312 av. Greene, Westmount, ☎ 514/935–2717 or 800/267–0373) stocks mostly watches, jewelry, and silverware.

Milord Antiques (✉ 1870 rue Notre-Dame Ouest, Mile End, ☎ 514/933–2433) focuses on 18th- and 19th-century furniture and also has some porcelain and crystal.

Rowntree (✉ 780 av. Atwater, Mile End, ☎ 514/933–5030) is filled with European country-style furniture and accessories.

Ruth Stalker (✉ 4447 rue Ste-Catherine Ouest, Westmount, ☎ 514/931–0822) is the place for high-quality Canadian furniture and exquisitely carved hunting decoys.

Le Village Antiquaires (✉ 1708 rue Notre-Dame Ouest, Mile End, ☎ 514/931–5121) is shared by several dealers, including specialists in furniture, jewelry, books, and vintage clothing. Galerie du Louvre merits a special visit for its beautiful antique stained glass.

Viva Gallery (✉ 1970 rue Notre-Dame Ouest, Mile End, ☎ 514/932–3200), where Asian antique furniture and art take center stage, has a wide selection of carved tables, benches, and armoires.

Art

Montréal brims with art galleries that present work by local luminaries as well as international artists. The Downtown area has a wide choice; Vieux-Montréal is also rich in galleries, which usually specialize in Québecois and First Nations work.

Edifice Belago (✉ 372 rue Ste-Catherine Ouest, Downtown), in a nondescript building, is in essence a mall for art galleries showing established and upcoming artists. **Galerie René Blouin** (☎ 514/393–9969) is one of the best galleries for contemporary art. **Galerie Trois Points** (☎ 514/866–8008) shows the work of national and international contemporary artists. Both galleries are on the fifth floor.

Galerie Art & Culture (✉ 227 rue St-Paul Ouest, Vieux-Montréal, ☎ 514/843–5980) specializes in Canadian landscapes.

Galerie des Arts Relais des Époques (✉ 234 rue St-Paul Ouest, Vieux-Montréal, ☎ 514/844–2133) sells modern and abstract works by contemporary Montréal painters.

Galerie de Bellefeuille (✉ 1367 av. Greene, Westmount, ☎ 514/933–4406) has a knack for discovering important new talents.

Galerie de Chariot (✉ 446 Place Jacques-Cartier, Vieux-Montréal, ☎ 514/875–6134) has a spectacular selection of Inuit carvings and drawings.

Galerie Elena Lee Verre (✉ 1460 rue Sherbrooke Ouest, Square Mile, ☎ 514/844–6009) is the city's leading dealer in glassworks.

Galerie Walter Klinkhof (✉ 1200 rue Sherbrooke Ouest, Square Mile, ☎ 514/288–7306) shows established artists.

La Guilde Graphique (✉ 9 rue St-Paul Ouest, Vieux-Montréal, ☎ 514/844–3438) has an exceptional selection of original prints, engravings, and etchings.

Books and Stationery

Bibliomania (✉ 460 rue Ste-Catherine Ouest, Rm. 406, Downtown, ☎ 514/933–8156) includes some out-of-print gems among its extensive shelves of secondhand books. It also has engravings, postcards, and other printed collectibles.

Chapters (✉ 1171 rue Ste-Catherine Ouest, Downtown, ☎ 514/849–8825) stocks one of the largest selections of books and magazines in the city, as well as CD-ROMs and stationery, and has a Starbucks café. Book signings are frequent.

Double Hook (✉ 1235A av. Greene, Westmount, ☎ 514/932–5093) has been selling Canadian books—from fiction and poetry to children's books, cookbooks, and business tomes—since 1974.

L'Essence du Papier (✉ 4160 rue St-Denis, Plateau Mont-Royal, ☎ 514/288–9691), with its selection of imported and handmade papers, is a reminder that letter-writing can be an art form. Here are pens suited to all tastes and budgets as well as waxes and stamps with which to seal any romantic prose that you might be inspired to produce. It also offers a wide selection of placecards, invitations, and journals.

Ex Libris (✉ 1628B rue Sherbrooke Ouest, Square Mile, ☎ 514/932–1689) houses a fine collection of secondhand books in an elegant, gray stone building.

Indigo (✉ 1500 av. McGill College, Downtown, ☎ 514/281–5549) is mainly about books and magazines, but the chain has branched out into CD-ROMs, videos, cards, gifts, and housewares. This location also has a large children's section.

Paragraphe (✉ 2220 av. McGill College, Square Mile, ☎ 514/845–5811) is the biggest and most successful independent bookstore in the city.

S. W. Welch (✉ 3878 blvd. St-Laurent, Plateau Mont-Royal, ☎ 514/848–9358) has a wide selection of old books that range from religion and philosophy to mysteries and science fiction.

The Word (✉ 469 rue Milton, Downtown, ☎ 514/845–5640), deep in the McGill University neighborhood, is a timeless shop with sagging shelves that specializes in previously owned books on art, philosophy, and literature. Leave your credit cards at home—the owner here tallies his bills by hand.

Clothing

Aime Com Moi (⊠ 150 av. Mont-Royal Est, Plateau Mont-Royal, ☎ 514/982–0088) sells exclusive men's and women's clothing created by Québec designers.

BCBG MAXAZRIA (⊠ 1300 rue Ste-Catherine Ouest, Downtown, ☎ 514/733–4470) fits right into Montréal's avant-garde attitude. Max Azria's super-stylish clothing, shoes, and handbags make a statement without risking a fashion "faux pas."

Chas. Johnson & Sons (⊠ 1184 Phillips Pl., Downtown, ☎ 514/878–1931) has on hand three expert kilt makers who can cut any tartan to any size. This downtown shop also rents Highland formal gear for all occasions and sells sporrans, skean-dhus, dirks, doublets, and day jackets, as well as a full line of classic British menswear.

Club Monaco (⊠ Les Cours Mont-Royal, 1455 rue Peel, Downtown, ☎ 514/499–0959) specializes in urban attire—some of which might do in the office—for men and women.

Diffusion Griff 3000 (⊠ 350 rue St-Paul Est, Vieux-Montréal, ☎ 514/398–0761) is Anne de Shalla's showcase for leading Québecois fashion designers.

Jean Airoldi (⊠ 4455 rue St-Denis, Plateau Mont-Royal, ☎ 514/287–6524) is one of Quebec's most talented clothing designers. The shop that bears his name specializes in classic yet chic women's fashions. Made-to-measure is available.

Kanuk (⊠ 485 rue Rachel Est, Plateau Mont-Royal, ☎ 514/527–4494) has developed a line of coats and sleeping bags that could keep an arctic explorer warm. But it also sells elegant winter clothes that are designed for layering and are suitable for any city or town where the temperature dips below freezing. The brand has become something of a status symbol among the shivering urban masses. Many fine retailers carry Kanuk coats, but you can also buy them at the display room over the factory.

Mains Folles (⊠ 4427 rue St-Denis, Plateau Mont-Royal, ☎ 514/284–6854) sells tropical dresses, skirts, and blouses imported from Bali.

Revenge (⊠ 3852 rue St-Denis, Plateau Mont-Royal, ☎ 514/843–4379) carries well-crafted original fashions for women by Québecois designers.

Roots (⊠ 1035 rue Ste-Catherine Ouest, Downtown, ☎ 514-845–7995) is a fashion darling, thanks to its quality materials and approachable, sometimes retro look.

Scandale (⊠ 3639 blvd. St-Laurent, Plateau Mont-Royal, ☎ 514/842–4707) has cutting-edge fashions, each piece an original by Québecois designer Georges Lévesque and created on-site. Here also is one of the most lurid window displays in the city.

Tilley Endurables (⊠ 1050 av. Laurier Ouest, Outremont, ☎ 514/272–7791) sells the famous, Canadian-designed Tilley hat and other easy-care travel wear.

Winners (⊠ 6900 rue Decarie, Côte St-Luc, ☎ 514/733–4200), a discount designer clothing store, has turned shopping into a sport. And now that it carries housewares, leaving empty-handed is even more difficult.

CHILDREN'S

Oink Oink (⊠ 1343 av. Greene, Westmount, ☎ 514/939–2634) carries the latest fashions as well as toys for infants and children. It's fun to hear how the staff answers the phone.

FURS

Montréal is one of the fur capitals of the world. Close to 85% of Canada's fur manufacturers are based in the city, as are many of their retail outlets. Many of them are clustered along rue Mayor and boulevard de Maisonneuve between rues de Bleury and Aylmer.

Alexandor (⊠ 2055 rue Peel, ☎ 514/288–1119), nine blocks west of the main fur-trade area, caters to the downtown trade.

Birger Christensen at Holt Renfrew (⊠ 1300 rue Sherbrooke Ouest, Downtown, ☎ 514/842–5111) is perhaps the most exclusive showroom in the city, with prices to match.

Marcel Jodoin Fourrures (⊠ 1228 rue St-Denis, Downtown, ☎ 514/288–1683) has a wide selection of nearly new (under five years old), previously owned fur coats, jackets, and stoles, most of which go for less than the cost of an imitation.

McComber Grosvenor (⊠ 402 blvd. de Maisonneuve Ouest, Downtown, ☎ 514/288–1255), two of Montréal's biggest fur merchants, have merged to create this showroom filled with beautiful mink coats and jackets.

LINGERIE

Collange (⊠ 1 Westmount Square, Westmount, ☎ 514/933–4634) carries lacy goods of the designer variety.

Deuxième Peau (Second Skin; ⊠ 4457 rue St-Denis, Plateau Mont-Royal, ☎ 514/842–0811), as its name suggests, sells lingerie so fine you don't notice you're wearing it. While you're feeling brave and beautiful, kill two birds with one stone and try on a bathing suit.

Lyla (⊠ 400 av. Laurier Ouest, Outremont, ☎ 514/271–0763) has seductively lacy lingerie.

VINTAGE

Boutique Encore (⊠ 2165 rue Crescent, Downtown, ☎ 514/849–0092), in business for about 50 years, retains its popularity by maintaining a good selection of designer labels. Although best known for its nearly new women's fashions, it now includes the big names for men.

Eva B (⊠ 2013 blvd. St-Laurent, Downtown, ☎ 514/849–8246) has a vast collection of clothes. If your fantasy is being a flapper, or you miss the '60s, turn back the clock and perk up your wardrobe.

Cigars

Casa del Habano (⊠ 1434 rue Sherbrooke Ouest, Downtown, ☎ 514/849–0037) stocks the finest cigars Cuba produces. Note that U.S. law forbids Americans from buying Cuban products.

Davidoff (⊠ 1458 Sherbrooke Ouest, Downtown, ☎ 514/289–9118) stocks the best names in cigars as well as a fine collection of smoking accessories and humidors.

H. Poupart (⊠ 1385 Ste-Catherine Ouest, Downtown, ☎ 514/842–5794) has been supplying Montrealers with the best tobacco the world has to offer for almost 100 years. Be it cigars, cigarettes, chewing and pipe tobaccos, or snuff, you can find a large selection here.

Fabrics

Créations Nicole Moisan (⊠ 4324 rue St-Denis, Plateau Mont-Royal, ☎ 514/284–9506) has miles and miles of lace, with thousands of patterns to choose from, all from Europe. Custom orders are available.

Food

Charcuterie/Boucherie Hongroise (⊠ 3843 blvd. St-Laurent, Plateau Mont-Royal, ☎ 514/844–6734), family-owned and -operated, smokes and cures its own bacon and hams, plus a wide selection of German, Polish, and Hungarian sausages.

Marché Jean Talon (⊠ 7015 rue Casgrain, Little Italy, ☎ 514/277–1588), an outdoor market, has some of the best produce in the city. In springtime it's almost overrun with gardeners rushing to procure the best plants and seeds. The market itself is surrounded by butchers, bakers, and other shopkeepers who have set up businesses on the market outskirts.

Marché Atwater (Atwater Market; ⊠ 138 av. Atwater, Mile End, ☎ 514/937–7754), at the bottom of Atwater, gets shipments of the freshest produce available from farmers who arrive in the wee morning hours. Before dawn breaks, chefs are haggling to carry off the best of the available crop. The next round of shoppers is the early risers hoping to be rewarded for their sacrifice with a good selection and a little solitude. Most of this market's shopkeepers are within the two-story complex, well-suited to rainy-day browsing.

Marché de Westmount (⊠ 1 Westmount Sq., Westmount, ☎ no phone) is an indoor market with shops selling pastries, cheeses, pâtés, fruits, cakes, and chocolates. You can assemble a picnic and eat it at one of the little tables scattered among the stalls.

Milano (⊠ 6862 blvd. St-Laurent, Little Italy, ☎ 514/273–8558) offers one of the largest cheese selections in the city as well as fresh pasta of all kinds. An entire wall is devoted to olive oils and vinegars; there are also a butcher and a big produce section.

Nino (⊠ 3667 blvd. St-Laurent, Plateau Mont-Royal, ☎ 514/844–7630) is hectic on weekends, when shoppers pack the narrow aisles scanning the shelves for spices, pickles, hams, and kitchen gadgets of all sorts.

Gifts

Desmarais et Robitaille (⊠ 60 rue Notre-Dame Ouest, Vieux-Montréal, ☎ 514/845–3194), a store that supplies churches with vestments and liturgical items, also has Québecois carvings and handicrafts and tasteful religious articles.

L'Empreinte Coopérative (⊠ 272 rue St-Paul Est, Vieux-Montréal, ☎ 514/861–4427) has fine Québec handicrafts.

Home Furnishings

Caban (⊠ 777 rue Ste-Catherine Ouest, Downtown, ☎ 514/844–9300), a sister store of clothing retailer Club Monaco, carries mainly laid-back yet stylish furnishings and home accessories.

L'Institut de Design de Montréal (⊠ 350 rue St-Paul Est, Vieux-Montréal, ☎ 514/866–2436) has an amusingly innovative collection of kitchen brushes, buckets, CD-storage racks, clocks, bathroom equipment, and so forth.

Jeunes d'Ici (⊠ 134 av. Laurier Ouest, Outremont, ☎ 514/270–5512) has furniture and decorating accessories for children of all ages.

Rita R. Giroux (⊠ 206 rue St-Paul Ouest, Vieux-Montréal, ☎ 514/844–4714) makes flamboyant creations with fresh, dried, and silk flowers.

Ungava Factory Outlet (⊠ 10 av. des Pins Ouest, Suite 112, Plateau Mont-Royal, ☎ 514/287–9276) manufactures Canadian-down comforters, sold at wholesale prices here. Custom orders are accepted.

Housewares

Ares Kitchen and Baking Supplies (⊠ 2355 Trans-Canada Hwy., Pointe Claire, ☎ 514/695–5225) can provide just about any kitchen gadget that you might be looking for, as well as top-of-the-line kitchen equipment that would make a professional chef's flame burn brighter.

Danesco (⊠ 18111 Trans-Canada Hwy., Kirkland, ☎ 514/694–0950) is a manufacturer and importer of kitchen equipment and tableware. It operates an outlet out of its head office where you can find great deals on everything from pots and pans to cutlery and linen napkins.

The Linen Chest (⊠ 625 rue Ste-Catherine Ouest, Downtown, ☎ 514/

282–9525) has one of the largest selections of competitively priced china, crystal, and cutlery in the city—affectionately known as "The Great Wall of China." Down comforters and bedding are also a specialty.

Jewelry

Birks (✉ 1240 Phillips Sq., Downtown, ☎ 514/397–2511) has, since 1879, helped shoppers mark special occasions. Be it an engagement ring or a wedding or retirement gift, a blue Birks box is a welcome sight for its recipient.

Kaufmann de Suisse (✉ 2195 rue Crescent, Downtown, ☎ 514/848–0595) has fine jewelry wrought by expert craftspeople.

Hemsleys Jewellers (✉ 660 rue Ste-Catherine Ouest, ☎ 514/866–3706) is Canada's oldest jeweler—in operation since 1870. The family-run business takes pride in an approachable attitude and reasonable prices. The selection and prices range wide, from small tokens to original creations. Private shopping is available.

Music

Cheap Thrills (✉ 2044 Metcalfe, Downtown, ☎ 514/844–8988) sells good secondhand CDs and has a wide selection of secondhand books at bargain prices.

HMV (✉ 1020 rue Ste-Catherine Ouest, Downtown, ☎ 514/875–0765) carries mainstream music and a limited amount of imports.

Steve's Music Store (✉ 51 rue St-Antoine Ouest, Downtown, ☎ 514/878–2216), a shabby warren of five storefronts, is jammed with just about everything you need to be a rock star.

Shoes

Pegabo Shoes (✉ 770 rue McGill College, Downtown, ☎ 514/861–4324) is a true Montréal success story. Aldo Bensadoun opened his first Pegabo store in 1972. His shoe empire now includes more than 600 stores across Canada, operating under the names Pegabo, Simard et Voyer, Aldo, Globo, StoneRidge, and Transit. Pegabo is more high-end than others. There are numerous Pegabo stores around Montréal.

Tony's Shoe Shop (✉ 1346 av. Greene, Westmount, ☎ 514/935–2993), a Montréal institution for the finely shod foot, places stylish imports beside elegantly sensible footwear.

Sporting Goods and Clothing

Boutique Classique Angler (✉ 414 rue McGill, Downtown, ☎ 514/878–3474) has everything anglers need for fly fishing, from rods and reels to feathers for tying flies. Owner Peter Ferago has great advice on where to fish.

Canadiens Boutique Centre Bell (✉ 1250 rue de la Gauchetière, Downtown, ☎ 514/989–2836) sells hockey sticks, posters, pucks, authentic jerseys, and other memorabilia, all bearing the emblem of the world's most storied hockey team.

Lucie Favreau Sports Memorabilia (✉ 1904 rue Notre-Dame Ouest, Downtown, ☎ 514/989–5117) is the place to search for your own sports-hall-of-fame items, such as an autographed hockey stick or 1950s football poster.

Toys and Games

Cerf Volanterie (✉ 2019 Moreau, Hochelaga-Maisonneuve, ☎ 514/845–7613) has sturdy, gloriously colored kites made by Claude Thibaudeau. He signs the kites and guarantees them for three years. Visits are by appointment only.

Jouets Choo-Choo (✉ 940 blvd. Ste-Jean, Pointe Claire, ☎ 514/697–7550) has quality European toys and educational games at this shop 20 minutes from downtown.

MONTRÉAL A TO Z

To research prices, get advice from other travelers, and book travel arrangements, visit www.fodors.com.

AIR TRAVEL TO AND FROM MONTRÉAL

Major airlines serving Montréal include Air Canada, American Airlines, British Airways, Continental, Delta, El Al, Northwest, and US Airways.

Note that when you depart by plane, you must pay a $15 airport tax (for capital improvements); you can pay cash or with a credit card.

AIRPORTS AND TRANSFERS

Dorval International, 22½ km (14 mi) west of the city, handles all scheduled foreign and domestic flights and some charter operations. Mirabel International, 54½ km (34 mi) northwest of the city, serves most charter and cargo traffic.

➤ AIRPORT INFORMATION: **Dorval International Airport** (✉ 975 blvd. René-Vachon, Dorval, ☎ 514/394–7377). **Mirabel International Airport** (✉ 12600 rue Aérogare, Mirabel, ☎ 514/394–7377).

AIRPORT TRANSFER
A taxi from Dorval International to downtown costs about $28; from Mirabel, about $56. All taxi companies in Montréal must charge the same rates by law. L'Aerobus is a much cheaper alternative into town from Mirabel and Dorval. Shuttle service from Mirabel to the terminal next to the Gare Centrale, at 777 rue de la Gauchetière, is frequent and costs only $20 ($30 round-trip). The shuttle from Dorval runs about every half hour and stops at Le Centre Sheraton, the Marriott, Le Reine Elizabeth, and the central bus terminal. It costs $11 ($19.75 round-trip).

➤ SHUTTLE: **L'Aerobus** (☎ 514/931–9002).

BUS TRAVEL TO AND FROM MONTRÉAL

Greyhound Lines and its subsidiaries provide service to Montréal from various U.S. cities; Greyhound Canada has service from Toronto and points west in Canada. SMT & Acadian Lines arrives from eastern Canada. All buses arrive at and depart from the city's downtown bus terminal, the Station Central d'Autobus Montréal, which connects with the Berri-UQAM Métro station. Terminal staff have schedule and fare information for all bus service from Montréal, including the patchwork of independent companies that provide service to all Québec and some Ontario destinations.

➤ BUS INFORMATION: **Greyhound Canada** (☎ 800/661–8747). **Greyhound Lines** (☎ 800/231–2222). **SMT & Acadian Lines** (☎ 800/567–5151). **Station Central d'Autobus Montréal** (✉ 505 blvd. de Maisonneuve Est, Berri-UQAM, ☎ 514/842–2281).

BUS TRAVEL WITHIN MONTRÉAL

STCUM (Société de Transport de la Communauté Urbaine de Montréal) administers the buses as well as the Métro, so the same tickets and transfers (free) are valid on either service. You should be able to get within a few blocks of anywhere in the city on one fare. At this writing, rates are $2.25 for a single ticket, $9 for six tickets, and $48.50 for a monthly pass. Visitors can buy a day pass for $7 or a three-day pass for $14. They're available at some major hotels and at Berri-UQAM and some other downtown stations.

➤ BUS INFORMATION: **Société de Transport de la Communauté Urbaine de Montréal** (STCUM; ☎ 514/288–6287).

CAR RENTAL

➤ MAJOR AGENCIES: **Avis** (☎ 800/879–2847; ✉ Dorval International, ☎ 514/636–1902; ✉ 1225 rue Metcalfe, Downtown, ☎ 514/866–7906; ✉ Mirabel International, ☎ 450/476–3481). **Budget** (☎ 800/268–8900; ✉ Dorval International, ☎ 514/636–0052; ✉ Mirabel International, ☎ 450/476–2687). **Discount** (☎ 514/286–1554 or 800/263–2355). **Dollar** (✉ Mirabel International, ☎ 514/633–4467; ✉ 1155 rue Guy, Downtown, ☎ 514/344–5858). **Enterprise** (☎ 800/562–2886; ✉ 1005 rue Guy, Downtown, ☎ 514/931–3722; ✉ Dorval International, ☎ 514/633–1433). **Hertz** (☎ 800/263–0600 or 514/842–8537; ✉ Mirabel International, ☎ 450/476–3385; ✉ Dorval International, ☎ 514/636–9530). **National Car Rental** (☎ 514/878–2771 or 800/387–4747). **National Tilden** (☎ 514/878–2771 or 800/387–4747). **Thrifty** (✉ Dorval International, ☎ 514/631–5567; ✉ Mirabel International, ☎ 450/476–0496). **Via Route** (✉ 5180 av. Papineau, ☎ 514/871–1166).

CAR TRAVEL

Montréal is accessible from the rest of Canada via the Trans-Canada Highway (Highway 1), which enters the city from the east and west via Routes 20 and 40. The New York State Thruway (I–87) becomes Route 15 at the Canadian border, and then it's 47 km (29 mi) to the outskirts of Montréal. U.S. I–89 becomes two-lane Route 133, which eventually joins Route 10, at the border. From I–91 from Massachusetts via New Hampshire and Vermont, you must take Routes 55 and 10 to reach Montréal. At the border you must clear Canadian Customs, so be prepared with proof of citizenship (with photo I.D.) and your vehicle's ownership papers. On holidays and during the peak summer season, expect to wait up to a half hour or more at the major crossings.

In winter, remember that your car may not start on extra-cold mornings unless it has been kept in a heated garage.

➤ CONTACT: **Touring Club de Montréal–AAA, CAA, RAC** (☎ 514/861–7111).

PARKING

Montréal police have a diligent tow-away and fine system for cars double-parked or stopped in no-stopping zones downtown during rush hours and business hours. A parking ticket usually costs between $35 and $40. All Montréal parking signs are in French, so brush up on your *gauche* (left), *droit* (right), *ouest* (west), and *est* (east). If your car is towed while illegally parked, it will cost an additional $35 to retrieve it. Be especially alert in winter: Montréal's street plowers are ruthless in dealing with any parked cars in their way. If they don't tow them, they'll bury them. When parking in residential neighborhoods, beware of the alternate side of the street parking rules.

RULES OF THE ROAD

Once you're in Québec, the road signs are in French, but they're designed for everyone to understand them. The speed limit is posted in kilometers; on highways the limit is 100 kph (about 62 mph), and the use of radar-detection devices is prohibited. There are heavy penalties for driving while intoxicated, and drivers and front-seat passengers must wear over-the-shoulder seat belts. New York, Maine, and Ontario residents should drive with extra care in Québec: traffic violations in the province are entered on their driving records back home (and vice versa).

If you drive in the city, remember three things: Québec law forbids you to turn right on a red light, Montrealers are notorious jaywalkers, and the city has some crater-sized potholes.

DISCOUNTS AND DEALS

The Montréal museum pass allows access to 19 major museums. A day pass costs $15, a three-day pass $28; family passes are $30 for one day and $60 for three days. They are available at museums or Centre Info-Touriste, at 1001 Square Dorchester.

EMERGENCIES

The U.S. Consulate has a list of various medical specialists in the Montréal area. Call ☎ 514/398–9695 in advance to make sure the Consulate is open. The emergency Consulate number is ☎ 514/981–5059.

There's a dental clinic on avenue Van Horne that's open 24 hours; Sunday appointments are for emergencies only.

Many pharmacies are open until midnight, including Jean Coutu and Pharmaprix locations. Some are open around the clock, including the Pharmaprix on chemin de la Côte-des-Neiges.

➤ DENTISTS: **Dental clinic** (✉ 3546 av. Van Horne, Côte-des-Neiges, ☎ 514/342–4444).

➤ EMERGENCY SERVICES: **Ambulance, fire, police** (☎ 911). **Québec Poison Control Centre** (☎ 800/463–5060).

➤ HOSPITAL: **Montréal General Hospital** (✉ 1650 av. Cedar, Downtown, ☎ 514/937–6011).

➤ LATE-NIGHT PHARMACIES: **Jean Coutu** (✉ 501 rue Mont-Royal Est, Quartier Latin, ☎ 514/521–1058; ✉ 5510 chemin de la Côte-des-Neiges, Côte-des-Neiges, ☎ 514/344–8338). **Pharmaprix** (✉ 1500 rue Ste-Catherine Ouest, Downtown, ☎ 514/933–4744; ✉ 5157 rue Sherbrooke Ouest, NDG, ☎ 514/484–3531; ✉ 901 rue Ste-Catherine Est, Village, ☎ 514/842–4915; ✉ 5122 chemin de la Côte-des-Neiges, Côte-des-Neiges, ☎ 514/738–8464).

GAY AND LESBIAN TRAVELERS

Montréal has one of the most visible gay communities in North America. Much of the scene centers on the Village, a once gritty neighborhood that's become dramatically rejuvenated. On the Plateau, whose shops and eateries also draw plenty of gays and lesbians, is L'Androgyne, an inviting little bookshop with an excellent selection of lesbian, gay, and feminist titles, in both French and English. The French-language newspapers *RG* (www.rgmag.com) and *Fugues* (www.fugues.com), which has a limited English-language section, and the feminist/lesbian magazine *Gazelle* include events listings, culture, and news. The gay and lesbian bilingual Web site www.directiongayquebec.com is another good resource.

➤ CONTACT: **L'Androgyne** (✉ 1436 rue Amherst, Village, ☎ 514/842–4765).

LODGING

The room-reservation service of Hospitality Canada can help you find a room in one of 80 hotels, motels, and B&Bs. Tourisme Québec also operates a room-booking service.

➤ TOLL-FREE NUMBERS: **Hospitality Canada** (☎ 800/665–1528). **Tourisme Québec** (☎ 877/266–5687, WEB www.bonjourquebec.com).

B&BS

Bed and Breakfast à Montréal represents more than 50 homes in downtown and in the elegant neighborhoods of Westmount and Outremont. Downtown B&B Network represents 75 homes and apartments, mostly around the downtown core and along rue Sherbrooke, that have one or more rooms available for visitors.

➤ RESERVATION SERVICES: **Bed and Breakfast à Montréal** (✉ Marian Kahn, Box 575, Snowdon Station, H3X 3T8, ☎ 514/738–9410 or 800/

738–4338, FAX 514/735–7493, WEB www.bbmontreal.com). **Downtown B&B Network** (⊠ Bob Finkelstein, 3458 av. Laval, H2X 3C8, ☎ 514/ 289–9749 or 800/267–5180, WEB www.bbmontreal.qc.ca).

SUBWAY TRAVEL

The Métro, or subway, is clean, quiet (it runs on rubber wheels), and safe, and it's heated in winter and cooled in summer. As in any city, visitors should be alert and attentive to personal property such as purses and wallets. The Métro is also connected to the 29 km (18 mi) of the Underground City. Each of the 65 Métro stops has been individually designed and decorated; Berri-UQAM has stained glass, and at Place d'Armes a small collection of archaeological artifacts is exhibited. The stations between Snowdon and Jean-Talon on the Blue Line are worth a visit, particularly Outremont, with its glass-block design. Each station connects with one or more bus routes, which cover the rest of the island.

Free maps may be obtained at Métro ticket booths. Try to get the *Carte Réseau* (System Map); it's the most complete. Transfers from Métro to buses are available from the dispenser just beyond the ticket booth inside the station. Bus-to-bus and bus-to-Métro transfers may be obtained from the bus driver. The Société de Transport de la Communauté Urbaine de Montréal does operate an automated line for information on bus and Métro schedules, but in French only.

FARES AND SCHEDULES

Métro hours on the Orange, Green, and Yellow lines are weekdays 5:30 AM–12:58 AM, Saturday 5:30 AM–1:28 AM, and Sunday 5:30 AM–1:58 AM. The Blue Line runs daily 5:30 AM–11 PM. Trains run as often as every three minutes on the most crowded lines—Orange and Green— at rush hours.

The STCUM, or Société de Transport de la Communauté Urbaine de Montréal, administers both the Métro and the buses, so the same tickets and transfers, which are free, are valid on either service. You should be able to get within a few blocks of anywhere in the city on one fare. Rates are $2 for a single ticket, $8.50 for six tickets, $48.50 for a monthly pass, $7 for a day pass, and $14 for a three-day pass. They're available at some of the bigger hotels, at most corner variety stores, at Berri-UQAM, and at some other downtown stations.
➤ SUBWAY INFORMATION: **Société de Transport de la Communauté Urbaine de Montréal** (STCUM; ☎ 514/288–6287).

TAXES

A $15 airport tax (for capital improvements) is charged when you leave. You can pay cash or with a credit card.

TAXIS

Taxis in Montréal all run on the same rate: $2.50 minimum and $1.10 per km (½ mi). They're usually reliable, although they may be difficult to find on rainy nights after the Métro has closed. Each has on its roof a white or orange plastic sign that is lit when available and off when occupied.

TOURS

BOAT TOURS

From May through October, Amphi Tour offers a unique one-hour tour of Vieux-Montréal and the Vieux-Port on both land and water in an amphibious bus. Bateau-Mouche runs four harbor excursions and an evening supper cruise daily May through October. The boats are reminiscent of the ones that cruise the canals of the Netherlands—wide-

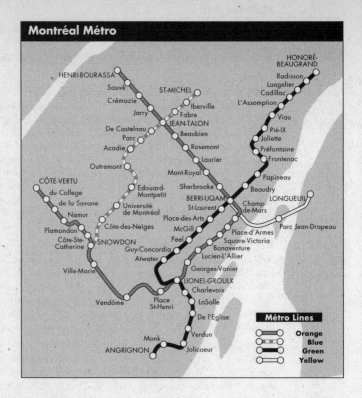

beamed and low-slung, with a glassed-in passenger deck. Boats leave from the Jacques Cartier Pier at the foot of Place Jacques-Cartier in the Vieux-Port.

➤ FEES AND SCHEDULES: **Amphi Tour** (☎ 514/849–5181 or 514/386–1298). **Bateau-Mouche** (☎ 514/849–9952).

BUS TOURS

Gray Line offers nine different tours of Montréal from June to October and one tour during other months. It has pickup service at the major hotels and at Info-Touriste (1001 Sq. Dorchester).

Imperial Tours' double-decker buses follow a nine-stop circuit of the city. You can get off and on as often as you like and stay at each stop as long as you like. There's pickup service at major hotels.

➤ FEES AND SCHEDULES: **Gray Line** (☎ 514/934–1222). **Imperial Tours** (☎ 514/871–4733).

CALÈCHE RIDES

Open horse-drawn carriages—fleece-lined in winter—leave from Place Jacques-Cartier, Square Dorchester, Place d'Armes, and rue de la Commune. An hour-long ride costs about $50, although slow days mean better bargaining opportunities.

TRAIN TRAVEL

The Gare Centrale, on rue de la Gauchetière between rues University and Mansfield (behind Le Reine Elizabeth), is the rail terminus for all trains from the United States and from other Canadian provinces. It is connected underground to the Bonaventure Métro station. The Amtrak *Adirondack* leaves New York's Penn Station every morning for the 10½-hour trip through scenic upstate New York to Montréal. Amtrak also has bus connections with the *Vermonter* in St. Albans, Vermont. VIA Rail connects Montréal with all the major cities of Canada,

including Québec City, Halifax, Ottawa, Toronto, Winnipeg, Edmonton, and Vancouver.
➤ Train Information: **Amtrak** (☎ 800/872–7245). **VIA Rail** (☎ 514/989–2626, 888/842–7245, 800/361–5390 in Québec).

TRANSPORTATION AROUND MONTRÉAL
Public transportation is easily the best and cheapest way to get around. Finding your way around Montréal by car is not difficult, as the streets are laid out in a fairly straightforward grid and one-way streets are clearly marked. But parking isn't easy, and the narrow cobbled streets of Vieux-Montréal can be a trial. It's much easier to park near a Métro station and walk and use public transit.

TRAVEL AGENCIES
➤ Local Agents: **American Express** (✉ 1141 blvd. de Maisonneuve Ouest, Downtown, ☎ 514/284–3300). **Canadian Automobile Club** (✉ 1180 rue Drummond, Downtown, ☎ 514/861–5111). **Vacances Tourbec** (✉ 595 blvd. de Maisonneuve Ouest, Downtown, ☎ 514/842–1400). **Voyages Campus** (✉ McGill University, 3480 rue McTavish, Downtown, ☎ 514/398–0647).

VISITOR INFORMATION
Centre Info-Touriste, on Square Dorchester, has extensive tourist information on Montréal and the rest of the province of Québec, as well as a currency-exchange service and Internet café. It's open June 1 to early September, daily 7:30–8, and September to May 31, daily 9–6. The Vieux-Montréal branch is open mid-October to mid-May, daily 9–5, and daily 9–7 the rest of the year.

Tourisme-Montréal has information on city attractions and events. The very trendy Plateau Mont-Royal district has its own tourist association. The Hochelaga-Maisonneuve tourist association has information on attractions and events in the colorful district around the Stade Olympique.
➤ Tourist Information: **Centre Info-Touriste** (✉ 1001 Sq. Dorchester, Downtown, ☎ 514/873–2015 or 800/363–7777; ✉ 174 rue Notre-Dame Est, at pl. Jacques-Cartier, Vieux-Montréal, ☎ 514/873–2015). **Hochelaga-Maisonneuve tourist association** (☎ 514/256–4636, WEB www.tourismemaisonneuve.qc.ca). **Plateau Mont-Royal tourist association** (☎ 514/840–0926 or 888/449–9944, WEB www.tpmr.qc.ca). **Tourisme-Montréal** (☎ 514/844–5400, WEB www.tourism-montreal.org).

3 QUÉBEC CITY

Whether you're strolling along the Plains
of Abraham or exploring the Vieux-Port,
Québec City gives you a feeling for centuries
of history and French civilization. The city,
which has one of the most spectacular
settings in North America, is perched on a
cliff above a narrow point in the St. Lawrence
River. It is the capital of, as well as the oldest
municipality in, the province of Québec.

Updated by
Elizabeth
Thompson

N O EXCURSION TO FRENCH-SPEAKING Canada is complete without a visit to exuberant, romantic Québec City, which can claim one of the most beautiful natural settings in North America. The well-preserved Vieux-Québec (Old Québec) is small and dense, steeped in four centuries of history and French tradition. The ramparts that once protected the city, 17th- and 18th-century buildings, and numerous parks and monuments are here. The government of Québec has completely restored many of the centuries-old buildings of Place Royale, one of the oldest districts on the continent. Because of the site's immaculate preservation as the only fortified city remaining in North America north of Mexico, UNESCO has designated Vieux-Québec a World Heritage Site.

Perched on a cliff above a narrow point in the St. Lawrence River, Québec City is the oldest municipality in Québec province. In the 17th century the first French explorers, fur trappers, and missionaries came here to establish the colony of New France. Today it still resembles a French provincial town in many ways; its family-oriented residents have strong ties to their past. An estimated 96% of the Québec City region's population of more than 650,000 list French as their mother tongue.

In 1535 French explorer Jacques Cartier first came upon what the Algonquin people called Kebec, meaning "where the river narrows." New France, however, was not actually founded in the vicinity of what is now Québec City until 1608, when another French explorer, Samuel de Champlain, recognized the military advantages of the location and set up a fort. On the banks of the St. Lawrence, on the spot now called Place Royale, this fort developed into an economic center for fur trade and shipbuilding. Twelve years later, Champlain realized the French colony's vulnerability to attacks from above and expanded its boundaries to the top of the cliff, where he built the fort Château St-Louis on the site of the present-day Château Frontenac.

During the early days of New France, the French and British fought for control of the region. In 1690, when an expedition led by Admiral Sir William Phipps arrived from England, Comte de Frontenac, New France's most illustrious governor, defied him with the statement, "Tell your lord that I will reply with the mouth of my cannons."

The French, preoccupied with scandals at the courts of Louis XV and Louis XVI, gave only grudging help to their possessions in the New World. The French colonists built walls and other military structures and had the strong defensive position on top of the cliff, but they still had to contend with Britain's naval supremacy. On September 13, 1759, the British army, led by General James Wolfe, scaled the colony's cliff and took the French troops led by General Louis-Joseph Montcalm by surprise. The British defeated the French in a 20-minute battle on the Plains of Abraham, and New France came under British rule.

The British brought their mastery of trade to the region. During the 18th century, Québec City's economy prospered because of the success of the fishing, fur-trading, shipbuilding, and timber industries. Wary of new invasions, the British continued to expand upon the fortifications left by the French. They built a wall encircling the city and a star-shaped citadel, both of which mark the city's urban landscape today. The constitution of 1791 established Québec City as the capital of Lower Canada until the 1840 Act of Union united Upper and Lower Canada and made Montréal the capital. Québec City remained under British rule until 1867, when the Act of Confederation united several Canadian provinces (Québec, Ontario, New Brunswick, and Nova Scotia) and established Québec City as capital of the province of Québec.

In the mid-19th century the economic center of eastern Canada shifted west from Québec City to Montréal and Toronto. Today, government is Québec City's main business: about 27,000 full- or part-time civil-service employees work and live in the area. Office complexes continue to spring up outside the older part of town; modern malls, convention centers, and imposing hotels now cater to a business clientele.

In 2001, surrounding suburbs such as Ste-Foy and Sillery were merged with Québec City. The merger, which is being phased in, could result in changes to many street names around the city over the next few years.

Pleasures and Pastimes

Dining
Gone are the days when Québec City dining consisted mostly of classic French and hearty Québecois cuisine served in restaurants in the downtown core. Nowadays the city's finest eateries, found both inside and outside the city's walls, offer lighter contemporary fare, often with Asian or Italian as well as French and Québecois influences. There are still fine French restaurants, though, and you can sample French-Canadian cuisine composed of robust, uncomplicated dishes that make use of the region's bounty of foods, including fowl and wild game (quail, caribou, venison), maple syrup, and various berries and nuts. Other specialties include *cretons* (pâtés), *tourtière* (meat pie), and *tarte au sucre* (maple-syrup pie).

Lodging
With more than 35 hotels within its walls and an abundance of family-run bed-and-breakfasts, Québec City has many options. Landmark hotels stand as prominent as the city's most historic sites; modern high-rises outside the ramparts have spectacular views of the old city. Another choice is to immerse yourself in the city's historic charm by staying in an old-fashioned inn where no two rooms are alike.

Walking
Québec City is a wonderful place to wander on foot. Impressive vistas of the Laurentian Mountains and the St. Lawrence River are revealed on a walk along the city walls or a climb to the city's highest point, Cap Diamant, near the Citadelle. It's possible to spend days investigating the narrow cobblestone streets of Vieux-Québec, visiting historic sites, or browsing for local arts and crafts in the boutiques of quartier Petit-Champlain. A stroll on the Promenade des Gouverneurs and the Plains of Abraham provides a view of the river as well as the Laurentian foothills and the Appalachian Mountains.

EXPLORING QUÉBEC CITY

Québec City's split-level landscape divides Upper Town on the cape from Lower Town, along the shores of the St. Lawrence. If you look out from the Terrasse Dufferin boardwalk in Upper Town, you will see the rooftops of Lower Town buildings directly below. Separating these two sections of the city is steep and precipitous rock, against which were built more than 25 *escaliers* (staircases). A *funiculaire* (funicular) climbs and descends the cliff between Terrasse Dufferin and the Maison Louis-Jolliet in Lower Town. There's plenty to see in the oldest sections of town, as well as in the modern city beyond the walls.

Numbers in the text correspond to numbers in the margin and on the Upper and Lower Towns (Haute-Ville, Basse-Ville), Outside the Walls, and Île d'Orléans maps.

Great Itineraries

Whether you take a weekend or almost a week, there's enough history, scenery, and entertainment for even the most seasoned traveler. On a weekend or four-day trip, you can take in the historic sites of Vieux-Québec, walking along ancient streets and the boardwalk by the river before dining at some of the city's fine restaurants. A longer stay allows you to explore some lovely places beyond the city.

IF YOU HAVE 2 DAYS

With only a couple of days, you should devote one day to Lower Town, where you can view the earliest site of French civilization in North America, and the second day to Upper Town, where more of the later British influence can be seen. On Day 1, stroll through the narrow streets of the Quartier Petit-Champlain, visiting the Maison Chevalier and browsing through the many handicraft boutiques. Moving on to Place Royale, head for the Église Notre-Dame-des-Victoires; in summer there's almost always entertainment in the square. On Day 2, take the time to view the St. Lawrence River from Terrasse Dufferin and visit the impressive buildings of Upper Town, where 17th- and 18th-century religious and educational institutions predominate.

IF YOU HAVE 4 DAYS

A four-day trip allows you to wander farther afield, outside the walls of the old city. On Day 3, watch the pomp and ceremony of the changing of the guard at the Citadelle; roam the Plains of Abraham, site of the battle that decided the fate of New France; and tour the National Assembly, where battles for power are still being waged. On Day 4, you can take an in-depth look at the Musée du Québec or the Musée de la Civilisation. Then see the city from a different vantage point—aboard a horse-drawn *calèche* or from a walk atop the ramparts. In summer, do what the locals do—grab a seat on an outdoor *terrasse*, sip a cool drink, and watch the world go by.

IF YOU HAVE 6 DAYS

A trip this length gives you time to experience some of Québec's scenic countryside. Follow the itinerary above for a four-day trip. On Day 5, you could spend more time exploring Vieux-Québec. Or you could take historic avenue Royale (Route 360) east to Montmorency Falls, higher than Niagara. Afterward, you can explore the farms and woodlands of Île d'Orléans. On Day 6, do something you've never done before. In summer, you can take a boat cruise along the St. Lawrence or raft down the Jacques Cartier River. In winter, strap on skis and head to Mont Ste-Anne. Try snowmobiling, dogsledding, or even ice climbing at Montmorency Falls.

Upper Town

The most prominent buildings of Québec City's earliest European inhabitants, who set up the city's political, educational, and religious institutions, stand here. Haute-Ville, or Upper Town, became the political capital of the colony of New France and, later, of British North America. Historic buildings with thick stone walls, large wood doors, copper roofs, and majestic steeples fill the heart of the city.

A Good Walk

Begin your walk where rue St-Louis meets rue du Fort at **Place d'Armes** ①, a large plaza bordered by government buildings. To your

100

Metropolitan Québec City

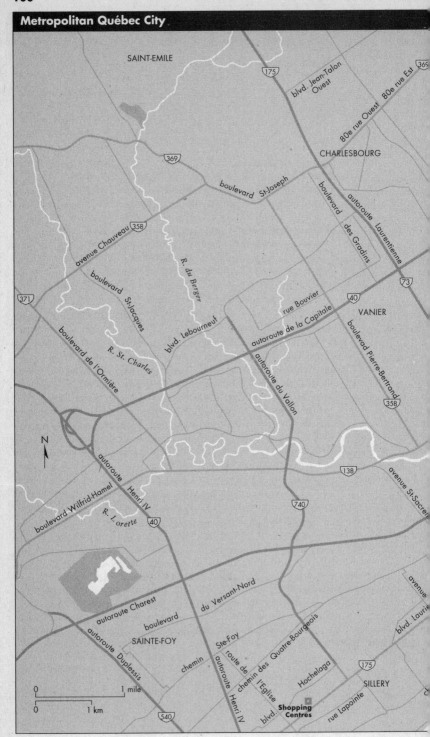

SAINT-EMILE

175

blvd. Jean-Talon Ouest

80e rue Ouest · 80e rue Est · 369

CHARLESBOURG

369

boulevard St-Joseph

boulevard des Gradins

autoroute Laurentienne

avenue Chauveau

358

boulevard St-Jacques

R. du Berger

73

371

boulevard de l'Ormière

R. St. Charles

blvd. Lebourneuf

rue Bouvier

40

VANIER

autoroute de la Capitale

autoroute du Vallon

boulevard Pierre-Bertrand

358

N

138

avenue St-Sacrer

autoroute Henri IV

boulevard Wilfrid-Hamel

R. Lorette

40

740

autoroute Charest

du Versant-Nord

avenue

boulevard

SAINTE-FOY

Ste-Foy

chemin des Quatre-Bourgeois

blvd. Laurie

autoroute Duplessis

chemin

route de

chemin de l'Église

autoroute Henri IV

Hochelaga

175

SILLERY

0   1 mile

0   1 km

540

blvd.

**Shopping
Centres**

rue Lapointe

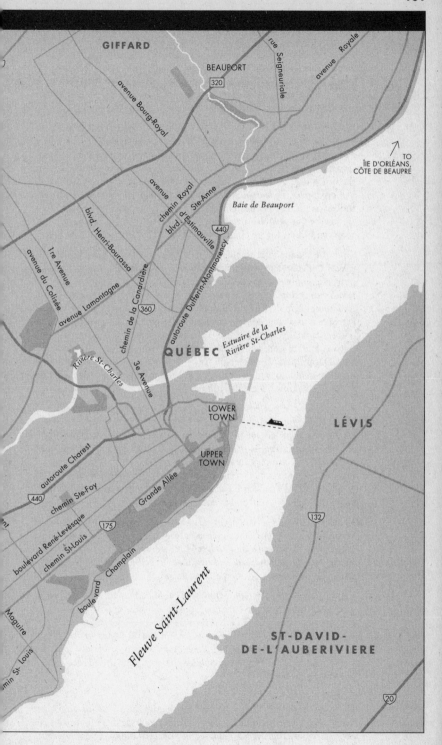

GIFFARD

BEAUPORT

avenue Bourg-Royal

rue Seigneuriale

avenue Royale

320

chemin Royal

avenue

blvd. d'Estimauville

blvd. Henri-Bourassa

chemin Ste-Anne

Baie de Beauport

TO
ÎLE D'ORLÉANS,
CÔTE DE BEAUPRÉ

440

1-re Avenue

avenue du Colisée

avenue Lamontagne

chemin de la Canardière

360

autoroute Dufferin-Montmorency

Estuaire de la
Rivière St-Charles

QUÉBEC

Rivière St-Charles

3e Avenue

LOWER
TOWN

LÉVIS

UPPER
TOWN

autoroute Charest

440

chemin Ste-Foy

Grande Allée

boulevard René-Lévesque

chemin St-Louis

175

132

boulevard Champlain

Maguire

chemin St-Louis

Fleuve Saint-Laurent

ST-DAVID-
DE-L'AUBERIVIERE

20

right is the colony's former treasury building, **Maison Maillou,** interesting for its 18th-century architecture. Maison Kent, where the terms of the surrender of Québec to the British were signed in 1759, is a little farther along, at 25 rue St-Louis. Québec City's most celebrated landmark, **Fairmont Le Château Frontenac** ②, an impressive green-turreted hotel, stands south of Place d'Armes. As you head to the boardwalk behind the Frontenac, notice the glorious bronze statue of Champlain, standing where he built his residence.

Walk south along the boardwalk called the **Terrasse Dufferin** ③, enlivened by street performers in summer, for a panoramic view of the city and its surroundings. As you pass to the southern side of the Frontenac, you arrive at a small park called **Jardin des Gouverneurs** ④. From the north side of the park, follow rue Haldimand and turn left on rue St-Louis, past the **Musée d'Art Inuit Brousseau**; then make a right and follow rue du Parloir until it intersects with tiny rue Donnacona. Here stands the **Couvent des Ursulines** ⑤, a private school that houses a museum and has a lovely chapel next door.

Take rue Donnacona to rue des Jardins and visit the **Holy Trinity Anglican Cathedral** ⑥, a dignified church with precious objects on display. Next come two buildings interesting for their art deco details: the **Hôtel Clarendon** ⑦, on the corner of rue des Jardins and rue Ste-Anne, and, next door, the **Edifice Price** ⑧. Continue along rue Ste-Anne up to rue St-Stanislas and **Morrin College** ⑨, which now houses the Literary and Historical Society library. Walk along rue St-Stanislas and turn left onto rue Dauphine, to the **Chapelle des Jésuites** ⑩, at the corner of rues Dauphine and d'Auteuil. Turn right on rue d'Auteuil and head down the hill to rue St-Jean and the entrance to the **Parc de l'Artillerie** ⑪, a complex of 20 military, industrial, and civilian buildings.

On your way out of Artillery Park, turn left, away from the walls, and walk along rue St-Jean, one of Québec City's most colorful thoroughfares; turn left on rue Collins. The cluster of stone buildings at the end of the street is the **Monastère des Augustines de l'Hôtel-Dieu de Québec** ⑫, which can be toured. Turn right onto rue Charlevoix, then left on rue Hamel to rue des Remparts. **Maison Montcalm** ⑬, the famous general's former home, is to the right, on rue des Remparts between rues Hamel and St-Flavien.

Continue along rue des Remparts and then turn right on rue Ste-Famille. When you reach côte de la Fabrique, look for the iron entrance gates of the **Séminaire du Québec** ⑭. Head west across the courtyard to the **Musée de l'Amérique Française** ⑮. Next, visit the seminary's Chapelle Extérieure, at its west entrance.

The historic **Basilique Notre-Dame-de-Québec** ⑯, which has an ornate interior, is nearby at the corner of rues Ste-Famille and de Buade. Turn left on rue de Buade, then cross the street halfway down the block and wander through the outdoor art gallery of **rue du Trésor** ⑰. At the end of the alley, turn left on rue Ste-Anne and wind up your walk (and rest your feet) with a 30-minute recap of the six sieges of Québec City at the **Musée du Fort** ⑱.

TIMING
Plan on spending at least a day visiting the sites and museums in Upper Town. Lunchtime should find you around Parc de l'Artillerie and rue St-Jean, where there is a good selection of restaurants. Those who prefer a leisurely pace could take two days, stopping to watch street performers and enjoying long lunches. May through October are the best months for walking, July and August being the busiest.

Sights to See

⑯ Basilique Notre-Dame-de-Québec. This basilica has the oldest parish in North America, dating from 1647. It's been rebuilt three times: in the early 1700s, when François de Montmorency Laval was the first bishop; in 1759, after cannons at Lévis fired upon it during the siege of Québec; and in 1922, after a fire. The basilica's somberly ornate interior includes a canopy dais over the episcopal throne, a ceiling of painted clouds decorated with gold leaf, richly colored stained-glass windows, and a chancel lamp that was a gift of Louis XIV. The large and famous crypt was Québec City's first cemetery; more than 900 people are interred here, including 20 bishops and four governors of New France. Samuel de Champlain is believed to be buried near the basilica: archaeologists have been searching for his tomb since 1950. In summer the indoor Act of Faith sound-and-light show uses the basilica as a backdrop to tell the history of the city and the basilica. *16 rue de Buade, Upper Town,* ☎ *418/692–2533 church, 418/694–4000 show.* ◻ *Basilica free, crypt $1, sound-and-light show $7.50.* ☉ *Mid-Oct.– Apr., daily 7:30–4:30; May–mid-Oct., weekdays 7:30–3, weekends 7:30– 6; sound-and-light show May 1–Oct.15, weekdays 3:30–8:30, weekends 6:30–8:30.*

⑩ Chapelle des Jésuites (Jesuits' Chapel). Built in 1820 from plans by architect François Baillairgé, the chapel, with its sculptures and paintings, is considered one of the monuments of Québec art of the period. Sculptor Pierre-Noël Levasseur contributed the mid-18th-century wooden statues of the Blessed Virgin and St. Joseph, which predate the chapel; the delicately carved high altar was designed by architect Eugène Taché. ✉ *20 rue Dauphine, Upper Town,* ☎ *418/694–9616.* ◻ *Free.* ☉ *Weekdays 11–1:30.*

❺ Couvent des Ursulines (Ursuline Convent). The site of North America's oldest teaching institution for girls, still a private school, was founded in 1639 by French nun Marie de l'Incarnation and laywoman Madame La Peltrie. The convent has many of its original walls still intact, and houses a museum and a little chapel. The **Chapelle des Ursulines** (Ursuline Chapel; ✉ 10 rue Donnacona, ☎ no phone) is where French general Louis-Joseph Montcalm was buried after he died in the 1759 battle that decided the fate of New France. In September 2001, Montcalm's remains were transferred to rest with those of his soldiers at the Hôpital Général de Québec's cemetery, at 260 blvd. Langelier. The exterior of the Ursuline Chapel was rebuilt in 1902, but the interior contains the original chapel, which took sculptor Pierre-Noël Levasseur from 1726 to 1736 to complete. The votive lamp was lit in 1717 and has never been extinguished. The chapel is open May through October, Tuesday through Saturday 10–11:30 and 1:30–4:30, Sunday 1:30– 4:30. Admission is free. The **Musée des Ursulines** (✉ 12 rue Donnacona, ☎ 418/694–0694) is the former residence of one of the convent's founders, Madame de la Peltrie. It provides an informative perspective on 120 years of the Ursulines' life under the French regime, from 1639 to 1759. It took an Ursuline nun nine years of training to attain the level of a professional embroiderer; the museum contains magnificent pieces of ornate embroidery, such as altar frontals with gold and silver threads intertwined with semiprecious jewels. Admission is $5. May through September the museum is open Tuesday through Saturday 10–noon and 1–5, Sunday 1–5; in October and November and February through April it's open Tuesday through Sunday 1–4:30. Next door to the museum is the **Centre Marie-de-l'Incarnation** (✉ 10 rue Donnacona, ☎ 418/694–0413), a center with an exhibit and books for sale on the life of the Ursulines' first superior, who came from France and cofounded the convent. The center is open May through the end

104

Upper and Lower Towns (Haute-Ville, Basse-Ville)

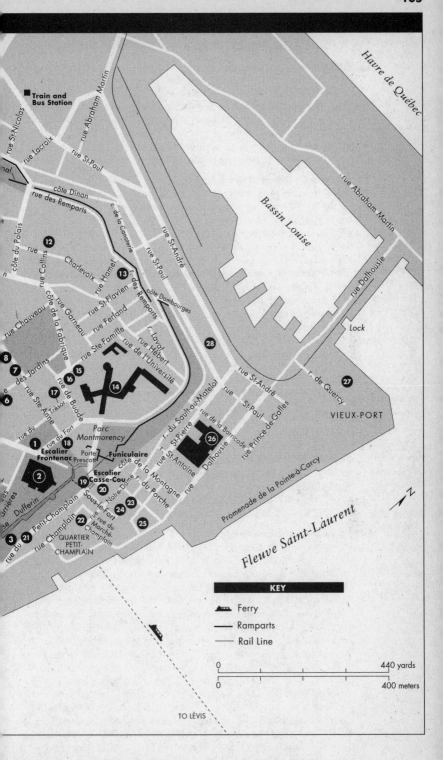

Havre de Québec

Train and
Bus Station

rue St-Nicolas
rue Lacroix
rue Abraham Martin
rue St-Paul

côte Dinan
rue des Remparts
e. de la Canoterie

Bassin Louise

rue Abraham Martin

côte du Palais
rue Collins
rue St-André
rue St-Paul
côte Dambourges

12

Charlevoix
rue Hamel
13
r. des Remparts

rue Chauveau
côte de la Fabrique
rue Garneau
rue St-Flavien
rue Ferland
rue Ste-Famille
rue Hébert
r. Laval
côte Dambourges
rue de l'Université

rue Dalhousie

Lock

8
7
des Jardins
15
16
14
28
rue St-André
r. de Quercy
27

6
rue Ste-Anne
rue de Buade
17
rue du Trésor

rue St-Paul
St-Paul

VIEUX-PORT

rue du Fort
Parc
Montmorency
r. du Sault-au-Matelot
rue de la Barricade
r. Prince-de-Galles

1
18
**Escalier
Frontenac**
Porte
Prescott
Funiculaire
r. St-Pierre
r. St-Antoine
26
rue Dalhousie

2
19
**Escalier
Casse-Cou**
côte de la Montagne
r. du Porche

Dufferin
20
Notre-Dame

24
23

Promenade de la Pointe-à-Carcy

Petit-Champlain
Sous-le-Fort
25

3
21
22
rue du Marché-
Champlain
rue du
Champlain
QUARTIER
PETIT-
CHAMPLAIN

Fleuve Saint-Laurent

N

KEY	
🚢	Ferry
—	Ramparts
—	Rail Line

0   440 yards
0   400 meters

TO LÉVIS

of October Tuesday through Saturday 10–11:30, Sunday 1:30–4:30; February through April it's open Tuesday through Sunday 1:30–4:30. ⊠ *18 rue Donnacona, Upper Town.*

⑧ Edifice Price (Price Building). The city's first skyscraper, a 15-story art deco structure, was built in 1929 and served as headquarters of the Price Brothers Company, the lumber firm founded in Canada by Sir William Price. Don't miss the interior: exquisite copper plaques depict scenes of the company's early pulp and paper activities, and the two maple-wood elevators are '30s classics. In 2001, the 16th and 17th floor of the building were converted into an official residence for Québec's premier. Only the lobby is open to the public. ⊠ *65 rue Ste-Anne, Upper Town.*

★ **② Fairmont Le Château Frontenac.** Québec City's most celebrated landmark, this imposing green-turreted castle with its copper roof stands on the site of what was the administrative and military headquarters of New France. It owes its name to the Comte de Frontenac, governor of the French colony between 1672 and 1698. Looking at the magnificence of the château's location, you can see why Frontenac said, "For me, there is no site more beautiful nor more grandiose than that of Québec City." Samuel de Champlain, who founded Québec City in 1608, was responsible for Château St-Louis, the first structure to appear on the site of the Frontenac; it was built between 1620 and 1624 as a residence for colonial governors. In 1784 Château Haldimand was constructed here, but it was demolished in 1892 to make way for Château Frontenac. The latter was built as a hotel in 1893, and it was considered remarkably luxurious at that time: guest rooms contained fireplaces, bathrooms, and marble fixtures, and a special commissioner purchased antiques for the establishment. The hotel was designed by New York architect Bruce Price, who also worked on Québec City's Gare du Palais (rail station) and other Canadian landmarks. The addition of a 20-story central tower in 1925 completed the Frontenac. It has accumulated a star-studded guest roster, including Queen Elizabeth and Ronald Reagan as well as Franklin Roosevelt and Winston Churchill, who convened here in 1943 and 1944 for two wartime conferences. Guides dressed in 19th-century costumes conduct tours of the hotel's luxurious interior. ⊠ *1 rue des Carrières, Upper Town,* ☎ *418/691–2166.* ▭ *Tours $6.50.* ⊙ *Tours: May–Oct. 15, daily 10–6; Oct. 16–Apr., weekends noon–5 or on demand.*

⑥ Holy Trinity Anglican Cathedral. This stone church dates from 1804 and was one of the first Anglican cathedrals built outside the British Isles. Its simple, dignified facade is reminiscent of London's St. Martin-in-the-Fields. The cathedral's land was originally given to the Recollet fathers (Franciscan monks from France) in 1681 by the king of France for a church and monastery. When Québec came under British rule, the Recollets made the church available to the Anglicans for services. Later, King George III of England ordered construction of the present cathedral, with an area set aside for members of the royal family. A portion of the north balcony still remains exclusively for the use of the reigning sovereign or her representative. The church houses precious objects donated by George III; wood for the oak benches was imported from the Royal Forest at Windsor. The cathedral's impressive rear organ has 3,058 pipes. On Sunday mornings the cathedral has traditional English bell ringing. ⊠ *31 rue des Jardins, Upper Town,* ☎ *418/692–2193.* ▭ *Free.* ⊙ *Mid-May–June, daily 9–6; July–Aug., daily 9–8; Sept.–early Oct., weekdays 10–6; Nov.–mid-May, services only; Sun. services in English at 11 AM, in French at 9:30 AM.*

⑦ Hôtel Clarendon. One of the city's finest art deco structures is the Clarendon, Québec's oldest hotel. Although the hotel dates from 1866, it was reconstructed in its current style—with geometric patterns of stone and wrought iron decorating its interior—in 1930. ⊠ *57 rue Ste-Anne, at rue des Jardins, Upper Town,* ☎ *418/692–2480.*

❹ Jardin des Gouverneurs (Governors' Park). In this small park just south of the Château Frontenac stands the **Wolfe-Montcalm Monument,** a 50-ft obelisk that is unique because it pays tribute to both a winning (English) and a losing (French) general. The monument recalls the 1759 battle on the Plains of Abraham, which ended French rule of New France. British general James Wolfe lived only long enough to hear of his victory; French general Louis-Joseph Montcalm died shortly after Wolfe with the knowledge that the city was lost. During the French regime the public area served as a garden for the governors who resided in Château St-Louis. On the south side of the park is **avenue Ste-Geneviève,** lined with well-preserved Victorian houses dating from 1850 to 1900. Several have been converted to old-fashioned inns.

Maison Maillou. The colony's former treasury building typifies the architecture of New France with its sharply slanted roof, dormer windows, concrete chimneys, shutters with iron hinges, and limestone walls. Built between 1736 and 1753, it stands at the end of **rue du Trésor.** Maison Maillou now houses the Québec City Chamber of Commerce and is not open for tours. ⊠ *17 rue St-Louis, Upper Town.*

⓭ Maison Montcalm. This was the home of French general Louis-Joseph Montcalm from 1758 until the capitulation of New France. A plaque dedicated to the general is on the right side of the house. ⊠ *Rue des Remparts between rues Hamel and St-Flavien, Upper Town. Closed to public.*

⓬ Monastère des Augustines de l'Hôtel-Dieu de Québec (Augustine Monastery). Augustine nuns arrived from Dieppe, France, in 1639 with a mission to care for the sick in the new colony. They established the first hospital north of Mexico, the **Hôtel-Dieu,** the large building west of the monastery. The **Musée des Augustines** (Augustine Museum) is in hospital-like quarters with large sterile corridors leading into a ward that has a large exhibit of antique medical instruments, such as a pill-making device. Upon request the Augustines also offer guided tours of the **chapel** (1800) and the cellars used by the nuns as a shelter, beginning in 1695, during bombardments by the British. During the Second World War, the cellars hid national treasures that had been smuggled out of Poland for safekeeping. At this writing, the museum is expected to be closed throughout 2003 for renovations and plans to reopen in 2004, with the addition of a new cultural center. ⊠ *32 rue Charlevoix, Upper Town,* ☎ *418/692–2492.* ⊠ *Museum free, guided tour $3.* ☉ *Tues.–Sat. 9:30–noon and 1:30–5, Sun. 1:30–5.*

★ ❾ Morrin College. This stately gray stone building was Québec City's first prison (the cells are still in the basement); wrongdoers were hanged outside the front door. In 1868 it was turned into one of the city's early private schools, Morrin College. The **Literary and Historical Society library** has been on the site since then. Its superb collection includes some of the earliest books printed in North America, and the librarian's desk once belonged to Sir Georges-Étienne Cartier, one of Canada's fathers of Confederation. A statue of Gen. James Wolfe, on the second-floor balcony that wraps around the interior of the library, dates from 1779. The society, founded in 1824, is the oldest of its kind in North America and a forerunner to Canada's National Archives. ⊠ *44 rue Chausée des Ecossais, Upper Town,* ☎ *418/694–9147.* ⊠ *Free.* ☉ *Tues., Thurs.–Fri. 9:30–4:30, Wed. 9:30–6:30, weekends 10–4.*

Musée d'Art Inuit Brousseau. The first museum south of the Arctic circle to be dedicated exclusively to Inuit art and culture includes some surviving examples of art from more than 200 years ago and shows how it has evolved following contact with white people. The collection includes artifacts and many styles of works by Inuit artists, shaped from materials such as walrus tusks, bone, caribou antlers, soapstone, basalt, and serpentine. ⊠ *39 rue St-Louis, Upper Town,* ☎ *418/694-1828.* ⊡ *$6.* ⊙ *Daily 9:30–5:30.*

⑮ Musée de l'Amérique Française. Housed in a former student residence of the Québec Seminary, Laval University, this museum focuses on the history of the French in North America. You can view about 20 of the museum's 400 landscape and still-life paintings, some from as early as the 15th century, along with rare Canadian money from colonial times and scientific instruments acquired for the purposes of research and teaching. The museum's 3,500-year-old mummy is expected to be out on loan for much of 2003. Historical documents and movies tell stories as well. A former chapel is used for exhibits, conferences, and cultural activities. ⊠ *2 côte de la Fabrique, Upper Town,* ☎ *418/692-2843.* ⊡ *$4, free Tues. early Sept.–June 23.* ⊙ *June 24–early Sept., daily 9:30–5; early Sept.–June 23, Tues.–Sun. 10–5.*

NEED A
BREAK? The stone-walled **Bistro Le Figaro** (⊠ 32 rue St-Louis, Upper Town, ☎ 418/692–4191), on the corner of rues des Jardins and St-Louis, is a good place to sample delicious salads, pastries, and desserts.

⑱ Musée du Fort. This museum's sole exhibit is a sound-and-light show that reenacts the area's important battles, including the battle of the Plains of Abraham and the 1775 attack by American generals Arnold and Montgomery. ⊠ *10 rue Ste-Anne, Upper Town,* ☎ *418/692-1759.* ⊡ *$6.75.* ⊙ *Apr. 1–Oct. 31, daily 10–5; Nov.–Jan., by reservation; Feb.–Mar., Thurs.–Sun. 11–4.*

★ **⑪ Parc de l'Artillerie** (Artillery Park). This national historic park showcases four buildings—all that remains of what was once a complex of up to 20 military, industrial, and civilian structures situated to guard the St. Charles River and the Old Port. The earliest buildings served as headquarters for the French garrison. When they were overtaken by the British, in 1759, they were used as barracks for British troops—30 years earlier than the first barracks used in England. In 1765, the Royal Artillery Regiment were stationed there, giving the fortress its name.The area served as an industrial complex providing ammunition for the Canadian army from 1882 until 1964. At the former **powder magazine,** which in 1903 was replaced by a shell foundry, you can see a detailed model of the buildings, streets, and military structures of Québec City in 1808, rendered by two surveyors in the office of the Royal Engineers Corps. Sent to officials in Britain in 1813, the model was intended to prove the strategic importance of Québec to garner more money for expanding the city's fortifications. The **Dauphin Redoubt,** named in honor of the son of Louis XIV (the heir apparent), was constructed from 1712 to 1748. It served as a barracks for the French and English garrisons until 1784-85, when it became an officers' mess for the Royal Artillery Regiment. The **Officers' Quarters,** a dwelling for Royal Artillery officers until 1871 when the British army departed, illustrates military family life during the British regime. **Les Dames de Soie** (The Ladies of Silk; ☎ 418/692–1516), in a former cannon warehouse, allows you to watch porcelain dolls being made and view an exhibit on the history of dolls. From June 24 to early September, it's open Monday through Saturday 9:30–6 and Sunday 11–6; the rest of the year it's open Tuesday through Saturday 10–5. Admission is free and you can visit it separately from Artillery Park. ⊠ *2 rue d'Auteuil, Upper Town,* ☎ *418/648–4205,* WEB *www.parkscanada.qc.ca/artillery.* ⊡ *$4.* ⊙ *Apr., Wed.–Sun 10–5; May–Oct., daily 10–5.*

❶ Place d'Armes. For centuries, this square atop a cliff has been used for parades and military events. Upper Town's most central location, the plaza is bordered by government buildings; at its west side is the majestic **Ancien Palais de Justice** (Old Courthouse), a Renaissance-style building from 1887. The plaza is on land that was occupied by a church and convent of the Recollet missionaries (Franciscan monks), who in 1615 were the first order of priests to arrive in New France. The Gothic-style **fountain** at the center of Place d'Armes pays tribute to their arrival. ⊠ *Rues St-Louis and du Fort, Upper Town.*

❿⃝ Rue du Trésor. The road that colonists took on their way to pay rent to the king's officials is now a narrow alley where colorful prints, paintings, and other artworks are on display. You won't necessarily find masterpieces, but this walkway is a good stop for a souvenir sketch or two—more than a few artists got their start selling their work here. In summer, activity on this street and nearby rue Ste-Anne, lined with eateries and boutiques, starts early in the morning and continues until late at night. Stores stay open, artists paint, and street musicians perform as long as there is an audience, even if it's 1 AM. At 8 rue du Trésor is the **Québec Experience** (☎ 418/694–4000), a multimedia sound-and-light show that traces Québec's history from the first explorers until modern days; the cost is $7.50.

⓮ Séminaire du Québec. Behind these gates lies a tranquil courtyard surrounded by austere stone buildings with rising steeples; these structures have housed classrooms and student residences since 1663. François de Montmorency Laval, the first bishop of New France, founded Québec Seminary to train priests in the new colony. In 1852 the seminary became Université Laval, the first Catholic university in North America. In 1946 the university moved to a larger campus in suburban Ste-Foy. Today priests live on the premises, and Laval's architecture school occupies part of the building. The on-site **Musée de l'Amerique Francaise** gives tours ($4) of the seminary grounds and the interior during the summer. Tours start from the museum at 2 côte de la Fabrique. The small Second Empire–style chapel, **Chapelle Extérieure** (Outer Chapel), at the west entrance of Québec Seminary, was built in 1888 after fire destroyed the original 1750 chapel. Joseph-Ferdinand Peachy designed the chapel; its interior is patterned after that of the Église de la Trinité in Paris. ⊠ *1 côte de la Fabrique, Upper Town,* ☎ *418/692–3981.* ⊙ *Tours June 24–early Sept., daily 9:45–3:45.*

❸ Terrasse Dufferin. This wide boardwalk with an intricate wrought-iron guardrail has a panoramic view of the St. Lawrence River, the town of Lévis on the opposite shore, Île d'Orléans, and the Laurentian Mountains. It was named for Lord Dufferin, governor of Canada between 1872 and 1878, who had this walkway constructed in 1878. The **Promenade des Gouverneurs,** which skirts the cliff and leads up to Québec's highest point, Cap Diamant, and also to the Citadelle, begins at its western end.

Lower Town

New France first began to flourish in the streets of the Basse-Ville, or Lower Town, along the banks of the St. Lawrence River. These streets became the colony's economic crossroads, where furs were traded, ships came in, and merchants established their residences. Despite the status of Lower Town as the oldest neighborhood in North America, its narrow and time-worn thoroughfares have a polished look. In the 1960s, after a century of decay as the commercial boom moved west and left the area abandoned, the Québec government committed millions of dollars to restore the district to the way it had been during the days of New France. Today the area is undergoing a renaissance. Modern boutiques, restaurants, galleries, and shops catering to tourists occupy the former warehouses and residences.

A Good Walk

Begin this walk on the northern end of rue du Petit-Champlain, at **Maison Louis-Jolliet** ⑲ at the foot of the **Escalier Casse-Cou.** The **Verrerie La Mailloche** ⑳ is across the street, where master glassblowers create contemporary works of art. Heading south on **rue du Petit-Champlain** ㉑, the city's oldest street, notice the cliff on the right that borders this narrow thoroughfare, with Upper Town on the heights above. At the point where rue du Petit-Champlain intersects with boulevard Champlain, make a U-turn to head back north on rue Champlain. One block farther, at the corner of rue du Marché-Champlain, is **Maison Chevalier** ㉒, a stone house in the style of urban New France. Walk east to rue Notre-Dame, which leads directly to **Place Royale** ㉓, formerly the heart of New France. The interpretation center here has exhibits on life in the colony. The small stone church at the south side of Place Royale is the **Église Notre-Dame-des-Victoires** ㉔, the oldest church in Québec.

On the east side of Place Royale, take rue de la Place, which leads to an open square, **Place de Paris** ㉕. Head north on rue Dalhousie until you come to the **Musée de la Civilisation** ㉖, devoted to Québecois culture and civilization. Walk east toward the river to the **Vieux-Port de Québec** ㉗, at one time the busiest port on the continent. The breezes from the St. Lawrence provide a cool reprieve on a hot summer's day, and you can browse through a farmers' market here. You are now in the ideal spot to explore Québec City's **antiques district** ㉘.

In summer walk west along rue St-Paul, all the way past the train station built in 1915 in the style of the castles in France's Loire Valley, and turn left on rue Vallière to **L'Ilot des Palais** ㉙, an archaeological museum that has the remnants of the first two palaces of the French colonial intendants (administrators).

TIMING
This is a good day of sightseeing. A morning stroll takes you to two of the city's most famous squares, Place Royale and Place de Paris. You can see the city from the Lévis ferry, if you wish, or pause for lunch before touring the Musée de la Civilisation and the antiques district. After browsing along rue St-Paul, explore L'Ilot des Palais, open in summer.

Sights to See

㉘ **Antiques district.** Antiques shops cluster around rues St-Pierre and St-Paul. Rue St-Paul was once part of a business district where warehouses, stores, and businesses abounded. After World War I, shipping and commercial activities plummeted; low rents attracted antiques dealers. Today numerous cafés, restaurants, and art galleries have turned this area into one of the town's more fashionable sections.

㉔ **Église Notre-Dame-des-Victoires** (Our Lady of Victory Church). The oldest church in Québec stands on the site of Samuel de Champlain's first residence, which also served as a fort and trading post. The church was built in 1688 and has been restored twice. Its name comes from two French victories against the British: one in 1690 against Admiral

William Phipps and another in 1711 against Sir Hovendon Walker. The interior contains copies of paintings by European masters such as Van Dyck, Rubens, and Boyermans; its altar resembles the shape of a fort. A scale model suspended from the ceiling represents *Le Brezé*, the boat that transported French soldiers to New France in 1664. The side chapel is dedicated to Ste-Geneviève, the patron saint of Paris. ✉ *Pl. Royale, Lower Town,* ☎ *418/692–1650.* ☞ *Free.* ☉ *Mid-May–mid-Oct., daily 9–5, except during mass (Sun. at 10:30 and noon), marriages, and funerals; mid-Oct.–mid-May, daily 10–4, except during mass, marriages, and funerals.*

Escalier Casse-Cou. The steepness of the city's first iron stairway, an ambitious 1893 design by city architect and engineer Charles Baillairgé, is ample evidence of how it got its name: Breakneck Steps. The 170 steps were built on the site of the original 17th-century stairway that linked the Upper Town and Lower Town during the French regime. Today shops and restaurants can be found at various levels.

㉙ **L'Ilot des Palais.** More than 300 years of history have been laid bare at this archaeological museum on the site of the first two palaces of New France's colonial intendants. (The translation of the museum name means "the palace block.") The first palace, erected as a brewery by Jean Talon in 1669, was turned into the intendant's residence in 1685 and destroyed by fire in 1713. In 1716, a second palace was built facing the first. It was later turned into a modern brewery, but the basement vaults remain and now house an archaeology exhibit and a multimedia display. ✉ *8 rue Vallière, Lower Town,* ☎ *418/691–6092.* ☞ *$3.* ☉ *June 24–early Sept., daily 10–5.*

OFF THE
BEATEN PATH

LÉVIS–QUÉBEC FERRY – En route to the opposite shore of the St. Lawrence River, you get a striking view of Québec City's skyline, with the Château Frontenac and the Québec Seminary high atop the cliff. The view is even more impressive at night. ✉ *Rue Dalhousie, 1 block south of pl. de Paris, ,* ☎ *418/644–3704.* ☞ *Winter $2, summer $2.50.*

㉒ **Maison Chevalier.** This old stone house was built in 1752 for shipowner Jean-Baptiste Chevalier. The house's style, of classic French inspiration, clearly reflects the urban architecture of New France. The fire walls, chimneys, vaulted cellars, and original wood beams and stone fireplaces are noteworthy. ✉ *50 rue du Marché-Champlain, Lower Town,* ☎ *418/643–2158.* ☞ *Free.* ☉ *May–June 23, Tues.–Sun. 10–5; June 24–Oct. 21, daily 9:30–5; Oct. 22–Apr., weekends 10–5.*

㉑ **Maison Louis-Jolliet.** The first settlers of New France used this house, built in 1683, as a base for further westward explorations. Today it's the lower station of the funicular. A monument commemorating Louis Jolliet's discovery of the Mississippi River in 1672 stands in the park next to the house. The **Escalier Casse-Cou** is at the north side of the house. ✉ *16 rue du Petit-Champlain, Lower Town.*

★ ☾ ㉖ **Musée de la Civilisation** (Museum of Civilization). Wedged into the foot of the cliff, this spacious museum with a striking limestone-and-glass facade has been artfully designed by architect Moshe Safdie to blend into the landscape. Its campanile echoes the shape of the city's church steeples. The museum's innovative exhibits explore aspects of Québec's culture. Some tell the story of how the first settlers lived, and how they survived such harsh winters. Others illustrate the extent to which the Roman Catholic Church dominated the people and explain the evolution of Québec nationalism. *Nous, les Premières Nations* (*Encounter with the First Nations*) looks at the 11 aboriginal nations that inhabit Québec. Several of the shows, with their imaginative use of artwork, video screens, computers, and sound, appeal to both adults and children. The museum's thematic, interactive approach also extends to exhibits of an international nature. From May 2003 to February 2004 the museum is to host an exhibit on the Middle Ages with artifacts from six European museums. ☒ *85 rue Dalhousie, Lower Town,* ☎ *418/ 643–2158,* WEB *www.mcq.org.* ☒ *$7, free Tues. Labor Day–June 23.* ☉ *June 24–Labor Day, daily 9:30–6:30; Sept.–June 23, Tues.–Sun. 10– 5.*

㉕ **Place de Paris.** A black-and-white geometric sculpture, *Dialogue avec l'Histoire* (*Dialogue with History*) dominates this square and is a newcomer (1987) to these historic quarters. A gift from France, the sculpture is on the site where the first French settlers landed. ☒ *Rue Dalhousie, Lower Town.*

NEED A BREAK?   Beer has been brewed in Québec since the early 17th century and **L'I-nox** (☒ 37 quai St-André, Lower Town, ☎ 418/692–2877) carries on the tradition with a combination brew pub and beer museum. Cherry-red columns and a stainless-steel bar contrast with exposed stone and brick walls, blending the old and the new. Outside, there's a large sunny terrace that's open in summer. L'Inox offers many of its own beers brewed on site as well as most other beverages, both alcoholic and not. Food is limited to European-style hot dogs served in baguettes or plates of Québec cheeses. If you reserve in advance, you can also take a guided tour of the brewery ($5) and partake in a taste test.

★ ☟ ㉓ **Place Royale.** Formerly the homes of wealthy merchants, houses with steep Normandy-style roofs, dormer windows, and several chimneys encircle this cobblestone square. Until 1686 the area was called Place du Marché, but its name changed when a bust of Louis XIV was erected at its center. During the late 1600s and early 1700s, when Place Royale was continually under threat of attacks from the British, the colonists progressively moved to higher and safer quarters atop the cliff in Upper Town. Yet after the French colony fell to British rule in 1759, Place Royale flourished again with shipbuilding, logging, fishing, and fur trading. The Fresque des Québecois, a 4,665-square-ft trompe-l'oeil mural depicting 400 years of Québec's history, is to the east of the square, at the corner of rue Notre-Dame and côte de la Montagne. An information center, the **Centre d'Interpretation de Place Royale** (☒ 27 rue Notre-Dame, Lower Town, ☎ 418/646–3167) includes exhibits, a multimedia show, and a Discovery Hall with a replica of a 19th-century home where children can try on period costumes. Admission is $3, free on Tuesday from early September to June 23. It's open daily 9:30–5 June 24 to early September. The rest of the year it's open 10–5, closed on Monday.

㉑ **Rue du Petit-Champlain.** The oldest street in the city was the main street of a former harbor village, with trading posts and the homes of rich merchants. Today it has pleasant boutiques and cafés. Natural-fiber weaving, Inuit carvings, hand-painted silks, and enameled copper crafts are some of the local specialties that are good buys here.

☟ ⓴ **Verrerie La Mailloche.** The glassblowing techniques used in this combination workshop, boutique, and museum are as old as Ancient Egypt, but the results are contemporary. In the workshop, master glassblower Jean Vallières and his assistants turn 1,092°C (2,000°F) molten glass into works of art and answer questions. Examples of Vallières's work have been presented by the Canadian government to visiting dignitaries such as Queen Elizabeth and former president Ronald Reagan. ☒ *58 rue Sous-le-Fort, Lower Town,* ☎ *418/694–0445.*

Free. ☉ *Workshop June–Oct., Wed.–Sun. 10–4:30; Nov.–May, weekdays 10–4:30. Boutique regular store hrs in winter, daily 9 AM– 10 PM in summer.*

㉗ **Vieux-Port de Québec** (Old Port of Québec). Today this historic 72-acre area encompasses several parks. The old harbor dates from the 17th century, when ships first arrived from Europe bringing supplies and settlers to the new colony. At one time this port was among the busiest on the continent: between 1797 and 1897, Québec shipyards turned out more than 2,500 ships, many of which passed the 1,000-ton mark. The port saw a rapid decline after steel and steam replaced wood and the channel to Montréal was deepened to allow larger boats to reach a good port upstream. You can stroll along the riverside promenade, where merchant and cruise ships dock. At the port's northern end, where the St. Charles meets the St. Lawrence, a lock protects the marina in the Louise Basin from the generous Atlantic tides that reach even this far up the St. Lawrence. In the northwest section of the port, the **Old Port of Québec Interpretation Center** (✉ 100 quai St-André, Lower Town, ☎ 418/648–3300) presents the history of the port in relation to the lumber trade and shipbuilding. Admission to the center is $3; it's open daily May to Labor Day 10–5, early September to October 6 1–5, and by reservation only October 7 through April. From June 22 through August 31, guides in 19th-century costume conduct walking tours of the port ($8). The **Marché du Vieux-Port** (Old Port Market), where farmers sell their fresh produce and cheese, as well as handicrafts, is at the port's northwestern tip. The market, near quai St-André, is open daily 8–8 in summer. Some of the stalls stay open in winter, 9–4.

The Fortifications

In the 20th century, Québec City grew into a modern metropolis outside the confines of the city walls. Beyond the walls lies a great deal of the city's military history, in the form of its fortifications and battlements, as well as a number of museums and other attractions.

A Good Walk

Start close to Porte St-Louis (St-Louis Gate) at the Parc de l'Esplanade, part of the **Fortifications of Québec National Historic Site** ㉚ and the site of a former military parade ground. From here you can tour the walls of the old city, North America's only walled city north of Mexico. From the powder magazine in the park, head south on côte de la Citadelle, which leads directly to **La Citadelle** ㉛, a historic fortified base. Retrace your steps on côte de la Citadelle to **Grande Allée** ㉜. Once you pass through the Porte St-Louis, turn left on avenue Georges VI past the concrete building that once housed the premier's offices to the historic and scenic **Parc des Champs-de-Bataille** ㉝. Head up the hill to the Cap Diamant. Here at the observation point you have a spectacular view of the St. Lawrence River and the cliff that British general James Wolfe and his troops scaled to win the 1759 battle that decided the fate of New France. The exact point where Wolfe's forces made the ascent is just to the west of the plains at Gilmour Hill. Retrace your steps down the hill and turn left along avenue Georges VI.

Look left as you walk along avenue Georges VI to see the **Plains of Abraham** ㉞, site of the famous battle. The neatly tended garden **Parc Jeanne d'Arc** ㉟ is a little farther along, on the right. To the left, toward the south end of the park, stands **Tour Martello No. 1** ㊱, a stone defense tower. Continue along avenue Georges VI past where it turns into avenue de Bernières. Tour Martello No. 2 is to the right, up avenue Taché. Continue heading west along avenue de Bernières to avenue Wolfe-

114

Outside the Walls

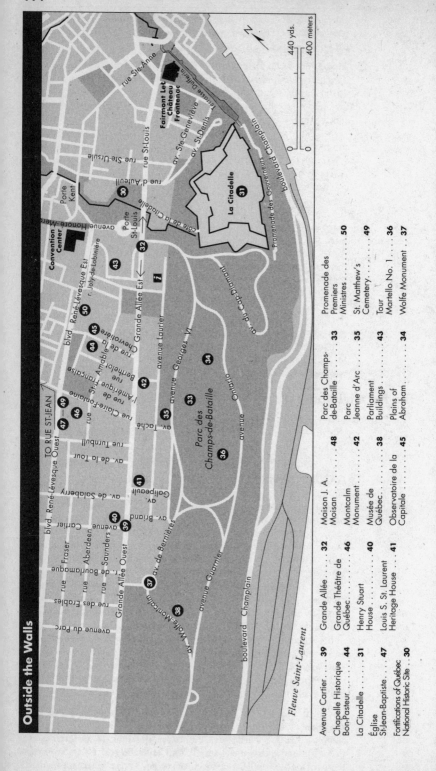

Montcalm, where you come to the tall **Wolfe Monument** ㊲, which marks the place where the British general died.

Turn left on avenue Wolfe-Montcalm to visit the **Musée de Québec** ㊳. Attached to the museum, the Centre d'Interpretation du Parc des Champs-de-Bataille has a multimedia show on the battles that took place on the site.

From the museum, head north on avenue Wolfe-Montcalm, turning right on Grande Allée and walking a block to **avenue Cartier** ㊴. Across the street, at the corner of avenue Cartier, is the **Henry Stuart House** ㊵, which once marked the city's outskirts. Near the corner of avenue Cartier and Grande Allée, note the simple white house with green trim that was once the home of the well-known painter Cornelius Krieghoff. Today it's a private home, not open to the public. Continue east along Grande Allée to 201 Grande Allée Est where you can visit the **Louis S. St. Laurent Heritage House** ㊶, home of Louis St. Laurent, prime minister of Canada from 1948–57. Continue east to Cours du Général-de-Montcalm, where you arrive at the **Montcalm Monument** ㊷. Farther along the Grande Allée, past the bars and restaurants, is the Manège Militaire, a turreted armory built in 1888 that is still a drill hall for the Royal 22nd Regiment. You can return on Grande Allée to your starting point or cross the street to begin the walk outside the walls.

TIMING

This walk takes a half-day, or a full day if you begin by walking the walls of the city. In summer you should try to catch the colorful 10 AM changing of the guard at the Citadelle. For lunch try one of the many restaurants around avenue Cartier or bring a picnic and eat on the Plains of Abraham.

Sights to See

㊴ **Avénue Cartier.** Here you can indulge in the pleasures offered by the many good restaurants, clubs, and cafés lining the street.

㉛ **La Citadelle** (Citadel). Built at the city's highest point, on Cap Diamant, the Citadel is the largest fortified base in North America still occupied by troops. The 25-building fortress was intended to protect the port, prevent the enemy from taking up a position on the Plains of Abraham, and provide a refuge in case of an attack. Having inherited incomplete fortifications, the British sought to complete the Citadel to protect themselves against retaliations from the French. By the time the Citadel was completed in 1832, the attacks against Québec City had ended. Since 1920 the Citadel has served as a base for the Royal 22nd Regiment. Firearms, uniforms, and decorations from the 17th century are displayed in the **Royal 22nd Regiment Museum**, in the former powder magazine, built in 1750. If weather permits, you can watch the Changing of the Guard, a ceremony in which the troops parade before the Citadel in red coats and black fur hats. Admission to the Citadel and the museum is by guided tour only. ⊠ *1 côte de la Citadelle, Upper Town,* ☎ *418/694–2815.* ⊡ *$6.* ☉ *Apr.–mid-May, daily 10–4; mid-May–June, daily 9–5; July–Labor Day, daily 9–6; Sept., daily 9–4; Oct., daily 10–3; Nov.–Mar., groups only (reservations required). Changing of the guard June 24–Labor Day, daily 10 AM. Retreat ceremony July–Aug., Wed.–Sat. 6 PM.*

㉚ **Fortifications of Québec National Historic Site.** In the early 19th century, this was a clear space surrounded by a picket fence and poplar trees. Today you find the **Poudrière de l'Esplanade** (⊠ 100 rue St-Louis, Upper Town, ☎ 418/648–7016), the powder magazine that the British constructed in 1820 and an interpretation center with a multimedia video and a model depicting the evolution of the wall surrounding Vieux-

Québec. There's a $3 charge to enter the site, which is open 10–5 daily mid-May to October 6. The French began building ramparts along the city's natural cliff as early as 1690 to protect themselves from British invaders. However, the colonists had trouble convincing the French government back home to take the threat of invasion seriously, and by 1759, when the British invaded for control of New France, the walls were still incomplete. The British, despite attacks by the Americans during the War of Independence and the War of 1812, took a century to finish them. In summer the park can also be the starting point for walking the city's 4½ km (3 mi) of walls. There are two guided tours ($10 each). One starts at the interpretation center and the other at Terrasse Dufferin.

㉜ Grande Allée. One of the city's oldest streets, Grande Allée was the route people took from outlying areas to sell their furs in town. Now trendy cafés, clubs, and restaurants line the road. The street actually has four names: inside the city walls it's rue St-Louis; outside the walls, Grande Allée; farther west, chemin St-Louis; and farther still, boulevard Laurier.

OFF THE BEATEN PATH
GROSSE ÎLE NATIONAL PARK – For thousands of immigrants from Europe in the 1800s, the first glimpse of North America was the hastily erected quarantine station at Grosse Île—Canada's equivalent of Ellis Island. For far too many passengers on the plague-racked ships, particularly the Irish fleeing the potato famine, Grosse Île became a final resting place. Several buildings have been restored to tell the story of the tragic period of Irish immigration. During the time Grosse Île operated (1832–1937), 4.3 million immigrants passed through the port of Québec. **Croisieres Le Coudrier** (☎ 888/600–5554) has tours that depart from Québec City's Old Port for Grosse Île. Tours cost $48, which includes admission to the island. **Croisieres Lachance** (☎ 888/476–7734) runs a ferry that departs from Berthier sur Mer to Grosse Île for $35, which includes admission. From Québec City, head south on the Pierre Laporte Bridge and follow the signs for Autoroute 20 East for about an hour to Berthier-sur-Mer. Follow the signs to the marina. Reservations recommended to ensure a place on either ferry. ☎ 418/248–8888 or 800/463–6769. 🖃 $35–$48, ferry included. ☉ May–Oct., daily 9–6.

㊵ Henry Stuart House. Built in 1849, this Regency-style cottage was the home of the Stuart family from 1918 to 1987, when the Ministry of Culture designated it a historic monument. Much has remained unchanged since 1930. Most of the furniture was imported from England in the second half of the 19th century. ✉ 82 Grande Allée Ouest, Montcalm, ☎ 418/647–4347. 🖃 $5. ☉ June 24–Labor Day, daily 11–4; early Sept.–June 23, Sun. 1–5.

NEED A BREAK?
Halles Petit-Cartier (✉ 1191 av. Cartier, Montcalm, ☎ 418/688–1630), a food mall near the Henry Stuart House, has restaurants and shops that sell French delicacies—cheeses, pastries, breads, vegetables, and candies.

㊶ Louis S. St. Laurent Heritage House. A costumed maid or chauffeur greets you when you visit this elegant Grande Allée house, the former home of Louis S. St. Laurent, prime minister of Canada from 1948–1957. The house, opened to the public in 2002, uses period furnishings and multimedia touches to tell St. Laurent's story and illustrate the lifestyle of upper-crust families in 1950's Québec City. ✉ 201 Grande Allée Est, Montcalm, ☎ 418/648–4071. 🖃 $3.50. ☉ June 15–Sept. 2, daily 10–5:30; Sept. 3–June 14, Wed. through Sun. 10–5:30.

42 **Montcalm Monument.** France and Canada joined together to erect this monument honoring Louis-Joseph Montcalm, the general who claimed his fame by winning four major battles in North America. His most famous battle, however, was the one he lost, when the British conquered New France on September 13, 1759. Montcalm was north of Québec City at Beauport when he learned that the British attack was imminent. He quickly assembled his troops to meet the enemy and was wounded in battle in the leg and stomach. Montcalm was carried into the walled city, where he died the next morning. ⊠ *Pl. Montcalm, Montcalm.*

★ **38** **Musée de Québec** (Québec Museum). A neoclassical Beaux Arts showcase, the museum has more than 22,000 traditional and contemporary pieces of Québec art. The portraits by artists well known in the area, such as Jean-Paul Riopelle (1923–2002), Jean-Paul Lemieux (1904–1990), and Horatio Walker (1858–1938), are particularly notable. The museum's very formal, dignified building in Parc des Champs-de-Bataille was designed by Wilfrid Lacroix and erected in 1933 to commemorate the tercentennial of the founding of Québec. The museum renovated the original building, incorporating the space of an abandoned prison dating from 1867. A hallway of cells, with the iron bars and courtyard still intact, has been preserved as part of a permanent exhibition on the prison's history. ⊠ *1 av. Wolfe-Montcalm, Montcalm,* ☎ *418/643–2150,* WEB *www.mdq.org.* ⊠ *Free; $10 for special exhibits.* ☉ *Sept.–May, Tues. and Thurs.–Sun. 10–5, Wed. 10–9; June–Aug., Thurs.–Tues. 10–6, Wed. 10–9.*

33 **Parc des Champs-de-Bataille** (Battlefields Park). One of North America's largest and most scenic parks, this 250-acre area of gently rolling slopes has unparalleled views of the St. Lawrence River. Within the park and west of the Citadel are the **Plains of Abraham,** the site of the famous 1759 battle that decided the fate of New France.

35 **Parc Jeanne d'Arc.** An equestrian statue of Joan of Arc is the focus of this park, which is bright with colorful flowers in summer. A symbol of courage, the statue stands in tribute to the heroes of 1759 near the place where New France was lost to the British. The park also commemorates the Canadian national anthem, "O Canada"; it was played here for the first time on June 24, 1880. ⊠ *Avs. Laurier and Taché, Montcalm.*

★ ☺ **34** **Plains of Abraham.** This park, named after the river pilot Abraham Martin, is the site of the famous 1759 battle that decided the fate of New France. People cross-country ski here in winter and in-line skate in summer. The interpretation center, attached to the Musée de Québec, is open year-round; in summer a bus driven by a guide portraying Abraham Martin provides an entertaining tour—with commentary in French and English—around the Plains of Abraham. At the **Discovery Pavilion** (835 ave. Wilfrid Laurier, ☎ 418/648–4071, ☉ mid-June–mid-Oct. daily 9–5:30, mid-Oct.–mid-June daily 9–5), the multimedia display Canada Odyssey tells 400 years of Canada's history and has a second floor with computer games, videos, and displays focusing on the biological and scientific history of the area. Call the Discovery Pavilion for tour departure times. ⊠ *Tour $3.50.* ☉ *Tours June 16–Sept. 2, daily 10–5:30; June 1–15 and Sept. 3–mid-Oct., weekends 10–5:30.*

36 **Tour Martello No. 1** (Martello Tower No. 1). Of the 16 Martello towers in Canada, four were built in Québec City because the British government feared an invasion after the American Revolution. Tour Martello No. 1, which exhibits the history of the four structures, was built between 1802 and 1810. **Tour Martello No. 2,** at avenues Taché and Laurier, has Council of War, a three-hour weekend mystery dinner show with a military theme. Tour No. 3 guarded westward entry to the city, but it was demolished in 1904. Tour No. 4 is on rue Lavigueur overlooking the St. Charles River but is not open to the public. ⊠ *South end of Parc Jeanne d'Arc, Montcalm.* 🖾 *$3.50.* ⊘ *Mid-June–Sept., daily 10–5:30.*

③⑦ **Wolfe Monument.** This tall monument marks the place where the British general James Wolfe died in 1759. Wolfe landed his troops about 3 km (2 mi) from the city's walls; 4,500 English soldiers scaled the cliff and opened fire on the Plains of Abraham. Wolfe was mortally wounded in battle and was carried behind the lines to this spot. ⊠ *Rue de Bernières and av. Wolfe-Montcalm, Montcalm.*

Outside the Walls

Although its economy is slowly diversifying, Québec City continues to revolve around the provincial government and the provincial government revolves around the National Assembly, one of the oldest parliaments in the world. One of the city's trendiest neighborhoods is down the hill on St. Jean Street.

A Good Walk

Start at the **Parliament Buildings** ㊸, home of the National Assembly, headquarters of the provincial government. As you leave the legislature, turn right and then right again onto the Grande Allée. The modern concrete building across the street once held the offices of Québec's premier. Now it houses the Treasury Board, which controls the government's purse strings. As you walk along the Grande Allée, look to the right to see a statue of former Québec premier Maurice Duplessis, who ruled the province with an iron fist from 1936 to 1939 and again from 1944 to 1959. At the corner of Grande Allée and Des Parlementaires sits the Parc de la Francophonie, dedicated to French-speaking countries around the world. Turn right on rue de la Chevrotière and walk past rue St-Amable. The **Chapelle Historique Bon-Pasteur** ㊹, a church surrounded by office buildings, is on the west side of the street. The entrance to Edifice Marie-Guyart is across the street; its observation tower, **Observatoire de la Capitale** ㊺, provides a spectacular view.

Turn left on boulevard René-Lévesque Est and walk two blocks past the Parc de l'Amérique-Française, dedicated to places in North America with a French-speaking population. At the corner, the modern concrete building is the **Grande Théâtre de Québec** ㊻, a performing-arts center. Turn right at rue Claire-Fontaine, cross the street and walk down the hill to rue St-Jean, where the **Église St-Jean-Baptiste** ㊼ dominates the neighborhood. Turn right and stroll down rue St-Jean past trendy shops in century-old buildings to **Maison J. A. Moisan** ㊽, which claims the title of the oldest grocery store in North America. Farther down the street you arrive at **St. Matthew's Cemetery** ㊾, the city's oldest remaining graveyard. Cut through the cemetery to rue St-Simon, walk up the hill, cross the street, and turn right on boulevard René-Lévesque. In summer you can end your walk by crossing the street and strolling along the raised **Promenade des Premiers Ministres** ㊿, which tells the stories of Québec's premiers. On the right, at the corner of des Parlementaires is the Honoré Mercier building which now houses offices of Québec's premier. Past the National Assembly, at the end of the promenade is a statue of René Lévesque, the diminutive late premier who is considered the father of Québec's independence movement.

TIMING

This walk should take a half-day. From March through June and from October through December, you should pause to listen to the cut and thrust of debates or Question Period in the National Assembly. For lunch, dine among decision-makers at the legislature's Le Parlementaire restaurant or in one of the many interesting and affordable restaurants along rue St-Jean.

Sights to See

🟢 **Aquarium du Québec.** The aquarium, about 10 km (6 mi) from the city center, is set to reopen in January 2003 with a focus on Nordic fish, marine mammals, and polar bears, including a replica of a subarctic ocean. A wooded picnic ground makes this spot ideal for a family outing. ⊠ *1675 av. des Hôtels, Ste-Foy,* ☎ *418/659–5266.*

44 Chapelle Historique Bon-Pasteur. Charles Baillargé designed this slender church with a steep sloping roof in 1868. Its ornate Baroque-style interior has carved-wood designs elaborately highlighted in gold leaf. The chapel houses 32 religious paintings created by the nuns of the community from 1868 to 1910. Classical concerts are performed here. ⊠ *1080 rue de la Chevrotière, Montcalm,* ☎ *418/641–1069.* ▣ *Free.* ☾ *Weekdays 8:30–4; ask at the office on weekdays to see chapel Sun. 10–1, before and after musical artists' mass, which begins at 10:45.*

★ **47 Église St-Jean-Baptiste.** Architect Joseph-Ferdinand Peachy's crowning glory, this church was inspired by the facade of the Église de la Trinité in Paris and rivals the Basilique Notre-Dame-de-Québec in beauty and size. The first church on the site, built in 1847, burned in the 1881 fire that destroyed much of the neighborhood. Seven varieties of Italian marble were used in the soaring columns, statues, and pulpit of the present church, which dates from 1884. Its 36 stained-glass windows consist of 30 sections each, and the organ, like the church, is classified as a historic monument. October to June 23 and outside regular opening hours, knock at the **presbytery** (⊠ 490 rue St-Jean, St. Jean Baptiste) to see the church. ⊠ *410 rue St-Jean, St. Jean Baptiste,* ☎ *418/525–7188.* ☾ *June 24–Sept., weekdays 10–4:30, Sun. 9–4.*

46 Grande Théâtre de Québec. Opened in 1971, the theater incorporates two main halls, named for 19th-century Canadian poets. Louis Frechette was the first Québec poet and writer to be honored by the French Academy; Octave Crémazie stirred the rise of Québec nationalism in the mid-19th century. A three-wall mural by Québec sculptor Jordi Bonet depicts Death, Life, and Liberty. Bonet wrote "La Liberté" on one wall to symbolize the Québecois' struggle for freedom and cultural distinction. ⊠ *269 blvd. René-Lévesque Est, Montcalm,* ☎ *418/643–8111.*

OFF THE BEATEN PATH

ICE HOTEL – At this hotel constructed completely of ice and snow, you can tour the art galleries of ice sculptures, get married in the chapel, lounge in the hot tub, have a drink at the bar made of ice, then nestle into a sleeping bag on a bed lined with deer skins for a night's sleep. The first of its kind in North America, the hotel is open mid-January to March 31. A night's stay, including equipment (like an extra-insulated sleeping bag), four-course supper, breakfast, and a welcome cocktail is around $230 per person. ⊠ *Duchesnay Ecotourism Station, 143 route Duchesnay, Ste Catherine de la Jacques Cartier (about 20 minutes west of Québec City),* ☎ *418/875–4522 or 877/505–0423,* 🌐 *www.icehotel-canada.com.*

🟢 **Jardin Zoologique du Québec.** This zoo is especially scenic because of the DuBerger River, which traverses the grounds. Closed until June 2003, the zoo plans to specialize in birds when it reopens. ⊠ *9300 rue de la Faune, Charlesbourg,* ☎ *418/622–0313.*

48 Maison J. A. Moisan. Founded in 1871 by Jean-Alfred Moisan, this store claims the title of the oldest grocery store in North America. The original display cases, woodwork, tin ceilings, and antiques preserve that old-time feel. The store's many products include difficult-to-find delicacies from other regions of Québec. ⊠ *699 rue St-Jean, St. Jean Baptiste,* ☎ *418/522–0685.*

NEED A
BREAK?   **La Piazzeta** (⊠ 707 rue St-Jean, St. Jean Baptiste, ☎ 418/529–7489), with its delicious thin-crust square pizzas, is just one of the many good and affordable restaurants along the stretch of rue St-Jean near Maison J. A. Moisan.

㊺ Observatoire de la Capitale. This observation gallery is atop Edifice Marie-Guyart, Québec City's tallest office building. The gray, modern concrete tower, 31 stories tall, has by far the best view of the city and the environs. There's an express elevator. ⊠ *1037 rue de la Chevrotière, Montcalm,* ☎ *418/644–9841.* 🎫 *$4.* ⊘ *Daily 10–5; closed Mon. Oct. 15–June 24.*

★ **㊸ Parliament Buildings.** Erected between 1877 and 1884, these buildings are the seat of L'Assemblée Nationale (the National Assembly) of 125 provincial representatives. Québec architect Eugène-Étienne Taché designed the stately buildings in the late-17th-century Renaissance style of Louis XIV, with four wings set in a square around an interior court. In front of the Parliament, statues pay tribute to important figures of Québec history: Cartier, Champlain, Frontenac, Wolfe, and Montcalm. There's a 30-minute tour (in English, French, or Spanish) of the President's Gallery, the Parlementaire restaurant, the Legislative Council Chamber, and the National Assembly Chamber, which is blue, white, and gold. ⊠ *Av. Honoré-Mercier and Grande Allée, Door 3, Montcalm,* ☎ *418/643–7239,* WEB *www.assnat.qc.ca.* 🎫 *Free.* ⊘ *Guided tours weekdays 9–4:30; late June–early Sept. also open weekends 10–4:30.*

㊿ Promenade des Premiers Ministres. Inaugurated in 1997, the promenade has a series of panels that tell the story (in French) of the premiers who have led the province and their contributions to its development. ⊠ *Parallel to blvd. René-Lévesque Est between rue de la Chevrotière and the Parliament Buildings, Montcalm. Closed in winter.*

㊾ St. Matthew's Cemetery. The burial place of many of the earliest English settlers in Canada was established in 1771 and is the oldest cemetery remaining in Québec City. Closed in 1860, it has been turned into a park. Next door, St. Matthew's Anglican Church is now a public library. It has a book listing most of the original tombstone inscriptions, including those that disappeared to make way for the city's modern convention center. ⊠ *755 rue St-Jean, St. Jean Baptiste,* ☎ *no phone.*

DINING

Most restaurants have a selection of dishes à la carte, but more creative specialties are often found on the table d'hôte, a two- to four-course meal chosen daily by the chef. This can also be an economical way to order a full meal. At dinner many restaurants will offer a *menu dégustation* (tasting menu), a five- to seven-course dinner of the chef's finest creations. In French-speaking Québec City, an *entrée*, as the name suggests, is an entry into a meal, or an appetizer. It is followed by a *plat principal*, which is the main dish. Lunch generally costs about 30% less than dinner, and many of the same dishes are available. Lunch is usually served 11:30 to 2:30, dinner 6:30 until about 11. You should tip at least 15% of the bill.

CATEGORY	COST*
$$$$	over $32
$$$	$22–$32
$$	$13–$21
$	under $13

per person, in Canadian dollars, for a main course at dinner

Upper Town

$$$–$$$$ ✕ **La Maison Gastronomique Serge Bruyère.** The Grand Table, serving classic French cuisine with a Québec twist, put Québec City on the map of great gastronomic cities. Opened in 1980 by the late Serge Bruyère, a native of France, it continues to benefit from his reputation. One highlight is the *menu découvert* (literally "discovery menu"), an eight-course meal for about $95. Among Chef Martin Còté's dishes are *aiguillettes* (thin strips) of roasted duck with foie gras or loin of veal from Charlevoix with Parma ham. The adjacent bistro **Chez Livernois** shares the kitchen but is less formal and less expensive. ⊠ *1200 rue St-Jean, Upper Town,* ☎ *418/694–0618. AE, D, DC, MC, V.*

$$$–$$$$ ✕ **Le Saint-Amour.** Light spills in through an airy atrium at this relaxed
★ restaurant, where acclaimed chef Jean-Luc Boulay travels the world gathering inspiration for such creations as caribou steak grilled with wild berries and served with poached pears in red wine, and beef tenderloin with a sauce made from port wine and a local blue cheese. Sauces are generally light, with no flour or butter. The $80 menu découvert has nine courses, and the table d'hôte has five. An extensive wine list has 650 choices ranging from $28 to $5,200 a bottle. ⊠ *48 rue Ste-Ursule, Upper Town,* ☎ *418/694–0667. Reservations essential. AE, DC, MC, V.*

$$–$$$$ ✕ **Aux Anciens Canadiens.** This establishment is named for a book by Philippe-Aubert de Gaspé, who once resided here. The house, dating from 1675, has waitresses in period cóstume and five dining rooms with different themes. For example, the *vaisselier* (dish room) is bright and cheerful, with colorful antique dishes and a fireplace. People come for the authentic French-Canadian cooking; hearty specialties include duck in maple glaze, Lac St-Jean meat pie, and maple-syrup pie with fresh cream. One of the best deals is a three-course meal for $13.75, served from noon until 6 PM. ⊠ *34 rue St-Louis, Upper Town,* ☎ *418/ 692–1627. AE, DC, MC, V.*

$$–$$$$ ✕ **Le Continental.** If Québec City had a dining Hall of Fame, Le Continental would be there among the best. Since 1956, the Sgobba family has been serving superb Continental cuisine. Deep-blue walls, mahogany paneling, and crisp white tablecloths create a stately air, and house specialties such as orange duckling and filet mignon are flambéed at your table. ⊠ *26 rue St-Louis, Upper Town,* ☎ *418/694–9995. AE, D, DC, MC, V.*

$–$$$ ✕ **Portofino Bistro Italiano.** By joining two 18th-century houses, owner James Monti has created a cozy Italian restaurant with a bistro flavor. The room is distinctive: burnt-sienna walls, soccer flags hanging from the ceiling, a wood pizza oven set behind a semicircular bar, deep-blue tablecloths and chairs. Not to be missed are the thin-crust pizza and its accompaniment of oils flavored with pepper and oregano, and *pennini al'arrabiata*—tubular pasta with a spicy tomato sauce. Save room for the homemade tiramisu—ladyfingers dipped in espresso with a whipped-cream and mascarpone-cheese filling. From 3 PM–7 PM the restaurant serves a beer and pizza meal for about $11. ⊠ *54 rue Couillard, Upper Town,* ☎ *418/692–8888. AE, D, DC, MC, V.*

122

Québec City Dining and Lodging

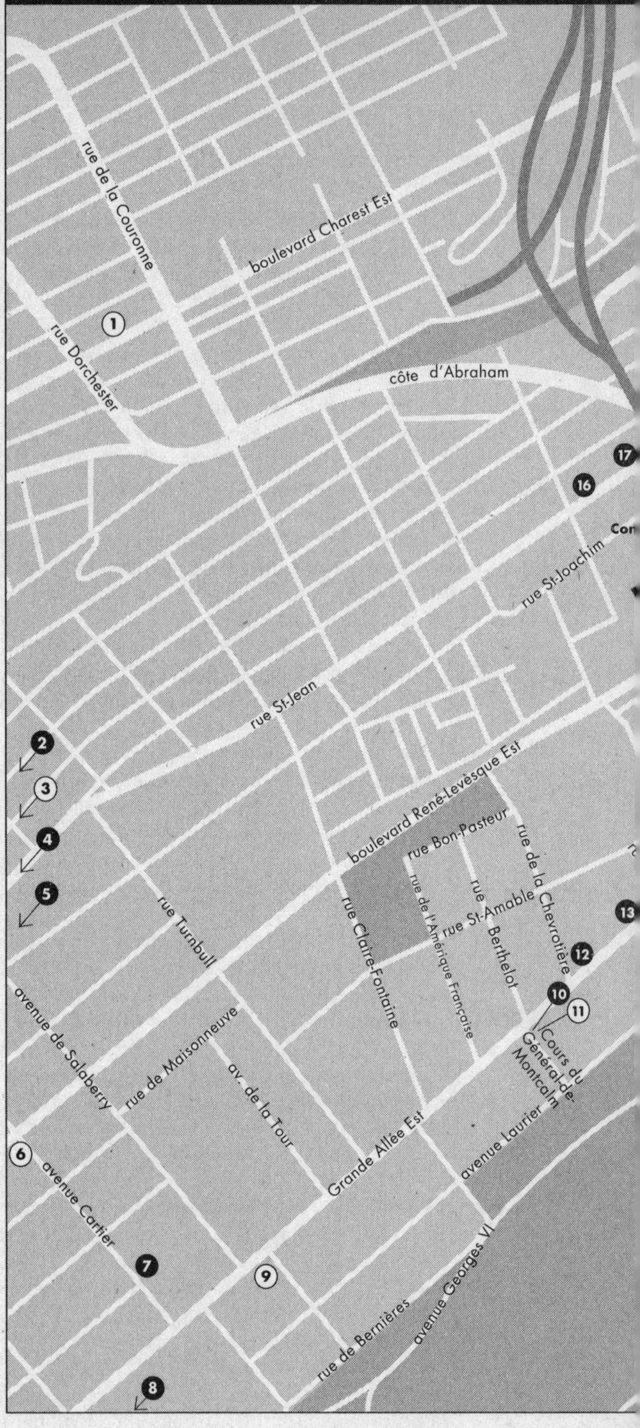

côte d'Abraham

rue de la Couronne

rue Dorchester

boulevard Charest Est

rue St-Joachim

Cor

rue St-Jean

boulevard René-Lévesque Est

rue Bon-Pasteur

rue de la Chevrotière

rue de l'Amérique Française

rue St-Amable

Berthelot

rue Claire-Fontaine

rue Turnbull

avenue de Salaberry

rue de Maisonneuve

av. de la Tour

Grande Allée Est

avenue Laurier

Cours du
Général-de
Montcalm

avenue Cartier

rue de Bernières

avenue Georges VI

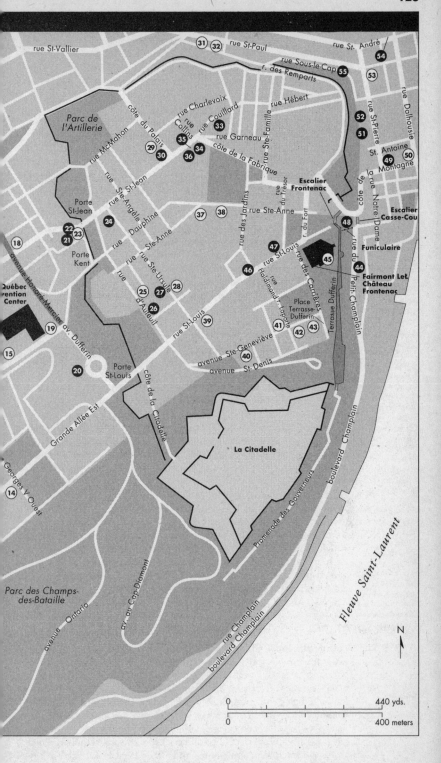

$-$$ ✕ **Les Frères de la Côte.** With its central location, Mediterranean influence, and reasonable prices, this busy bistro is a favorite among politicians and the journalists who cover them. The menu, inspired by the south of France, changes constantly, but osso bucco and a tender leg of lamb are among the regular choices. If you sit near the back, you can watch the chefs at work. This kitchen is often among those open the latest. ⊠ *1190 rue St-Jean, Upper Town,* ☎ *418/692–5445. AE, D, MC, V.*

$-$$ ✕ **Le Petit Coin Latin.** Tucked into a quiet street off bustling rue St-Jean, Le Petit Coin Latin, with its dark wood furniture, stone walls, and background music of French *chansonniers,* has the look and feel of a Parisian neighborhood café. Low prices and generous portions attract a diverse clientele, including many students. In summer there's a sunny, secluded courtyard terrace. The menu ranges from morning croissants, *chocolatines* (a chocolate-filled pastry), or eggs Benedict, to all-you-can-eat raclette, the restaurant's specialty. In between, there are plenty of low-cost options, including sandwiches, quiches, and salads. ⊠ *8½ rue Ste-Ursule, Upper Town,* ☎ *418/692–2022. MC, V.*

$ ✕ **Casse-Crêpe Breton.** Crepes in generous proportions are served in
★ this busy café-style restaurant. From a menu of more than 20 fillings, pick your own chocolate or fruit combinations; design a larger meal with cheese, ham, and vegetables; or sip a bowl of Viennese coffee topped with whipped cream. Many tables surround three round griddles at which you watch your creations being made. Crepes made with two to five fillings cost less than $6.15. This place is popular with tourists and locals alike, and there can be lines to get in at peak hours and seasons. ⊠ *1136 rue St-Jean, Upper Town,* ☎ *418/692–0438. Reservations not accepted. No credit cards.*

$ ✕ **Chez Temporel.** Tucked behind rue St-Jean and côte de la Fabrique, this smoky café perfumed with the aroma of fresh coffee is an experience *très français.* Its appearance is rustic, with wooden tables, chairs, and benches; a tiny staircase leads to an upper level. Croissants are made in-house; the staff will fill them with Gruyère and ham or anything else. Equally delicious are the *croques monsieur* (grilled ham-and-cheese sandwiches) and quiche Lorraine. ⊠ *25 rue Couillard, Upper Town,* ☎ *418/694–1813. V.*

$ ✕ **L'Elysée Mandarin.** A 19th-century home has been transformed into an elegant Chinese mandarin's garden where you can sip jasmine tea to the strains of soothing Asian music. Owner David Tsui uses rosewood and even imported stones from China to emulate his native Yanchao, a city near Shanghai known for training great chefs. Among the restaurant's Szechuan specialties are beef fillets with orange flavoring and crispy chicken with ginger sauce. The crispy duck with five spices is also delicious. ⊠ *65 rue d'Auteuil, Upper Town,* ☎ *418/692–0909. AE, DC, MC, V.*

Lower Town

$$$-$$$$ ✕ **Laurie Raphaël.** Classic yet unpretentious, this local hot spot has cool white linen tablecloths and sheer white drapery that contrasts warm burgundy accents. Chef Daniel Vézina is a star of Québec cuisine who makes frequent television appearances and has been chosen to cook for such high-profile individuals as President George W. Bush (at the Summit of the Americas in 2001). He is known for innovative recipes that mix classic French cuisine with international flavors. Among his creations are roulade of caribou and duck foie gras with cranberry juice and port served with apple purée and grilled Portobello, and an Australian rack of lamb with a shallot sauce, blue potatoes from Charlevoix, and goat cheese. There's a seven-course menu dégustation for $79, with

wines to complement each course available by the glass. The wine list ranges from $25 to $400 a bottle. ⊠ *117 rue Dalhousie, Lower Town,* ☎ *418/692–4555. AE, D, DC, MC, V. Closed first 2 wks of Jan. and Sun.–Mon. in winter.*

$$$–$$$$ ✕ **Le Marie Clarisse.** This restaurant at the bottom of Escalier Casse-Cou near Place Royale is known for unique seafood dishes, such as halibut with nuts and honey and scallops with port and paprika. A good game dish is usually on the menu, such as the deer and beef duo with berries and sweet garlic. The *menu du jour* has about seven entrées; dinner includes soup, salad, dessert, and coffee. Wood-beam ceilings, stone walls, and a fireplace make this one of the coziest spots in town. ⊠ *12 rue du Petit-Champlain, Lower Town,* ☎ *418/692–0857. Reservations essential. AE, DC, MC, V. No lunch weekends Oct.–Apr.*

$$$ ✕ **L'Initiale.** Sophistication and gracious service places L'Initiale in
★ good standing to rival the great tables of Europe. The modernity of its simple lines and light colors blend with its historic location. Widely spaced tables favor intimate dining. Chef Yvan Lebrun has brought a spit over from his native France, which produces a unique taste, particularly with lamb. The constantly changing menu follows the whims of the chef and the season. There's also an eight-course menu gastronomique for $76. Try the escalope de foie gras or the Québec lamb. For dessert, many small treats are attractively presented on a single plate. ⊠ *54 rue St-Pierre, Lower Town,* ☎ *418/694–1818. AE, DC, MC, V.*

$$–$$$ ✕ **L'Echaudé.** A chic beige-and-green bistro, L'Echaudé attracts a mix
★ of business and tourist clientele because of its location between the financial and antiques districts. Lunch offerings include *cuisse de canard confit* (duck confit) with french fries and fresh salad. Highlights of the three-course brunch are eggs Benedict and tantalizing desserts. The decor is modern, with hardwood floors, a mirrored wall, and a stainless-steel bar where you dine atop high stools. ⊠ *73 Sault-au-Matelot, Lower Town,* ☎ *418/692–1299. AE, DC, MC, V. No Sun. brunch mid-Oct.–mid-May.*

$$–$$$ ✕ **Le Mesclun.** When Frédéric Casadei and Cendrine Bailly vacationed in Québec City in 2000 they fell so much in love with the city that they moved here. Now they combine their two loves—the city and Provencale cuisine from their native France—in this sunny restaurant tucked away on a side street in Lower Town. Trained at Thonons-les-Bains, the oldest hotel school in France, Casadei specializes in dishes such as maigret of duck in peppercorn sauce, daube of beef provencale, bouillabaisse, or crème brûlée with vanilla. ⊠ *93 Sault-au-Matelot, Lower Town,* ☎ *418/692–0600. Reservations recommended. AE, MC, V. Closed Sun.–Mon. in winter, Sun. lunch in summer, and 2 wks in Nov. and in Apr.*

$–$$ ✕ **Le Cochon Dingue.** The boulevard Champlain location of this chain, a cheerful café whose name translates to The Crazy Pig, is across the street from the ferry in Lower Town. Sidewalk tables and indoor dining rooms artfully blend the chic and the antique; black-and-white checkerboard floors contrast with ancient stone walls. Café fare includes delicious mussels, *steak-frites* (steak with french fries), thick soups, and apple pie with maple cream. ⊠ *46 blvd. Champlain, Lower Town,* ☎ *418/692–2013;* ⊠ *46 blvd. René-Lévesque Ouest, Montcalm,* ☎ *418/ 523–2013;* ⊠ *1326 av. Maguire, Sillery,* ☎ *418/684–2013. AE, DC, MC, V.*

$ ✕ **Le Buffet de L'Antiquaire.** Hearty home cooking, generous portions, and rock-bottom prices have made this no-frills, diner-style eatery a Lower Town institution. As the name suggests, it's in the heart of the antiques district. In summer it has a small sidewalk terrace where you can sit and watch the shoppers stroll by. It's also a good place to sample traditional Québecois dishes such as tourtière. Desserts, such as the triple-layer orange cake, are homemade and delicious. ⊠ *95 rue St-Paul, Lower Town,* ☏ *418/692–2661. AE, MC, V.*

Outside the Walls

$$–$$$$ ✕ **L'Astral.** A spectacular view of Québec City is the chief attraction at this revolving restaurant atop the Hôtel Loews Le Concorde. L'Astral has wooed well-known chefs such as Jean-Claude Crouzet away from other restaurants and introduced a constantly evolving menu promoting local products—filet of Breton pork from the Beauce with polenta, Parmesan, and a garden herb sauce, for example, or rack of Charlevoix lamb with cabbage, dried fruits, and cumin sauce. L'Astral offers a varied three-course table d'hôte but no à la carte menu. ⊠ *1225 Cours du Général-de Montcalm, Montcalm,* ☏ *418/647–2222. AE, D, DC, MC, V.*

$–$$$$ ✕ **Il Teatro.** Québec's stars come out regularly at this upscale Italian restaurant just outside the St. Jean gate. Chances are the person sitting at the next table may be singing on stage at the adjacent Capitole theater after dinner, or be in town to promote his or her latest record, film, or play. The drama is enhanced by royal blue stagelike curtains and cherry-red chairs. Pastas are made on site and the basil is so fresh you can practically see it growing in a showcase window. Try the spaghetti with scampi or the *ossobuco d'agnello alle erbe* (lamb osso buco with herbs). ⊠ *972 rue St. Jean, Carré d'Youville,* ☏ *418/694– 9996. Reservations essential. AE, DC, MC, V.*

$$$ ✕ **Louis Hébert.** With its fine French cuisine and convenient location on the bustling Grande Allée, this restaurant has long been popular with many of Québec's top decision-makers. Dining areas range from the very public summer terrace to discreet second-floor meeting rooms, a solarium with bamboo chairs, and a cozy dining room with exposed stone walls and warm wood accents. In winter, chef Hervé Toussaint's roast lamb in a nut crust with Stilton and port is a favorite. In summer, seafood dishes, such as lobster and fresh pasta with a white-wine and basil cream sauce, are favored. ⊠ *668 Grande Allée Est, Montcalm,* ☏ *418/525–7812. AE, D, DC, MC, V.*

$$–$$$ ✕ **La Fenouillère.** Although this restaurant is connected to a standard
★ chain hotel, inside there's an elegant, spacious dining room with a view of the Pierre Laporte bridge. Chefs Yvon Godbout and Bernard St. Pierre serve a constantly rotating table d'hôte, going out of their way to offer seasonal products. The house specialty is salmon, but lamb is done to a turn and is very popular among the restaurant's regular customers. ⊠ *Hotel Best Western Aristocrate, 3100 chemin St-Louis, Ste-Foy,* ☏ *418/653–3886. AE, DC, MC, V.*

$$–$$$ ✕ **Le Paris Brest.** This busy restaurant on Grande Allée serves a gregarious crowd attracted to its tastefully prepared French dishes. Traditional fare, such as a warm salad with escargots and sweetbreads, and steak tartare, are presented artistically. Some popular choices are lamb with *herbes de Provence* and beef Wellington. A generous side platter of vegetables accompanies à la carte and main-course dishes; wine prices range from $22 to $700. Angular halogen lighting and soft yellow walls add a fresh, modern touch to the historic building. ⊠ *590 Grande Allée Est, Montcalm,* ☏ *418/529–2243. AE, DC, MC, V.*

$–$$$ ✕ **Le Graffiti.** A good alternative to Vieux-Québec dining, this colorful French restaurant with bright gold, red, and royal blue accents is housed in an upscale food mall. Large windows look out onto avenue Cartier. On the seasonal menu are such dishes as *escalope de veau Graffiti* (thin slices of veal) with white wine, cream, and crushed tomatoes, or angel-hair pasta with pesto, pine nuts, black olives, and sun-dried tomatoes. The table d'hôte is reasonably priced. ✉ *1191 av. Cartier, Montcalm,* ☎ *418/529–4949. AE, DC, MC, V.*

$–$$$ ✕ **Montego Resto Club.** The sun shines year-round at this trendy bistro where Californian, Italian, French, and Szechuan cuisine share the bill. The red-and-yellow Sante Fe style pays close attention to detail; each rainbow-colored light is a work of art. Every dish is presented with a creative twist as well. The inventive menu lists escalope of veal with mushrooms and hazelnuts or Californian filet of beef with salsa, morello cherries, and cantaloupe. Montego Resto Club is a 10-minute drive west of Vieux-Québec. ✉ *1460 av. Maguire, Sillery,* ☎ *418/688–7991. AE, D, DC, MC, V.*

$–$$ ✕ **Le Parlementaire.** With its magnificent Beaux Arts interior and ★ some of the most reasonable prices in town, the National Assembly's restaurant is nevertheless one of the best-kept secrets in Québec City. Chef Réal Therrien prepares contemporary cuisine that employs products from Québec's various regions. Although the restaurant is usually open Tuesday through Friday for breakfast and a three-course table d'hôte lunch, hours follow the National Assembly's schedule and can vary (it's sometimes open for dinner during the legislature's intensive sessions in June and December). It is wise to call ahead. ✉ *Av. Honoré-Mercier and Grande Allée Est, Door 3, Montcalm,* ☎ *418/643–6640. AE, MC, V. June 24–Labor Day closed weekends; Labor Day–June 23 closed Sat.–Mon.; usually no dinner.*

$–$$ ✕ **La Playa.** More than 90 different martinis and a brick-walled courtyard terrace that's heated in spring and fall make this restaurant on trendy rue St-Jean a popular choice. The West Coast influence is evident in the cuisine and in the design. Pasta can be combined with any one of 38 sauces, including the Bangkok, with shrimp, chicken, peanut, and coconut sauce, or the Île d'Orléans, with smoked duck and goat cheese. ✉ *780 rue St-Jean, St. Jean Baptiste,* ☎ *418/522–3989. AE, DC, MC, V. Closed Mon. in winter.*

$–$$ ✕ **La Pointe des Amériques.** Adventurous pizza lovers should explore the fare at this bistro. Some pizza combos (marinated alligator, smoked Gouda, Cajun sauce, and hot peppers is one of them) are strange. But don't worry—there are more than 27 different pizzas as well as meat and pasta dishes, soups, salads, and Southwest cuisine. The original brick walls of the century-old building just outside the St-Jean Gate contrast boldly with modern mirrors and artsy wrought-iron lighting. Connected to the downtown restaurant is the Biloxi Bar, which has the same menu. ✉ *964 rue St-Jean, Carré d'Youville,* ☎ *418/694–1199;* ✉ *2815 blvd. Laurier, Ste-Foy,* ☎ *418/658–2583. AE, DC, MC, V.*

$ ✕ **Chez Cora.** Spectacular breakfasts decorated with mounds of fresh ★ fruit are the specialty at this sunny chain restaurant. Whimsy is everywhere, from the plastic chicken decorations to the inventive dishes, often named after the customers and family members who inspired them. Try the Eggs Ben et Dictine, which has smoked salmon, or the Gargantua—two eggs, sausage, ham, pancakes, *cretons* (pâtés), and baked beans. Kids love the Banana Surprise, a banana wrapped in a pancake with chocolate or peanut butter and honey. The restaurant also serves light lunch fare such as salads and sandwiches. ✉ *545 rue de l'Église, St. Roch,* ☎ *418/524–3232. AE, DC, MC, V. No dinner.*

$ ✕ **Chez Victor.** It's no ordinary burger joint: this cozy café with brick and stone walls attracts an arty crowd to trendy rue St-Jean. Lettuce, tomatoes, onions, mushrooms, pickles, hot mustard, mayonnaise, and a choice of cheeses (mozzarella, Swiss, blue, goat, and cream) top hearty burgers. French fries are served with a dollop of mayo and poppy seeds. Salads, sandwiches, and a daily dessert also are available. ✉ *145 rue St-Jean, St. Jean Baptiste,* ☎ *418/529–7702. MC, V.*

$ ✕ **Le Commensal.** At this upscale cafeteria, you serve yourself from an outstanding informal vegetarian buffet and then grab a table in the vast dining room, where brick walls and green plants add a touch of class. Plates are weighed to determine the price. Hot and cold dishes run the gamut of health-conscious cooking and include stir-fry tofu and ratatouille with couscous. ⊠ *860 rue St-Jean, St. Jean Baptiste,* ☎ *418/ 647–3733. AE, DC, MC, V.*

LODGING

Be sure to make a reservation if you visit during peak season (May through September) or during the Winter Carnival, in February. During especially busy times, hotel rates usually rise 30%. From November through April, many lodgings offer weekend discounts and other promotions.

CATEGORY	COST*
$$$$	over $200
$$$	$150–$200
$$	$100–$150
$	under $100

All prices are for a standard double room at high season—excluding 7% GST, 7.5% provincial sales tax, a $2-per-night hotel tax, and an optional service charge—in Canadian dollars.

Upper Town

$$$$ 🏨 **Fairmont Le Château Frontenac.** Towering above the St. Lawrence
★   River, the Château Frontenac is Québec City's most renowned landmark. Its public rooms—from the intimate piano bar to the 700-seat ballroom reminiscent of the Hall of Mirrors at Versailles—have the opulence of years gone by. Reserve well in advance, especially late June to mid-October. More expensive deluxe or Frontenac premier rooms have views of the river, but all rooms are elegantly furnished and well maintained. At Le Champlain, classic French cuisine is served by waiters in traditional French costumes. Because the hotel is a tourist attraction, the lobby can be quite busy. ⊠ *1 rue des Carrières, Upper Town G1R 4P5,* ☎ *418/692–3861 or 800/441–1414,* FAX *418/692–1751,* WEB *www.fairmont.com. 586 rooms, 32 suites. 2 restaurants, snack bar, room service, some in-room hot tubs, minibars, cable TV with movies and video games, indoor pool, hair salon, health club, spa, piano bar, shops, baby-sitting, laundry service, concierge, parking (fee), some pets allowed. AE, DC, MC, V.*

$$–$$$$ 🏨 **Hôtel Manoir Victoria.** This European-style hotel with a good fitness center is well situated near the train station. Its discreet, old-fashioned entrance gives way to a large, wood-paneled foyer. Three rooms have whirlpool baths and electric fireplaces, as do the three suites. Some packages include a substantial buffet breakfast. ⊠ *44 côte du Palais, Upper Town G1R 4H8,* ☎ *418/692–1030 or 800/463–6283,* FAX *418/ 692–3822,* WEB *www.manoir-victoria.com. 142 rooms, 3 suites. 2 restaurants, in-room data ports (some), in-room hot tubs (some), minibars, cable TV with movies and video games, indoor pool, health club, massage, sauna, baby-sitting, dry cleaning, concierge, Internet, meeting rooms, parking (fee); no-smoking rooms. AE, D, DC, MC, V.*

$$–$$$$ 🏨 **Hôtel Palace Royal.** A soaring indoor atrium with balconies overlooking a tropical garden, swimming pool, and hot tub lends a dramatic air to this luxury hotel. Its eclectic design blends everything from Asian to art deco. Elegant rooms with antique gold accents have views of either Old Town or the atrium. Views of the river can be had

from rooms on the 7th floor and up. Four rooms are adapted for clients with disabilities. ✉ *775 av. Honoré-Mercier, Carré d'Youville G1R 6A5,* ☎ *418/694–2000 or 800/567–5276,* FAX *418/380–2553,* WEB *www.jaro.qc.ca. 74 rooms, 160 suites. Restaurant, in-room data ports, refrigerators, cable TV with movies, indoor pool, health club, bar, meeting rooms, parking (fee). AE, DC, MC, V.*

$–$$$$ 🔲 **Hôtel Le Clos St-Louis.** Winding staircases and crystal chandeliers add to the Victorian elegance of this centrally located inn, which was formed by combining two 1845-era houses. All the rooms have antiques or antique reproductions, and six have decorative fireplaces. Nine rooms have romantic four-poster beds, and seven have whirlpool baths. The small but attractive rooms with shared baths on the top floor are less expensive. ✉ *69 rue St-Louis, Upper Town G1R 3Z2,* ☎ *418/694–1311 or 800/ 461–1311,* FAX *418/694–9411,* WEB *www.clossaintlouis.com. 25 rooms, 21 with bath. In-room data ports, parking (fee); no air-conditioning in some rooms, no phones in some rooms, no TV in some rooms, no smoking. AE, DC, MC, V. CP.*

$$$ 🔲 **L'Hôtel du Capitole.** In 1992, this turn-of-the-20th-century theater just outside the St-Jean Gate was transformed into an exclusive lodging, an Italian bistro, and a 1920s cabaret-style dinner theater, Théâtre Capitole. The glitzy showbiz theme, with stars on the doors, has attracted Québec celebrities, including Céline Dion. Rooms are small and simple, highlighted with a few rich details. Painted ceilings have a blue-and-white sky motif, and white down-filled comforters dress the beds. ✉ *972 rue St-Jean, Carré d'Youville G1R 1R5,* ☎ *418/694–4040 or 800/363–4040,* FAX *418/694–1916,* WEB *www.lecapitole.com. 37 rooms, 1 suite. Restaurant, room service, in-room data ports, minibars, cable TV, in-room VCRs, 2 theaters, baby-sitting, dry cleaning, laundry service, business services, meeting rooms, parking (fee). AE, DC, MC, V.*

$$–$$$ 🔲 **Hôtel Cap Diamant.** An eclectic collection of vintage furniture and ★ ecclesiastical accents—stained glass from a church, a confessional door, even the odd angel—complement the decorative marble fireplaces, stone walls, and hardwood floors at this hotel. In the morning you can bring coffee, orange juice, and muffins to your room or dine in a sunroom that overlooks one of the old city's few gardens. Stairs to third-floor rooms are a bit steep but there is a baggage lift. ✉ *39 av. Ste-Geneviève, Upper Town G1R 4B3,* ☎ *418/694–0313,* FAX *418/ 694–1187,* WEB *www.hcapdiamant.qc.ca. 12 rooms. Refrigerators, cable TV; no room phones, dry cleaning, laundry service, no smoking. MC, V. CP.*

$$–$$$ 🔲 **Hôtel Clarendon.** Built in 1866, the Clarendon is the oldest hotel still in operation in Québec City, and has been refurbished in its original art deco and art nouveau styles, most notably in the public areas. Some guest rooms have period touches, while others are more modern. About half the rooms have excellent views of Old Québec, and others look out onto a courtyard. ✉ *57 rue Ste-Anne, Upper Town G1R 3X4,* ☎ *418/692–2480 or 888/554–6001,* FAX *418/692–4652,* WEB *www.hotelclarendon.com. 143 rooms. Restaurant, in-room data ports, cable TV with movies and video games, massage, bar, meeting rooms, parking (fee). AE, D, DC, MC, V.*

$$–$$$ 🔲 **Manoir Sur le Cap.** No two rooms are alike in this elegant 19th-century inn with beautiful views of Governors' Park and the St. Lawrence River. Built in 1837 as a private home, it was severely damaged in 1849 by a fire that razed the neighborhood. It was rebuilt the same year by George Mellis Douglas, the medical superintendent at Grosse Île. Rooms are light and airy with antiques and hardwood floors. Some have brass beds, brick walls, or small balconies. A two-story condo apartment at the rear has a double whirlpool tub and a small balcony with a view of the river. ✉ *9 av. Ste-Geneviève, Upper Town G1R 4A7,*

☎ *418/694–1987 or 866/694–1987,* ⒻⒶⓍ *418/627–7405,* ⓦⒺⒷ
*www.manoir-sur-le-cap.com. 13 rooms, one apartment. 2 restaurants,
some in-room data ports, some microwaves, cable TV; no air-conditioning in some rooms, no room phones, no smoking. AE, MC, V.*

$–$$$ ⊞ **Hôtel Château Bellevue.** Behind the Château Frontenac, this hotel
has comfortable accommodations at reasonable prices in a good loca-
tion. Guest rooms are modern, with standard hotel furnishings; many
have a view of the St. Lawrence River. The rooms vary considerably in
size (many are a bit cramped), and package deals are available. ✉ *16
rue de la Porte, Upper Town G1R 4M9,* ☎ *418/692–2573 or 800/463–
2617,* ⒻⒶⓍ *418/692–4876,* ⓦⒺⒷ *www.old-quebec.com/bellevue. 58 rooms.
In-room data ports, cable TV, dry cleaning, meeting room, free park-
ing. AE, D, DC, MC, V.*

$–$$ ⊞ **Hôtel Marie Rollet.** In the heart of Vieux-Québec, this intimate little inn built in 1876 by the Ursuline Order has warm woodwork and
antique charm. It is one of the few hotels in the old town to have two
rooms with working fireplaces. A rooftop terrace has a garden view.
✉ *81 rue Ste-Anne, Upper Town G1R 3X4,* ☎ *418/694–9271 or
800/275–0338,* ⓦⒺⒷ *www.hotelmarierollet.com. 10 rooms. Cable TV,
parking (fee); no room phones, no smoking. MC, V.*

$–$$ ⊞ **Manoir d'Auteuil.** One of the more lavish manors in town, this
lodging was originally a private home. A major renovation in 1957 re-
instated many of its art deco and art nouveau details. An ornate
sculpted iron banister wraps around four floors, and guest rooms
blend modern design with the art deco structure. Each room is different; one was formerly a chapel, and another has a tiny staircase leading to its bathroom. Two rooms have showers with seven showerheads.
Some rooms look out onto the wall between the St-Louis and St-Jean
gates. Rooms on the fourth floor are smaller, and thus less expensive.
✉ *49 rue d'Auteuil, Upper Town G1R 4C2,* ☎ *418/694–1173,* ⒻⒶⓍ *418/
694–0081,* ⓦⒺⒷ *www.quebecweb.com/dauteuil. 16 rooms. In-room
data ports, cable TV, parking (fee); no smoking. AE, D, DC, MC, V.
CP.*

$–$$ ⊞ **Manoir Ste-Geneviève.** Quaint and elaborately decorated, this hotel
dating from 1880 stands near the Château Frontenac, on the southwest corner of Governors' Park. The Victorian-style interior is decorated with fanciful wallpaper and stately English manor furnishings,
such as marble lamps, large wooden bedposts, and velvet upholstery.
Front rooms have views of the park and the St. Lawrence River. ✉ *13
av. Ste-Geneviève, Upper Town G1R 4A7,* ☎ ⒻⒶⓍ *418/694–1666 or* ☎
877/694–1666, ⓦⒺⒷ *www.quebecweb.com/msg. 9 rooms. Some kitchenettes, cable TV, parking (fee); no room phones. AE, MC, V.*

$ ⊞ **Hôtel Acadia.** Tasteful period furnishings and exposed brick walls
combine with modern comforts to make this a good centrally located,
low-cost option. The romantic, more expensive suites have double whirlpool tubs—and sparkling wine. In summer, breakfast is served on a
rooftop terrace. ✉ *43 rue Ste-Ursule, Upper Town G1R 4E4,* ☎ *418/
694–0280 or 800/463–0280,* ⒻⒶⓍ *418/694–0458,* ⓦⒺⒷ *www.hotelacadia.
com. 37 rooms, 31 with bath; 4 suites. In-room data ports (some), in-
room hot tubs (some), cable TV, dry cleaning, Internet, parking (fee),
some pets allowed; no air-conditioning in some rooms. AE, D, DC,
MC, V.*

Lower Town

$$$$ ⊞ **Auberge St-Antoine.** This charming little find is within comfortable
walking distance of all Vieux-Québec's attractions. The hotel, which
opened in 1992, seems much older than it is because of its location in
an old maritime warehouse and its generally rustic appearance. Each

room is styled differently (many have themes, such as the Captaine, decorated as a ship's captain's quarters, or the Sorbet room, in yellow, pink, and green) but all have a combination of antiques and contemporary pieces. Some rooms have river views; some have terraces. The buffet-style Continental breakfast (not included in the room rate) is extensive. ✉ *10 rue St-Antoine, Lower Town G1K 4C9,* ☎ *418/692–2211 or 888/692–2211,* FAX *418/692–1177,* WEB *www.saint-antoine.com. 84 rooms, 11 suites. In-room data ports, cable TV, meeting rooms, parking (fee). AE, DC, MC, V.*

$$$$ ⊞ **Hotel Dominion 1912.** Sophistication and attention to the smallest
★ detail prevail at this boutique hotel—from the custom-designed swing-out night tables in the modern rooms to the white goose-down duvets and the custom umbrellas in each room. Built in 1912 as a warehouse, the hotel has rooms on higher floors with views of either the St. Lawrence River or of the Old Town. ✉ *126 rue St-Pierre, Lower Town G1K 4A8,* ☎ *418/692–2224 or 888/833–5253,* FAX *418/692–4403,* WEB *www.hoteldominion.com. 60 rooms. In-room data ports, minibars, cable TV, baby-sitting, dry cleaning, concierge, Internet, business services, meeting rooms, parking (fee). AE, DC, MC, V. CP.*

$$–$$$ ⊞ **Hôtel Le Saint-Paul.** Perched at the edge of the antiques district, near art galleries and the train station, this European-style hotel was transformed from a 19th-century office building in 1998. Comfortable rooms have hunter green carpeting, standard hotel furnishings, and bedspreads with a Renaissance motif of characters in period dress. Some rooms have exposed brick walls. ✉ *229½ rue St-Paul, Lower Town G1K 3W3,* ☎ *418/694–4414 or 888/794–4414,* FAX *418/694–0889,* WEB *www.lesaintpaul.qc.ca. 23 rooms, 3 suites. Restaurant, in-room data ports, cable TV, meeting rooms. AE, DC, MC, V.*

$–$$ ⊞ **Hôtel Belley.** Modern artwork by local artists is everywhere in this modest little hotel tucked above the Belley Tavern, a stone's throw from the train station and the antiques district. Built as a private home around 1842, the building has housed various taverns uninterrupted since 1868. The current hotel was added in 1987. Rooms are simple, with exposed brick walls and beamed ceilings. Downstairs, the old-fashioned tin ceilings and modern furniture attract a café crowd. Five apartments are also available in a separate building. ✉ *249 rue St-Paul, Lower Town G1K 3W5,* ☎ *418/692–1694 or 888/692–1694,* FAX *418/692–1696,* WEB *www.oricom.ca/belley. 8 rooms, 5 apartments. Restaurant, in-room data ports, cable TV, parking (fee). AE, D, MC, V.*

Outside the Walls

$$$–$$$$ ⊞ **Hilton Québec.** Just opposite the National Assembly, the spacious Hilton rises from the shadow of Parliament Hill. The lobby, which can be busy at times, has a bar and an open-air restaurant. The hotel is next to the Parliament Buildings and connected to the convention center and a mall, Place Québec, which has more than 30 shops and restaurants. Standard yet modern rooms have tall windows; those on upper floors have fine views of Vieux-Québec. Stay on an executive floor, and you're entitled to a free breakfast and an open bar from 5 to 10 PM. ✉ *1100 blvd. René-Lévesque Est, Montcalm G1K 7K7,* ☎ *418/647–2411, 800/447–2411 within Canada,* FAX *418/647–6488,* WEB *www.hilton.com. 535 rooms, 36 suites. Restaurant, room service, in-room data ports, minibars, cable TV with movies and video games, pool, health club, massage, sauna, bar, baby-sitting, dry cleaning, laundry service, concierge, business service, meeting rooms, parking (fee), some pets allowed; no-smoking floors. AE, D, DC, MC, V.*

$$$–$$$$ ⊞ **Hôtel Radisson Québec.** This large establishment opposite the Parliament Buildings has standard rooms and business-class rooms. A

Continental breakfast is included for business-class rooms, which have in-room Internet access and ergonomic desk chairs. The hotel occupies the first 12 floors of a tall office complex; views of Vieux-Québec are limited to the higher floors. ⊠ *690 blvd. René-Lévesque Est, Montcalm G1R 5A8,* ☎ *418/647–1717, 888/884–7777, 800/333–3333,* FAX *418/647–2146,* WEB *www.radisson.com. 371 rooms, 6 suites. Restaurant, some in-room data ports, cable TV with movies and video games, pool, health club, sauna, dry cleaning, Internet, meeting rooms, some pets allowed, parking (fee). AE, D, DC, MC, V.*

$$–$$$$ ★ 🏨 **Hôtel Loews Le Concorde.** When Le Concorde was built in 1974, the shockingly tall concrete structure aroused controversy because it supplanted 19th-century Victorian homes. But the hotel's excellent location, on Grande Allée—where cafés, restaurants, and bars dot the street—has ensured its longevity. Celebrity guests have ranged from the Rolling Stones to President George W. Bush. Rooms are larger than average, with good views of Parc des Champs-de-Bataille (Battlefields Park) and the St. Lawrence River. Nearly all rooms have been redone in a combination of modern and traditional furnishings. This hotel is one of the few in the city that welcomes pets. ⊠ *1225 Cours du Général-de Montcalm, Montcalm G1R 4W6,* ☎ *418/647–2222 or 800/ 463–5256,* FAX *418/647–4710,* WEB *www.loewshotels.com. 386 rooms, 18 suites. 2 restaurants, room service, minibars, cable TV with movies, pool, health club, bar, baby-sitting, laundry service, business services, parking (fee), some pets allowed. AE, D, DC, MC, V.*

$$–$$$ 🏨 **Hôtel Royal William.** Like its namesake, the first Canadian steamship to cross the Atlantic in 1833, the Royal William brings the spirit of technology and innovation to this hotel designed with the business traveler in mind. Rooms have two phone lines, a fax connection, plus a high-speed Internet port. The meeting rooms on each floor have Internet connections and several are equipped for video conferencing. Throughout, the style is art deco with a modern twist. Five minutes from Vieux-Québec, the hotel is in the low-rent St-Roch district, where hip young artists, academics, and techies are replacing the panhandlers. ⊠ *360 blvd. Charest Est, St. Roch G1K 3H4,* ☎ *418/521–4488 or 888/541–0405,* FAX *418/521–6868,* WEB *www.royalwilliam.com. 44 rooms. Restaurant, in-room data ports, in-room safes, minibars, gym, library, baby-sitting, dry cleaning, Internet, meeting rooms, parking (fee); no-smoking floors. AE, D, DC, MC, V.*

$$ ★ 🏨 **Château Bonne Entente.** In a grassy residential parkland area with a duck pond, this English-style country inn is off the beaten path but worth the trip. Wings were added to what was originally a private home. In keeping with the hotel's English roots, hunter greens and burgundies adorn the rooms, and tea and biscuits are served every afternoon near the fireplace in the wood-paneled tearoom. In the newer wing, some rooms have multijet showers, and two suites have fireplaces. Two family suites have colorful bunk beds for kids. The hotel is 20 minutes from downtown, with a shuttle service. ⊠ *3400 chemin Ste-Foy, Ste-Foy G1X 1S6,* ☎ *418/653–5221 or 800/463–4390,* FAX *418/653–3098,* WEB *www.chateaubonneentente.com. 119 rooms, 17 suites. 2 restaurants, tennis court, outdoor pool, gym, outdoor hot tub, sauna, spa, ice-skating, bar, baby-sitting, playground, dry cleaning, Internet, meeting rooms, free parking. AE, D, DC, MC, V.*

$$ ★ 🏨 **Hôtel Relais Charles-Alexandre.** Sunny bay windows, hardwood floors, and furniture handmade by Québec artisans combine to make you feel as if you're staying in a family home. The elegance and reasonable prices at the three-story hotel, as well as its convenient location (a 10-15 minute walk from the old city), make it advisable to reserve several weeks in advance for stays from May through October. Continental breakfast is served in a small art gallery. There are no elevators. ✉ *91 Grande Allée Est, Montcalm G1R 2H5,* ☎ *418/523–1220,* FAX *418/523–9556,* WEB *www.quebecweb.com/rca/introang.html. 23 rooms. Meeting room, parking (fee); no room phones, no smoking. AE, MC, V. CP.*

$–$$ ⊡ **Hôtel Château Laurier.** The spacious lobby at this former private home has brown leather sofas and easy chairs and wrought-iron and wood chandeliers. All rooms have sleigh beds with paisley-inspired bedspreads in green, beige, or blue. Rooms in the newer section are a bit larger than those in the old; deluxe rooms have fireplaces and double whirlpool baths. Some rooms look out on the Plains of Abraham; more have a view of the National Assembly and the Upper Town. Busy Grande Allée is crowded with popular restaurants and trendy bars. ✉ *1220 pl. Georges V Ouest, Montcalm G1R 5B8,* ☎ *418/522–8108 or 800/ 463–4453,* FAX *418/524–8768,* WEB *www.oldquebec.com/laurier. 151 rooms, 3 suites. Restaurant, in-room data ports, in-room hot tubs (some), massage, bar, baby-sitting, dry cleaning, business services, meeting rooms, free parking; no-smoking floors. AE, D, DC, MC, V.*

$ ⊡ **Toast & French Bed & Breakfast.** If you would like to take advantage of your visit to Québec City to learn French, then this is the place to stay. In addition to large, comfortable rooms, owner France Levasseur, a certified French teacher, offers breakfast as well as tailor-made, on-site French lessons. Tours can be arranged to help you discover Québec City and introduce you to the neighborhood. Rooms in this centrally located third-floor home have hardwood floors and are tastefully decorated; two have private bathrooms. Canadian tax receipts are available for French lessons, which aren't included in room rates. ✉ *1020 av. Cartier, Montcalm G1R 2S4,* ☎ *418/523–9365,* FAX *418/ 523–6706,* WEB *www.quebecweb.com/toast&french. 4 rooms. Parking (fee); no room phones, no TV in some rooms, no smoking. AE, DC, MC, V. CP.*

NIGHTLIFE AND THE ARTS

Considering its size, Québec City has a good variety of cultural institutions, from the renowned Québec Symphony Orchestra to several small theater companies. The arts scene changes significantly depending on the season. From September through May, a steady repertory of concerts, plays, and performances is presented in theaters and halls. In summer, indoor theaters close to make room for outdoor stages. For arts and entertainment listings in English, consult the *Québec Chronicle-Telegraph,* published on Wednesday. The French-language daily newspaper *Le Soleil* has listings on a page called "Agenda." Also, *Voir* (www.voir.ca), a French-language weekly devoted to arts listings and reviews, appears on the street every Thursday.

Billetech (WEB www.billetech.com), which has outlets throughout the city, sells tickets for most shows. Hours vary. Outlets exist at: Bibliothèque Gabrielle-Roy (✉ 350 rue St-Joseph Est, St. Roch, ☎ 418/691– 7400); Colisée Pepsi (✉ Parc de l'Expocité, 250 blvd. Wilfrid-Hamel, Limoilou, ☎ 418/691–7211); Comptoir postal Le Soleil (✉ pl. Laurier, 2nd floor, Ste-Foy, ☎ 418/656–6095); Grand Théâtre de Québec (✉ 269 blvd. René-Lévesque Est, Montcalm, ☎ 418/643–8131 or 877/ 643–8131); Palais Montcalm (✉ 995 pl. d'Youville, Carré d'Youville, ☎ 418/670–9011); Salle Albert-Rousseau (✉ 2410 chemin Ste-Foy, Ste-Foy, ☎ 418/659–6710); and Théâtre Capitole (✉ 972 rue St-Jean, Carré d'Youville, ☎ 418/694–4444).

The Arts

Dance

Dancers appear at Bibliothèque Gabrielle-Roy, Salle Albert-Rousseau, and the Palais Montcalm. **Grand Théâtre de Québec** (✉ 269 blvd. René-Lévesque Est, Montcalm, ☎ 418/643–8131) presents a dance series with Canadian and international companies.

Film

Most theaters present French and American films dubbed into French. **Cineplex Odeon Ste-Foy** (✉ 1200 blvd. Duplessis, Ste-Foy, ☎ 418/871–1550) almost always shows some films in English. **Cinéma Star Cité** (✉ 1150 blvd. Duplessis, Ste-Foy, ☎ 418/874–0066) is a megaplex that usually shows English films. **IMAX Theatre** (✉ Galeries de la Capitale, 5401 blvd. des Galeries, Lebourgneuf, ☎ 418/627–4629, 418/627–4688, 800/643–4629) has extra-large-screen movies—educational fare on scientific, historical, and adventure topics—and translation headsets. **Le Clap** (✉ 2360 chemin Ste-Foy, Ste-Foy, ☎ 418/650–2527) has a repertoire of foreign, offbeat, and art films.

Music

Tickets for children's concerts at the **Joseph Lavergne auditorium** must be purchased in advance at the **Bibliothèque Gabrielle-Roy** (✉ 350 rue St-Joseph Est, St. Roch, ☎ 418/691–7400). Popular music concerts are often booked at the **Colisée Pepsi** (✉ Parc de l'Expocité, 250 blvd. Wilfrid-Hamel, Limoulou, ☎ 418/691–7211).

Maison de la Chanson (✉ Théâtre Petit Champlain, 68 rue du Petit-Champlain, Lower Town, ☎ 418/692–4744) is a fine spot to hear contemporary Francophone music.

L'Orchestre Symphonique de Québec (Québec Symphony Orchestra; ✉ 269 blvd. René-Lévesque Est, Montcalm, ☎ 418/643–8131) is Canada's oldest. It performs at Louis-Frechette Hall in the Grand Théâtre de Québec.

For classical concerts at the **Salle de l'Institut Canadien** (✉ 42 Chaussée des Ecossais, Upper Town), buy tickets in advance at the Palais Montcalm.

MUSIC FESTIVALS

An annual highlight is the July **Festival d'Eté International de Québec** (☎ 418/523–4540, WEB www.infofestival.com), an 11-day music festival with more than 400 shows and concerts (most of them free), from classical music to Francophone song and street performers. Events are held in more than 10 locations, including outdoor stages and public squares. Dates for 2003 are July 3–13.

The streets of Québec City's Lower Town are transported back in time during the **Fêtes de la Nouvelle France** (☎ 418/694–3311, WEB www.nouvellefrance.qc.ca), a five-day festival that re-creates the days of New France. Events, ranging from an old-time farmers' market to games, music, demonstrations, and spontaneous skits are held throughout the old city and everywhere you will see people in period costume. Dates for 2003 are August 6–10.

During the **Québec City International Festival of Military Bands** (☎ 418/694–5757), in August, the streets of Old Québec resound with military airs. Bands from several countries participate in the four-day festival, which includes a gala parade. Shows—most of them free—are held in Vieux-Québec or just outside the walls. Dates for 2003 are August 21–24.

Theater

Most theater productions are in French. The theaters listed here schedule shows September to April.

Grand Théâtre de Québec (✉ 269 blvd. René-Lévesque Est, Montcalm, ☎ 418/643–8131) offers classic and contemporary plays staged by the leading local company, le Théâtre du Trident (☎ 418/643–5873). **Palais Montcalm** (✉ 995 pl. d'Youville, Carré d'Youville, ☎ 418/670–9011), a municipal theater outside St-Jean Gate, presents a broad range of productions.

A diverse repertoire, from classic to comedy, is staged at **Salle Albert-Rousseau** (✉ 2410 chemin Ste-Foy, Ste-Foy, ☎ 418/659–6710). **Théâtre Le Capitole** (✉ 972 rue St-Jean, Carré d'Youville, ☎ 418/694–4444), a restored cabaret-style theater, schedules pop music and musical comedy shows. **Théâtre Périscope** (✉ 2 rue Crémazie Est, Montcalm, ☎ 418/529–2183), a multipurpose theater, stages about 125 shows a year, including performances for children.

In summer, **open-air concerts** are presented at Place d'Youville (just outside St-Jean Gate) and on the Plains of Abraham.

Nightlife

Québec City nightlife centers on the clubs and cafés of rue St-Jean, avenue Cartier, and Grande Allée. In winter, evening activity becomes livelier as the week nears its end, beginning on Wednesday. As warmer temperatures set in, the café–terrace crowd emerges, and bars are active seven days a week. Most bars and clubs stay open until 3 AM.

Bars and Lounges

One of the city's most romantic spots is the Château Frontenac's **Bar St-Laurent** (✉ 1 rue des Carrières, Upper Town, ☎ 418/692–3861), with soft lights, a panoramic view of the St. Lawrence, and a fireplace. The rhythms at **Chez Maurice** (✉ 575 Grande Allée Est, 2nd floor, Montcalm, ☎ 418/647–2000) have attracted stars such as Mick Jagger and the Backstreet Boys. **Cosmos Café** (✉ 575 Grande Allée Est, Montcalm, ☎ 418/640–0606) is a lively club and restaurant. With its brick walls and wine cellar–like atmosphere, **Les Voutes de Napoleon** (✉ 680 Grande Allée Est, Montcalm, ☎ 418/640–9388) is a popular place to listen to Québecois music and taste beer from local microbreweries.

L'Inox (✉ 37 quai St-André, Lower Town, ☎ 418/692–2877) is a popular Lower Town brew pub where patrons can sample beers brewed on-site. Some of them, like Transat and Viking, were developed to mark special events. Inside are billiard tables; outside there's a summer terrace. **Le Pub Saint-Alexandre** (✉ 1087 rue St-Jean, Upper Town, ☎ 418/694–0015), a popular English-style pub, serves 40 kinds of single malt scotch and 200 kinds of beer, 20 on tap. Perched on the cliff just above the increasingly trendy St. Roch district, **Les Salons d'Edgar** (✉ 263 rue St. Vallier Est, St. Roch, ☎ 418/523–7811) attracts a 30-something crowd with its eclectic music—everything from salsa beats and tango music to jazz and techno sounds. It's closed in July and August.

Dance Clubs

Patrons at **Vogue** (✉ 1170 rue d'Artigny, Montcalm, ☎ 418/529–9973) move to techno and pop beats at the second-story dance club. There's a little bit of everything—from live rock bands to loud disco—at **Chez Dagobert** (✉ 600 Grande Allée Est, Montcalm, ☎ 418/522–0393), a large, popular club. Electronic music and a trendy vibe have made **Le Sonar** (✉ 1147 av. Cartier, Montcalm, ☎ 418/640–7333) one of the hottest dance clubs in town.

Folk, Jazz, and Blues

French-Canadian and Québecois folk songs fill **Chez Son Père** (⊠ 24 rue St-Stanislas, Upper Town, ☎ 418/692–5308), a smoky pub on the second floor of an old building in the Latin Quarter. Singers perform nightly. The first jazz bar in Québec City, **L'Emprise at Hôtel Clarendon** (⊠ 57 rue Ste-Anne, Upper Town, ☎ 418/692–2480) is the preferred spot for enthusiasts. The art deco style sets the mood for Jazz Age rhythms.

OUTDOOR ACTIVITIES AND SPORTS

Scenic rivers and nearby mountains (no more than 30 minutes by car) make Québec City ideal for the sporting life. For information about sports and fitness, contact the **Québec City Tourist Information Office** (⊠ 835 av. Laurier, Montcalm G1R 2L3, ☎ 418/649–2608). The **Québec City Bureau of Culture, Recreation and Community Life** (⊠ 275 rue de l'Eglise, 4ᵉ, St. Roch G1K 6G7, ☎ 418/691–6284) has information about municipal facilities.

Sprawling between Laurier Ave. and the cliffs in the Montcalm district, the 250-acre **Parc des Champs-de-Bataille** (Battlefields Park) has panoramic views of the St. Lawrence River, and has trails for running, biking, in-line skating, and cross-country skiing, plus walking paths, volleyball courts, and open fields. Bordering the St. Charles River, **Cartier-Brébeuf Park** (⊠ 175 rue de l'Espinay), in the Limoilou district, is popular with runners, hikers, cyclists, and cross-country skiiers.

Participant Sports and Outdoor Activities

Biking

The number of bike paths and trails in the Québec City area has mushroomed in recent years; detailed maps are available at tourism offices. Bike paths along rolling hills traverse **Parc des Champs-de-Bataille** (Battlefields Park), which encompasses the Plains of Abraham, at the south side of the city. Ambitious cyclists can head for the 22-km-long (14-mi-long) **Corridor des Cheminots,** which runs from Limoilou near Vieux-Québec to the picturesque community of Shannon. Paths along the **Côte de Beaupré,** beginning at the confluence of the St. Charles and St. Lawrence rivers, are especially scenic. They begin northeast of the city at rue de la Verandrye and boulevard Montmorency or rue Abraham-Martin and Pont Samson (Samson Bridge) and continue 10 km (6 mi) along the coast to Montmorency Falls. **Mont Ste-Anne,** site of the 1998 world mountain-biking championship and annual World Cup races, has 150 km (93 mi) of mountain-bike trails, 14 downhill runs, a gondola, and an extreme mountain biking park.

From the end of March to mid-October, you can rent bicycles, including helmets and locks, for $25 a day or $17 for four hours at **Vélo Passe-Sport** (⊠ 22 côte du Palais, Upper Town, ☎ 418/692–3643), which also gives guided bike tours of the area.

Boating

Manoir St-Castin (⊠ 99 chemin du Tour du Lac, Lac Beauport, ☎ 418/841–4949), at Lac Beauport, has canoes, kayaks, and pedal boats. Follow Route 73 north of the city to Lac Beauport and then take Exit 157, boulevard du Lac. Just west of Québec City, on the St. Lawrence River, canoes, pedal boats, and small sailboats can be rented at **Parc Nautique du Cap-Rouge** (⊠ 4155 chemin de la Plage Jacques Cartier, Cap Rouge, ☎ 418/650–7770).

Dogsledding

Aventures Nord-Bec (✉ 665 rue St-Aimé, St-Lambert de Lévis, ☎ 418/889–8001), 30 minutes from the bridges south of the city, can teach you how to mush in the forest. A half-day—including initiation, dogsledding, and a snack—is $85. Overnight camping trips are available.

Fishing

Permits are needed for fishing in Québec. Most sporting-goods stores and all Walmarts and Canadian Tire stores sell permits. **Latulippe** (✉ 637 rue St-Vallier Ouest, St. Roch, ☎ 418/529–0024) sells permits and also stocks a wide selection of hunting and fishing equipment. The **Société de la Faune et les Parcs** (✉ 675 blvd. René-Lévesque Est, Montcalm, ☎ 418/521–3830, WEB www.fapaq.gouv.qc.ca) publishes a pamphlet on fishing regulations and is available at ministry offices and where permits are sold.

Réserve Faunique des Laurentides (☎ 418/528–6868, 800/665–6527 fishing reservations, FAX 418/528–8833, WEB www.sepaq.com), a wildlife reserve with good lakes for fishing, is approximately 48 km (30 mi) north of Québec City via Route 73. Reserve a boat 48 hours in advance by phone.

Golf

The Québec City region has 18 golf courses, and most are open to the public. Reservations are essential in summer. The 18-hole, par-72 course at **Club de Golf de Cap-Rouge** (✉ 4600 rue St-Felix, ☎ 418/653–9381) is one of the closest courses to Québec City. **Club de Golf de Mont Tourbillon** (✉ 55 montée du Golf, Lac Beauport, ☎ 418/849–4418), a par-70, 18-hole course, is 20 minutes from the city by car via Route 73 North (Lac Beauport exit). **Le Grand Vallon** (✉ 100 rue Beaumont, Beaupré, ☎ 418/827–4653), a half-hour drive north of Québec City, has one of the best 18-hole, par-72 courses in the region.

Health and Fitness Clubs

One of the city's most popular health clubs is **Club Entrain** (✉ pl. de la Cité, 2600 blvd. Laurier, Ste-Foy, ☎ 418/658–7771). Facilities, available for a daily fee of $11.50, include a weight room with Nautilus, sauna, whirlpool, aerobics classes, and squash courts. **Hilton Québec** (✉ 1100 blvd. René-Lévesque Est, Montcalm, ☎ 418/525–9909) has a health club with weights, exercise machines, a sauna, and a year-round heated outdoor pool available to nonguests for a $10 fee. Nonguests can use the health-club facilities at **Hôtel Radisson Québec** (✉ 690 blvd. René-Lévesque Est, Montcalm, ☎ 418/647–1717), including weights, sauna, whirlpool, and an outdoor heated pool (in summer), for $5. At the **YWCA** (✉ 855 av. Holland, St. Sacrement, ☎ 418/683–2155), pool facilities cost $2.50 for nonmembers.

Hiking and Jogging

Parc Cartier-Brébeuf (✉ 175 rue de l'Espinay, Limoilou, ☎ 418/648–4038), north of Vieux-Québec along the banks of the St. Charles River, is connected to about 13 km (8 mi) of hiking trails. It's also a historic site with a reconstruction of a native longhouse. For mountainous terrain, head 19 km (12 mi) north on Route 73 to **Lac Beauport.** Along with Parc des Champs-de-Bataille (Battlefields Park) and Parc Cartier-Brébeuf, **Bois-de-Coulonge Park** (✉ 1215 chemin St-Louis, Sillery, ☎ 418/528–0773) is one of the most popular places for jogging.

Horseback Riding

Excursions et Mechoui Jacques Cartier (✉ 978 av. Jacques-Cartier Nord, Tewkesbury, ☎ 418/848–7238), also known for rafting, offers summer and winter horseback riding. A summer excursion includes an hour of instruction and three hours of riding; the cost is $45.

Ice-Skating

The ice-skating season is usually December through March.Try the **Patinoire de la Terrasse** adjacent to the Château Frontenac (☎ 418/692–2955), open 11–11; it costs $2 to skate and skates can be rented for $5 daily (including skating). **Place d'Youville,** outside St-Jean Gate, has an outdoor rink that's open November through April. Nighttime skating is an option at **Village Vacances Valcartier** (✉ 1860 blvd. Valcartier, St-Gabriel-de-Valcartier, ☎ 418/844–2200), although closing times vary.

Outfitters

Outdoor enthusiasts flock to **Latulippe** (✉ 637 rue St-Vallier Ouest, St. Roch, ☎ 418/529–0024) for its wide selection of clothing and equipment for such open-air pursuits as hiking, camping, snowmobiling, hunting, and fishing.

Rafting

The Jacques Cartier River, about 48 km (30 mi) northwest of Québec City, provides good rafting. **Les Excursions et Mechoui Jacques Cartier** (✉ 978 av. Jacques-Cartier Nord, Tewkesbury, ☎ 418/848–7238) runs rafting trips on the river from May through October. Tours originate from Tewkesbury, a half-hour drive from Québec City. A half-day tour costs less than $35; wet suits are $16. In winter, you can slide on inner tubes for about $19 a day.

Village Vacances Valcartier (✉ 1860 blvd. Valcartier, St-Gabriel-de-Valcartier, ☎ 418/844–2200) has excursions on the Jacques Cartier River from May through September. A three-hour excursion costs $35 plus $16 to rent a wet suit. It also offers hydro speeding—running the rapids on surfboards—and quieter family river tours.

Skiing

Brochures about ski centers in Québec are available at the **Québec Tourism and Convention Bureau** or by calling ☎ 877/266–5687. The **Hiver Express** (☎ 418/525–5191) winter shuttle is a taxi service between major hotels in Vieux-Québec, ski centers, and the Village Vacances Valcartier. It leaves hotels in Vieux-Québec at 8 AM and 10 for the ski hills, 10 for Valcartier, and returns at 4:30 PM. The cost is $23; reserve and pay in advance at hotels.

CROSS-COUNTRY

Parc des Champs-de-Bataille (Battlefields Park), which you can reach from Place Montcalm, has scenic, marked cross-country skiing trails. Thirty ski centers in the Québec area offer 2,000 km (1,240 mi) of groomed trails and heated shelters; for information, call **Regroupement des Stations de Ski de Fond** (☎ 418/653–5875, WEB www.rssfrq.qc.ca). **Le Centre de Randonnée à Skis de Duchesnay** (✉ 143 rue de Duchesnay, St-Catherine-de-Jacques-Cartier, ☎ 418/875–2711), north of Québec City, has marked trails totaling 150 km (93 mi). **Mont Ste-Anne** (☎ 418/827–4561), 40 km (25 mi) northeast of Québec City, is the second-largest cross-country ski center in North America, with 27 trails; 224 km (139 mi) for skiing and 135 km (84 mi) of trails for skating stride. **Lac Beauport,** 19 km (12 mi) north of the city, has more than 20 marked trails (150 km, or 93 mi); contact **Les Sentiers du Moulin** (✉ 99 chemin du Moulin, Lac Beauport, ☎ 418/849–9652).

DOWNHILL

Three downhill ski resorts, all with night skiing, are within a 30-minute drive of Québec City. There are 25 trails and a vertical drop of 734 ft at the relatively small **Le Relais** (✉ 1084 blvd. du Lac, Lac Beauport, ☎ 418/849–1851), where you can buy lift tickets by the hour. **Mont Ste-Anne** (✉ 2000 blvd. Beaupré, Beaupré, ☎ 418/827–4561,

800/463–1568 lodging) is one of the largest resorts in eastern Canada, with a vertical drop of 2,050 ft, 56 downhill trails, a halfpipe for snowboarders, a terrain park, and 13 lifts including a gondola. **Station Touristique Stoneham** (✉ 1420 av. du Hibou, Stoneham, ☎ 418/848–2411), with a vertical drop of 1,380 ft, is known for its long, easy slopes. It has 30 downhill runs and 10 lifts as well as a terrain park and two halfpipes.

Snowmobiling

Québec is the birthplace of the snowmobile, and with 32,000 km (18,600 mi) of trails, it is one of the best places in the world to practice this activity. Two major trails, the Trans-Québec Snowmobile Trail and the 1,300-km (806-mi) Fur Traders Tour, run just north of Québec City. Trail maps are available at tourist offices. Snowmobiles can be rented near Mont Ste-Anne, a half-hour drive north of the city, at **Centre de Location de Motoneiges du Québec** (15 blvd. du Beaupré, Beaupré, ☎ 418/827–8478), starting at $40 for an hour or $100 a day plus taxes, insurance, and gas. **SM Sport** (113 blvd. Valcartier, Loretteville, ☎ 418/842–2703) will pick you up from several downtown hotels. Prices start at $20 per person. Snowmobile rental prices begin at $45 plus tax for an hour or $135 per day, plus $15 insurance and cost of gas.

Snow Slides

At **Glissades de la Terrasse** (☎ 418/692–2955), adjacent to the Château Frontenac, a wooden toboggan takes you down a 700-ft snow slide. The cost is $2 per ride per adult and $1.25 for children under six.

Use inner tubes or carpets on any of 42 snow slides at **Village Vacances Valcartier** (✉ 1860 blvd. Valcartier, St-Gabriel-de-Valcartier, ☎ 418/844–2200, WEB www.valcartier.com), or join 6 to 12 others for a snow-raft ride down one of three groomed trails or take a dizzying ride on the Tornado, a giant inner tube seating eight that spins down the slopes. Rafting and sliding costs $22 per day, $24 with skating. Trails open daily 10 AM. Closing times vary.

Tennis and Racquet Sports

At **Montcalm Tennis Club** (✉ 901 blvd. Champlain, Sillery, ☎ 418/687–1250), southwest of Québec City, four indoor and seven outdoor courts are open weekdays from 7 AM and weekends from 8 AM to midnight. **Tennisport** (✉ 6280 blvd. Hamel, Ancienne Lorette, ☎ 418/872–0111) has nine indoor tennis courts, two squash courts, one racquetball court, and eight badminton courts.

Water Parks

Village Vacances Valcartier (✉ 1860 blvd. Valcartier, St-Gabriel-de-Valcartier, ☎ 418/844–2200) has one of the largest water parks in Canada, with 23 water slides, a wave pool, and the Amazon, a tropical river adventure. On Everest, one of the highest slides in North America, bathers shoot down at speeds of up to 50 mph. Admission is $25 a day for those at least 52 inches tall, $16 for those under 52 inches.

Winter Carnival

One winter highlight is the **Carnaval de Québec** (✉ 290 rue Joly, GIL 1N8, ☎ 418/626–3716, WEB www.carnaval.qc.ca). The whirl of activities over three weekends in January and/or February includes night parades, a snow-sculpture competition, and a canoe race across the St. Lawrence River. You can participate in or watch every activity imaginable in the snow from dogsledding to ice climbing. Dates for 2003 are Jan. 31–Feb. 16.

Spectator Sports

Tickets for sporting events can be purchased at **Colisée Pepsi** (⊠ Parc de l'Expocité, 250 blvd. Wilfrid-Hamel, Limoilou, ☎ 418/691–7211). You can order tickets for many events through **Billetech** (WEB www.billetech.com).

Baseball

The **Capitales de Québec** (⊠ Stade Municipal, 100 rue du Cardinal Maurice-Roy, St. Roch, ☎ 418/521–2255 or 877/521–2244), part of the Northern League, play Single A professional baseball from May 24 through September in this old-fashioned ballpark built in 1938.

Harness Racing

There's horse racing at **Hippodrome de Québec** (⊠ Parc de l'Expocité, 250 blvd. Wilfrid-Hamel, Limoilou, ☎ 418/524–5283).

SHOPPING

On the fashionable streets of Québec City, shopping is European-style. The boutiques and specialty shops clustered along narrow streets such as rue du Petit-Champlain, and rues de Buade and St-Jean in the Latin Quarter, have one of the most striking historic settings on the continent. Prices in Québec City tend to be on a par with those in Montréal and other North American cities. The city's attractions for shoppers traditionally have been antiques, furs, and works by local artisans rather than bargains, but the exchange rate for the U.S. dollar and sales-tax rebates available to international visitors make shopping particularly tempting. When sales occur, they are usually listed in the French daily newspaper *Le Soleil*.

Interest has grown in the highly collectible art and sculpture of the Inuit, usually rendered in soapstone. For the best price and a guarantee of authenticity, purchase Inuit and other native crafts in the province where they originate. Many styles are now attributed to certain tribes and are mass-produced for sale in galleries and shops miles away from their regions of origin. At the very top galleries you can be assured of getting pieces done by individual artists, though the prices will be higher than in the provinces of origin. The Canadian government has registered the symbol of an igloo as a mark of a work's authenticity. Be sure this Canadian government sticker or tag is attached before you make your purchase.

Stores are generally open Monday through Wednesday 9:30–5:30, Thursday and Friday until 9, Saturday until 5, and Sunday noon–5. In summer, shops may be open seven days, and most have later evening hours.

Department Stores

Most large department stores can be found in the malls of suburban Ste-Foy. **La Baie** (⊠ pl. Laurier, Ste-Foy, ☎ 418/627–5959) is Québec's version of the Canadian Hudson's Bay Company conglomerate, founded in 1670 by Montréal trappers Pierre Radisson and Médard Chouart des Groseilliers. Today La Baie carries clothing for the entire family and household wares. **Holt Renfrew & Co., Ltd.** (⊠ pl. Ste-Foy, Ste-Foy, ☎ 418/656–6783), one of the country's more exclusive stores, carries furs in winter, perfume, and tailored designer collections for men and women. **Simons** (⊠ 20 côte de la Fabrique, Upper Town, ☎ 418/692–3630; ⊠ pl. Ste-Foy, Ste-Foy, ☎ 418/692–3630), one of Québec City's oldest family stores, used to be its only source for fine British woolens and tweeds; now the store also has a large selection of designer clothing, linens, and other household items.

Shopping Malls

An indoor amusement park with a roller coaster and an IMAX theater attracts families to the **Galeries de la Capitale** (⊠ 5401 blvd. des Galeries, Lebourgneuf, ☎ 418/627–5800), with 250 stores, about a 20-minute drive from Vieux-Québec. **Place Québec** (⊠ 880 autoroute Dufferin-Montmorency, Upper Town, ☎ 418/529–0551) is a multilevel shopping complex and convention center with more than 30 stores and restaurants; it's connected to the Hilton Québec.

The following shopping centers are approximately a 15-minute drive west along Grande Allée. **Place de la Cité** (⊠ 2600 blvd. Laurier, Ste-Foy, ☎ 418/657–6920) has 150 boutiques, services, and restaurants. With 350 stores and a wide variety, the massive **Place Laurier** (⊠ 2700 blvd. Laurier, Ste-Foy, ☎ 418/653–9318) is your best bet for one-stop shopping. Designer labels and upscale clothing are easy to find at **Place Ste-Foy** (⊠ 2450 blvd. Laurier, Ste-Foy, ☎ 418/653–4184), which has 130 stores.

Quartier Petit-Champlain (☎ 418/692–2613) in Lower Town is a pedestrian mall with some 45 boutiques, local businesses, and restaurants. This popular district is the best area for native Québec arts and crafts, such as wood sculptures, weavings, ceramics, and jewelry. **Pauline Pelletier** (⊠ 38 rue du Petit-Champlain, Lower Town, ☎ 418/692–4871) specializes in porcelain, particularly her comical golden porcelain cats. **Pot-en-Ciel** (⊠ 27 rue du Petit-Champlain, Lower Town, ☎ 418/692–1743) carries an eclectic assortment of unique ceramics and tablewares.

Specialty Stores

Antiques

Québec City's antiques district is centered on rues St-Paul and St-Pierre, across from the Old Port. French-Canadian, Victorian, and art deco furniture along with clocks, silverware, and porcelain are some of the rare collectibles found here. Authentic Québec pine furniture, characterized by simple forms and lines, is rare and costly.

Engravings, maps, and prints of Québec and Canada, and white ironstone are the specialties at **Les Antiquités du Matelot** (⊠ 137 rue St-Paul, Lower Town, ☎ 418/694–9585). **Antiquités Marcel Bolduc** (⊠ 74 rue St-Paul, Lower Town, ☎ 418/694–9558) is the largest antiques store on rue St-Paul. Antique books, most of them in French, can be found at **Argus Livres Anciens** (⊠ 160 rue St-Paul, Lower Town, ☎ 418/694–2122). **Boutique Aux Mémoires Antiquités** (⊠ 105 rue St-Paul, Lower Town, ☎ 418/692–2180) has a good selection of Victorian and Edwardian pieces, plus silver, porcelain, curiosities, paintings, and bronzes. You're not likely to find any bargains here, but **Gérard Bourguet Antiquaire** (⊠ 97 rue St-Paul, Lower Town, ☎ 418/694–0896) has the best selection in Québec City of authentic 18th- and 19th-century Québec pine furniture. **L'Héritage Antiquité** (⊠ 110 rue St-Paul, Lower Town, ☎ 418/692–1681) is probably the best place in the neighborhood to find good Québecois furniture, clocks, oil lamps, porcelain, and ceramics.

Art

Aux Multiples Collections (⊠ 69 rue Ste-Anne, Upper Town, ☎ 418/692–1230) has Inuit art and antique wood collectibles. **Galerie Brousseau**

et Brousseau (⊠ 35 rue St-Louis, Upper Town, ☎ 418/694–1828) has fine Inuit art. In Lower Town, **Galerie Madeleine Lacerte** (⊠ 1 côte Dinan, Lower Town, ☎ 418/692–1566) sells contemporary art and sculpture. A source for less expensive artwork or work by promising young artists is **rue du Trésor,** where local artists display their sketches, paintings, and etchings. Good portraits of Québec City and the region are plentiful.

Books

English-language books are difficult to find in Québec City. **Librairie du Nouveau Monde** (⊠ 103 rue St-Pierre, Lower Town, ☎ 418/694– 9475) stocks titles in French and some in English. **Librairie Smith** (⊠ 2700 blvd. Laurier, Ste-Foy, ☎ 418/653–8683), in the Place Laurier mall, has both English and French books. In the Place de la Cité mall, **La Maison Anglaise** (⊠ 2600 blvd. Laurier, Ste-Foy, ☎ 418/654–9523) carries English-language titles only, specializing in fiction.

Clothing

Le Blanc Mouton (⊠ 51 Sous le Fort, Lower Town, ☎ 418/692–2880), in Quartier Petit-Champlain, specializes in unique creations for women by Québec designers, including accessories and handcrafted jewelry. **François Côté Collection** (⊠ 1200 Germain des Prés, Ste-Foy, ☎ 418/ 657–1760) is a chic boutique with fashions for men. **Louis Laflamme** (⊠ 1192 rue St-Jean, Upper Town, ☎ 418/692–3774) has a large selection of stylish men's clothes. **La Maison Darlington** (⊠ 7 rue de Buade, Upper Town, ☎ 418/692–2268) carries well-made woolens, dresses, and other items for men, women, and children by fine names in couture.

Crafts

Crafts by Québec artisans at **Regard d'Ici** (⊠ pl. Québec, 880 autoroute Dufferin-Montmorency, Upper Town, ☎ 418/522–0360) includes jewelry, clothing, leather goods, and decorative items. **Les Trois Colombes Inc.** (⊠ 46 rue St-Louis, Upper Town, ☎ 418/694–1114) sells handmade items, including clothing made from handwoven fabric, native and Inuit carvings, furs, and ceramics.

Food

Chocolate becomes a work of art at **Choco-Musée Érico** (⊠ 634 rue St-Jean, St. Jean Baptiste, ☎ 418/524–2122), where *chocolatier* Éric Normand crafts whatever you like out of chocolate within a few days.

Fur

The fur trade has been an important industry here for centuries. Québec City is a good place to purchase high-quality furs at fairly reasonable prices. The department store **J. B. Laliberté** (⊠ 595 rue St-Joseph Est, St. Roch, ☎ 418/525–4841) carries furs. Since 1894, one of the best furriers in town has been **Richard Robitaille Fourrures** (⊠ 329 rue St. Paul, Lower Town, ☎ 418/681–7297).

Gifts

Collection Lazuli (⊠ 774 rue St-Jean, St. Jean Baptiste, ☎ 418/525– 6528; ⊠ Pl. de la Cité, 2600 blvd. Laurier, Ste-Foy, ☎ 418/652–3732) offers a good choice of unusual art objects and jewelry from around the world.

Jewelry

Joaillier Louis Perrier (⊠ 48 rue du Petit-Champlain, Lower Town, ☎ 418/692–4633) has Québec-made gold and silver jewelry. Exclusive handmade jewelry can be found at **Zimmermann** (⊠ 46 côte de la Fabrique, Upper Town, ☎ 418/692–2672).

SIDE TRIPS FROM QUÉBEC CITY

Several easy excursions show you another side of the province and provide more insight into its past. The spectacular Montmorency Falls can be seen in a day trip. A drive around the Île d'Orléans, east of the city, is an easy way to experience rural Québec. The farms, markets, and churches here evoke the island's long history. The island can be toured in an energetic day, though rural inns make it tempting to extend a visit.

Côte de Beaupré and Montmorency Falls

As legend tells it, when explorer Jacques Cartier first caught sight of the north shore of the St. Lawrence River in 1535, he exclaimed, *"Quel beau pré!"* ("What a lovely meadow!"), because the area was the first inviting piece of land he had spotted since leaving France. Today this fertile meadow, first settled by French farmers, is known as Côte de Beaupré (Beaupré Coast), stretching 40 km (25 mi) east from Québec City to the famous pilgrimage site of Ste-Anne-de-Beaupré. Historic Route 360, or avenue Royal, winds its way from Beauport to St-Joachim, east of Ste-Anne-de-Beaupré. The impressive Montmorency Falls are midway between Québec City and Ste-Anne-de-Beaupré.

Montmorency Falls

51 *10 km (6 mi) east of Québec City.*

As it cascades over a cliff into the St. Lawrence River, the Montmorency River (named for Charles de Montmorency, who was a governor of New France) is one of the most beautiful sights in the province. The falls, at 274 ft, are 50% higher than Niagara Falls. A cable car runs to the top of the falls in **Parc de la Chute-Montmorency** (Montmorency Falls Park) from late April to early November. During very cold weather, the falls' heavy spray freezes and forms a giant loaf-shape ice cone known to Québecois as the Pain du Sucre (Sugarloaf); this phenomenon attracts sledders and sliders from Québec City. Ice climbers come to scale the falls; from late December through mid-March, a school trains novices to make the ascent. In the warmer months, you can visit an observation tower in the river's gorge that is continuously sprayed by a fine drizzle from water pounding onto the cliff rocks. The top of the falls can be observed from avenue Royale. In late July and early August, the skies above the falls light up with **Les Grands Feux Loto-Québec** (WEB www.lesgrandsfeux.com), an international competition with fireworks set to music.

The park is also historic. The British general Wolfe, on his way to conquer New France, set up camp here in 1759. In 1780, Sir Frederick Haldimand, then the governor of Canada, built a summer home—now a good restaurant called Manoir Montmorency—on top of the cliff. Prince Edward, Queen Victoria's father, rented this villa from 1791 to 1794. Unfortunately, the structure burned down several years ago; what stands is a re-creation. ✉ *2490 av. Royale, Beauport,* ☎ *418/663–3330,* WEB *www.chutemontmorency.qc.ca.* ✉ *Cable car $7.50 round-trip, car parking $7.50.* ☉ *Cable car Jan. 27–Apr. 13, weekends 9–4 (to Sugarloaf slide); Apr. 14–June 16 and Aug. 26–Oct. 20, daily 8:30–7; June 17–Aug. 25, daily 8:30 AM–9 PM; Dec. 26–Jan. 5, daily 9–4.*

OFF THE
BEAUTEN PATH **MUSÉE DE L'ABEILLE** – Things are buzzing at this economuseum devoted to bees and honey. A giant glassed-in hive with a tube leading outdoors allows you to get a close look at life inside a beehive. On the bee safari, guides take a hive apart, explaining how it works and how bees behave, before taking you indoors to taste honey wines. You can also taste

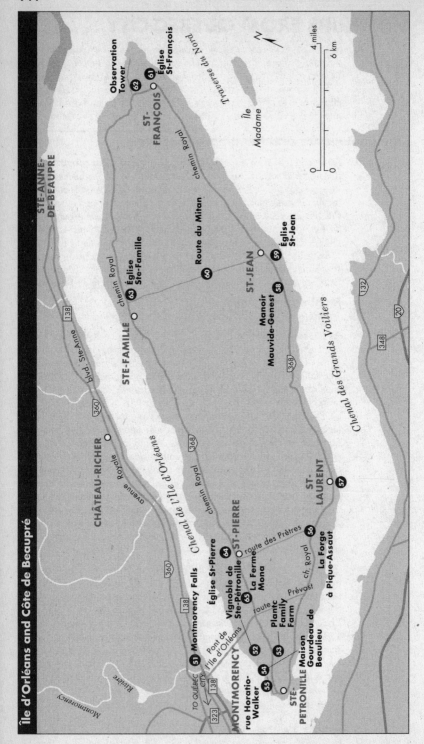

Île d'Orléans and Côte de Beaupré

STE-ANNE-DE-BEAUPRÉ

Observation Tower

Église St-François

ST-FRANÇOIS

Traverse du Nord

Île Madame

4 miles

6 km

N

138

blvd Ste-Anne

360

Église Ste-Famille

Route du Mitan

Église St-Jean

ST-JEAN

STE-FAMILLE

chemin Royal

chemin Royal

Manoir Mauvide-Genest

368

CHÂTEAU-RICHER

avenue Royale

Chenal de l'Île d'Orléans

chemin Royal

368

132

348

20

Chenal des Grands Voiliers

ST-LAURENT

Montmorency Falls

Église St-Pierre

ST-PIERRE

Vignoble de Ste-Pétronille

La Ferme Mona

route des Prêtres

138

360

138

Pont de l'Île d'Orléans

route Prévost

ch. Royal

La Forge à Pique-Assaut

Plante Family Farm

Maison Gourdeau de Beaulieu

MONTMORENCY

rue Horatio-Walker

STE-PÉTRONILLE

TO QUÉBEC CITY

323

Rivière Montmorency

51

42

61

63

60

59

58

57

56

64

65

52

53

54

55

honey made from different kinds of flowers, from clover to blueberry. ✉
8862 blvd. Ste-Anne, Château-Richer, ☎ *418/824–4411 or 877/
499–4411,* ⓦⒺⒷ *www.musee-abeille.qc.ca.* ✆ *Museum free, bee safari
$3.* ☉ *Bee safari June 24–Labor Day.*

Côte de Beaupré and Montmorency Falls A to Z

CAR TRAVEL

To reach Montmorency Falls, take Route 440 (Autoroute Dufferin–
Montmorency) east from Québec City approximately 9½ km (6 mi) to
the exit for Montmorency Falls.

TOURS

Autocar Dupont-Gray Line leads day excursions along the Côte de
Beaupré, with stops at Montmorency Falls and the Ste-Anne-de-Beaupré
basilica. The cost is about $37 plus taxes per person.
➤ FEES AND SCHEDULES: **Autocar Dupont-Gray Line** (☎ 418/649–
9226).

VISITOR INFORMATION

At the Beaupré Coast Interpretation Center, in a former convent, guides
in New France costumes explain displays on the history of the region.
Admission is $3. The Center is open from June 21 to Sept. 29, daily
10–5. During the rest of the year, the Center is open by reservation only.
Québec City Tourist Information has a bureau in Beauport, in Montmorency Falls Park. It's open June 3 to mid-October, daily 9–5.
➤ TOURIST INFORMATION: **Beaupré Coast Interpretation Center** (✉
7976 av. Royale, Château-Richer, ☎ 418/824–3677). **Québec City
Tourist Information** (✉ 4300 blvd. Ste-Anne/Rte. 138, ☎ no phone).

Île d'Orléans

The Algonquins called it Minigo, the "Bewitched Place," and over the
years the island's tranquil rural beauty has inspired poets and painters.
The Île d'Orléans is only 15 minutes from downtown Québec City, but
a visit here is one of the best ways to get a feel for traditional life in
rural Québec. Centuries-old homes and some of the oldest churches
in the region dot the road that rings the island. Île d'Orléans is at its
best in summer when the boughs of trees in lush orchards bend under
the weight of apples, plums, or pears, and the fields are bursting with
strawberries and raspberries. Roadside stands sell woven articles,
maple syrup, baked goods, jams, fruits, and vegetables. You can also
pick your own produce at about two dozen farms. The island, immortalized by one of its most famous residents, the late poet and songwriter Félix Leclerc, is still fertile ground for artists and artisans.

The island was discovered at about the same time as Québec City, in
1535. Explorer Jacques Cartier noticed an abundance of vines and called
it the Island of Bacchus, after the Greek god of wine. (Today, native
Québec vines are being crossbred with European varieties at Ste-
Pétronille's fledgling vineyard.) In 1536 Cartier renamed the island in
honor of the duke of Orléans, son of the French king François I. Its
fertile soil and abundant fishing made it so attractive to settlers that
its population once exceeded Québec City's.

Île d'Orléans, about 8 km (5 mi) wide and 34 km (21 mi) long, is composed of six small villages that have sought over the years to retain
their identities. The island's bridge to the mainland was built in 1935,
and in 1970 the island was declared a historic area to protect it from
urban development.

Ste-Pétronille

17 km (10½ mi) northeast of Québec City.

The lovely village of Ste-Pétronille, the first to be settled on Île d'Orléans, lies to the west of the bridge to the island. Founded in 1648, the community was chosen in 1759 by British general James Wolfe for his headquarters. With 40,000 soldiers and a hundred ships, the English bombarded French-occupied Québec City and Côte de Beaupré.

In the late 19th century, the English population of Québec developed Ste-Pétronille into a resort village. This area is considered to be the island's most beautiful, not only because of its spectacular views of Montmorency Falls and Québec City but also for the Regency-style English villas and exquisitely tended gardens.

🟝 At the **Vignoble de Ste-Pétronille,** hardy native Québec vines have been crossbred with three types of European grapes to produce a surprisingly good dry white wine as well as a red and a rosé. A guided tour of the vineyard includes a tasting. ⊠ *1A chemin du Bout de l'Ile,* ☎ *418/828–9554.* 🔲 *Guided tour $2.50.* ☉ *June–mid-Oct., daily 10–6; mid-Apr.–May and Nov.–Dec., weekends 11–5.*

🟝 At **Plante family farm** (⊠ 20 chemin du Bout de l'Île, ☎ 418/828–9603) you can stop to pick apples and strawberries (in season) or buy fresh fruits, vegetables, and apple cider.

🟝 The island's first home, the **Maison Gourdeau de Beaulieu** (⊠ 137 chemin du Bout de l'Ile) was built in 1648 for Jacques Gourdeau de Beaulieu, who was the first *seigneur* (a landholder who distributed lots to tenant farmers) of Ste-Pétronille. Remodeled over the years, this white house with blue shutters now incorporates both French and Québecois styles. Its thick walls and dormer windows are characteristic of Breton architecture, but its sloping bell-shape roof, designed to protect buildings from large amounts of snow, is typically Québecois. The house is not open to the public.

🟝 The tiny street called **rue Horatio-Walker,** off chemin Royal, was named after the early-19th-century painter known for his landscapes of the island. Walker lived on this street from 1904 until his death in 1938. At 11 and 13 rue Horatio-Walker are his home and workshop, but they are not open to the public.

DINING AND LODGING

$$ ✕🏨 **La Goéliche.** This English-style country manor, rebuilt in 1996–97 following a fire, stands steps away from the St. Lawrence River. Antiques decorate the cozy, elegant rooms, all with river views. Sinks are in the rooms instead of the baths to maximize space. Classic French cuisine includes calf sweetbreads with honey and lime sauce, garnished with hazelnuts, and quail baked in a creamy pear and celery sauce. The romantic dining room overlooks the river; an enclosed terrace is open year-round. The apartments have cable TV. ⊠ *22 chemin du Quai,* ☎ *418/828–2248 or 888/511–2248,* 𝖥𝖠𝖷 *418/828–2745,* 𝖶𝖤𝖡 *www.goeliche.ca. 14 rooms, 2 apartments. Restaurant, fans, minibars (some), pool, Internet, meeting rooms, free parking; no air-conditioning. AE, DC, MC, V.*

SHOPPING

Chocolaterie de l'Ile d'Orléans (⊠ 150 chemin du Bout de l'Ile, ☎ 418/828–2252) combines Belgian chocolate with local ingredients to create handmade treats. Some choices are chocolates filled with maple butter or the *framboisette* made from raspberries. In summer try the homemade ice creams and sherbets.

St-Laurent de l'Ile d'Orléans

9 km (5½ mi) northeast of Ste-Pétronille.

Founded in 1679, St-Laurent is one of the island's maritime villages. Until as late as 1935, residents here used boats as their main means of transportation. **La Forge à Pique-Assaut** (⊠ 2200 chemin Royal, ☎ 418/828–9300) belongs to the talented and well-known local artisan Guy Bel, who has done ironwork restoration for Québec City. He was born in Lyon, France, and studied there at the École des Beaux Arts. From June to mid-October, daily 9–5, you can watch him work; his stylish candlesticks, chandeliers, fireplace tools, and other ironwork are for sale. Call ahead for reservations in winter.

The **Parc Maritime de St-Laurent,** at a former boatyard, is where craftspeople specializing in boatbuilding practiced their trade. Now you can picnic here and visit the Chalouperie Godbout (Godbout Longboat), which houses a complete collection of tools used during the golden era of boatbuilding. ⊠ *120 chemin de la Chalouperie,* ☎ *418/828–9672.* ⊠ *$3.* ☉ *June 24–Labor Day, daily 10–5; Sept.–early Oct., weekends 10–4 or by reservation; mid-May–mid-June by reservation.*

The tall, inspiring **Église St-Laurent,** which stands next to the village marina on chemin Royal, was built in 1860 on the site of an 18th-century church that had to be torn down. One of the church's procession chapels is a miniature stone replica of the original. ⊠ *1532 chemin Royal,* ☎ *418/828–2551.* ⊠ *Free, guided tour of religious art $1.* ☉ *Summer, daily 9–5.*

DINING AND LODGING

$$ ✕ **Moulin de St-Laurent.** This is an early 18th-century stone mill where you can dine in the herb-and-flower garden out back. Scrumptious snacks, such as quiches, bagels, and salads, are available at the café-terrace. Evening dishes include local game such as *aiguillettes de pintade au cassis et rhubarbe,* thin strips of guinea hen with cassis and rhubarb. ⊠ *754 chemin Royal,* ☎ *418/829–3888 or 888/629–3888. AE, DC, MC, V. Closed mid-Oct.–mid-Apr.*

$$ ✕ **Le Canard Huppé.** As the inn's name suggests, its contemporary
★ cuisine usually includes at least one dish with duck, such as Barbarie Duck with clover honey, fresh thyme, and wood garlic. Chef Maïka Courval also showcases dishes made with ingredients from local producers—for example, a salad of smoked eel and sturgeon or quail raised on Ile d'Orléans stuffed with mushrooms from the island and madeira. Upstairs, each of the inn's rooms has unusual antiques and original paintings by Québec City–area artists. Deluxe rooms are in a separate building and have fireplaces, whirlpool tubs, and a river view. ⊠ *2198 chemin Royal,* ☎ *418/828–2292 or 800/838–2292,* FAX *418/828–0966,* WEB *www.canard-huppe.com. 15 rooms, 1 suite. Restaurant, cable TV in some rooms, meeting room; no air-conditioning in some rooms, no room phones. AE, DC, MC, V. CP.*

St-Jean

12 km (7 mi) northeast of St-Laurent.

The southernmost point of the island, St-Jean is a village whose inhabitants were once river pilots and navigators. Most of its small, homogeneous row homes were built between 1840 and 1860. Being at sea most of the time, the sailors didn't need large homes and plots of land, as did the farmers.

St-Jean's beautiful Normandy-style manor, **Manoir Mauvide-Genest,** was built in 1734 for Jean Mauvide (surgeon to Louis XV) and his wife, Marie-Anne Genest. Most notable about this house, which still has its original thick walls, ceiling beams, and fireplaces, is the degree to which it has held up over the years. In 2002 the house reopened to the public as an interpretation center of New France's seigneurial regime, with 18th-century furniture, a multimedia presentation, and tours with guides dressed in 18th-century costumes. ⊠ *1451 chemin Royal,* ☎ *418/829–2630.* ☞ *$5.* ⊙ *May–Nov., daily 10–4:30.*

59 At the eastern end of the village is **Église St-Jean,** a massive granite structure with large red doors and a towering steeple built in 1749. The church resembles a ship; it's big and round and appears to be sitting right on the river. Paintings of the patron saints of seamen line the interior walls. The church's cemetery is also intriguing, especially if you can read French. Back in the 18th century, piloting the St. Lawrence was a dangerous profession; the cemetery tombstones recall the tragedies of lives lost in these harsh waters. ⊠ *2001 chemin Royal,* ☎ *418/828–2551.* ☞ *Free.* ⊙ *Summer, daily 10–5.*

60 Outside St-Jean, chemin Royal crosses **route du Mitan,** the most beautiful on the island. In old French, *mitan* means "halfway." This road, dividing the island in half, has views of acres of tended farmland, apple orchards, and maple groves. If you need to end your circuit of the island here, take route du Mitan, which brings you to Ste-Famille; head west on chemin Royal to return to the bridge to the mainland.

St-François
12 km (7 mi) northeast of St-Jean.

Sprawling open fields separate 17th-century farmhouses in St-François, the island's least-toured and most rustic village. This community at the eastern tip of the island was originally settled mainly by farmers. St-François is also the perfect place to visit one of the island's *cabanes à sucre* (maple-sugaring shacks), found along chemin Royal. Stop at a hut for a tasting tour; sap is gathered from the maple groves and boiled until it turns to syrup. When it's poured on ice, it tastes like a delicious toffee. The maple syrup season is from late March through April.

61 **Église St-François** (⊠ 341 chemin Royal, ☎ 419/828–2551), built in 1734, is one of eight provincial churches dating from the French regime. At the time the English seized Québec City in 1759, General James Wolfe knew St-François to be a strategic point along the St. Lawrence. Consequently, he stationed British troops here and used the church as a military hospital. In 1988 a car crash set the church on fire and most of the interior treasures were lost. A separate children's cemetery stands as a silent witness to the difficult life of early residents. The church is open 10–5 in summer.

62 A picnic area with a wood **observation tower** is perfectly situated for viewing the majestic St. Lawrence. In spring and fall, wild Canada geese can be seen here. The area is about 2 km (1 mi) north on chemin Royal from St-François Church.

Ste-Famille
14 km (9 mi) west of St-François.

The village of Ste-Famille, founded in 1661, has exquisite scenery, including abundant apple orchards and strawberry fields with views of Côte de Beaupré and Mont Ste-Anne in the distance. But it also has plenty of historic charm, claiming the area's highest concentration of stone houses dating from the French regime.

63 The impressive **Église Ste-Famille,** constructed in 1749, is the only church in Québec province to have three bell towers at the front. Its ceiling was redone in the mid-19th century with elaborate designs in wood and gold. The church also holds a famous painting, *L'Enfant Jésus Voyant la Croix (Baby Jesus Looking at the Cross),* done in 1670 by Frère Luc (Father Luc), who was sent from France to decorate churches in the area. ⊠ *3915 chemin Royal,* ☎ *418/828–2656.* ⊠ *Free.* ☉ *Summer, daily 11–5.*

St-Pierre

14 km (9 mi) southwest of St-Famille.

St-Pierre, established in 1679, is set on a plateau that has the island's most fertile land. The town has long been the center of traditional farming industries. The best products grown here are potatoes, asparagus, and corn. In 2002 the Espace Félix Leclerc—an exhibit by day and a *boîte à chansons* (combination of a coffee house and bar with live performances) by night—was opened to honor the former singer and songwriter who made St-Pierre his home. If you continue west on chemin Royal, just up ahead is the bridge back to the mainland and Route 440.

(64) Église St-Pierre, the oldest on the island, dates from 1717. It's no longer open for worship, but it was restored during the 1960s and is open to visitors. Many original components are still intact, such as benches with compartments below where hot bricks and stones were placed to keep people warm in winter. Félix Leclerc (1914–88), the first Québecois singer to make his mark in Europe, is buried in the cemetery nearby. ⊠ *1249 chemin Royal,* ☎ *418/828–9824.* ⊠ *Free.* ☉ *July daily 9–6, May–June and August–October daily 10–5.*

(65) La Ferme Monna has won international awards for its crème de cassis de l'Île d'Orléans, a liqueur made from black currants. The farm offers free samples of the strong, sweet cassis or one of its black-currant wines; the tour explains how they are made. In summer there is a terrace overlooking the river where you can sample foods made with cassis. ⊠ *723 chemin Royal,* ☎ *418/828–1057.* ⊠ *Free; guided tours $4.* ☉ *Mid-June–Sept., daily 10–6; Mar. and Oct.–Dec., weekends 10–5.*

Île d'Orléans A to Z

CAR TRAVEL

From Québec City, take Route 440 (Autoroute Dufferin–Montmorency) northeast. After a drive of about 10 km (6 mi) take the Pont de l'Île d'Orléans (a bridge) to the island. The main road, chemin Royal (Route 368), extends 67 km (42 mi) through the island's six villages, turning into chemin du Bout de l'Île in Ste-Pétronille.

Parking can sometimes be a problem, but you can leave your car in the church parking lot and explore each village on foot.

EMERGENCIES

Centre Médical Prévost is the principal medical clinic on the island.
➤ HOSPITAL: **Centre Médical Prévost** (⊠ 1015 Rte. Prévost, St-Pierre, ☎ 418/828–2213).

LODGING

Reservations are necessary at the island's 40 B&Bs, which cost about $55–$125 per night for a double-occupancy room. The Chamber of Commerce has a referral service for B&Bs.
➤ RESERVATION REFERRAL SERVICE: **Chamber of Commerce** (☎ 418/828–9411).

TOURS

The island's Chamber of Commerce rents a cassette tape or compact disc for $10 a day with an interesting 108-minute tour of the island by car; it's available at the tourist kiosk.

Québec City tour companies, including Autocar Dupont-Gray Line, run bus tours of the western tip of the island, combined with sightseeing along the Côte de Beaupré.

➤ FEES AND SCHEDULES: **Autocar Dupont-Gray Line** (☎ 418/649–9226).

VISITOR INFORMATION

Any of the offices of the Québec City Region Tourism and Convention Bureau can provide information on tours and accommodations on the island. The island's Chamber of Commerce operates a tourist-information kiosk at the west corner of côte du Pont and chemin Royal in St-Pierre. Look for the question mark.

➤ TOURIST INFORMATION: **Chamber of Commerce** (✉ 490 côte du Pont, ☎ 418/828–9411, 866/941–9411, WEB www.iledorleans.com).

QUÉBEC CITY A TO Z

To research prices, get advice from other travelers, and book travel arrangements, visit www.fodors.com.

AIR TRAVEL TO AND FROM QUÉBEC CITY

Continental flies directly to Québec City from Newark. American Eagle has flights daily from Boston. Air Canada and its subsidiary, Jazz, fly to Québec City with stops in Montréal, Toronto, or Ottawa.

AIRPORTS AND TRANSFERS

Jean Lesage International Airport is about 19 km (12 mi) from downtown.

➤ AIRPORT INFORMATION: **Jean Lesage International Airport** (✉ 500 rue Principale, Ste-Foy, ☎ 418/640–2600, WEB www.aeroportdequebec.com).

AIRPORT TRANSFERS

The ride from the airport into town should be no longer than 30 minutes. If you're driving from the airport, take Route 540 (Autoroute Duplessis) to Route 175 (blvd. Laurier), which becomes Grande Allée and leads right to Vieux-Québec. The ride is about 30 minutes and may be only slightly longer (45 minutes or so) during rush hours (7:30–8:30 AM into town and 4–5:30 PM leaving town).

Private limo service is expensive, starting at $55 for the ride from the airport into Québec City. Try Groupe Limousine A-1. Taxis are available immediately outside the airport exit near the baggage-claim area. A ride into the city costs about $24.50. Two local taxi firms are Taxi Québec and Taxi Coop de Québec, the largest company in the city.

➤ TAXIS AND SHUTTLES: **Groupe Limousine A-1** (✉ 361 rue des Commissaires Est, St. Roch, ☎ 418/523–5059). **Taxi Coop de Québec** (✉ 496 2ᵉ av., Limoilou, ☎ 418/525–5191). **Taxi Québec** (✉ 975 8ᵉ av., Limoilou, ☎ 418/522–2001).

BOAT AND FERRY TRAVEL

The Québec–Lévis ferry crosses the St. Lawrence River to the town of Lévis. Although the crossing takes 15 minutes, waiting time can increase that to an hour. The cost is $2 in winter and $2.50 in summer. The first ferry from Québec City leaves daily at 6:30 AM from the pier at rue Dalhousie, across from Place Royale. Crossings run every half hour from 7:30 AM until 6:30 PM, then hourly until 2:20 AM. From April through November, the ferry adds extra service every 10 to 20 minutes during rush hours (7–10 AM and 3–6:45 PM). Schedules can change. Check the Web site.

➤ BOAT AND FERRY INFORMATION: **Québec–Lévis ferry** (☎ 418/644–3704, WEB www.traversiers.gouv.qc.ca).

BUS TRAVEL TO AND FROM QUÉBEC CITY

Orléans Express Inc. provides service between Montréal and Québec City daily.

Buses from Montréal to Québec City depart daily on the hour from 6 AM–8 PM, with additional nightly trips at 9:30, 10:30, and midnight. Buses from Québec City to Montréal depart daily on the hour from 7 AM–8 PM, and also at 9:30 and 11 PM nightly; Wednesday through Sunday, you have the option of a midnight bus to Montréal. At this writing, the three-hour one-way ticket is $42.56, and a round-trip ticket is $63.26 as long as you return within 10 days and do not travel on Friday or certain days during holiday periods. Otherwise, the price is double the one-way fare. Tickets can be purchased only at terminals.
➤ TERMINALS: **Québec City Terminal** (✉ 3020 rue Abraham Martin, Lower Town, ☎ 418/525–3000). **Ste-Foy Terminal** (✉ 3001 chemin Quatre Bourgeois, Ste-Foy, ☎ 418/650–0087). **Terminus Voyageur** (✉ 505 blvd. de Maisonneuve Est, Downtown Montréal, ☎ 514/842–2281).

BUS TRAVEL WITHIN QUÉBEC CITY

The city's transit system, the Réseau de Transport de la Capitale, runs buses approximately every 10 minutes to an hour, stopping at major points around town.

The cost is $2.25; you need exact change. For a discount on your fare, buy bus tickets at a major convenience store for $1.80 ($5.10 for a day pass). Terminals are in Lower Town at Place Jacques-Cartier and outside St-Jean Gate at Place d'Youville in Upper Town. Timetables are available at some visitor information offices and at Place Jacques Cartier.
➤ BUS INFORMATION: **Réseau de Transport de la Capitale** (☎ 418/627–2511).

BUSINESS HOURS

In winter, many attractions and shops change their hours, so it's a good idea to call ahead. Most banks are open Monday through Wednesday 10–3 and close later on Thursday and Friday. Museum hours are typically 10–5, with longer evening hours in summer. Most are closed on Monday.

CAR RENTAL

➤ MAJOR AGENCIES: **Hertz Canada** (✉ Jean Lesage International Airport, ☎ 418/871–1571; ✉ 44 Côte du Palais, Upper Town, ☎ 418/694–1224, 800/263–0600 in English, 800/263–0678 in French). **National** (✉ Jean Lesage International Airport, ☎ 418/871–1224; ✉ 295 rue St-Paul, Lower Town, ☎ 418/694–1727). **Via Route** (✉ 2605 blvd. Wilfrid-Hamel, Duberger, ☎ 418/682–2660).

CAR TRAVEL

Montréal and Québec City are linked by Autoroute 20 on the south shore of the St. Lawrence River and by Autoroute 40 on the north shore. On both highways, the ride between the two cities is about 240 km (149 mi) and takes about three hours. U.S. I–87 in New York, U.S. I–89 in Vermont, and U.S. I–91 in New Hampshire connect with Autoroute 20. Highway 401 from Toronto links up with Autoroute 20.

Driving northeast from Montréal on Autoroute 20, follow signs for Pont Pierre-Laporte (Pierre Laporte Bridge) as you approach Québec City. After you've crossed the bridge, turn right onto boulevard Laurier (Route 175), which becomes the Grande Allée leading into Québec City.

A car is necessary only if you plan to visit outlying areas. Automated seasonal information about roads is available November through April by calling ☎ 418/684–2363.

PARKING

The narrow streets of the old city leave few two-hour metered parking spaces available. However, several parking garages at central locations charge about $12 a day on weekdays or $6 for 12 hours on weekends. Main garages are at City Hall, Place d'Youville, Edifice Marie-Guyart, Place Québec, Château Frontenac, rue St-Paul, and the Old Port.

EMERGENCIES

Centre Hospitalier Universitaire de Québec is the city's largest institution and incorporates the teaching hospitals the Pavillon CHUL in Ste-Foy and the Pavillon Hôtel-Dieu, the main hospital in Vieux-Québec.

If you don't have an emergency but require medical assistance, you can avoid long hospital waits at the Clinique Médecine de Famille. The walk-in clinic is open weekdays 8 AM–9 PM and weekends 9 AM–1 PM.

Clinique Dentaire Darveau, De Blois, and Tardif is open for dental services Monday and Tuesday 8–8, Wednesday 8–5, Thursday 8–6, and Friday 8–4. Summer hours are Monday to Thursday 8–5 and Friday 8–4. Call for an appointment. Pharmacie Brunet, north of Québec City in the Charlesbourg district, is open 8 AM–midnight.

➤ DOCTORS AND DENTISTS: **Clinique Dentaire Darveau, De Blois, and Tardif** (✉ 1175 rue Lavigerie, Edifice Iberville 2, Room 100, Ste-Foy, ☎ 418/653–5412). **Clinique Médecine de Famille** (✉ 1000 chemin Ste-Foy, Suite 116, St. Sacrement, ☎ 418/688–1385).

➤ EMERGENCY SERVICES: **Distress Center** (☎ 418/686–2433). **Fire, police** (☎ 911 or 418/691–7722). **Poison Center** (☎ 418/656–8090). **Provincial police** (☎ 418/310–4141).

➤ HOSPITALS: **Centre Hospitalier Universitaire de Québec, Pavillon CHUL** (✉ 2705 blvd. Laurier, Ste-Foy, ☎ 418/656–4141, 418/654–2114 emergencies). **Centre Hospitalier Universitaire de Québec, Pavillon Hôtel-Dieu** (✉ 11 côte du Palais, Upper Town, ☎ 418/691–5151, 418/691–5042 emergencies).

➤ LATE-NIGHT PHARMACY: **Pharmacie Brunet** (✉ Les Galeries Charlesbourg, 4250 1ʳᵉ av., Charlesbourg, ☎ 418/623–1571).

ENGLISH-LANGUAGE MEDIA
BOOKS

➤ BOOKSTORES: **La Maison Anglaise** (✉ pl. de la Cité, 2600 blvd. Laurier, Ste-Foy, ☎ 418/654–9523).

LODGING
B&BS

Québec City has many accommodations in hostels and B&Bs, which increasingly are known as Couette & Cafés. To guarantee a room during the peak season, reserve in advance. Québec City Tourist Information has B&B listings.

➤ RESERVATION SERVICE: **Québec City Tourist Information** (✉ 835 av. Wilfrid-Laurier, G1R 2L3, ☎ 418/649–2608).

MONEY MATTERS

ATMs, or *guichets automatiques,* are widely available throughout Québec City and technical difficulties or running out of cash are rare. ATMs accept many types of bank cards and are generally linked to international banking networks such as Cirrus.

BANKS

From May through September, Caisse Populaire Desjardins de Québec is open weekends 9–6, in addition to weekday hours.
➤ CONTACT: **Caisse Populaire Desjardins de Québec** (✉ 19 rue des Jardins, Upper Town, ☎ 418/522–6806).

CURRENCY EXCHANGE

Echange de Devises Montréal is open September to mid-June, daily 9–5, and mid-June to early September, daily 8:30–7:30.
➤ EXCHANGE SERVICE: **Echange de Devises Montréal** (✉ 12 rue Ste-Anne, Upper Town, ☎ 418/694–1014).

TAXIS AND LIMOUSINES

Taxis are stationed in front of major hotels and the Hôtel de Ville (City Hall), along rue des Jardins, and at Place d'Youville outside St-Jean Gate. Passengers are charged an initial $2.50, plus $1.20 for each kilometer (½ mi). For radio-dispatched cars, try Taxi Coop de Québec or Taxi Québec.

Limousines are another option. Groupe Limousine A-1 has 24-hour service.
➤ TAXI AND LIMOUSINE COMPANIES: **Groupe Limousine A-1** (✉ 361 rue des Commissaires Est, St. Roch, ☎ 418/523–5059). **Taxi Coop de Québec** (☎ 418/525–5191). **Taxi Québec** (☎ 418/522–2001).

TOURS

Tours can include Montmorency Falls, whale-watching, and Ste-Anne-de-Beaupré in addition to sights in Québec City; combination city and harbor-cruise tours are also available. Québec City tours operate year-round; excursions to outlying areas may operate only in summer.

BOAT TOURS

Croisières AML Inc. runs day and evening cruises on the St. Lawrence River aboard the MV *Louis-Jolliet*. The 1½- to 3-hour cruises run from May through mid-October and start at $24 plus tax.
➤ FEES AND SCHEDULES: **Croisières AML Inc.** (✉ Pier Chouinard, 10 rue Dalhousie, beside the Québec–Lévis ferry terminal, Lower Town, ☎ 418/692–1159).

BUS TOURS

Tickets for Autocar Dupont–Gray Line bus tours can be purchased at most major hotels. Tours depart across the square from the Château Laurier Hotel (✉ 1230 pl. Georges V). The company also offers guided tours in a minibus or trolley. Tours run year-round and cost $25–$85. Call for a reservation and the company will pick you up at your hotel.
➤ FEES AND SCHEDULES: **Autocar Dupont–Gray Line** (☎ 418/649–9226 or 888/558–7668).

WALKING TOURS

Adlard Tours leads walking tours of the old city through the narrow streets that buses cannot enter. The $14 cost includes a refreshment break; unilingual tours are available in many languages. Tours leave from 12 rue Ste-Anne. Ghost Tours of Québec give ghoulish 90-minute evening tours of Québec City murders, executions, and ghost-sightings. Costumed actors lead the $15 tours, in English or French, from May through October.
➤ FEES AND SCHEDULES: **Adlard Tours** (✉ 13 rue Ste-Famille, Upper Town, ☎ 418/692–2358). **Ghost Tours of Québec** (✉ 41½ rue d'Auteuil, Upper Town, ☎ 418/692–9770).

TRAIN TRAVEL

VIA Rail, Canada's passenger rail service, runs daily trains from Montréal to Québec City. The train arrives at the 19th-century Gare du Palais, in the heart of the old city.

Trains from Montréal to Québec City and from Québec City to Montréal run four times daily on weekdays, three times daily on weekends. The trip takes less than three hours, with a stop in Ste-Foy. Tickets can be purchased in advance at any VIA Rail office, travel agent, at the station before departure, or online at www.viarail.ca. The basic one-way fare, including taxes, is $63.26.

First-class service costs $119.63 each way and includes early boarding, seat selection, and a three-course meal with wine. One of the best deals, subject to availability, is the round-trip ticket bought 10 days in advance for $82.82.

➤ TRAIN INFORMATION: **Gare du Palais** (✉ 450 rue de la Gare du Palais, Lower Town, ☎ no phone). **VIA Rail** (☎ 418/692–3940, 800/561–3949 from U.S., 800/361–5390 within Canada).

TRANSPORTATION AROUND QUÉBEC CITY

Walking is the best way to explore the city. Vieux-Québec measures 11 square km (about 4 square mi), and most historic sites, hotels, and restaurants are within the walls or a short distance outside. City maps are available at visitor information offices.

La Belle Epoque, Balades en Calèche et Diligence, and Les Calèches du Vieux-Québec are three calèche companies. You can hire a calèche at Place d'Armes near the Chateau Frontenac, at the St. Louis gate, or on rue d'Auteuil between the St-Louis and Kent gates. If you call ahead, some companies can also pick you up at your hotel. Some drivers talk about Québec's history and others don't; if you want a storyteller, ask for one in advance. The cost is about $60 including all taxes for a 45-minute tour of Vieux-Québec.

➤ FEES AND SCHEDULES: **Balades en Calèche et Diligence** (☎ 418/624–3062). **La Belle Epoque** (☎ 418/687–6653). **Les Calèches du Vieux-Québec** (☎ 418/683–9222).

TRAVEL AGENCIES

➤ LOCAL AGENTS: **American Express** (✉ pl. Laurier, 2700 blvd. Laurier, Ste-Foy, ☎ 418/658–8820). **Voyages Claire Champoux** (✉ 1050 blvd. René-Lévesque, Suite 411, Montcalm, ☎ 418/522–5234).

VISITOR INFORMATION

The Québec City Region Tourism and Convention Bureau has two visitor information centers that are open year-round and a mobile information service that operates between mid-June and September 7 (look for the mopeds with a big question mark). The Québec City information center is open June 24 to early September, daily 8:30–7:30; early September to mid-October, daily 8:30–6:30; and mid-October through June 23, Monday through Thursday and Saturday 9–5, Friday 9–6, and Sunday 10–4. The Ste-Foy information center is open the same hours; look for big question marks as signage. The Québec government tourism department, Tourisme Québec, has a center that is open daily 9–6 from September 3 to March 31 and 8:30–7:30 April 1 to September 2.

➤ TOURIST INFORMATION: **Québec City Tourist Information** (✉ 835 av. Laurier, Montcalm G1R 2L3, ☎ 418/649–2608, WEB www.quebecregion.com). **Ste-Foy** (✉ 3300 av. des Hôtels, Ste-Foy G1W 5A8, ☎ 418/651–2891). **Québec Government Tourism Department** (✉ 12 rue Ste-Anne, Place d'Armes, Upper Town, ☎ 877/266–5687, WEB www.bonjour-quebec.com).

4 PROVINCE OF QUÉBEC

THE LAURENTIANS, THE EASTERN TOWNSHIPS, CHARLEVOIX, THE GASPÉ PENINSULA

Québec has a distinct personality forged by its French heritage and culture. The land, too, is memorable: within its boundaries lie thousands of lakes and rivers—the highways for explorers, fur traders, and pioneers. The Laurentians with their ski resorts and the forested coastline of the Gulf of St. Lawrence are the playground of La Belle Province. Echoes of the past remain in the charming rural communities of the Eastern Townships and Charlevoix, and the rugged beauty and isolation of Gaspé are unsurpassed in the province.

A MONG THE PROVINCES OF CANADA, Québec is set apart by its strong French heritage, a matter not only of language but of customs, religion, and political structure. Québec covers a vast area—almost one-sixth of Canada's total—although the upper three-quarters is only sparsely inhabited. Outside Montréal and Québec City, serenity and natural beauty abound in the province's innumerable lakes, streams, and rivers; in its farmlands and villages; in its great mountains and deep forests; and in its rugged coastline along the Gulf of St. Lawrence. Though the winters are long, activities from skiing to snowmobiling lure residents and visitors outdoors.

Updated by
Carolyn
Jackson

The first European to arrive in Québec was French explorer Jacques Cartier in 1534; another Frenchman, Samuel de Champlain, arrived in 1603 to build French settlements in the region; and Jesuit missionaries followed. In 1663 Louis XIV of France proclaimed Canada a crown colony—New France, and the land was allotted to French aristocrats and administrators in large grants called *seigneuries*.

Tenants, known as *habitants*, settled on the farms belonging to those who received the grants, the *seigneurs*. The Roman Catholic Church took on an importance that went beyond religion. Priests and nuns acted as doctors, educators, and arbiters among the habitants, and as liaisons between French-speaking fur traders and English-speaking merchants. An important church priority in Québec, one emphasized after the British conquest of 1759, was *survivance*—the survival of the French people and their culture.

Québec's threats to secede from the Canadian union are part of a long-standing tradition of independence. Although the British won control of Canada in the French and Indian War in 1763, Parliament passed the Québec Act in 1774. The act ensured the continuation of French civil law in Québec and left provincial authority in the hands of the Roman Catholic Church. In general the law preserved the traditional French-Canadian way of life. Tensions between French- and English-speaking Canada continued throughout the 20th century, however, and in 1974 the province proclaimed French its sole official language, much the same way the provinces of Manitoba and Alberta had taken steps earlier in the century to make English their sole official language. Québec is part of the Canadian union and a signatory to its original constitution, but it hasn't accepted the changes made in that document during the 1980s. Two attempts to get Québec to sign the revised constitution in the 1990s failed.

The ability to speak French can make a visit to the province more pleasant—many locals, at least in rural areas, don't speak English. If you don't speak French, arm yourself with a phrase book or at least a knowledge of some basic phrases. It's also worth your while to sample the regional Québecois cuisine, for this is a province where food is taken seriously.

Pleasures and Pastimes

Dining

In the countryside, a number of inns, including some in the Eastern Townships, provide food that can compete with any served in the cities for freshness and creativity. Whether you choose a mixed-game pie such as *cipaille* or a sweet–salty dish like ham with maple syrup, you won't soon forget your meals here. Cooking in the province tends to be hearty: cassoulet, *tourtières* (meat pies), onion soup, and apple pie head up menus. Maple syrup, much of it produced locally, is a mainstay of Québecois dishes. Cloves, nutmeg, cinnamon, and pepper—spices used by the first settlers—haven't gone out of style. When you're in Québec, do as the locals do and order the table d'hôte, a several-course package deal that is often less expensive than ordering a comparable amount of food à la carte and may give you a chance to sample some special dishes.

The Eastern Townships are one of Québec's foremost regions for fine cuisine, and chefs at the finer Laurentian inns have attracted an international following. Early reservations are essential. Monday or Tuesday is not too soon to book weekend tables at the best provincial restaurants.

More-casual fare such as a croissant and an espresso, or *poutine,* a heaped plate of *frites* (french fries) smothered with gravy and melted cheese curds, are available from sidewalk cafés and fast-food emporiums.

CATEGORY	COST*
$$$$	over $32
$$$	$22–$32
$$	$13–$21
$	under $13

per person, in Canadian dollars, for a main course at dinner

Lodging
Accommodations in the province range from resort hotels in the Laurentians and elegant Relais & Châteaux properties in the Eastern Townships to simple motels and *auberges* (inns) in the heart of the Gaspé. Year-round or in high season (winter in the Laurentians and other ski areas, summer elsewhere), many inns operate on the Modified American Plan (MAP) and include two meals, usually breakfast and dinner, in the cost of a night's stay. Be sure to ask what's included, and expect prices to be lower off-season. In addition, some inns require a minimum two-night stay; always ask.

CATEGORY	COST*
$$$$	over $200
$$$	$150–$200
$$	$100–$150
$	under $100

All prices are for a standard double room at high season—excluding optional service charge, 7% GST, and 7.5% provincial tax—in Canadian dollars.

Outdoor Activities and Sports
FISHING
More than 60 outfitters (some of whom are also innkeepers) work in the northern Laurentians area, where provincial parks and game sanctuaries abound. Pike, walleye, and lake and speckled trout are plentiful just a three-hour drive north of Montréal. Open year-round in most cases, lodging facilities range from luxurious, first-class resorts to log cabins. As well as supplying trained guides, all provide services and equipment to allow both neophytes and experts the best possible fishing in addition to boating, swimming, river rafting, windsurfing, ice fishing, cross-country skiing, or hiking.

RAFTING
The Rivière Rouge in the Laurentians rates among the best rivers for rafting in North America. Just an hour's drive north of Montréal, the Rouge cuts across the rugged Laurentians through canyons and alongside beaches. April through October you can experience what traversing the region must have meant in the days of the voyageurs, though today's trip is much safer and more comfortable.

James
Bay

Lac
Albanel

Kesagami
Lake

Harricana R.

Lac
Mistassini

(109)

Matagami

(113)

Lac
Albanel

QUÉBEC

(167)

Lake
Abitibi

La Sarre

(109)

Parent
Lake

Mistassini

(111)
Amos

Réservoir
de Gouin

Saint-
Félicien

Lac
St-Jean

(101)

Noranda

(117)

(113)

Chambord

(169)

Malartic
Val-d'Or

Louvicourt

New Liskeard

Parc Provincial
de la Vérendrye

(155)

Réserve
des Lau

(101)

La Tuque

Lac
Kipawa

Manouane

(11)

(117)

Parc Provincial
du Mont-
Tremblant

Parc Nat.
de Mauricie

Québec

(17)
Mattawa

Ottawa R.

Mont-Laurier

St-Zénon

Trois-
Rivières

Algonquin
Prov. Park

Pembroke

(117)

(105)

(309)

St-Jovite

St-Donat

(40) (132) (20)

Victorio

(11)

(60)

(60) (62)

(17)

Parc Nat.
de Gatineau

Ste-Agathe-
des-Monts

Sorel

Richmond

Hawkesbury

(158)

Laval

(112)

Hull

(17)

Dorion

(10)

Sherbrooke

(29)

Ottawa

Montréal

ONTARIO

(28)

(62)

(41)

(31)

Rideau

Cornwall

CANADA

(15) (133)

(55)

Coe

(7)

U.S.

(91)

Lake
Simcoe

(401)

Massena

VERMONT

(7)

Ogdensburg

St. Regis R.

Lake Champlain

(93)

(401)

Lake Ontario

NEW YORK

(87)

NEW
HAMPSH

Niagara
Falls

Rochester

Hudson R.

(91)

Buffalo

(90)

(90)

(90)

Genesee R.

(15)

(81)

MASSACHUSETTS

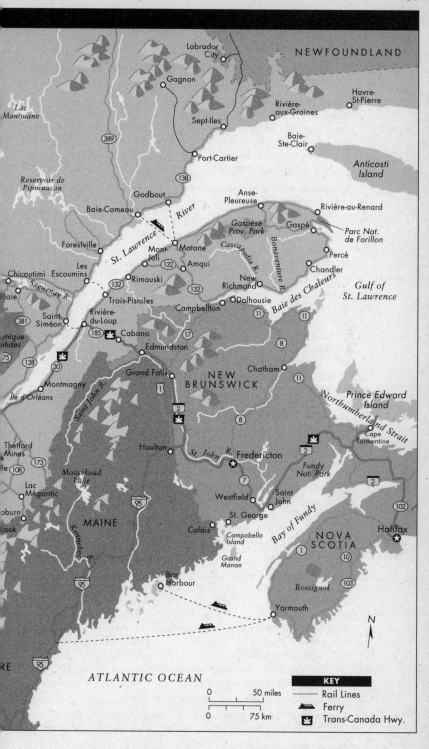

NEWFOUNDLAND

Labrador City

Gagnon

Havre-St-Pierre

Rivière-aux-Graines

Sept-Îles

Baie-Ste-Clair

Lac Manouane

Anticosti Island

Port-Cartier

389

138

Reservoir de Pipmuacan

Godbout

Anse-Pleureuse

Rivière-au-Renard

Baie-Comeau

St. Lawrence River

Gaspése Prov. Park

Gaspé

Parc Nat. de Forillon

Forestville

Mont-Joli

Matane

Cascapedia R.

Bonaventure R.

Percé

Les Escoumins

132

Amqui

Chandler

Chicoutimi

Rimouski

New Richmond

Gulf of St. Lawrence

Saguenay R.

132

132

Baie des Chaleurs

Baie

Trois-Pistoles

Dalhousie

11

Campbellton

381

Saint-Siméon

Rivière-du-Loup

11

nique tides

185

Cabano

17

75

138

20

Edmundston

8

Grand Falls

Chatham

Montmagny

NEW BRUNSWICK

11

Île d'Orléans

Prince Edward Island

Northumberland Strait

2

Cape Tormentine

Thetford Mines

Houlton

8

173

St. John R. Fredericton

2

108

le

7

Fundy Nat. Park

Lac Mégantic

Moosehead Lake

95

Saint John

2

oburn

Westfield

102

ook

MAINE

St. George

Bay of Fundy

NOVA SCOTIA

Halifax

Calais

Campobello Island

1

10

Grand Manan

Rossignol

103

Bar Harbour

95

Yarmouth

N

ATLANTIC OCEAN

KEY	
—	Rail Lines
🚢	Ferry
🛡	Trans-Canada Hwy.

0   50 miles

0   75 km

95

RE

SKIING

The Laurentians are well known internationally as a downhill destination, from St-Sauveur to majestic Mont-Tremblant. Night skiing is
available on some slopes. Cross-country skiing is popular throughout
the area from December to the end of March, especially at Val David,
Val Morin, and Estérel. Each has a cross-country ski center and at least
a dozen groomed trails.

The Eastern Townships have more than 1,000 km (620 mi) of cross-
country trails. Three inns here offer a week-long package of cross-country treks from one inn to another. The area is also popular as a downhill
ski center, with ski hills on four mountains that dwarf anything the
Laurentians have to offer, with the exception of Mont-Tremblant.

Charlevoix has three main ski areas with excellent facilities for both
downhill and cross-country skiers.

Lift ticket prices vary by resort, and the cost is often included in hotel
packages. Expect to pay about $40 per day. Road names near ski areas
are seldom labeled (they're up the mountain, where else?) but the signage is extremely good, with ski symbols and distance clearly marked.

Sugar Shacks

Every March the combination of sunny days and cold nights causes
the sap to run in the maple trees. *Cabanes à sucre* (sugar shacks) go
into operation, boiling the sap collected from the trees in buckets
(now, at some places, complicated tubing and vats do the job). The many
commercial enterprises scattered over the area host "sugaring offs" and
tours of the process, including tapping the maple trees, boiling the sap
in vats, and *tire sur la neige*, pouring hot syrup over cold snow to give
it a taffy consistency just right for "pulling" and eating. A number of
cabanes serve hearty meals of ham, baked beans, and pancakes, all
drowned in maple syrup.

Exploring Québec

Two major recreational areas attract stressed-out urbanites and anyone else who wants to relax: the Laurentians and the Eastern Townships. The Laurentians resort area, which begins 60 km (37 mi) north
of Montréal, has fine ski hills and thousands of miles of wilderness.
The Eastern Townships, in a southern corner of the province, have outdoor activities on ski slopes and lakes and in provincial parks. The Townships, which start 80 km (50 mi) east of Montréal, also offer cultural
attractions.

Charlevoix is often called the Switzerland of Québec because of its landscape, which includes mountains, valleys, streams, and waterfalls.
Charming villages line the north shore of the St. Lawrence River for
about 200 km (124 mi)—from Ste-Anne-de-Beaupré, east of Québec
City, to the Saguenay River. The knobby Gaspé Peninsula is where the
St. Lawrence River meets the Gulf of St. Lawrence. This isolated peninsula, which begins about 200 km (124 mi) east of Québec City, has a
wild beauty all its own: mountains and cliffs tower above its beaches.
The drive around the Gaspé is 848 km (526 mi).

*Numbers in the text correspond to numbers in the margin and on the
Laurentians (les Laurentides), Eastern Townships (les Cantons de l'Est),
and Montérégie, Charlevoix, and Gaspé Peninsula (Gaspésie) maps.*

Great Itineraries

IF YOU HAVE 2 DAYS

If you have only a few days for a visit, you'll need to concentrate on
one area, and the Laurentians, outside Montréal, are a good choice.

This resort area has recreational options (depending on the season) that include golf, hiking, and great skiing. Pick a resort town to stay in, whether it's ⌧ **St-Sauveur-des-Monts** ④, ⌧ **Ste-Adèle** ⑥, or ⌧ **Mont-Tremblant** ⑩ near the vast **Parc Provincial du Mont-Tremblant,** and use that as a base to visit some of the surrounding towns. There's good eating and shopping here—and even a reconstructed historic village in Ste-Adèle.

If your starting point is Québec City, you could take two days to explore the towns of Charlevoix east of the city, with an overnight in the elegant resort town ⌧ **La Malbaie** ㉕.

IF YOU HAVE 5 DAYS

You can combine a taste of the Eastern Townships with a two-day visit to the Laurentians. Get a feeling for the Laurentians by staying overnight in ⌧ **St-Sauveur-des-Monts** ④ or ⌧ **Ste-Adèle** ⑥ and exploring surrounding towns such as **St-Jérôme** ③ and **Morin Heights** ⑤. Then head back south of Montréal to the Townships, which extend to the east along the border with New England. Overnight in ⌧ **Granby** ⑪ or ⌧ **Bromont** ⑫: Granby has a zoo and Bromont is known for its factory outlets. The next day, you can shop in pretty **Knowlton** ⑭ (look for signs to Lac Brome) and explore regional history in such towns as **Valcourt** ⑮, where a museum is dedicated to the inventor of the snowmobile. Spend a night or two in the appealing resort town of ⌧ **Magog** ⑱, along Lac Memphrémagog, or the quieter ⌧ **North Hatley** ⑲, on Lac Massawippi. You'll have good dining in either. Save a day for some outdoor activity, whether it's golfing, skiing, biking on former railroad lines, or hiking.

IF YOU HAVE 10–12 DAYS

A longer visit can show you a number of regions in Québec, but you must do some driving between them. You can spend a few days in either the Laurentians or the Eastern Townships before heading east to Québec City and historic Charlevoix, the heart of what was New France, along the St. Lawrence River. The drive from Montréal or Sherbrooke to Québec City is more than 240 km (149 mi); 33 km (20 mi) to the east lies **Ste-Anne-de-Beaupré** ㉒, with its famous basilica. Colonial-era homes and farmhouses dot several Charlevoix villages; some are still homes, and others are now theaters, museums, or restaurants. Spend time in ⌧ **Baie St-Paul** ㉓ and ⌧ **La Malbaie** ㉕, or just drive lovely roads such as Route 362. In season you can whale-watch in **Tadoussac** ㉖. To get to the Gaspé Peninsula, you have to cross the St. Lawrence River. An hour-long ferry ride from St-Siméon, between La Malbaie and Tadoussac, takes you to Rivière-du-Loup. From there it's a day to get to ⌧ **Carleton** ㉗ on the Gaspé's southern shore. The peninsula offers one of the most scenic drives in North America; you can stop in ⌧ **Percé** ㉘ and spend a day visiting **l'Île Bonaventure,** which has a fascinating bird colony.

When to Tour Québec

The Laurentians are mainly a winter skiing destination, but you can drive up from Montréal to enjoy the fall foliage; to hike, bike, or play golf; or to engage in spring skiing—and still get back to the city before dark. The only slow periods are early November, when there isn't much to do, and June, when there is plenty to do but the area is plagued by blackflies (admittedly less of a problem thanks to effective biological-control programs).

The Eastern Townships are best in fall, when the foliage is at its peak. The region borders Vermont and has the same dramatic colors. It's possible to visit wineries at this time, but you should call ahead to see if visitors are welcome during the harvest, which can be busy. Charlevoix is lovely in fall, but winter is particularly magical—although the steep and narrow roads aren't great. In summer there is a special silvery light, born of the mountains and the proximity of the sea, which attracts many painters.

Summer is really the only time to tour the Gaspé. Some attractions have already closed by Labor Day (September 1), and few hotels are open during winter. The weather can be harsh, too, and driving the coast road can be difficult.

THE LAURENTIANS

Updated by
Paul Karr

The Laurentians (les Laurentides) are divided into two major regions: the Lower Laurentians (les Basses Laurentides) and the Upper Laurentians (les Hautes Laurentides). But don't be fooled by the designations; they don't signify great driving distances. Avid skiers might call Montréal a bedroom community for the Laurentians, which start just 60 km (37 mi) to the north. The range dates to the Precambrian era (more than 600 million years ago). These rocky hills are relatively low, but they include eminently skiable hills, with a few peaks above 2,500 ft. World-famous Mont-Tremblant, at 3,150 ft, is the tallest.

The P'tit Train du Nord—the former railroad line that is now a 200-km (124-mi) linear park used by cyclists, hikers, skiers, and snowmobilers—made it possible to transport settlers and cargo easily to the Upper Laurentians. It also opened the area up to skiing by the early 20th century. Before long, trainloads of skiers replaced settlers and cargo as the railway's major trade. Initially a winter weekend getaway for Montrealers who stayed at boardinghouses and fledgling resorts and skied its hills, the Upper Laurentians soon began attracting international visitors.

Ski lodges and private family cottages for wealthy city dwellers were accessible only by train until the 1930s when Route 117 was built. Today there is an uneasy peace between the longtime cottagers who want to restrict development and resort entrepreneurs who want to expand. At the moment, commercial interests seem to be prevailing. A number of large hotels have added indoor pools and spa facilities, and efficient highways have brought the country even closer to the city—45 minutes to St-Sauveur, 1½–2 hours to Mont-Tremblant.

The Lower Laurentians start almost immediately outside Montréal and are rich in historic and architectural landmarks. Towns such as St-Eustache and Oka are home to the manors, mills, churches, and public buildings seigneurs built for themselves and their habitants.

The resort area truly begins at St-Sauveur-des-Monts (Exit 60 on Autoroute 15) and extends as far north as Mont-Tremblant, where it turns into a wilderness of lakes and forests best visited with an outfitter. Guides that offer fishing trips are concentrated around Parc Provincial du Mont-Tremblant. To the first-time visitor, the hilly areas around St-Sauveur, Ste-Adèle, Morin Heights, Val Morin, and Val David up to Ste-Agathe-des-Monts form a pleasant hodgepodge of villages, hotels, and inns that seem to blend one into another.

Oka

❶ *40 km (25 mi) west of Montréal.*

To promote piety among the native people, the Sulpicians erected the **Calvaire d'Oka** (Oka Calvary; ⊠ Rte. 344, ☎ no phone), representing the Stations of the Cross, between 1740 and 1742. Three of the

The Laurentians (les Laurentides)

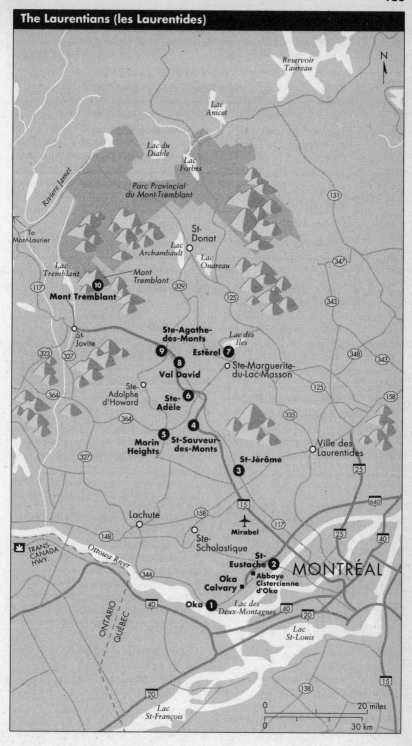

N

Reservoir Taureau

Lac Anicet

Lac du Diable

Lac Forbes

Parc Provinçial du Mont-Tremblant

Rivière Janet

To Mont-Laurier

St-Donat

Lac Archambault

Lac Ouareau

Lac Tremblant

Mont Tremblant

10 **Mont Tremblant**

St-Jovite

Ste-Agathe-des-Monts

Lac des Iles

9

Estérel 7

Ste-Marguerite-du-Lac-Masson

8

Val David

Ste-Adolphe d'Howard

6

Ste-Adèle

4

5

Morin Heights

St-Sauveur-des-Monts

Ville des Laurentides

St-Jérôme

3

Lachute

Ste-Scholastique

Mirabel

TRANS-CANADA HWY.

Ottowa River

St-Eustache 2

MONTRÉAL

Oka Calvary ■ Abbaye Cistercienne d'Oka

Oka 1

Lac des Deux-Montagnes

ONTARIO
QUÉBEC

Lac St-Louis

Lac St-François

0   20 miles

0   30 km

seven chapels are still maintained, and every September 14 since 1870 Québecois pilgrims have congregated here to participate in the half-hour ceremony that proceeds on foot to the calvary's summit. A sense of the divine is inspired as much by the magnificent view of Lac des Deux-Montagnes as by religious fervor.

The **Abbaye Cistercienne d'Oka** is one of the oldest North American abbeys. In 1887 the Sulpicians donated about 865 acres of their property near the Oka Calvary to the Trappist monks, who had arrived in New France in 1880 from Bellefontaine Abbey in France. Within 10 years they had built their monastery and transformed this land. Trappists established the Oka School of Agriculture, which operated until 1960, and are still famous for making Oka cheese today. The monastery is a noted prayer retreat. The gardens and chapel are open to visitors. ⊠ *1600 chemin d'Oka,* ☎ *450/479–8361,* WEB *www.abbayeoka.com.* 🖅 *Free.* 🕙 *Chapel Mon.–Sat. 4 AM–8 PM; gardens and boutique weekdays 9:30–4:30, Sat. 9:30–4.*

Parc Provincial d'Oka, surrounded by rolling hills, has a lake fringed by a sandy beach with picnic areas and hiking and biking trails. There are 800 camp sites here and this is a good place for kayaking, canoeing, fishing, and, in winter, snowshoeing and cross-country skiing. ⊠ *2020 chemin Oka,* ☎ *450/479–8365, 450/479–8337 activities,* WEB *www.sepaq.com.* 🖅 *$3.50 plus $5 per car.* 🕙 *Daily 8–8.*

If you're traveling with children, take a quick detour on the ferry across Lac des Deux Montagnes to **Hudson,** an attractive hamlet where the fire hydrants are decorated with human "faces." In winter, when there is an ice "bridge" across the water—it's even more fun for youngsters from warmer climes who may never have experienced this characteristically Canadian way of crossing a frozen lake.

Lodging

$$$–$$$$ 🏨 **Hotel du Lac Carling.** The modern but classically furnished hotel is near Lachute (about 40 km, or 25 mi, northwest of Oka). Besides a large sports center and 20 km (12 mi) of cross-country ski trails, there's an excellent par-72 golf course. On the doorstep to 5,000 acres of wilderness, the hotel is owned by a German real-estate magnate. The rooms have oil paintings and priceless antiques shipped from his various estates, and his daughter, Janet Hildebrand, runs the property. ⊠ *2255 Rte. 327, Pinehill, J0V 1A0,* ☎ *450/533–9211 or 800/661–9211,* FAX *450/533–4495,* WEB *www.laccarling.com. 91 rooms, 9 suites. Restaurant, minibars, room TVs, 18-hole golf course, pool, gym, sauna, spa, racquetball, squash, cross-country skiing, bar. AE, DC, MC, V. MAP.*

St-Eustache

❷ *25 km (16 mi) northeast of Oka, 15 km (9 mi) north of Montréal.*

One of the most important and tragic battles in Canadian history was fought here during the 1837 Rebellion. After the British conquest of 1759, French Canadians had been confined to preexisting territories and the new townships were allotted exclusively to the English. Adding to this insult was the government's decision to tax all imported products from England, which made them prohibitively expensive. The result? In 1834 the French Canadian Patriot party defeated the British party locally. Lower Canada, as it was then known, became a hotbed of tension between the French and English.

Rumors of rebellion were rife, and in December 1837, some 2,000 English soldiers led by General Colborne were sent in to put down the "army" of North Shore patriots by surrounding St-Eustache. Jean-Olivier

Chénier and his 200 patriots took refuge in the local church, which Colborne's cannons bombed. Chénier and 80 of his followers were killed during the battle, and more than 100 of the town's buildings were looted and burned by Colborne's soldiers. Traces of shots fired by the English army cannons are visible on the facade of **Église St-Eustache** (St-Eustache Church; ⊠ 123 rue St-Louis).

Most of the town's period buildings are open to the public. The oldest structure in St-Eustache is the **Moulin Légaré** (⊠ 232 rue St-Eustache, ☎ 450/472–9529), a flour mill that dates back to 1762. Designated a National Historic Site, it's the oldest working mill in Canada. Wheat and buckwheat are still ground on the premises.

The **Manoir Globensky,** a handsome white manor house built in 1903 (once a private residence), includes exhibits about the Rebellion. Guided tours start at 1 and 3 daily. There's also a free brochure that can be used for a good self-guided tour. ⊠ *235 rue St-Eustache,* ☎ *450/974–5166,* WEB *www.tourisme-st-eustache.com.* 🖃 *$3.* ☉ *Late June–early Sept., Tues.–Fri. 9–5, weekends 10–5.*

St-Jérôme

❸ *25 km (16 mi) north of St-Eustache, 48 km (30 mi) north of Montréal.*

Founded in 1834, St-Jérôme is a thriving economic center and cultural hub. The town first gained prominence in 1868 when Curé Antoine Labelle became pastor of this parish on the shores of the Rivière du Nord. Curé Labelle devoted himself to opening up northern Québec to French Canadians. Between 1868 and 1890, he founded 20 parish towns—an impressive achievement given the harsh conditions of this vast wilderness. But his most important legacy was the famous P'tit Train du Nord railroad line, which he persuaded the government to build in order to open St-Jérôme to travel and trade.

Le P'tit Train du Nord, immortalized by singer Felix Leclerc, spurred settlement into what was then virgin wilderness. In the 1920s and 1930s, it also boosted the just-emerging tourist industry. "Snow trains" used to carry Montrealers into the hinterland to enjoy what was then a trendy new sport. By the beginning of the 1940s, some 10,000 skiers were wending their way northward every weekend—nothing compared with today's numbers, of course, but a record at the time.

The Le P'tit Train du Nord no longer exists, but in 1996 the track was transformed into the 200-km (124-mi) **Linear Park.** From the moment it opened, the park proved hugely popular. By the end of 1997, it had already attracted more than 1 million visitors. The well-signposted trail starts at the former railway station (1 place de la Gare) in St-Jérôme and is used mostly by cyclists (walkers use it at their peril, because the bikers fairly hurtle along). The path runs all the way to Mont-Laurier in the north. It's flanked by mileage markers, so that cyclists can track their progress (or ride just parts of the trail); some of the old railway stations and historic landmarks along the route have been converted into places where *velo-touristes* (bike tourists) can stop for a snack. In winter, cross-country skiers and snowmobilers use the trail.

St-Jérôme's **promenade,** a boardwalk stretching 4 km (2½ mi), follows the Rivière du Nord from rue de Martigny bridge to rue St-Joseph bridge. Descriptive plaques en route highlight episodes of the Battle of 1837, a French–Canadian uprising.

Centre d'Exposition du Vieux-Palais, housed in the old courthouse, has changing exhibits of contemporary art and mostly features artists from

Québec. ⊠ *185 rue du Palais,* ☎ *450/432–7171.* 🔄 *Free.* ☉ *Sun. and Tues.–Fri. noon–5, Sat. 9–5.*

Parc Régional de la Rivière-du-Nord was created as a nature retreat. Trails through the park lead to the spectacular **Wilson Falls.** The Pavillon Marie-Victorin has summer weekend displays and workshops devoted to nature, culture, and history. You can hike, bike, cross-country ski, snowshoe, or snow slide here. ⊠ *1051 blvd. International,* ☎ *450/ 431–1676.* 🔄 *$3.* ☉ *Sept. 2–late May, daily 9–5; late May–Sept. 1, daily 9–8.*

Outdoor Activities and Sports

Para Vision (⊠ C.P. 95, Bellefeuille J7Z 5T7, ☎ 450/438–0855, WEB www.para-vision.qc.ca), a parachute school with a flying center in Bellefeuille, 15 minutes from St-Jérôme, caters to novices and seasoned flyers alike. Courses ($250 to $275 per person) are limited to ages 16 and up.

St-Sauveur-des-Monts

❹ *25 km (16 mi) north of St-Jérôme, 63 km (39 mi) north of Montréal.*

Since the early 1980s, St-Sauveur-des-Monts, a focal point for area resorts, has changed from a sleepy Laurentian village of 4,000 residents to a thriving year-round town attracting some 30,000 cottagers and visitors on weekends. Its main street, rue Principale, once dotted with quaint French restaurants, now has dozens of eateries at all price levels; they serve everything from lamb brochettes to spicy Thai cuisine. The narrow strip is so choked with cars and tourists in summer that it has earned the sobriquet Crescent Street of the North, after the action-filled street in Montréal. Despite all this development, St-Sauveur has maintained some of its charming, rural character.

In winter, skiing is the main event. Mont-St-Sauveur, Mont-Avila, Mont-Gabriel, and Mont-Olympia all offer special season passes and programs, and some ski-center passes can be used at more than one center in the region. Blue signs on Route 117 and Autoroute 15 indicate where the ski hills are.

🌀 Just outside St-Sauveur, the **Mont-St-Sauveur Water Park** and tourist center keeps children occupied with slides, a giant wave pool, a shallow wading pool, snack bars, and more. The rafting river attracts the older, braver crowd; the nine-minute ride follows the natural contours of steep hills and requires about 12,000 gallons of water to be pumped per minute. On the tandem slides, plumes of water flow through figure-eight tubes. ⊠ *350 rue St-Denis,* ☎ *514/871–0101 or 800/363–2426,* WEB *www.montsaintsauveur.com.* 🔄 *Full day $28, half-day (begins at 3 PM) $22, after 5 PM $15.* ☉ *Early June–early Sept., daily 10–7.*

Dining and Lodging

$$–$$$ ✕ **Le Bifthèque.** French-Canadians flock to this local institution (with outposts throughout the province) for perfectly aged steaks and other hearty fare. In the heart of St-Sauveur, this branch also serves lamb loin with Dijon mustard and trout stuffed with crab and shrimp. The list of wines is long. Children have their own menu. Pick up steaks to go at the meat counter if you're staying somewhere you can grill your own. ⊠ *86 rue de la Gare,* ☎ *450/227–2442. AE, MC, V. No lunch Sun.– Thurs.*

$–$$ ✕🏨 **Relais St-Denis.** A traditional sloping Québecois roof tops this comfortable, traditional inn where every guest room has a fireplace. Junior suites have whirlpool baths, too. The inn houses two restaurants.

La Reine Victoria creates a romantic atmosphere and serves multicourse meals with an emphasis on local ingredients and French flair. La Bourgogne serves Sunday brunch, hosts weekly dinner dances, and caters to a business breakfast crowd during the week. ⌧ *61 rue St-Denis, J0R 1R4,* ☎ *450/227–4766 or 888/997–4766,* FAX *450/227–8504,* WEB *www.relaisst-denis.com. 21 rooms, 20 suites. 2 restaurants, room TVs, pool, bar, meeting rooms. MC, V. BP.*

Outdoor Activities and Sports

La Vallée de Saint-Sauveur is the collective name for the ski area north of the village of St-Sauveur-des-Monts. The area is especially well known for its night skiing. **Mont St-Sauveur** (⌧ 350 rue St-Denis, St-Sauveur-des-Monts, ☎ 800/363–2426, 450/227–4671, 514/871–0101, WEB www.montsaintsauveur.com) has nine lifts and a vertical drop of 762 ft. Adjacent to the Mont St-Sauveur ski resort and sharing an owner is **Mont Avila** (⌧ 500 chemin Avila, Piedmont, ☎ 450/227–4671 or 514/871–0101, WEB www.montavila.com).

Station de Ski Mont-Habitant (⌧ 12 blvd. des Skieurs, St-Sauveur-des-Monts, ☎ 866/887–2637 or 450/227–2637, WEB www.monthabitant.com) has 14 trails, three lifts, and a vertical drop of 660 ft.

Shopping

Factorerie St-Sauveur (⌧ 100 rue Guindon; Autoroute 15, Exit 60; ☎ 450/227–1074) is a factory outlet mall with more than 25 stores. Canadian, American, and European manufacturers sell goods, from designer clothing to household items, at reduced prices. **Rue Principale** has shops, fashion boutiques, and café terraces with bright awnings and flowers. Housed in a former bank, **Solo Mode** (⌧ 239B rue Principale, ☎ 450/227–1234) carries international fashion labels such as Byblos.

Morin Heights

❺ *10 km (6 mi) west of St-Sauveur-des-Monts, 73 km (45 mi) northwest of Montréal.*

The town's architecture and population reflect its Anglo settlers' heritage: most residents are English-speaking. Morin Heights has escaped the overdevelopment of neighboring St-Sauveur but still encompasses a range of restaurants, bookstores, boutiques, and craft shops to explore.

In summer, windsurfing, swimming, and canoeing on the area's two lakes are popular. You can also head for the region's golf courses (including the 18-hole links at Mont-Gabriel), campgrounds at Val David, Lacs Claude, and Lafontaine, and beaches. In fall and winter, come for the foliage and the alpine and Nordic skiing.

Dining and Lodging

$$–$$$ ✕▥ **Auberge le Clos Joli.** This farmhouse turned country inn two ★ minutes from the ski slopes is considered one of the top hostelries in the Laurentians. Original art by Québecois painters adorns the cozy, intimate auberge, which is run by the Roux family. The dining room ($$$–$$$$) has a fireplace. The menu is based on French cuisine but with local touches; dishes may include soufflé of wild mushrooms with port, homemade duck or rabbit pâté, and layers of smoked salmon and trout flavored with warm goat cheese. ⌧ *19 chemin du Clos Joli, J0R 1H0,* ☎ *450/226–5401. 9 rooms. Restaurant; no air-conditioning, no room TVs. AE, MC, V. MAP.*

Outdoor Activities and Sports

The vertical drop at **Ski Morin Heights** (⌧ 231 rue Bennett, ☎ 450/227–2020, WEB www.skimorinheights.com), near Exit 60 of Autoroute

15 North, is 660 ft and there are six lifts. Although this is a downhill skiing center, snowboarding's growing popularity is in evidence here. A 44,000-square-ft chalet houses eateries, a pub, a day-care center, and equipment rental, but the center doesn't have lodging.

Ste-Adèle

❻ *12 km (7 mi) north of Morin Heights, 85 km (53 mi) north of Mont-réal.*

With a permanent population of more than 9,000, Ste-Adèle is the largest community in the lower part of the Laurentians and the service center for the region. A number of government offices and facilities for local residents are here: cinemas, shopping malls, and summer theater (in French). Of interest to visitors are the sports shops, boutiques, restaurants, and family-oriented amusements.

At **Au Pay des Merveilles,** fairy-tale characters such as Snow White, Little Red Riding Hood, and Alice in Wonderland wander the grounds, playing games with children. Small fry may also enjoy the petting zoo, wading pool, puppet theater, and rides. ⊠ *3595 rue de la Savane,* ☎ *450/229–3141,* WEB *www.paysmerveilles.com.* ⌨ *$15–$27.* ☉ *Early June–early Sept., daily 10–6.*

The Laurentians region has more than its share of water parks; Ste-Adèle started the trend with **Super Splash Sainte-Adèle.** On hot, humid weekends, Montrealers with families fill the water park, which has water slides, a wading pool, and the requisite wave pool. ⊠ *1791 blvd. Sainte-Adèle,* ☎ *450/229–2909,* WEB *www.supersplash.qc.ca.* ⌨ *$15.50.* ☉ *Late June–late Aug., daily 10–7.*

Dining and Lodging

$$$–$$$$ ✕ **La Clef des Champs.** The superior French cuisine (the owners come from France) and the romantic atmosphere are the draws at this family-owned restaurant tucked amid trees facing a mountain. Game dishes, such as medallions of roasted ostrich in a port-infused sauce and caribou in red-currant marinade, are a specialty. Good dessert choices include *gâteaux aux deux chocolats* (two-chocolate cake) and crème brûlée. ⊠ *875 chemin Ste-Marguerite,* ☎ *450/229–2857. AE, DC, MC, V. Closed Mon. Oct.–May.*

$$$–$$$$ ✕🗒 **L'Eau à la Bouche.** Superb service, stunning rooms awash with color, ★   and a terrace with a flower garden are highlights of this elegant inn. Guest rooms have Victorian, safari, Inuit, and other themes. Skiing is literally at the door as the inn faces Le Chantecler's slopes. The restaurant ($$$$) at this Relais & Chateaux property marries nouvelle cuisine and traditional Québecois cooking. The menu changes with the seasons, but it has included dishes such as foie gras with apple-cider sauce and red wine–marinated venison. ⊠ *3003 blvd. Ste-Adèle, J0R 1L0,* ☎ *450/229–2991,* FAX *450/229–7573,* WEB *www.leaualabouche.com. 23 rooms, 2 suites. Restaurant, in-room data ports, cable TV, pool. AE, DC, MC, V. EP.*

$$–$$$ ✕🗒 **Hôtel Mont-Gabriel.** At this 1,200-acre resort with a spa, you can relax in a cozy, modern room with a valley view or be close to nature in a log cabin with a fireplace. The French cuisine is first rate, with entrées such as salmon with braised leeks and pork with ginger and orange. Tennis, golf, and ski packages are available. On Jewish holidays, kosher meals can be served if you call in advance. ⊠ *1699 chemin du Mont Gabriel (Autoroute 15, Exit 64), J8B 1A5,* ☎ *450/229–3547 or 800/668–5253,* FAX *450/229–7034,* WEB *www.mont-gabriel.com. 125 rooms, 4 suites, 3 chalets. Restaurant, room service, room TVs with movies and video games, 18-hole golf course, 6 ten-*

nis courts, 1 indoor and 1 outdoor pool, spa. AE, DC, MC, V. EP.

$$$–$$$$ 🗹 **Le Chantecler.** This Montrealer favorite on Lac Ste-Adèle is nestled at the base of a mountain with 22 downhill ski runs. Trails begin almost at the hotel entrance. The rooms and chalets, furnished with Canadian pine, have a rustic appeal. ✉ *1474 chemin Chantecler, J0B 1A2,* ☎ *450/229–3555 or 888/916–1616,* FAX *450/229–5593,* WEB *www. lechantecler.com. 200 rooms, 15 suites, 3 chalets. Restaurant, in-room data ports, minibars, cable TV with movies and video games, 18-hole golf course, tennis court, indoor pool, spa, beach, boating, downhill skiing; no air-conditioning in some rooms. AE, D, DC, MC, V. EP.*

$–$$ 🗹 **Auberge & Spa Beaux Rêves.** Guest rooms at this full-service Québecois retreat have plenty of space in which to spread out. Furnishings are spare, but many of the suites have fireplaces. The outdoor hot tub and Finnish sauna are used all year. The restaurant serves light meals as well as a table d'hôte menu and fondue. Spa services include massage therapy and seaweed wraps. ✉ *2310 blvd. Ste-Adèle, J8B 2N5,* ☎ *450/229–9226 or 800/279–7679,* FAX *450/229–2999,* WEB *www. beauxreves.com. 7 rooms, 6 suites. Restaurant, hot tub, massage, sauna, meeting rooms; no air-conditioning in some rooms, no smoking. MC, V.*

Outdoor Activities and Sports

GOLF

The par-72, 18-hole **Club de Golf Chantecler** (✉ 2520 chemin du Golf, ☎ 450/229–3742) is off Exit 67 of Autoroute 15.

SKIING

Ski Chantecler (✉ 1474 rue Chantecler, Mont-Chantecler, ☎ 450/ 229–3555) has six lifts, 23 runs, and a vertical drop of 663 ft, in addition to 50 km (31 mi) of cross-country trails. **Ski Mont-Gabriel** (✉ 350 rue St-Denis, Monté Mont-Gabriel, St-Sauveur, ☎ 450/227–1100 or 800/363–2426, WEB www.skimontgabriel.com), 19 km (12 mi) northeast of Ste-Adèle, has eight lifts and 13 superb downhill trails—primarily for intermediate and advanced skiers. The vertical drop is 660 ft. **Station de Ski Côtes** (✉ Mont-Côtes, ☎ 450/229–2700) has six runs and a vertical drop of 392 ft.

Estérel

❼ *15 km (9 mi) north of Ste-Adèle, 100 km (62 mi) north of Montréal.*

The permanent population of Estérel is a mere 95 souls, but visitors to Hôtel l'Estérel—a resort off Route 370, at Exit 69 near Ste-Marguerite Station—swell that number throughout the year. Founded in 1959 on the shores of Lac Dupuis, the 5,000-acre estate was named Estérel by Baron Louis Empain because it evoked memories of his native village in Provence. Fridolin Simard bought the property and Hôtel l'Estérel soon became a household word for vacationers in search of a first-class resort area.

Dining and Lodging

$$–$$$$ ✕ **Bistro à Champlain.** An astonishing selection of wines—some 2,000—
★ has made the bistro famous. You can tour the cellars, where 35,000 bottles (at last count) had prices from $28 to $25,000. The restaurant is in a former general store built in 1864; paintings of Jean-Paul Riopelle adorn the walls. Next to the 150-seat dining room is a comfy lounge for cigar smokers. The *menu dégustation* (tasting menu) includes a different wine with each of several courses for $69. Typical dishes are marinated Atlantic smoked salmon and roast duckling with rosemary. ✉ *75 chemin Masson, Ste-Marguerite du Lac Masson,* ☎ *450/ 228–4988,* WEB *www.bistroachamplain.com. AE, DC, MC, V.*

\$\$\$–\$\$\$\$ 🏨 **Hôtel l'Estérel.** Dogsledding and an ice-skating disco are two of the more unusual options at this all-inclusive resort, and buses shuttle guests to nearby downhill ski sites. Comfortable air-conditioned rooms have a view of either the lake or the beautiful flower gardens. ⊠ *39 blvd. Fridolin Simard, J0T 1E0,* ☎ *450/228–2571 or 888/378–3735,* 🅵🅰🆇 *450/ 228–4977,* 🆆🅴🅱 *www.esterel.com. 124 rooms. Restaurant, room service, in-room data ports, room TVs with movies, 18-hole golf course, driving range, tennis court, indoor pool, gym, spa, beach, dock, bicycles, cross-country skiing, ice-skating, snowmobiling. AE, DC, MC, V. MAP.*

Val David

⑧   *18 km (11 mi) west of Estérel, 82 km (51 mi) north of Montréal.*

Besides being a center for arts and crafts, Val David is a rendezvous for mountain climbers, hikers, and campers. Children know Val David
☺ because of **Santa Claus Village.** At Santa Claus's summer residence kids can sit on Santa's knee and speak to him in French or English. On the grounds is a petting zoo (with goats, sheep, horses, and colorful birds), games, and bumper boats. ⊠ *987 rue Morin,* ☎ *819/322–2146 or 800/ 287–6635.* 🎟 *\$9.* 🕐 *Late May–early June, weekends 10–6; early June–late Aug., daily 10–6.*

Dining and Lodging

\$\$–\$\$\$ ✕ **Au Petit Poucet.** At this beloved Laurentians institution, you can savor traditional fare such as meatball ragout, maple-smoked ham, *cipaille* (a stew of game meats and chicken), pickled beets, pea soup, baked beans, and ham casserole. A dinner buffet is served on the weekend and features an even wider selection of high-calorie items. A maple-syrup pie is the perfect sweet (though not cloyingly so) ending. ⊠ *1030 Rte. 117,* ☎ *819/322—2246 or 888/334—2246. MC, V.*

\$\$–\$\$\$\$ ✕🏨 **Hôtel La Sapinière.** The homey, dark brown wood-frame hotel overlooks a fir-fringed lake (*sapin* is fir tree in French). Built by Léonidas Dufresne—father of the present owner—in 1936, the property has been modernized several times. Rooms, with country-style furnishings and pastel floral accents, come with such luxurious extras as thick terry bathrobes. You can relax in front of a blazing fire in one of several lounges. Sports options include canoes, mountain bikes (two trails run through the grounds), driving range, and tennis courts—all of which cost extra. The property is best known, however, for the French nouvelle cuisine in its fine dining room. The minimum stay is two nights. ⊠ *1244 chemin de la Sapinière, J0T 2N0,* ☎ *819/322–2020 or 800/ 567–6635,* 🅵🅰🆇 *819/322–6510,* 🆆🅴🅱 *www.sapiniere.com. 70 rooms. Restaurant, room service, in-room data ports, cable TVs, driving range, putting green, 3 tennis courts, pool, boating, mountain bikes. AE, DC, MC, V. MAP.*

\$–\$\$ 🏨 **La Maison de Bavière.** Colorful frescoes adorn the exterior shutters, doorways, and interior walls of this simple farmhouse with cheerful guest rooms. Teutonic composers inspired the names of the rooms, with the exception of the suite Alpenhaus, which has three floors and a private entrance. The tranquil riverside location is soothing. Cross-country skiing is available nearby. ⊠ *1470 chemin del la Rivière, J0T 2N0,* ☎ *819/322–3528,* 🆆🅴🅱 *www.maisondebaviere.com. 4 rooms, 1 suite. Fans; no room TVs. V. BP.*

Outdoor Activities and Sports

Mont-Alta (⊠ 2114 Rte. 117, ☎ 819/322–3206) has 22 runs and two lifts; the vertical drop is 587 ft. **Station de Ski Vallée-Bleue** (⊠ 1418 chemin Vallée-Bleue, ☎ 819/322–3427) has 17 runs and three lifts.

Shopping

The town is a haven for artists, many of whom open their studios to the public. **Atelier Bernard Chaudron, Inc.** (⊠ 2449 chemin de l'Île, ☎ 819/322–3944) sells hand-shaped lead-free pewter objets d'art such as oil lamps, plus hammered silver beer mugs, pitchers, and candleholders as well as some crystal. One of the most interesting annual events in Val David is **1001 Pots** (⊠ 2435 rue de l'Église, ☎ 819/322–6868, WEB www.1001pots.com), which showcases the Japanese-style pottery of Kinya Ishikawa—as well as pieces by many other Québec ceramicists—each summer from mid-July through mid-August.

Ste-Agathe-des-Monts

❾ *5 km (3 mi) north of Val David, 96 km (60 mi) northwest of Montréal.*

The sandy beaches of Lac des Sables are the most surprising feature of Ste-Agathe-des-Monts, a tourist town best known for its ski hills. Waterbound activities include canoeing, kayaking, swimming, and fishing. Ste-Agathe is also a stopover point on the Linear Park, the bike trail between St-Jérôme and Mont-Laurier.

Dining and Lodging

$$$–$$$$ ✕ **Chatel Vienna.** Owners Claudine and Clement Martins, from Grenoble, France, keep up tradition at this venerable Viennese restaurant, serving the popular Austrian and Continental fare that put the lakeside eatery on the map back in 1966. Home-smoked trout comes with an herb-and-spice butter and sautéed garden-fresh vegetables. Schnitzels, a sauerkraut plate, and venison are other options. Hot spiced wine, Czech pilsner beer, and dry Austrian and other international white wines are some of the beverage choices. In summer, you can enjoy the view from the patio of the century-old building. ⊠ *6 rue Ste-Lucie,* ☎ *819/ 326–1485. Reservations essential. MC, V.*

$–$$ ⌂ **Auberge du Lac des Sables.** A favorite with couples, this inn provides a quiet, relaxed atmosphere in a country setting with a magnificent view of Lac des Sables. All rooms have contemporary decor; suites have fireplaces and whirlpool baths. ⊠ *230 St-Venant, J8C 2Z7,* ☎ *819/326–3994 or 800/567–8329,* FAX *819/326–9159,* WEB *www.aubergedulac.com. 18 rooms, 5 suites. In-room data ports (some), in-room VCRs (some); no TV in some rooms MC, V. CP.*

$ ⚠ **Au Parc des Campeurs.** Near a lively resort area, this spacious campground has 30 sites with hook-ups for RVs. You can rent canoes and kayaks here. ⊠ *Tour du Lac and Rte. 329, J8C 1M9,* ☎ *819/324–0482. 556 sites. Miniature golf, tennis court, bicycles, volleyball, laundry facilities. MC, V.*

Outdoor Activities and Sports

Sailing is the favorite summer sport, especially during the **24 Heures de la Voile,** a weekend sailing competition that takes place each year in June. The sightseeing boat *Alouette* (⊠ Municipal Dock, rue Principale, ☎ 819/326–3656) offers guided tours of Lac des Sables.

Mont-Tremblant

❿ *25 km (16 mi) north of Ste-Agathe-des-Monts, 100 km (62 mi) north of Montréal.*

Mont-Tremblant, at more than 3,000 ft high, is the highest peak in the Laurentians and a major center for skiing. It's also the name of the village. The world-class resort area at the foot of the mountain, simply called Tremblant (www.tremblant.com), is spread around 14-km-long (9-mi-long) Lac Tremblant. *Ski* magazine consistently selects it as among the top ski resorts in eastern North America, and the area encompasses several golf courses, so it's not surprising that Tremblant has become the most fashionable vacation venue in Québec among sporty types. Its hub is a pedestrian-only village that looks a bit like a displaced Québec City. The buildings—constructed in the style of New France, with dormer windows and steep roofs—hold pubs, restaurants, boutiques, sports shops, a cinema, and accommodations ranging from hotels to self-catering condominiums. An indoor water-recreation complex includes pools, water slides, and whirlpool baths.

The mountain, and the hundreds of square miles of wilderness beyond, constitute the **Parc Provincial du Mont-Tremblant** (☎ 819/688–2281, WEB www.sepaq.com). Created in 1894, the park was the home of the Algonquin people, who called this area Manitonga Soutana, meaning "mountain of the spirits." Today it's a vast wildlife sanctuary of more than 400 lakes and rivers protecting about 230 species of birds and animals, including moose, deer, bear, and beaver. In winter its trails are used by cross-country skiers, snowshoers, and snowmobile enthusiasts. Moose hunting is allowed in season, and camping and canoeing are the main summer activities. Entrance to the park is free, and the main entry point is through the hamlet of St-Donat, about 45 minutes north of Mont-Tremblant, via routes 329 and 125.

Dining and Lodging

$$$$ ✕☒ **Club Tremblant.** Built as a private retreat in the 1930s by a wealthy American, this hotel is across the lake from the ski station at Mont-Tremblant. The original large log-cabin lodge is furnished in colonial style, with wooden staircases and huge stone fireplaces. The rustic but comfortable accommodation has excellent facilities, including a spa and an outstanding restaurant ($$$–$$$$) that serves French cuisine. The Saturday-night buffet features a wide selection of seafood. Both the main lodge and the deluxe condominium complex (with fireplaces, private balconies, kitchenettes, and split-level design), up the hill from the lodge, have magnificent views of Mont-Tremblant. ☒ *121 rue Cuttle, J0T 1Z0,* ☎ *819/425–2731,* FAX *819/425–9903,* WEB *www.clubtremblant.com. 113 rooms. Restaurant, in-room data ports, cable TV, tennis court, indoor pool, gym, spa. AE, MC, V. EP, MAP.*

$$$$ ✕☒ **Westin Resort–Tremblant.** The Westin, part of the Tremblant resort town and a short walk from the ski slopes, is plush and polished and often attracts a business crowd. Some guest rooms have fireplaces; most have balconies. At chic Le Soto ($$$), you can sample sushi in its many forms as well as entrées such as seared filet mignon in teriyaki sauce. Many menu items are tofu-based. ☒ *100 chemin Kandahar, J0T 1Z0,* ☎ *819/681–8000, 866/687–9330 from U.S.,* FAX *819/681–8001,* WEB *www.westin.com. 55 rooms, 71 suites. 2 restaurants, room service, in-room data ports, room TVs with movies and video games, kitchens (some), kitchenettes (some), microwaves, pool, hot tub, gym, baby-sitting, concierge, Internet, business services, meeting rooms; no-smoking rooms. AE, D, DC, MC, V. EP.*

$$–$$$$ ✕☒ **Auberge du Coq de Montagne.** Owners Nino and Kay Faragalli have earned a favorable reputation for their auberge on Lac Moore. The cozy, family-run inn is touted for its friendly service, hospitality, and modern accommodations. Year-round facilities and activities—on-site or nearby—include canoeing, kayaking, sailboarding, fishing, badminton, tennis, horseback riding, skating, and skiing. Kudos have also been garnered for the Italian cuisine served up nightly, which draws a local crowd. Menu offerings include tried-and-tested favorites such as veal marsala, veal *fiorentina* (cooked with spinach and cheese), and veal with tangy mushroom and pepper sauce. The chef also makes great

homemade pasta. Reservations are essential. ⊠ *2151 chemin Principal, C.P. 208, J0T 1Z0,* ☎ *819/425–3380 or 800/895–3380,* FAX *819/ 425–7846. 26 rooms, 6 chalets. Restaurant, gym, sauna, beach; no TV in some rooms. AE, MC, V. EP, MAP.*

$$–$$$$ ✕⊡ **Fairmont Tremblant.** The sporty but classy centerpiece of the
★ Tremblant resort area was built by Canadian Pacific Hotels (now under the prestigious Fairmont banner). Taking its cues from the historic railroad "castles" scattered throughout Canada, this contemporary hotel has wood paneling, copper and wrought-iron details, stained glass, and stone fireplaces. Skiers can zoom off the mountain right into the ground-level deli, near the full-service spa. Upstairs is dressier Le Loup-Garou restaurant ($$$$), where French touches are applied to locally sourced ingredients. Meat and game dominate the main courses. Elaborate themed buffets are the draw at the casual Windigo restaurant. ⊠ *Box 100, 3045 chemin Principal, J0T 1Z0,* ☎ *819/681–7000, 800/441–1414, 877/277–3767,* WEB *www.fairmont.com. 254 rooms, 62 suites. 2 restaurants, café, room service, kitchens (some), room TVs with movies and video games, 1 indoor and 1 outdoor pool, gym, outdoor hot tub, sauna, spa, bar, lobby lounge, shops, concierge, meeting rooms; no-smoking floors. AE, DC, MC, V. EP.*

$$–$$$$ ⊡ **Le Grand Lodge.** No expense has been spared at this Scandinavian-style log cabin all-suites hotel on 13½ acres on Lac Ouimet. The accommodations, from studios to two-bedroom suites, are spacious, with kitchenettes, stone fireplaces, and balconies that overlook the water. The indoor–outdoor café, which serves light fare, also looks out on the lake. The more formal Chez Borivage, which has a good wine cellar, specializes in French cuisine. Although the resort attracts a sizeable corporate clientele, it caters to families as well, with day-care facilities and a game room for teens. ⊠ *2396 rue Labelle, J8E 1T8,* ☎ *819/425–2734 or 800/ 567–6763,* FAX *819/425–9725,* WEB *www.legrandlodge.com. 112 suites. Restaurant, café, golf privileges, in-room data ports (some), room TVs with movies, indoor pool, gym, massage, steam room, boating, bicycles, badminton, shuffleboard, volleyball, baby-sitting, business services, meeting rooms; no-smoking rooms. AE, MC, V. EP.*

Outdoor Activities and Sports

With a 2,131-ft vertical drop, **Mont-Tremblant** (☎ 819/425–8711 or 819/681–2000, WEB www.tremblant.ca) offers 77 downhill trails, 11 lifts, and 90 km (56 mi) of cross-country trails. Downhill beginners favor the 6-km (4-mi) Nansen trail; experts often choose the Flying Mile on the south side and the Duncan and Expo runs on the mountain's north side. The speedy Duncan Express is a quadruple chairlift; there's also a heated, high-speed gondola.

On the other side of the mountain is the Versant Soleil (sunny slope). The area has a vertical drop of 1,905 ft and 15 runs (including much sought-after glade skiing) served by a state-of-the-art, high-speed quad chair that's capable of moving 2,250 people to the summit every hour. Sixty percent of the trails are for advanced skiers and 7% are classified for expert skiers only. The remainder are for skiers who consider themselves intermediate.

THE EASTERN TOWNSHIPS

Updated by
Carolyn
Jackson

The Eastern Townships (also known as les Cantons de l'Est, and formerly as l'Estrie) refers to the area in the southwest corner of the province of Québec—bordering Vermont, New Hampshire, and Maine. Its northern Appalachian hills, rolling down to placid lakeshores, were first home to the Abenaki natives, long before "summer people" built their cottages and horse paddocks. The Abenaki are gone, but the names they gave to the region's recreational lakes remain: Memphrémagog, Massawippi, Mégantic.

The Townships, as locals call them, were populated by Empire Loyalists fleeing the Revolutionary War and, later, the newly created United States of America. They wanted to continue living under the English king in British North America. It's not surprising that the covered bridges, village greens, white church steeples, and country inns are reminiscent of New England. The Loyalists were followed, around 1820, by the first wave of Irish immigrants (ironically, Catholics fleeing their country's union with Protestant England). Some 20 years later the potato famine sent more Irish pioneers to the Townships.

The area became more Francophone after 1850 as French Canadians moved in to work on the railroad and in the lumber industry. During the late 19th century, English families from Montréal and Americans from the border states began summering at cottages along the lakes. During Prohibition the area attracted even more cottagers from the United States. Lac Massawippi became a favorite summer resort of wealthy families, and those homes have since been converted into gracious inns and upscale bed-and-breakfasts.

Today the summer communities fill up with equal parts French and English visitors, though the year-round residents are primarily French. The locals are proud of their multiethnic heritage. They boast of "Loyalist tours" and Victorian gingerbread homes, and in the next breath direct visitors to the snowmobile museum in Valcourt, where in 1937, native French son Joseph-Armand Bombardier built the first *moto-neige* (snowmobile) in his garage. (Bombardier's other inventions became the basis for one of Canada's biggest industries—supplying New York City and Mexico City with subway cars and other rolling stock.)

Since the 1980s, the Townships have developed from a series of quiet farm communities and wood-frame summer homes to a thriving all-season resort area. In winter, skiers flock to seven downhill centers and more than 1,000 km (622 mi) of cross-country trails. Three inns—Manoir Hovey, Auberge Hatley, and the Ripplecove Inn—offer cross-country packages. Skiers can ski between the inns on a challenging trail that meanders through the woods for 32 km (20 mi). Still less crowded and commercialized than the Laurentians, the area has ski hills on four mountains that dwarf anything the Laurentians have to offer, with the exception of Mont-Tremblant. And compared to Vermont, ski-pass rates are still a bargain. Owl's Head, Mont-Orford, and Mont-Sutton have interchangeable lift tickets.

By early spring, the sugar shacks are busy with the new maple syrup. In summer, boating, swimming, sailing, golfing, rollerblading, hiking, and bicycling take over. And every fall the inns are booked solid with leaf peepers eager to take in the brilliant foliage.

The fall is also a good time to visit the wineries (though most are open all year). Because of its mild micro-climate, the Townships area has become one of the fastest-developing wine regions in Canada, with a dozen of the more than 30 wineries in Québec province. The wines don't quite measure up to the standards of Ontario's Niagara Peninsula or British Columbia's Okanagan Valley—at least not yet, as the industry is fairly young here—but wine makers produce some good hearty reds and sparkling whites that go well with the regional cuisine. Wine makers are also making some inroads with ice wine, a sweet dessert wine made—as the name suggests—from frozen grapes (they have a very high sugar content).

Granby

⑪ *80 km (50 mi) east of Montréal.*

Granby is the western gateway to the Eastern Townships and home to a notable zoo. It also hosts a number of annual festivals: the Festival of Mascots and Cartoon Characters (July), a great favorite with youngsters and families, and the Granby International, an antique-car competition held at the Granby Autodrome (also in July). The Festival International de la Chanson, a songfest of budding composers and performers that has launched several of Québec's current megastars, is a nine-day event in mid-September.

★ ℭ The **Jardin Zoologique de Granby** (Granby Zoo), one of the biggest attractions in the area, houses some 1,000 animals representing 225 species in a naturally landscaped setting. The Afrika pavilion, with its gorillas, lions, and birds, is a favorite with youngsters; they also love the camel rides and Amazoo—an aquatic park with turbulent wave pools and rides. At certain times of the day, keepers demonstrate the acrobatic skills of the birds of prey. The complex includes amusement rides and souvenir shops, as well as a playground and picnic area. ✉ *525 rue St-Hubert,* ☎ *450/372–9113,* ⓦ *www.zoogranby.com.* 🎫 *$21.95.* ⊙ *Mid-May–early Sept., daily 10–7; late Sept., weekends 10–6.*

Outdoor Activities and Sports

Biking is big here. The quiet back roads lend themselves to exploring the region on two wheels, as does the network of off-road trails. There are 450 km (279 mi) of bike-friendly trails, some linked to La Route Verte (The Green Route), a province-wide network that is being expanded by leaps and bounds. For details and a map, contact Vélo Québec (☎ 514/521–8356 or 800/567–8356, ⓦ www.routeverte.com). One of the most popular (and flattest) bike and in-line skating trails is the paved **l'Estriade,** which links Granby to Waterloo. The **Montérégiade** bike trail between Granby and Farnham is 21 km (13 mi) long.

Mountain biking is also popular in the Townships. The mountain-biking season kicks off in late May with the **Tour de la Montagne** (☎ 450/534–2453, ⓦ www.bromontbiking.com), a 25-km (15-mi) rally. Competitions for serious mountain bikers are held in summer.

Bromont

⑫ *78 km (48 mi) east of Montréal.*

This *station touristique* (tourist center) offers a wide range of activities in all seasons—boating, camping, golf, horseback riding, swimming, tennis, biking, canoeing, fishing, hiking, cross-country and downhill skiing, and snowshoeing. Bromont has the only night skiing in the Eastern Townships and a slope-side disco, Le Bromontais. The town also has more than 100 km (62 mi) of maintained trails for mountain bikers. A former Olympic equestrian site, Bromont hosts the **International Bromont Equestrian Competition** (☎ 450/534–3255, ⓦ www.internationalbromont.org.) every year in late June.

ℭ **Bromont Aquatic Park** is a water park with 15 rides and games, including the Corkscrew (self-explanatory) and the Elephant's Trunk (where kids shoot out of a model of an elephant's head). Slides are divided into four degrees of difficulty from easy to extreme, which is recommended for adults and older children only. Admission includes a chairlift ride to the top of the ski hill. September through late October it's open only for mountain biking. ✉ *Autoroute 10, Exit 78,* ☎ *450/534–2200,* ⓦ *www.skibromont.com.* 🎫 *$24.* ⊙ *Late May–Aug., daily 10–6:30, Sept.–late Oct., daily 10–4.*

Eastern Townships (les Cantons de l'Est) and Montérégie

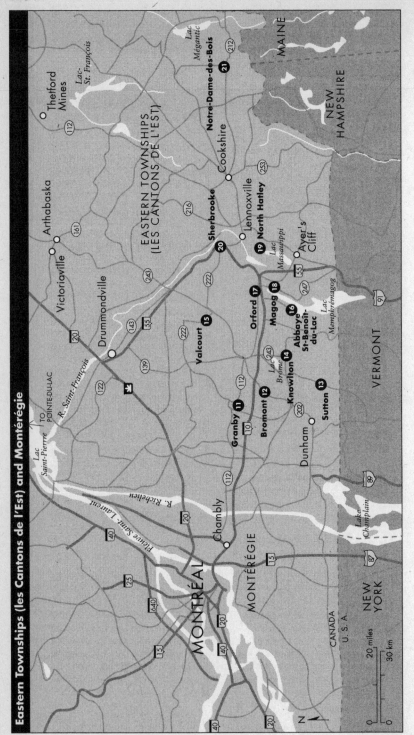

EASTERN TOWNSHIPS
(LES CANTONS DE L'EST)

MONTÉRÉGIE

MONTRÉAL

NEW HAMPSHIRE

MAINE

VERMONT

NEW YORK

CANADA
U.S.A.

Lac
Mégantic

Lac
St. François

Lac
Saint-Pierre

Lac
Massawippi

Lac
Brome

Lac
Memphrémagog

Lake
Champlain

Thetford
Mines

Arthabaska

Victoriaville

Drummondville

Sherbrooke

Notre-Dame-des-Bois

Cookshire

Lennoxville

North Hatley

Ayer's
Cliff

Orford

Magog

Abbaye
St-Benoît-
du-lac

Valcourt

Granby

Bromont

Knowlton

Dunham

Sutton

Chambly

TO
POINTE-DU-LAC

R. Saint-François

Fleuve Saint-Laurent

R. Richelieu

11 Granby
12 Bromont
13 Sutton
14 Knowlton
15 Valcourt
16 Abbaye St-Benoît-du-lac
17 Orford
18 Magog
19 North Hatley
20 Sherbrooke
21 Notre-Dame-des-Bois

20 miles

30 km

N

OFF THE
BEATEN PATH

SAFARI AVENTURE LOOWAK – The brainchild of butterfly collector Serge Poirier, this park sprawls over 500 acres of wooded land, 10 km (6 mi) from Bromont. It's a kind of Indiana Jones–theme guided tour where you head off into the bush to hunt for treasure and to look for downed planes. It's a great hit with little ones, but parents get caught up in the fantasy, too. Reservations are recommended. ✉ *475 Horizon Blvd. (off Exit 88 of Autoroute 10), Waterloo,* ☎ *450/539–0501,* WEB *www.safariloowak.qc. ca.* ✉ *Trips begin at $10 per person, minimum 4 people.*

DUNHAM – At least three wineries near the town of Dunham, about 20 km (12 mi) from Bromont on Route 202, offer tastings and tours. Call ahead for business hours, which can be erratic, especially in the autumn, when they're set around harvesting. **Vignoble Domaine Côtes d'Ardoise** (✉ 879 Rte. 202, Dunham, ☎ 450/295–2020) was one of the first wineries to set up shop, more than 20 years ago. The original, French owner encountered a lot of skepticism, but in time he proved that vines could be grown successfully in the region. Before walking through the vineyard at **Vignoble de l'Orpailleur** (✉ 1086 Rte. 202, Dunham, ☎ 450/295–2763, WEB www.orpailleur.ca.), stop by the ecomuseum to learn everything you ever wanted to know about the production of wine, from the growing of the grapes right up to the bottling process. There's also a gift shop and patio restaurant. **Vignoble Les Trois Clochers** (✉ 341 chemin Bruce, or Rte. 202, Dunham, ☎ 450/295–2034) produces a dry, fruity white from seyval grapes as well as several other white wines.

Lodging

$$$ 🏨 **Hôtel Château Bromont.** Massages, electropuncture, algae wraps, facials, and aromatherapy are just a few of the pampering services at this European-style resort spa. Rooms are large and comfortable, with contemporary furniture. Sunny Mediterranean colors dress the atrium walls, and center-facing rooms have balconies and window boxes. Greenery and patio furniture surround the swimming pool in the middle of the atrium. The restaurant Les Quatres Canards serves regional cuisine featuring duck, and has a panoramic view. ✉ *90 rue Stanstead, J2L 1K6,* ☎ *450/534–3433 or 800/304–3433,* FAX *450/534–0514,* WEB *www.chateaubromont.com. 144 rooms, 8 suites. 2 restaurants, cable TV with movies and video games, 1 indoor and 1 outdoor pool, hot tub, sauna, spa, badminton, racquetball, squash, volleyball, bar, Internet, meeting rooms. AE, D, DC, MC, V. EP, MAP.*

Outdoor Activities and Sports

The **Royal Bromont** (✉ 400 chemin Compton, ☎ 450/534–4653 or 888/281–0017, WEB www.royalbromont.com.) is an 18-hole, par-72, bent-grass course. Greens fees are $37–$58.

Station de Ski Bromont (✉ 150 rue Champlain, ☎ 450/534–2200, WEB www.skibromont.com), with 45 trails for downhill skiing, was the site of the 1986 World Cup Slalom. The vertical drop is 1,336 ft, and there are four lifts. Hiking and mountain biking are popular here in summer and early fall.

Shopping

Shopping for bargains is a popular weekend activity in the Townships; the **Bromont Flea Market** is the largest. (You can't miss the HUGE sign on Autoroute 10.) More than 1,000 vendors sell their wares—everything from T-shirts to household gadgets—each Saturday and Sunday from May to the end of October, and shoppers come from as far afield as Montréal and Vermont, just over the border.

Sutton

⑬ *106 km (66 mi) southeast of Montréal.*

Sutton is a well-established community with crafts shops, cozy eateries, and bars (La Paimpolaise is a favorite among skiers). Encircled by mountains, the town is best explored on foot; a circuit of 12 heritage sites makes an interesting walk past Loyalist-built homes and elegant shops. **Arts Sutton** (⬚ 7 rue Academy, ☎ 450/538–2563) is a long-established art gallery with works for sale.

Lodging

$ 🏠 **Auberge la Paimpolaise.** This alpine-style auberge on Mont-Sutton is 50 ft from the ski trails. It's nothing fancy, but the location is hard to beat. Rooms, some of which don't have phones, are simple, comfortable, and clean, with a woodsy appeal. All-inclusive weekend ski packages are available. ⬚ *615 rue Maple, J0E 2K0, ☎ 450/538–3213 or 800/263–3213, FAX 450/538–3970, WEB www.paimpolaise.com. 27 rooms, 1 suite. Dining room, cable TV, meeting rooms, some pets allowed (fee); no smoking. AE, DC, MC, V. EP, MAP.*

Outdoor Activities and Sports

GOLF

Reservations must be made in advance at **Les Rochers Bleus** (⬚ 550 Rte. 139, ☎ 450/538–2324, WEB www.lesrochersbleus.com), a par-72, 18-hole course. Its narrow fairways surrounded by mountains are a challenge. Greens fees are $18.25–$32.60.

HIKING

Au Diable Vert (⬚ 160 chemin Staines, Glen Sutton J0E 2K0, ☎ 450/538–5639 or 888/779–9090, WEB www.audiablevert.qc.ca) is a 200-acre mountainside site, 15 minutes from the village of Sutton, where the hiking trails look out over spectacular mountain scenery. Glen Sutton is between the Appalachians and Vermont's Green Mountains and the Missisquoi River runs through the middle. The centerpiece of Au Diable Vert is a rustic lodge, a converted, early-20th-century farmhouse with three bedrooms and a dormitory. (The lodge can accommodate 15 hikers.) Thirty campsites are also available.

SKIING

Mont-Sutton (⬚ Rte. 139 S, Autoroute 10, Exit 68, ☎ 450/538–2339, WEB www.montsutton.com) has 53 downhill trails, a vertical drop of 1,518 ft, and nine lifts. This ski area—one of the region's largest—attracts a die-hard crowd of mostly Anglophone skiers and snowboarders from Québec. Trails plunge and meander through pine, maple, and birch trees.

Knowlton (Lac Brome)

⑭ *101 km (63 mi) southeast of Montréal.*

Along the shore of Lac Brome, picturesque Knowlton makes a great stop for antiques, clothes, and gifts. The village is a treasure trove: high-quality boutiques, art galleries, and interesting little eateries fill renovated clapboard buildings painted every shade of the rainbow. The town also has several factory outlets. Distinctive Lake Brome duck is found on local menus and is celebrated in a gastronomic event in late September.

Dining and Lodging

$$ ✕🏠 **Auberge Knowlton.** The 12-room inn, at the main intersection in Knowlton, has been a local landmark since 1849, when it was a stagecoach stop on the road between Bolton Pass and Gilman's Corner. The current owners gutted the building but retained the historic exterior. The inn attracts a corporate clientele (the rooms have Internet access)

as well as vacationers and locals who like coming to the old, familiar hotel to celebrate special occasions. The on-site bistro, Le Relais ($$–$$$), serves local wines and cheeses and offers a wide range of duck dishes, such as warm duck salad served with gizzards. Confit du canard is made with the leg of duck, roasted slowly in the oven, then marinated in its own juices for several days before being reheated. The result is tender, tasty meat. ✉ *286 chemin Knowlton, J0E 1V0,* ☎ *450/242–6886,* FAX *450/242–1055,* WEB *www.cclacbrome.qc.ca/ak. 12 rooms. Restaurant, no air-conditioning in some rooms, in-room data ports, cable TV, Internet, meeting rooms, some pets allowed. AE, MC, V.*

Nightlife and the Arts

Théâtre Lac Brome (✉ 267 rue Knowlton, ☎ 450/242–2270 or 450/242–1395, WEB www.cclacbrome.qc.ca/tlb) stages plays, musicals, and productions of classic Broadway and West End hits. The company specializes in English productions but also has dabbled in bilingual productions and some new Canadian works. The 175-seat, air-conditioned theater is behind Knowlton's popular pub of the same name.

Outdoor Activities and Sports

Not far from Knowlton is **Golf Inverness** (✉ 511 chemin Bondville/Rte. 215, ☎ 450/242–1595 or 800/468–1595, WEB www.golfinverness.ca.), an 18-hole, par-71 course with an elegant 1915 clubhouse. Greens fees are $22–$42.

Many Montrealers come for the downhill skiing at **Mont-Glen** (✉ off Rte. 243, ☎ 450/243–6142 or 877/243–6142, WEB www.glen.qc.ca). The area has 32 trails, four lifts, and a vertical drop of 1,099 ft.

Shopping

Hurricane Grace (✉ 285 chemin Knowlton, ☎ 450/243–0164) carries original designer clothing for women and children. You can find handmade jewelry by Québec artisans at **Jules Perrier-Joaillier** (✉ 264 chemin Knowlton, ☎ 450/243–6444), at the same address as a Woolrich store. **L.L. Brome Factory Outlet** (✉ 91 rue Lakeside, ☎ 450/243–0123) carries well-made sports and casual clothing. Big and small kids should visit **Township Toy Trains** (✉ 5 chemin du Mont-Echo, ☎ 450/243–1881) to peruse its stock of trains and dollhouse miniatures. **Woolrich.pure laine** (✉ 264 chemin Knowlton, ☎ 450/243–0058) has classic imported wool garments.

Valcourt

🅖 *158 km (98 mi) east of Montréal.*

Valcourt is the birthplace of the inventor of the snowmobile, and the Eastern Townships are a world center for the sport, with more than 2,000 km (1,240 mi) of paths cutting through the woods and meadows. In February Valcourt hosts the **Valcourt Snowmobiling Grand Prix** (☎ 450/532–3443), a three-day event with competitions and festivities.

The **Musée Joseph-Armand Bombardier** displays innovator Bombardier's many inventions, including the snowmobile. ✉ *1001 av. Joseph-Armand Bombardier,* ☎ *450/532–5300,* WEB *www.museebombardier.com.* ✉ *$5.* ☉ *May–Aug., daily 10–5; Sept.–Apr., Tues.–Sun. 10–5.*

Abbaye St-Benoît-du-Lac

★ 🅗 *132 km (82 mi) southeast of Montréal.*

This abbey's slender bell tower juts up above the trees like a fairy-tale castle. Built by the Benedictines in 1912 on a wooded peninsula on Lac Memphrémagog, the abbey is home to some 60 monks who sell apples and sparkling apple wine from their orchards as well as distinctive cheeses: Ermite, St-Benoît, and ricotta. Gregorian prayers are sung daily and some masses are open to the public; call for the schedule. Dress modestly if you plan to attend vespers or other rituals, and avoid shorts. The monks might be traditionalists but they've joined the modern world with a comprehensive Web site that explains their way of life and spiritual practices. Guests wishing to experience a few days of retreat should reserve well in advance (a contribution of $35 per night is suggested). To get to the abbey from Magog, take Route 112 and follow the signs for the side road (Rural Route 2, or rue des Pères) to the abbey. ⊠ *R.R. 2,* ☎ *819/843–4080,* WEB *www.st-benoit-du-lac.com.* ☉ *Store open daily between services, except Sundays.*

Orford

🕑 *115 km (72 mi) east of Montréal.*

Orford is the township where the **Parc Provincial du Mont-Orford** (⊠ 3321 chemin du Parc, ☎ 819/843–6548 or 800/567–2772) lies. The park is in use year-round, whether for skiing, snowshoeing, camping, or hiking. An annual arts festival, Festival Orford, highlights classical music and chamber-orchestra concerts.

Since 1951, thousands of students have come to the **Orford Arts Centre** (3165 chemin du Parc, ☎ 819/843–8595, 800/567–6155 in Canada May–Aug., WEB www.arts-orford.org) to study and perform classical music in summer. Thirty-five public concerts are given during July and August. Canada's internationally celebrated Orford String Quartet originated here.

Lodging

$$–$$$ 🏨 **Auberge Estrimont.** An exclusive complex built of cedar, Auberge Estrimont has hotel rooms, condos, and larger chalets close to ski hills, riding stables, and golf courses. Every room in the hotel or in an adjoining condo unit has a fireplace and a private balcony. The attractive dining room serves Continental cuisine. The table d'hôte menu, priced at $30 per person, features such specialties as ostrich terrine, salmon-and-scallop roulade, and praline mousse. ⊠ *44 av. de l'Auberge, C.P. 98, J1X 6J3,* ☎ *819/843–1616 or 800/567–7320,* FAX *819/843–4909,* WEB *www.estrimont.qc.ca. 76 rooms, 7 suites. Restaurant, microwaves (some), cable TV, 2 tennis courts, 1 indoor and 1 outdoor pool, gym, hot tub, sauna, spa, badminton, racquetball, squash, bar, Internet, meeting rooms. AE, DC, MC, V.*

Outdoor Activities and Sports

Mont-Orford Ski Area (⊠ Rte. 141, ☎ 819/843–6548 or 800/567–2772), at the center of the provincial park, has plenty of challenges for alpine and cross-country skiers, from novices to veterans. It has 52 runs, a vertical drop of 1,782 ft, and eight lifts, as well as 56 km (35 mi) of cross-country trails, an 18-hole golf course, and a day-care center.

Magog

🕒 *118 km (74 mi) east of Montréal.*

At the northern tip of Lac Memphrémagog, a large body of water that reaches into northern Vermont, lies the bustling town of Magog, with bed-and-breakfasts, hotels, and restaurants. It has sandy beaches as well as activities that include boating, bird-watching, sailboarding, horseback riding, dogsledding, rollerblading, golfing, and snowmobiling. You might even see the lake's legendary sea dragon on one of the many lake cruises. It is said to have been sighted about 90 times since 1816.

The streets downtown are lined with century-old homes that have been converted into boutiques, stores, and dozens of eating places—from fast-food outlets to bistros serving Italian and French fare.

You can stroll or picnic (skate or cross-country ski in winter) in the scenic Linear Park. A trail for cyclists, walkers, and cross-country skiers hugs the lake, then parallels Route 112 before turning into an off-road recreational trail that leads into the Parc Provincial du Mont-Orford, 13½ km (8 mi) from town.

Magog is the site of one of the largest wineries in the province, **Le Cep d'Argent** (⊠ 1257 chemin de la Rivière, R.R. 5, ☎ 819/864–4441 or 877/864–4441, WEB www.cepdargent.com). The sparkling white wine is particularly good, and the dessert wine, which is similar to a port and flavored with a soupçon of maple syrup, makes a wonderful accompaniment to a plate of local cheese. This winery plays a leading role in the annual wine festival that's held in Magog in early September and has guided visits, a boutique, and tastings.

Dining and Lodging

$$$$ ✕⌂ **Ripplecove Inn.** The accommodations, service, and food at the
★ Ripplecove, 11 km (7 mi) south of Magog, are consistently excellent. The Europe-trained chef designs delicious Eastern Townships set menus that might consist of black tiger prawns flamed with brandy on fennel salad, marinated pheasant with morel cream sauce, panfried local trout with white wine and watercress emulsion, and crème brûlée with a crust of local maple syrup—for $59 a person. A seven-course gourmet menu is also available. ⊠ *700 rue Ripplecove, C.P. 246, Ayer's Cliff J0B 1C0,* ☎ *819/838–4296 or 800/668–4296,* FAX *819/838–5541,* WEB *www.ripplecove.com. 19 rooms, 4 suites, 3 cottages. Restaurant, cable TV (no TV in some rooms), pool, beach, windsurfing, boating, cross-country skiing, Internet, meeting room. AE, MC, V. MAP.*

$$–$$$ ✕⌂ **Auberge l'Étoile Sur-le-Lac.** All 53 rooms and 2 suites at this popular auberge on Magog's waterfront are modern. Some guest rooms have whirlpools and fireplaces. Large windows overlooking mountain-ringed Lac Memphrémagog make the restaurant bright and airy. In summer you can sit outside and take in the smells and sounds, as well as the beautiful view. House specialties include wild game and Swiss fondue. ⊠ *1150 rue Principale Ouest,* ☎ *819/843–6521 or 800/567–2727,* WEB *www.etoile-sur-le-lac.com. 53 rooms, 2 suites. Restaurant, cable TV, spa, boating, bicycles, hiking, ice-skating, meeting rooms. AE, DC, MC, V.*

$$–$$$$ ⌂ **Centre de Santé d'Eastman.** The oldest spa in Québec has evolved
★ from a simple health center into a bucolic haven for anyone seeking rest and therapeutic treatments, including weight-management counseling. Surrounded by 350 acres of rolling, wooded land in Eastman, 15 km (9 mi) west of Magog, the spa is an elegant, simple structure that brings to mind the soothing calm of a Japanese garden. Some bedrooms have fireplaces, large balconies, and views of Mont-Orford, but none have phones. In the restaurant, vegetarian dishes predominate, prepared with produce from the chef's garden, but innovative fish, rabbit, and chicken courses are also served from time to time. Nearby Eastman, an attractive hamlet with antiques and gift shops, is within walking distance. ⊠ *895 chemin des Diligences, Eastman J0E 1P0,* ☎ *450/297–3009 or 800/665–5272,* FAX *450/297–3370,* WEB *www.spa-eastman.com. 44 rooms. Dining room, pool, spa, cross-country skiing, meeting rooms; no air-conditioning in some rooms, no room TVs, no kids. AE, MC, V. MAP.*

Nightlife and the Arts

NIGHTLIFE

Magog is lively after dark, with bars, cafés, bistros, and restaurants to suit every taste and pocketbook. A patio bar at **Auberge Orford** (✉ 20 rue Merry Sud, ☎ 819/843–9361) overlooks the Magog River (you can moor your boat alongside it). Sometimes there's live entertainment. **Café St-Michel** (✉ 503 rue Principale Ouest, ☎ 819/868–1062), in a century-old building on the northeastern corner of the main street, is a cheery pub that serves Tex-Mex food and imported and local beers. *Chansonniers* (singers) belt out popular hits for a full house every weekend. **Le Chat du Moulinier** (✉ 101 rue du Moulin, ☎ 819/868–5678) is a hot spot in a cool location: a former factory on the waterfront. The jazz club (it also serves food) has exposed beams, exposed-brick walls with climbing vines, and a concrete dance floor with a grand piano in the center. **La Grosse Pomme** (✉ 270 rue Principale Ouest, ☎ 819/843–9365) is a multilevel complex with huge video screens, dance floors, and restaurant service. The **Liquor Store** (✉ 101 rue du Moulin, ☎ 819/868–4279), a dance club below Le Chat du Moulinier jazz club, has live entertainment. The huge windows, which illuminated the former factory building, give panoramic views of Lac Memphrémagog.

THE ARTS

Le Vieux Clocher de Magog (✉ 64 rue Merry Nord, ☎ 819/847–0470, WEB www.vieuxclocher.com) is one of two former churches converted into theaters by local impresario Bernard Caza. It headlines well-known comedians and singers. Most performances are in French, but big names, such as Jim Corcoran and Michel Rivard, perform here from time to time.

Outdoor Activities and Sports

GOLF

Golf du Mont Orford (✉ 3074 chemin du Parc, ☎ 819/843–5688, WEB www.mt-orford.com) is a venerable course—it was laid out in 1939. The 18-hole, par-70, 6,287-yard course winds around undulating, forested land; from many of the greens you can see the peak of Mont-Orford. Greens fees are $13–$35.

Golf Owl's Head (✉ 181 chemin du Mont Owl's Head, Mansonville, ☎ 450/292–3666 or 800/363–3342), close to the Vermont border, offers spectacular views. Laid out with undulating fairways and bent-grass greens and 64 sand bunkers, the 6,705-yard, 18-hole course (par-72), designed by Graham Cooke, is surrounded by mountain scenery. It's considered one of the best courses in Canada, and its club house, a stunning timber and fieldstone structure with five fireplaces and 45-ft-high ceilings, is a favorite watering hole for locals and visitors alike. Greens fees are $21–$45.

The **Manoir des Sables golf course** (✉ 90 av. des Jardins, Magog-Orford, ☎ 819/847–4299 or 800/567–3514, WEB www.hotel.manoirdessables.com) is a 6,120-yard, 18-hole, par-71 course built on a sandy base. You can play nine holes with a pro for $50.

SKIING

Owl's Head Ski Area (✉ Rte. 243 S; Autoroute 10, Exit 106; ☎ 450/292–3342 or 800/363–3342, WEB www.owlshead.com), on the Knowlton side of Lake Memphrémagog, is great for skiers seeking sparser crowds. It has seven lifts, a 1,782-ft vertical drop, and 41 trails, including a 4-km (2½-mi) intermediate run, the longest in the Eastern Townships.

North Hatley

⑲ *134 km (83 mi) east of Montréal.*

North Hatley, the small resort town on the tip of lovely Lac Massaw-ippi, has a theater and excellent inns and restaurants. Set among hills and farms, it was discovered by well-to-do vacationers early in the 20th century and has been drawing people ever since. A number of events such as "The Springtime in Music" series (early April–mid-June), con-certs held in Ste-Elizabeth church, and the North Hatley Antique Show (early July) are additional attractions.

Dining and Lodging

$–$$ ✕ **Café de Lafontaine.** A casual neighborhood spot, this café has a great atmosphere and attracts an artsy clientele. The food is on the light side—soups, salads, pastas, and the like—but on Saturday nights October through May, more-formal dinners are served and live entertainers (mostly from Montréal) come to play for the locals. The music pro-gram is eclectic—and so is the crowd. Recent lineups have included a Cuban trio, a Celtic group, and a jazz duo that played piano and dou-ble bass. ☒ *35 rue Principale,* ☎ *819/842–4242. MC, V.*

$–$$ ✕ **Pilsen Pub.** Québec's earliest microbrewery no longer brews beer on-site, but Massawippi pale and brown ales and a vast selection of microbrews and imports are on tap at this lively spot. Good pub food—pasta, homemade soups, burgers, and the like—is served in the upstairs restaurant and in the tavern, both of which overlook the water. ☒ *55 rue Principale,* ☎ *819/842–2971. AE, MC, V.*

$$$$ ✕⌂ **Auberge Hatley.** As befits a member of the prestigious Relais & ★   Châteaux chain, the service at this intimate and elegant country inn is consistently good. Some guest rooms in the 1903 country manor have whirlpool baths and fireplaces. Chef Alain Labrie specializes in re-gional dishes and has won numerous awards. The menu changes sea-sonally: the rich foie gras, piglet, and venison are recommended when available. Herbs and vegetables are grown in the inn's hydroponic greenhouse and turn up everywhere—there's even a carrot marmalade and a basil sherbet. You can dine in a corner of the kitchen, at the "chef's table," on weekends and watch the behind-the-scenes goings-on. The sommelier in charge of the more than 1,300 wines here is highly respected worldwide. ☒ *325 chemin Virgin, C.P. 330, J0B 2C0,* ☎ *819/842–2451 or 800/336–2451,* FAX *819/842–2907,* WEB *www.aubergehatley.com. 25 rooms. Restaurant, cable TV, pool, massage, boating, bicycles, hiking, Internet, meeting rooms; no kids under 7. AE, MC, V. Closed Jan. MAP.*

$$$$ ✕⌂ **Manoir Hovey.** Overlooking Lac Massawippi, this retreat maintains ★   the ambience of a private estate and provides the activities of a resort—many included in the room rates. Built in 1900, the manor was mod-eled after George Washington's home at Mount Vernon. Each guest room has a mix of antiques and more-modern wood furniture, richly printed fabrics, and lace trimmings; many have fireplaces and private balconies overlooking the lake. The restaurant serves exquisite Continental and French cuisine; try the endive–and–goat cheese tatin, fruit with cheese from the Benedictine Abbey, or sautéed venison loin with mushroom stuff-ing. There's also a light menu and a sommelier menu (six courses and six wines). ☒ *575 chemin Hovey, J0B 2C0,* ☎ *819/842–2421 or 800/ 661–2421,* FAX *819/842–2248,* WEB *www.manoirhovey.com. 40 rooms, 3 suites, 1 4-bedroom cottage. Restaurant, cable TV, tennis court, pool, beach, massage, mountain bikes, cross-country skiing, ice-skating, 2 bars, library, Internet, meeting rooms. AE, DC, MC, V. MAP.*

$–$$ ✕⌂ **Auberge Le Saint-Amant.** The cozy, 19th-century home is perched on a hill overlooking Lac Massawippi. Rooms at this B&B are hung with plants and furnished with antiques. The restaurant, which has a fireplace, seats about 50 people, but the food would do justice to a much bigger and fancier establishment. Jean-Claude, the chef-owner, whips up sophisticated fare at reasonable prices: rabbit terrine, sorrel-flavored salmon, sweetbreads in raspberry-vinegar sauce, and rack of lamb with cedar jelly. ✉ *3 chemin Côte Minton, J0B 2C0,* ☎ *819/842–1211. 3 rooms. Restaurant, pool, Internet, meeting rooms; no air-conditioning in some rooms, no room TVs. MC, V. MAP.*

Nightlife and the Arts

The **Piggery** (✉ 215 chemin Simard, off Rte. 108, ☎ 819/842–2432 or 819/842–2431, ⚏ www.piggery.com), a theater that was once a pig barn, reigns supreme in the Townships' cultural life. The venue, which has an on-site restaurant, often presents new plays by Canadian playwrights and experiments with bilingual productions. The season runs July through mid-September.

L'Association du Festival du Lac Massawippi (☎ 819/823–7810) presents an annual antiques and folk-art show in July. The association also sponsors classical music concerts at the Église Ste-Elizabeth in North Hatley on Sundays from late April through June and presents lively Sunday-afternoon band concerts at Dreamland Park June through August.

Sherbrooke

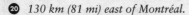 *130 km (81 mi) east of Montréal.*

The region's unofficial capital and largest city is Sherbrooke, named in 1818 for Canadian governor general Sir John Coape Sherbrooke. It was founded by Loyalists in the 1790s along the St-François River.

Sherbrooke has a number of art galleries and museums, including the **Musée des Beaux-Arts de Sherbrooke.** This fine-arts museum has a permanent exhibit tracing the history of art in the region from 1800 to the present. Changing shows display the works of regional artists. ✉ *241 rue Dufferin,* ☎ *819/821–2115.* ⚏ *$8.* ☉ *Tues. and Thurs.–Sun. 11–5, Wed. 11–9.*

The **Sherbrooke Tourist Information Center** (✉ 3010 King St. W, ☎ 819/821–1919) conducts animated tours, mainly in French, for groups from late June through early September. Call for reservations.

Sugar shacks near Sherbrooke give tours of their maple-syrup-producing operations in spring (call before visiting). **La Ferme Martinette** (✉ 1728 chemin Martineau, Coaticook, ☎ 819/849–7089 or 888/881–4561, ⚏ www.lafermemartinette.com), in the heart of Québec's dairy country, hosts "sugaring off" parties with traditional menus in March and April. Lisa Nadeau and her husband, Gérald Martineau, have 2,500 maple trees as well as a herd of 50 Holsteins. You can tour the farm in a trailer pulled by the tractor that belonged to Gérald's grandfather and fill up on the $16.95 all-you-can-eat traditional meal.

One of the oldest, most traditional maple-syrup operations in the Eastern Townships is **Sucrerie des Normand** (✉ 426 George Bonnalie, Eastman, ☎ 450/297–2659, ⚏ www.acbm.qc.ca/sucrerie), run by a third-generation farmer, Richard Normand. In Eastman, about a half-hour drive west of Sherbrooke, the farm is spread over 250 acres of wooded land (there are 9,000 maple trees). Visitors, who tour the property in horse-drawn carriages, can watch the "sugaring off" process—from the tapping of trees to the rendering down of the sweet liquid into this syrup and sugar. After the tour, Richard and his wife, Marlene, serve traditional Québecois food in a wood cabin, to the sounds of the harmonica and spoons.

Dining and Lodging

$$–$$$$ ✕ **La Falaise St-Michel.** A warmly decorated redbrick and wood room takes off any chill even before you sit down. Chef, and part-owner, Patrick Laigniel serves superb French cuisine. A large selection of wines complements the table d'hôte. Menu offerings at this award-winning restaurant, considered to be one of the best in town, include lamb, salmon, and Barbary duck. ⊠ *100 rue Webster (behind Banque Nationale),* ☎ *819/346–6339,* WEB *www.falaisestmichel.com. AE, DC, MC, V.*

$$–$$$ ✕ **Restaurant au P'tit Sabot.** The chef-owner of this establishment is a woman (still an uncommon occurrence in this part of the country); Anne-Marie Eloy designs adventurous menus using local ingredients such as wild boar, quail, and bison. The emphasis is on French cuisine; Anne-Marie is yet another local chef who hails from France. The serene decor and small dining area (it seats around 35 people) create an intimate, romantic atmosphere—a pleasant refuge from the busy and not very attractive shopping strip. ⊠ *1410 rue King Ouest,* ☎ *819/ 563–0262. AE, DC, MC, V.*

$ ⊞ **Bishop's University.** If you're on a budget, these students' residences, 5 km (3 mi) south of Sherbrooke, are a great place to stay in summer. The prices can't be beat, and the location near Sherbrooke is good for touring. The university's lovely grounds have architecture reminiscent of stately New England campuses. The 1857 Gothic-style chapel, paneled with richly carved ash, shows fine local craftsmanship. Reservations for summer guests are accepted as early as September, so book in advance. ⊠ *Box 5000, rue College, Lennoxville J1M 1Z7,* ☎ *819/822–9651,* FAX *819/822–9615,* WEB *www.ubishops.ca. 438 rooms, 10 apts. Restaurant, 9-hole golf course, tennis courts, indoor pool, gym. MC, V. Closed Sept.–mid-May.*

Nightlife and the Arts

The 600-seat **Centennial Theatre** (⊠ rue College, Lennoxville, ☎ 819/ 822–9692) at Bishop's University in Lennoxville, 5 km (3 mi) south of Sherbrooke, presents a roster of jazz, classical, and rock concerts, as well as opera, dance, mime, and children's theater. **Le Vieux Clocher de Sherbrooke** (⊠ 1590 rue Galt Ouest, ☎ 819/822–2102, WEB www.vieuxclocher.com), in a converted church, presents music, from classical to jazz, and a variety of theater and comedy.

Notre-Dame-des-Bois

㉑ *204 km (127 mi) east of Montréal.*

The big draw here is the observatory. Both amateur stargazers and serious astronomers are drawn to **Astrolab du Mont-Mégantic** (Mont-Mégantic's Observatory), in a beautifully wild and mountainous area. The observatory is at the summit of the Townships' second-highest mountain (3,601 ft), whose northern face records annual snowfalls rivaling any other in North America. A joint venture by the University of Montréal and Laval University, the observatory has a powerful telescope that allows scientists to observe celestial bodies 10 million times smaller than the human eye can detect. At the welcome center on the mountain's base, you can view an exhibition and a multimedia show to learn about the night sky. ⊠ *189 Rte. du Parc,* ☎ *819/888–2941,* WEB *www.astrolab.qc.ca.* ⊠ *$10, summit tour $12.* ☉ *Mid-May–early Sept., daily 10–7; summit tour: late June–early Sept., daily 8–11 PM.*

Dining and Lodging

$–$$ ✕⊞ **Aux Berges de l'Aurore.** Although this tiny B&B has attractive furnishings and spectacular views (it sits at the foot of Mont-Mégantic), the draw is the inn's cuisine. The restaurant ($$$$) serves a six-course meal using produce from the inn's huge garden, as well as local

wild game: boar, fish, hare, and caribou. ✉ *139 route du Parc,* ☎ *819/
888–2715,* WEB *www.auberge-aurore.qc.ca. 5 rooms. Restaurant, meeting rooms; no air-conditioning, no room TVs, no kids under 12. MC,
V. Closed Jan.–May.*

CHARLEVOIX

Stretching along the St. Lawrence River's north shore, east of Québec
City to the Saguenay River, Charlevoix embraces mountains rising from
the sea and a succession of valleys, plateaus, and cliffs cut by waterfalls, brooks, and streams. It was named the first populated UNESCO
World Biosphere Reserve in the world, in recognition of its unique combination of nature and culture. The roads wind into villages of picturesque houses and huge tin-roof churches. The area has attracted
summer visitors and artists for more than a century. In winter there
are opportunities for both downhill and cross-country skiing.

New France's first historian, the Jesuit priest François-Xavier de
Charlevoix, gave his name to the region. Charlevoix (pronounced
sharle-*vwah*) was first explored by Jacques Cartier, who landed in
1535, although the first colonists didn't arrive until well into the 17th
century. They developed a thriving shipbuilding industry, specializing
in the sturdy schooner called a *goélette,* which they used to haul everything from logs to lobsters up and down the coast in the days before
rail and paved roads. By the early 20th century, tourism had overtaken
shipbuilding as the backbone of the provincial economy; today wrecked
and forgotten goélettes lie along beaches in the region.

Ste-Anne-de-Beaupré

㉒ *33 km (20 mi) east of Québec City.*

On Route 138 approaching Charlevoix from Québec City is the tiny
town Ste-Anne-de-Beaupré, named for Québec's patron saint. Each year
more than a million pilgrims visit the region's most famous religious
★ site, the **Basilique Ste-Anne-de-Beaupré,** dedicated to the mother of the
Virgin Mary. The basilica is surrounded by aged, modest homes and
tacky souvenir shops that emphasize its grandeur.

The French brought their devotion to St. Anne (the patron saint of those
in shipwrecks) with them when they sailed across the Atlantic to New
France. In 1650 Breton sailors caught in a storm vowed to erect a chapel
in honor of this patron saint at the exact spot where they landed. The
present-day neo-Roman basilica constructed in 1923 was the fifth to
be built on the site where the sailors first touched ground. According
to local legend, St. Anne was responsible over the years for saving voy-
agers from shipwrecks in the harsh waters of the St. Lawrence. Trib-
utes to her miraculous powers can be seen in the shrine's various
mosaics, murals, altars, and ceilings. A bas-relief at the entrance depicts St. Anne welcoming her pilgrims, and ceiling mosaics represent
her life. Numerous crutches and braces posted on the back pillars
have been left by those who have felt the saint's healing powers.

The basilica, in the shape of a Latin cross, has two granite steeples jutting from its gigantic structure. Its interior has 22 chapels and 18 altars, as well as round arches and numerous ornaments in the Romanesque
style. The 214 stained-glass windows, completed in 1949 by French-
men Auguste Labouret and Pierre Chaudière, tell a story of salvation
through personages who were believed to be instruments of God over
the centuries. Other features of the shrine are intricately carved wood
pews decorated with various animals and several smaller altars (behind the main altar) dedicated to different saints.

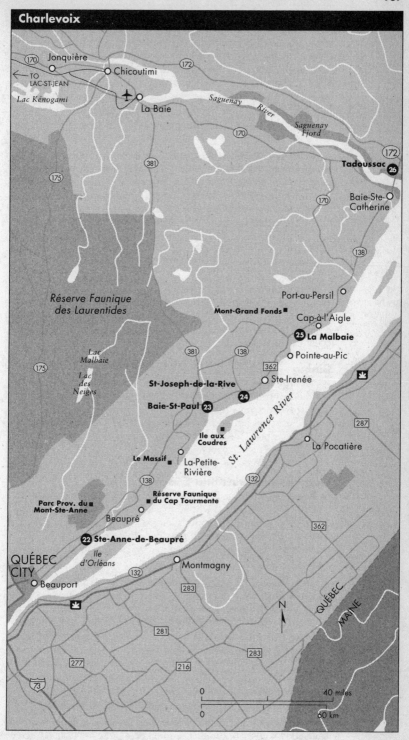

Charlevoix

170 Jonquière
Chicoutimi
172
← TO LAC-ST-JEAN
Lac Kénogami
La Baie
Saguenay River
170
Saguenay Fjord
172
381
Tadoussac 26
175
170
Baie-Ste-Catherine
138
Réserve Faunique
des Laurentides
Port-au-Persil
Mont-Grand Fonds ■
Cap-à-l'Aigle
25 La Malbaie
381
138
362
Pointe-au-Pic
Lac Malbaie
175
Lac des Neiges
St-Joseph-de-la-Rive
24
Ste-Irenée
Baie-St-Paul 23
St. Lawrence River
287
■ Ile aux Coudres
Le Massif ■
La-Petite-Rivière
La Pocatière
138
132
Réserve Faunique
du Cap Tourmente ■
362
Parc Prov. du ■
Mont-Ste-Anne
Beaupré
22 Ste-Anne-de-Beaupré
QUÉBEC CITY
Ile d'Orléans
Beauport
132
Montmagny
283
QUÉBEC
MAINE
N
281
277
283
73
216

0 _____ 40 miles
0 _____ 60 km

The original 17th-century wood chapel was built too close to the St. Lawrence and was swept away by river flooding. In 1676 the chapel was replaced by a stone church that was visited by pilgrims for more than a century, but this structure was demolished in 1872. The first basilica, which replaced the stone church, was destroyed by a fire in 1922. The following year architects Maxime Rosin from Paris and Louis N. Audet from Québec province designed the basilica that now stands. ⊠ *10018 av. Royale,* ☎ *418/827–3781.* ⊡ *Free.* ☉ *Reception booth May–Sept. 1, daily 6:30–9; Sept.–Apr., daily 6:30–5. Guided tours daily at 1 in summer; Sept.–mid-May, call to arrange tour.*

At the **Rèserve Faunique du Cap Tourmente** (Cap Tourmente Wildlife Reserve), about 8 km (5 mi) northeast of Ste-Anne-de-Beaupré, more than 800,000 greater snow geese gather every October and May, with an average of 100,000 per day. The park harbors hundreds of kinds of birds and mammals and more than 700 plant species. This enclave on the north shore of the St. Lawrence River has 18 km (11 mi) of hiking trails; naturalists give guided tours. ⊠ *St-Joachim,* ☎ *418/827–4591 Apr.–Oct., 418/827–3776 Nov.–Mar.* ⊡ *$5.* ☉ *Jan.–Oct., daily 8:30–5.*

OFF THE
BEATEN PATH

RÉSERVE FAUNIQUE DES LAURENTIDES – A wildlife reserve with good lakes for fishing, Réserve Faunique des Laurentides is approximately 48 km (30 mi) north of Québec City via Route 175. It's advisable to reserve a slot 48 hours ahead by phone or fax. ☎ *418/528–6868, 418/890–6527 fishing reservations,* ℻ *418/528–8833.*

Dining

$$$ ✕ **Auberge Baker.** A restaurant in a 150-year-old French-Canadian farmhouse blends the best of old and new. Antiques and old-fashioned woodstoves decorate the dining rooms, where you can sample traditional Québecois fare such as tourtière, pork hocks, meatball stew, and maple-sugar pie. The adventurous can opt for more-exotic dishes, including grilled ostrich with fir sauce. ⊠ *8790 chemin Royale, Château-Richer,* ☎ *418/824–4478 or 866/824–4478. AE, MC, V.*

Outdoor Activities and Sports

Le Massif (⊠ 1350 rue Principale, Petite-Rivière St-François, ☎ 418/632–5876 or 877/536–2774, ⟨WEB⟩ www.lemassif.com) is a three-peak ski resort that has the province's longest vertical drop—2,525 ft. The 20 trails (there are three lifts) are divided into runs for different levels, including one for extremely advanced skiers. Equipment can be rented on-site.

Mont-Ste-Anne (⊠ 2000 blvd. Beaupré, ☎ 418/827–4561 or 800/463–1568, ⟨WEB⟩ www.mont-sainte-anne.com), outside Québec City, is on the World Cup downhill circuit. It's one of the largest resorts in eastern Canada, with a vertical drop of 2,050 ft, 56 downhill trails, two halfpipes for snowboarders, a terrain park, and 13 lifts including a gondola. Cross-country skiing is also a draw here, with 21 trails totaling 224 km (139 mi). When the weather warms, mountain biking becomes the sport of choice. Enthusiasts can choose from 200 km (124 mi) of mountain-bike trails, 14 downhill runs (and a gondola to get back up to the top). Three bike runs are designated as "extreme zones."

Snowmobiles can be rented at **Centre de Location de Motoneiges du Québec** (15 blvd. Beaupré, Beaupré, ☎ 418/827–8478, ⟨WEB⟩ www.locationmotoneiges.com), near Mont Ste-Anne, starting at $60 per person (two to a snowmobile) for an hour or $180 per person for the day, including equipment.

Baie-St-Paul

❷❸ *60 km (37 mi) northeast of Ste-Anne-de-Beaupré.*

Baie-St-Paul, one of the oldest towns in the province, is popular with craftspeople and artists. The village, with its centuries-old mansard-roofed houses, sits by a river, on a wide plain encircled by high hills.

Boutiques and a handful of commercial galleries line the historic narrow streets in the town center; most have original artwork and handicrafts for sale. In addition, each August, more than a dozen artists from across Canada take part in "Symposium of Modern Art." The themes are different each time and the artists work together to create a giant canvas.

Jean-Paul Lemieux, Clarence Gagnon, and many more of Québec's greatest landscape artists depicted the area, and some of these works are for sale at the **Centre d'Art Baie-St-Paul** (⊠ 4 rue Ambroise-Fafard, ☎ 418/435–3681). The **Centre d'Exposition de Baie-St-Paul** (⊠ 23 rue Ambroise-Fafard, ☎ 418/435–3681, ⬛ $3) has rotating exhibits and programs, and it displays the work of various artists, some of them from the region.

Dining and Lodging

$$$–$$$$ ✕⊡ **Auberge la Maison Otis.** The calm and romantic accommodations
★   of this inn are housed in three buildings (the restaurant is in an old stone house) in the center of the village. Some of the country-style rooms have whirlpools, fireplaces, and antique furnishings. The restaurant ($$$$) serves creative, regionally oriented French cuisine, such as *ballotine de faisan,* pheasant stuffed with quail and served in venison sauce. The elegant, Norman-style house, which dates back to the mid-1850s, has a huge fireplace. ⊠ *23 rue St-Jean-Baptiste, G3Z 1M2,* ☎ *418/435–2255 or 800/267–2254,* ℻ *418/435–2464,* ⬛ *www.maisonotis.com. 30 rooms, 4 suites. Restaurant, cable TV, indoor pool, sauna, lounge, piano bar, Internet, meeting rooms; some pets allowed (fee). MC, V. MAP.*

En Route   From Baie-St-Paul, drivers have a choice of the open, scenic coastal drive on **Route 362** or the faster Route 138 to Pointe-au-Pic, La Malbaie, and Cap-à-l'Aigle. This section of Route 362 has memorable views of rolling hills—green, white, or ablaze with fiery hues, depending on the season—meeting the broad expanse of the "sea," as the locals like to call the St. Lawrence estuary.

St-Joseph-de-la-Rive

❷❹ *19 km (12 mi) northeast of Baie-St-Paul.*

A secondary road descends sharply into St-Joseph-de-la-Rive, with its line of old houses hugging the mountain base on the narrow shore road. The town has a number of peaceful inns and inviting restaurants. The small **Exposition Maritime** (Maritime Museum), in an old shipyard, commemorates the days of the St. Lawrence goélettes, the feisty little schooners that, until the 1950s, were the lifeblood of the region. In the mid-20th century, the roads through Charlevoix were little more than rugged tracks. (Indeed, they are still narrow and winding and are being upgraded.) Entire, very large families lived in cramped conditions aboard the boats. To modern eyes, it doesn't look like it was a comfortable existence, but the folklore of the goélettes, celebrated in poetry, paintings, and song, is part of the strong cultural identity of the region. ⊠ *305 place de l'Église,* ☎ *418/635–1131.* ⬛ *$3.* ⊙ *Mid-May–mid-June, weekdays 9–4, weekends 11–4; mid-June–Sept. 1, daily 9–5.*

A free, government-run ferry from the wharf in St-Joseph-de-la-Rive takes you on the 15-minute trip to **Île aux Coudres** (☎ 418/438–2743 ferry information), an island where Jacques Cartier's men gathered *coudres* (hazelnuts) in 1535. Since then, the island has produced many a goélette, and the families of former captains now run several small inns. Larger inns have folk-dance evenings. You can bike around the island (26 km/16 mi) and see windmills and water mills, or stop at boutiques selling paintings and handicrafts such as traditional handwoven household linens.

Lodging

$–$$ ⊡ **Hôtel Cap-aux-Pierres.** The traditional Canadian main building of this
★ hotel has a long veranda with river views. Comfortable accommodations also are available in a motel section, open only in summer. About a third of the rooms have river views. The hotel is one of several properties in the region run by the large, entrepreneurial Dufour family. The family has been in the business since the 1930s, when Louis Dufour and his wife, Alvine Desmeules, started taking in paying guests as a way to raise money to help support their 17 children. The restaurant serves a mix of Québec standards and French cuisine, and summer entertainment includes folk dancing on Saturday evening. ⊠ *246 chemin la Baleine, La Baleine, Île aux Coudres G0A 2A0,* ☎ *418/438–2711 or 800/463–5250,* FAX *418/438–2127,* WEB *www.hotelcapauxpierres.com. 98 rooms. Restaurant, miniature golf, tennis court, indoor-outdoor pool, spa, shuffleboard, bar, Internet, meeting rooms, some pets allowed (fee). AE, DC, MC, V. EP.*

Shopping

Papeterie St-Gilles (⊠ 354 rue F. A. Savard, ☎ 418/635–2430) produces handcrafted stationery using a 17th-century process. The paper factory, which is also a small museum, explains through photographs and demonstrations how paper is manufactured the old-fashioned way. Slivers of wood and flower petals are pressed into the paper sheets, which are as thick as the covers of a paperback book. The finished products—made into writing paper, greeting cards, and one-page poems or quotations—make beautiful, if pricey, gifts.

La Malbaie

㉕ *35 km (22 mi) northeast of St-Joseph-de-la-Rive.*

La Malbaie, one of the province's most elegant and historically interesting resort towns, was known as Murray Bay in an earlier era when wealthy Anglophones summered here and in the neighboring villages: Pointe-au-Pic, 3 km (2 mi) to the south, and Cap-à-l'Aigle, 3 km (2 mi) to the north. This area became popular with both American and Canadian politicians in the late 1800s when Ottawa Liberals and Washington Republicans partied decorously through the summer with members of the Québec judiciary. William Howard Taft built the "summer White House," the first of three summer residences in Pointe-au-Pic in 1894, when he was the American civil governor of the Philippines. He became the 27th president of the United States in 1908.

Now many Taft-era homes serve as handsome inns, guaranteeing an old-fashioned coddling, with such extras as breakfast in bed, whirlpool baths, and free shuttles to the ski areas in winter. Many serve lunch and dinner to nonresidents, so you can tour the area going from one gourmet delight to the next. The cuisine, as elsewhere in Québec, is genuine French or regional fare.

Musée de Charlevoix traces the region's history as a vacation spot in a series of exhibits and has been developing an excellent collection of local paintings and folk art. The museum's mission statement—"one museum, one passion: the people of this place"—pretty much sums up local pride. ⊠ *10 chemin du Havre, Pointe-au-Pic,* ☎ *418/665–4411.* ⬚ *$4.* ☽ *Late June–early Sept., daily 10–6; early Sept.–late June, Tues.–Fri. 10–5, weekends 1–5.*

The **Casino de Charlevoix,** one of three highly profitable gaming halls (the others are in Montréal and Hull), is operated by Loto-Québec, a province-owned lottery corporation. This is the smallest of the casinos, but it still hauls in almost 1 million visitors a year—some of them from Japan and Germany who stay at the Fairmont Le Manoir Richelieu, which is connected by a tunnel. There are 22 gaming tables and 780 slot machines. Minimum age is 18. ⊠ *Fairmont Le Manoir Richelieu, 183 rue Richelieu,* ☎ *418/665–5300 or 800/665–2274,* ⟨WEB⟩ *www.casino-de-charlevoix.com.* ☽ *Sun.–Thurs. 10 AM–2 AM, Fri.–Sat. 10 AM–3 AM.*

Dining and Lodging

$$$$ ✕⌂ **Auberge des 3 Canards.** The inn has made a name for itself in the region, not only for its accommodations but also for its fine restaurant. Rooms in a rustic-chic style have wicker furniture, brass beds, pine dressers, and chintz curtains; all have balconies and views over the St. Lawrence. In the restaurant, you might have boneless guinea fowl with maple syrup–and–spicy mustard sauce; maple-sugar pie and maple-flavored mousse are sweet dessert treats. ⊠ *115 côte Bellevue, Pointe-au-Pic G5A 1Y2,* ☎ *418/665–3761 or 800/461–3761,* ⟨FAX⟩ *418/ 665–4727,* ⟨WEB⟩ *www.auberge3canards.com. 34 rooms, 8 suites. Restaurant, cable TV, putting green, tennis court, pool, Internet, meeting rooms; no air-conditioning. AE, DC, MC, V. MAP.*

$$$–$$$$ ✕⌂ **Auberge la Pinsonnière.** An atmosphere of country luxury pre-
★ vails at this Relais & Châteaux inn with an impressive art collection. Every guest room is different—some have fireplaces, whirlpools, and king-size four-poster beds—but all overlook Murray Bay on the St. Lawrence River. The restaurant ($$$$) is excellent, and the auberge has one of the largest wine cellars in North America, housing 12,000 bottles. The haute cuisine doesn't come cheap; the appetizers, including foie gras with pear confit, duck ravioli, warm smoked-salmon salad, and braised sweetbreads, cost as much as the entrées in other establishments, but the dining experience is well worth the money. ⊠ *124 rue St-Raphael, Cap-à-l'Aigle G5A 1X9,* ☎ *418/665–4431 or 800/ 387–4431,* ⟨FAX⟩ *418/665–7156,* ⟨WEB⟩ *www.lapinsonniere.com. 25 rooms, 1 suite. 2 restaurants, cable TV, tennis court, indoor pool, spa, beach, 3 lounges, Internet, meeting rooms; no-smoking rooms. AE, MC, V. EP.*

$$$–$$$$ ⌂ **Fairmont Le Manoir Richelieu.** The Richelieu, an imposing castlelike
★ building sitting amid trees on a cliff overlooking the St. Lawrence River, has been offering first-class accommodations for nearly a century. Constructed in 1929 on the site of an earlier property, the hotel retains a classic elegance. There is a clubby after-dinner lounge where guests can smoke cigars and drink single malts or vintage ports, and the restaurants offer a wide range of food—from family fare to haute cuisine. The full-service spa has 22 treatment rooms, and the links-style golf course overlooks the St. Lawrence. A tunnel links the hotel to the Casino de Charlevoix. ⊠ *181 rue Richelieu, Pointe-au-Pic, G5A 1X7,* ☎ *418/665– 3703 or 800/463–2613,* ⟨FAX⟩ *418/665–3093,* ⟨WEB⟩ *www.fairmont.com. 405 rooms. 3 restaurants, TVs with movies and video games, 18-hole golf course, miniature golf, tennis court, 1 indoor and 1 outdoor pool, sauna, spa, mountain bikes, croquet, horseshoes, Ping-Pong, shuffle-board, volleyball, cross-country skiing, ice-skating, snowmobiling, bar, lounge, casino, children's programs (ages 4–12), concierge, concierge floor, Internet, meeting rooms, some pets allowed (fee); no-smoking floors. AE, DC, MC, V. EP.*

Nightlife and the Arts

Domaine Forget (⊠ 5 St-Antoine, Ste-Irenée, ☎ 418/452–8111, 418/452–3535, 888/336–7438, WEB www.domaineforget.com) is a music and dance academy with a 600-seat hall in Ste-Irenée, 15 km (9 mi) south of La Malbaie. Fine musicians from around the world, many of whom are teaching or studying at the school, perform during summer evening concerts and Sunday musical brunches. The Domaine also functions as a stopover for traveling musicians, who can take advantage of its rental studios.

Outdoor Activities and Sports

Club de Golf de Manoir Richelieu (⊠ 595 côte Bellevue, Pointe-au-Pic, ☎ 418/665–2526 or 800/463–2613) is a par-71, 6,225-yard, links-style 18-hole course. Greens fees start at $85.

Mont-Grand Fonds (⊠ 1000 chemin des Loisirs, ☎ 418/665–0095 or 877/665–0095, WEB www.quebecweb.com/montgrandfonds), 10 km (6 mi) north of La Malbaie, has 14 downhill slopes, a 1,105-ft vertical drop, and two lifts. It also has 160 km (99 mi) of cross-country trails. Two trails meet International Ski Federation standards, and the ski center hosts major competitions occasionally. Other sports available here are dogsledding, sleigh riding, ice-skating, and tobogganing.

Tadoussac

㉖ *71 km (44 mi) north of La Malbaie.*

The small town of Tadoussac shares the view up the magnificent Saguenay Fjord with Baie-Ste-Catherine across the river. The drive here from La Malbaie, along Route 138, leads past lovely villages and views along the St. Lawrence. Jacques Cartier made a stop at this point in 1535, and from 1600 to the mid-19th century it was an important meeting site for fur traders. Whale-watching excursions and cruises of the fjord now depart from Tadoussac, as well as from Chicoutimi, farther up the deep fjord.

As the Saguenay River flows from Lac St-Jean south toward the St. Lawrence, it has a dual character: Between Alma and Chicoutimi, the once rapidly flowing river has been harnessed for hydroelectric power; in its lower section, it becomes wider and deeper and flows by steep mountains and cliffs en route to the St. Lawrence. The small white beluga whale breeds in the lower portion of the Saguenay in summer. The many marine species that live in the confluence of the fjord and the seaway attract other whales, too, such as pilots, finbacks, humpbacks, and blues.

Sadly, the beluga is an endangered species; the whales, with 27 other species of mammals and birds and 17 species of fish, are being threatened by pollution in the St. Lawrence River. This has inspired a $100 million project funded by both the federal and provincial governments. The 800-square-km (309-square-mi) **Parc Marine du Saguenay–St-Laurent** (park office: ⊠ 182 rue de l'Église, ☎ 418/235–4703 or 800/463–6769), a marine park at the confluence of the Saguenay and St. Lawrence rivers, has been created to protect the latter's fragile ecosystem.

You can learn more about the whales and their habitat at the **Centre d'Interprétation des Mammifères Marin.** The interpretation center is run by members of a locally based research team and they're only too glad to answer questions. In addition, explanatory videos and exhibits (including a collection of whale skeletons) tell you everything there is to know about the mighty cetaceans. Whale news is posted at www.whales-online.net. ⊠ *108 rue Cale-Sèche,* ☎ *418/235–4701.* ⊠ *$5.50.* ☉ *July–Oct., daily 9–8; winter, daily noon–5.*

Outdoor Activities and Sports

Croisières AML (☎ 418/692–1159, 800/463–1292 July–Sept., WEB www.croisieresaml.com) offers three-hour whale-watching tours ($45). Cruises, in Zodiacs or larger boats, depart from Baie-Ste-Catherine and Tadoussac. The best period for seeing whales is July through September, although some operators extend the season at either end if whales are around.

THE GASPÉ PENINSULA

Jutting into the stormy Gulf of St. Lawrence like the battered prow of a ship, the Gaspé Peninsula (Gaspésie in French) remains an isolated region of unsurpassed wild beauty. Sheer cliffs tower above broad beaches, and tiny coastal fishing communities cling to the shoreline. Inland rise the Chic-Choc Mountains, eastern Canada's highest, the realm of woodland caribou, black bear, and moose. Townspeople in some areas speak mainly English.

The Gaspé was on Jacques Cartier's itinerary—he first stepped ashore in North America in the town of Gaspé in 1534—but Vikings, Basques, and Portuguese fishermen had come before. The area's history is told in countless towns en route. Acadians, displaced by the British from New Brunswick in 1755, settled Bonaventure; Paspébiac still has a gunpowder shed built in the 1770s to help defend the peninsula from American ships; and Empire Loyalists settled New Carlisle in 1784.

Today the area still seems unspoiled and timeless, a blessing for anyone dipping and soaring along the spectacular coastal highways or venturing on river-valley roads to the interior. Geographically, the peninsula is among the oldest lands on earth. A vast, mainly uninhabited forest covers the hilly hinterland. Local tourist officials can be helpful in locating outfitters and guides for fishing. The Gaspé has many parks, nature trails, and wildlife sanctuaries. The most accessible include Parc de l'Ile Bonaventure-et-du-Rocher-Percé (Bonaventure Island is a sanctuary for 250,000 birds); Parc National Forillon at the tip of the peninsula, with 50 km (31 mi) of trails and an interesting boardwalk; and the Parc Provincial de la Gaspésie. The provincial park includes the Chic-Choc Mountains and has terrain ranging from tundra to subalpine forest.

Carleton

㉗ *574 km (357 mi) northeast of Québec City.*

Windsurfers and sailors enjoy the breezes around the Gaspé; there are windsurfing marathons in the Baie des Chaleurs each summer.

The **Oratoire Notre-Dame-du-Mont Saint-Joseph** (Notre Dame Oratory), a chapel on Mont-St-Joseph, dominates this French-speaking city. There are lookout points and hiking trails around the site. The views, almost 2,000 ft above Baie des Chaleurs, are lovely.

Dining and Lodging

$–$$$ ✕☑ **Hostelerie Baie-Bleue.** The motel snuggles against a mountain beside the Baie des Chaleurs and has great views. Daily guided bus tours leave from the hotel June through September. In the large restaurant, La Seigneurie, chef Yvan Belzile prepares regional dishes, especially seafood. The table d'hôte won't break your budget, and the wine list is extensive and well chosen. ✉ *482 blvd. Perron, G0C 1J0,* ☎ *418/364–3355 or 800/463–9099,* FAX *418/364–6165,* WEB *www.baiebleue.com. 95 rooms. Restaurant, cable TV, tennis court, pool, beach, Internet, meeting rooms, some pets allowed; no air-conditioning, no-smoking rooms. AE, DC, MC, V.*

Gaspé Peninsula (Gaspésie)

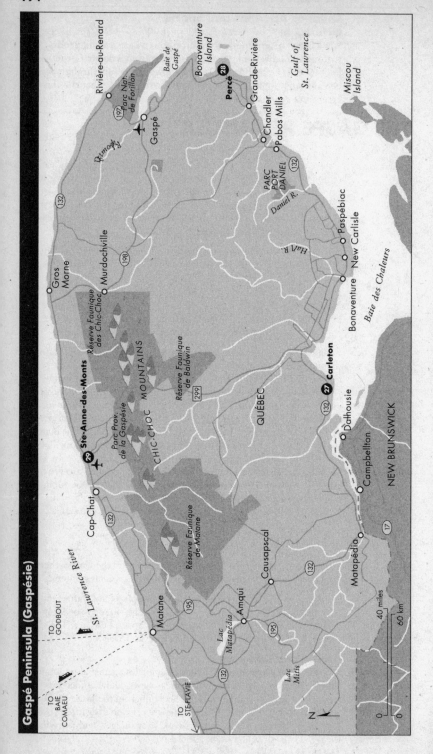

Percé

28 *193 km (120 mi) east of Carleton.*

A pretty fishing village, Percé has a number of attractions and can get busy in summer. The most famous sight in the region is the huge fossil-embedded rock offshore that the sea "pierced" thousands of years ago. There are many pleasant places to walk and hike near town, and it's also possible to do some fishing or take a whale-watching cruise.

★ The largest colony of gannets (large, fish-eating seabirds) in the world summers off Percé on **l'Île Bonaventure** (Bonaventure Island). From the wharf at Percé, you can join an organized tour to the island and walk the trails. Take binoculars and a camera; there are many kinds of seabirds. Several companies offer trips from Percé to Bonaventure Island.

Dining and Lodging

$$$ ✕ **La Sieur de Pabos.** You can get some of the best seafood in the province at this rustic restaurant overlooking Pabos Bay, about 40 km (25 mi) south of Percé. Try the *casserole aux fruits de mer* (seafood casserole) stuffed with shrimps and scallops and encased in potato. ⊠ *325 Rte. 132, Pabos Mills,* ☎ *418/689–4741. AE, DC, MC, V.*

$$$–$$$$ ⊞ **Hôtel La Normandie.** All but four rooms of this split-level motel face the ocean, with views of Percé Rock and Bonaventure Island. The location in the center of town puts shops and restaurants within walking distance; a beach and a municipal pool are also nearby. Third-floor rooms are the most spacious. ⊠ *221 Rte. 132 Ouest, C.P. 129, G0C 2L0,* ☎ *418/782–2112 or 800/463–0820,* FAX *418/782–2337,* WEB *www.normandieperce.com. 45 rooms. Restaurant, cable TV, lounge, Internet, meeting rooms; no air-conditioning. MC, V. Closed Nov.–mid-May. MAP.*

$–$$ ⊞ **La Bonaventure-sur-Mer Hotel.** The waterfront location with views of Percé Rock and Bonaventure Island makes up for the motel-standard decor. Some units have kitchenettes. The restaurant serves mainly beef and seafood dishes. ⊠ *261 Rte. 132, C.P. 339, G0C 2L0,* ☎ *418/ 782–2166 or 800/463–4212,* FAX *418/782–5323,* WEB *www.resperce.com. 90 rooms. Restaurant, cable TV, beach, meeting rooms; no air-conditioning in some rooms, no-smoking rooms. AE, DC, MC, V. Closed mid-Oct.–mid-May.*

$–$$ ⊞ **Motel Hotel La Côte Surprise.** Most rooms at this motel have views of Percé Rock and the village. Decor is standard in both motel and second-floor hotel units, but the private balconies and terraces are a plus. ⊠ *367 Rte. 132 Ouest, C.P. 159, G0C 2L0,* ☎ *418/782–2131 or 866/ 782–2131,* FAX *418/782–2626. 36 rooms. Dining room, snack bar, cable TV, lounge, Internet, meeting rooms, some pets allowed (fee); no air-conditioning, no-smoking rooms. AE, D, DC, MC, V. Closed Oct. 15–May. CP.*

$ ⊞ **Hôtel-Motel Rocher Percé.** The beach is a 10-minute walk from this hostelry. Picnic tables and chairs overlook Percé Rock and the sea. Some guest rooms have kitchenettes and sea views. The art gallery shows the work of local artists. ⊠ *111 Rte. 132 Ouest, C.P. 34, G0C 2L0,* ☎ *418/782–2330 or 888/467–3723,* FAX *418/782–2330. 4 hotel rooms, 14 motel rooms. Kitchenettes (some), some pets allowed, no air-conditioning in some rooms, no room phones, no-smoking rooms. MC, V. Closed Nov.–Apr. CP.*

Ste-Anne-des-Monts

29 *282 km (175 mi) northwest of Percé.*

The area south of this coastal town has Québec's highest peaks, the Chic-Choc Mountains. **Parc Provincial de la Gaspésie** (Gaspé Penin-

sula Provincial Park; ⊠ Rte. 299, ☎ 418/763–3301, WEB
www.sepaq.com) has climbing, heli-skiing, mountain hiking, and na-
ture-interpretation programs such as moose-watching. Overnight accommodation is available in cabins that sleep two to eight people and
are heated by wood-burning stoves. More-primitive huts and campsites also are available.

Lodging

$$ 🏠 **Gîte du Mont-Albert.** In the middle of the Chic-Choc Mountains,
this property is 40 km (25 mi) south of Ste-Anne-des-Monts, in the Parc
Provinçial de la Gaspésie. It's a perfect retreat for hiking, biking, horse-
back riding, or salmon fishing on the Ste-Anne River. The rooms are
similar to what you'd find in a European mountain lodge: basic and
modern, but comfortable. Cottages also are available. ⊠ *2001 Rte. du
Parc, Box 1150, G4V 2E4, ☎ 418/763–2288, 888/270–4483, 866/
727–2427. 48 rooms, 19 cottages. Restaurant, pool, sauna, hiking, cross-
country skiing, bar, meeting rooms; no air-conditioning in some rooms,
no TV in some rooms. AE, DC, MC, V. MAP.*

$ 🏠 **Riôtel Monaco-des-Monts.** This small hotel is near the entrance to
the Parc Provinçial de la Gaspésie and all its activities, from cross-
country skiing to biking; packages including some of the outdoor ac-
tivities are available. Half the rooms are motel-style; the rest are
plain-but-comfortable hotel rooms. The air-conditioned restaurant
is open 6 AM–10 PM. ⊠ *90 blvd. Ste-Anne, G4V 1R3, ☎ 418/763–
3321 or 800/463–7468, WEB www.riotel.com. 46 rooms. Restaurant,
cable TV with movies and video games, bicycles, bar, meeting rooms;
no air-conditioning in some rooms, no-smoking rooms. AE, DC, MC,
V. EP.*

PROVINCE OF QUÉBEC A TO Z

*To research prices, get advice from other travelers, and book travel ar-
rangements, visit www.fodors.com.*

AIR TRAVEL
Montréal and Québec City are the gateway cities.

BIKE TRAVEL
The Green Route, or La Route Verte, a 4,000-km (2,480-mi) path that
will run from northern Québec to the Gaspé and will also link up with
trails in New England and New York, is scheduled to be completed by
2005. More than half of the marked bikeways are already open. For
information and a map, contact Vélo Québec.
➤ CONTACT: **Vélo Québec** (☎ 514/521–8356 or 800/567–8356, WEB
www.routeverte.com).

BUS TRAVEL
Frequent bus service for the province is available from the central bus
station in downtown Montréal. Daily service to Granby, Lac-Mégan-
tic, Magog, and Sherbrooke in the Eastern Townships leaves from the
Montréal central bus station.

Voyageur is a province-wide bus line. Several smaller private compa-
nies also serve the regions and connect with Voyageur. The trip to Gaspé
Peninsula from Montréal takes 13 hours.

Limocar service departs for the Laurentians: L'Annonciation, Mont-
Laurier, Ste-Adèle, Ste-Agathe-des-Monts, and St-Jovite, among other
stops. Limocar also has a service to the Lower Laurentians region (in-

cluding St-Jérôme), departing from the Laval bus terminal at the Henri-Bourassa Métro stop in north Montréal.

➤ CONTACTS: **Limocar** (☎ 450/435–8899). **Montréal central bus station** (✉ 505 blvd. de Maisonneuve Est, Montréal, ☎ 514/842–2281). **Québec bus terminal** (✉ 320 rue Abraham-Martin, Québec City, ☎ 418/525–3000). **Voyageur** (☎ 514/842–2281, WEB www.voyageur.com).

CAR TRAVEL

Major entry points are Ottawa/Hull, U.S. 87 from New York State south of Montréal, U.S. 91 from Vermont into the Eastern Townships area, and the Trans-Canada Highway (Highway 1) just west of Montréal.

Québec has fine roads, and speedy drivers. The major highways are Autoroute des Laurentides 15, a six-lane highway from Montréal to the Laurentians; Autoroute 10 East from Montréal to the Eastern Townships; U.S. 91 from New England, which becomes Autoroute 55 as it crosses the border to the Eastern Townships; and Route 138, which runs from Montréal along the north shore of the St. Lawrence River. Road maps are available at Québec tourist offices.

Autoroute des Laurentides 15 and Route 117—a slower but more scenic secondary road at its northern end—lead to the Laurentians. Exit numbers on Autoroute 15 are the distance in kilometers from Montréal. Try to avoid traveling to and from the region Friday evening or Sunday afternoon, as you're likely to sit in traffic for hours.

Autoroute 10 East heads from Montréal through the Eastern Townships; from New England, U.S. 91 becomes Autoroute 55, a major road.

The main roads through the Charlevoix region are the scenic Route 362 and the faster Route 138.

On the Gaspé Peninsula, the Trans-Canada Highway (Highway 1) runs northeast along the southern shore of the St. Lawrence River to just south of Rivière-du-Loup, where the 270-km (167-mi) Route 132 hugs the dramatic coastline. At Ste-Flavie, follow the southern leg of Route 132. The entire distance around the peninsula is 848 km (526 mi).

EMERGENCIES

➤ CONTACTS: **Ambulance, fire, police** (☎ 911).
➤ HOSPITALS: **Centre Hospitalier de Charlevoix** (✉ 74 rue Ambroise-Fafard, Baie-Saint-Paul, ☎ 418/435–5150). **Centre Hospitalier de Gaspé** (✉ 215 blvd. York Ouest, Gaspé, ☎ 418/368–3301). **Centre Hospitalier Laurentien** (✉ 234 rue Saint-Vincent, Sainte-Agathe-des-Monts, ☎ 819/324–4000). **Centre Universitaire de Santé de l'Estrie** (CUSE; ✉ 560 rue Bowen Sud, Sherbrooke, ☎ 819/346–1110).

LODGING

CAMPING

Inquiries about camping in Québec's national parks should be directed to Canadian Heritage Parks Canada. Contact the individual park administration for camping in provincial parks. For information on camping in the province's private trailer parks and campgrounds, write for the free publication "Québec Camping," available from Tourisme Québec.

➤ CONTACTS: **Canadian Heritage Parks Canada** (✉ Box 6060, Passage du Chien d'Or, Québec City G1R 4V7, ☎ 418/648–4177 or 800/463–6769, WEB www.parkscanada.pch.gc.ca). **Tourisme Québec** (✉ Box 979, Montréal H3C 2W3, ☎ 514/873–2015 or 800/363–7777 or 877/266–5687, WEB www.bonjourquebec.com).

Agricotours, the Québec farm-vacation association, can provide lists of guest farms in the province.

➤ CONTACT: **Agricotours** (✉ 4545 av. Pierre-de-Coubertin, C.P. 1000, Succursale M, Montréal H1V 3R2, ☎ 514/252–3138, WEB www. agricotours.qc.ca).

OUTDOOR ACTIVITIES AND SPORTS

FISHING

Twenty outfitters are members of the Laurentian tourist association. The Fédération des Pourvoyeurs du Québec (Québec Outfitters Federation) has a list of outfitters that is available through tourist offices. Fishing requires a permit, available from the regional offices of the Ministère de l'Environnement et de la Faune (Ministry of the Environment and Wildlife), or at regional sporting-goods stores displaying an "authorized agent" sticker.

➤ CONTACTS: **Fédération des Pourvoyeurs du Québec** (✉ 5237 blvd. Hamel, Bureau 270, Québec City G2E 2H2, ☎ 418/877–5191, WEB www.fpq.com). **Ministère de l'Environnement et de la Faune** (✉ 675 blvd. René-Lévesque Est, Québec City G1R 5V7, ☎ 418/521–3830 or 800/561–1616, WEB www.menv.gouv.qc.ca).

MOUNTAIN CLIMBING

The Fédération Québécoise de la Montagne (Québec Mountain-Climbing Federation) has information about climbing, as do the province's tourist offices.

➤ CONTACT: **Fédération Québécoise de la Montagne** (✉ 4545 rue Pierre-de-Coubertin, C.P. 1000, Succursale M, Montréal H1V 3R2, ☎ 514/252–3004).

RIVER RAFTING

Aventure en Eau Vive, New World River Expeditions, and Aventure Riviere Rouge—specializing in white-water rafting at Rivière Rouge—are on-site at the trip's departure point near Calumet. (To get here, take Route 148 past Calumet; turn onto chemin de la Rivière Rouge until you see the signs for the access road to each rafter's headquarters.) All offer four- to five-hour rafting trips and provide transportation to and from the river site, as well as guides, helmets, life jackets, and, at the end of the trip, a much-anticipated meal. Most have facilities on-site or nearby for dining, drinking, camping, bathing, swimming, hiking, and horseback riding.

➤ CONTACTS: **Aventure en Eau Vive** (☎ 819/242–6084 or 800/567–6881). **Aventure Riviere** Rougè (☎ 450/533–6996 or 888/723–8484). **New World River Expeditions** (☎ 819/242–7238 or 800/361–5033, WEB www.newworld.ca).

SKIING

Lift tickets range from $34 to $52. For information about ski conditions, you can call Tourisme Québec and ask for the ski report.

➤ CONTACT: **Tourisme Québec** (☎ 800/363–7777).

SNOWMOBILING

Regional tourist offices have information about snowmobiling in their area, including snowmobile maps and lists of essential services. Snowmobilers who use trails in Québec must obtain an access pass or day user's pass for the trails. This increasingly popular activity is regulated by the Québec Federation of Snowmobiling Clubs.

Jonview Canada offers snowmobile tours in the Laurentians, in Charlevoix, and as far north as the James Bay region. Other weeklong packages may include dogsledding and ice fishing.

➤ CONTACTS: **Jonview Canada** (✉ 1134 rue Ste-Catherine Ouest, 12th floor, Montréal, ☎ 514/861–9190). **Québec Federation of Snowmobiling Clubs** (✉ Box 1000, 4545 av. Pierre-de-Coubertin, Montréal H1V 3R2, ☎ 514/252–3076).

TOURS

The Montréal Zoological Society is a nature-oriented group that runs lectures, field trips, and weekend excursions. Tours include whale-watching in the St. Lawrence estuary and hiking and bird-watching in national parks throughout Québec, Canada, and the northern United States.

Autocar Dupont-Gray Line leads day excursions along the Côte de Beaupré, with stops at Montmorency Falls and the Ste-Anne-de-Beaupré basilica. The cost is about $35 per person.

Trips from Percé to Bonaventure Island off the Gaspé Peninsula are offered by Croisières Baie de Gaspé and Les Bateliers de Percé.
➤ CONTACTS: **Autocar Dupont-Gray Line** (☎ 418/649–9226). **Les Bateliers de Percé** (☎ 418/782–2974). **Croisières Baie de Gaspé** (☎ 418/892–5500). **Montréal Zoological Society** (☎ 514/845–8317).

TRAIN TRAVEL

The railway line follows the coast. On the south shore, VIA trains stop at Rimouski, Mont-Joli, Matapédia, Carleton, Gaspé, and Percé.
➤ TRAIN INFORMATION: **VIA Rail** (☎ 514/989–2626, 800/361–5390 in Québec, 888/842–7245 outside Québec, WEB www.viarail.ca).

VISITOR INFORMATION

Tourisme Québec can provide information on specific towns' tourist bureaus.

In the Laurentians, the major tourist office is the Association Touristique des Laurentides, just off the Autoroute des Laurentides 15 at Exit 39. The office is open mid-June through August, daily 8:30–8; September to mid-June, Saturday through Thursday 9–5, Friday 9–7. The towns of L'Annonciation, Labelle, Mont-Tremblant, St-Jovite, Ste-Agathe-des-Monts, St-Eustache, St-Adolphe-d'Howard, and Val David have year-round regional tourist offices. Seasonal tourist offices (open mid-June to early September) are in Grenville, Lachute, St-Jérôme, Oka, Notre-Dame-du-Laus, Saint-Sauveur, Sainte-Marguerite-du-Lac-Masson, Nominique, Lac-du-Cerf, and Ferme Neuve.

In the Eastern Townships, year-round regional provincial tourist offices are in Bromont, Granby, Magog-Orford, Sherbrooke, Sutton, Ulverton, and at Exit 68 off Autoroute 10. Seasonal tourist offices (open June to early September) are in Coaticook, Danville, Dunham, Eastman, Frelighsburg, Granby, Lambton, La Patrie, Masonsville, Birchton, Cowansville, Dudswell, Lac-Brome (Foster), Waterloo, and Pike River. The schedules of seasonal bureaus are irregular, so it's a good idea to contact the Association Touristique des Cantons de l'Est before visiting. This association also provides lodging information.

On the way from Québec City to Charlevoix, look for the Beaupré Coast Interpretation Center off Highway 360 in Château-Richer. The old mill Petit-Pré (built in 1695) serves as the backdrop for guides in New France costumes to explain displays on the history of the region. Admission is $2.50. The center is open from mid-June to mid-October, daily 10–5 (by reservation only the rest of the year).
➤ TOURIST INFORMATION: **Association Touristique des Cantons de l'Est** (✉ 20 rue Don Bosco Sud, Sherbrooke J1L 1W4, ☎ 819/820–2020 or 800/355–5755, WEB www.easterntownships.cc). **Association Touristique**

de la Gaspésie (⊠ 357 rte. de la Mer, Ste-Flavie G0J 2L0, ☎ 418/775–2223 or 800/463–0323, WEB www.tourisme-gaspesie.com). **Association Touristique des Laurentides** (⊠ 14142 rue de la Chapelle, Mirabel J7J 2C8, ☎ 450/436–8532 or 800/561–6673, WEB www.laurentides.com). **Association Touristique Régionale de Charlevoix** (⊠ 495 blvd. de Comporté, C.P. 275, La Malbaie G5A 1T0, ☎ 418/665–4454, WEB www.tourisme-charlevoix.com). **Beaupré Coast Interpretation Center** (⊠ 7977 av. Royale, Château-Richer J5A 1T8, ☎ 418/824–3677). **Tourisme Québec** (⊠ 1001 Square-Dorchester, #100, C.P. 979, Montréal H3C 2W3, ☎ 800/363–7777).

INDEX

Icons and Symbols

★ Our special recommendations

✕ Restaurant

▭ Lodging establishment

✕▭ Lodging establishment whose restaurant warrants a special trip

☺ Good for kids (rubber duck)

☞ Sends you to another section of the guide for more information

⊠ Address

☏ Telephone number

☉ Opening and closing times

💶 Admission prices

Numbers in white and black circles ③ ❸ that appear on the maps, in the margins, and within the tours correspond to one another.

NOTES

Fodor's Key to the Guides

America's guidebook leader publishes guides for every kind of traveler.
Check out our many series and find your perfect match.

Fodor's Gold Guides

America's favorite travel-guide series
offers the most detailed insider reviews
of hotels, restaurants, and attractions
in all price ranges, plus great background information, smart tips, and
useful maps.

Fodor's Road Guide USA

Big guides for a big country—the
most comprehensive guides to
America's roads, packed with places
to stay, eat, and play across the
U.S.A. Just right for road warriors,
family vacationers, and cross-country
trekkers.

COMPASS AMERICAN GUIDES

Stunning guides from top local writers
and photographers, with gorgeous
photos, literary excerpts, and colorful
anecdotes. A must-have for culture
mavens, history buffs, and new residents.

Fodor's CITYPACKS

Concise city coverage with a foldout
map. The right choice for urban travelers
who want everything under one cover.

Fodor's EXPLORING GUIDES

Hundreds of color photos bring your
destination to life. Lively stories lend
insight into the culture, history, and
people.

Fodor's POCKET GUIDES

For travelers who need only the essen-
tials. The best of Fodor's in pocket-size
packages for just $9.95.

Fodor's To Go

Credit-card–size, magnetized color
microguides that fit in the palm
of your hand—perfect for "stealth"
travelers or as gifts.

Fodor's FLASHMAPS

Every resident's map guide. 60 easy-
to-follow maps of public transit, parks,
museums, zip codes, and more.

Fodor's CITYGUIDES

Sourcebooks for living in the city:
Thousands of in-the-know listings for
restaurants, shops, sports, nightlife,
and other city resources.

Fodor's AROUND THE CITY WITH KIDS

68 great ideas for family days,
recommended by resident parents.
Perfect for exploring in your own
backyard or on the road.

Fodor's ESCAPES

Fill your trip with once-in-a-lifetime
experiences, from ballooning in
Chianti to overnighting in the
Moroccan desert. These full-color
dream books point the way.

Fodor's FYI

Get tips from the pros on planning
the perfect trip. Learn how to pack,
fly hassle-free, plan a honeymoon
or cruise, stay healthy on the road,
and travel with your baby.

Fodor's Languages for Travelers

Practice the local language before
hitting the road. Available in phrase
books, cassette sets, and CD sets.

Karen Brown's Guides

Engaging guides to the most charming
inns and B&Bs in the U.S.A. and Europe,
with easy-to-follow inn-to-inn itineraries.

Baedeker's Guides

Comprehensive guides, trusted since
1829, packed with A–Z reviews and
star ratings.